Same difference

Women's studies books of related interest

Bureaucrats, Technocrats, Femocrats
Anna Yeatman

Dissenting Opinions
Regina Graycar

Educating Girls: Practice and Research
Edited by Gilah C. Leder and Shirley N. Sampson

Female Crime: The Construction of Women in Criminology
Ngaire Naffine

Feminine/Masculine and Representation
Edited by Terry Threadgold and Anne Cranny-Francis

For and Against Feminism: A personal journey into feminist theory and history
Ann Curthoys

Frogs and Snails and Feminist Tales
Bronwyn Davies

Gender and Power: Society, the Person and Sexual Politics
R.W. Connell

Law and the Sexes: Explorations in Feminist Jurisprudence
Ngaire Naffine

Playing the State: Australian feminist interventions
Edited by Sophie Watson

Populate and Perish: Australian Women's Fight for Birth Control
Stefania Siedlecky and Diana Wyndham

Secretaries Talk: Sexuality, Power and Work
Rosemary Pringle

Sexual Subversions: Three French feminists
Elizabeth Grosz

Short-changed: Women and economic policies
Rhonda Sharp and Ray Broomhill

Sisters in Suits: Women and Public Policy in Australia
Marian Sawer

Staking a Claim: Feminism, bureaucracy and the state
Suzanne Franzway, Dianne Court and R.W. Connell

Same difference

Feminism and sexual difference

Carol Lee Bacchi

ALLEN & UNWIN

First published in 1990
Allen & Unwin Pty Ltd
9 Atchison Street, St Leonards, NSW 2065 Australia

National Library of Australia
Cataloguing-in-Publication entry:

Bacchi, Carol Lee, 1948–   .
    Same difference: feminism and sexual difference.
    Bibliography
    Includes index.
    ISBN 0 04 442152 4.
    1. Feminism. I. Title.
305.4

Library of Congress Catalog Card Number: 89-46322

Set in 10.5/11.5 pt by Graphicraft Typesetters Ltd., Hong Kong
Printed by South Wind Productions, Singapore
10   9   8   7   6   5   4   3   2

...do we want to continue reorganizing the relationship of difference to sameness through a dialectics of valorization, or is there a way to break down the overdetermined metaphors which continue to organize our perceptions of reality.

Alice Jardine, 'Prelude' to
The Future of Difference
1980, xxvi

I am not saying: if such-and-such facts of nature were different people would have different concepts (in the sense of a hypothesis). But: if anyone believes that certain concepts are absolutely the correct ones, and that having different ones would mean not realizing something that we realize—then let him imagine certain very general facts of nature to be different from what we are used to, and the formation of concepts different from the usual ones will become intelligible to him.

Ludwig Wittgenstein in
Staten, *1984: 160*

To Sam, Ngaire, Alison,
Carol and Stephen

Contents

Acknowledgements

The way in which the research for this book was conducted means that I have an unusually large number of people to thank. Many of their names appear in the Appendix which contains the list of all those who generously gave of their time to permit me an interview. I would also like to thank the myriad office staff and research officers who helped to set up these interviews.

Most of the research was conducted during my study leave and I therefore thank the University of Adelaide for this time and for the additional support of grants in both 1987 and 1988 which enabled me to employ much-needed research assistance. Another grant from the Office of the Status of Women in Canberra assisted with the Australian side of the research. I am indebted to my chief research assistant, Kathy Edwards, both for the research she conducted and for many stimulating conversations on the subject.

A number of colleagues, too numerous to list, have offered helpful comments and ideas. In America I would single out Marion Palley, Sandra Harding and Guy Alchon of the University of Delaware. In Adelaide my sincere thanks to my good friends Ngaire Naffine, Carol Johnson, Alison Mackinnon, Stephen McDonald and Sandra Holton. The ever enthusiastic and efficient work of the women who typed the manuscript, Christine Hill, Ruth Ellickson, and Kerrin Croft, was much appreciated. To Sam, thanks for your patience and encouragement.

Preface

The idea for this book grew out of my teaching and research over the last twenty years. Initially I trained as a historian. My PhD thesis which became a book (Bacchi, 1983) studied the ideology of the woman suffrage movement. Over the last six years I have been working in women's politics and feminist theory. A long view of the women's movement began to emerge. I recognised recurring problems and approaches. The sameness/difference theme (whether women were the same as or different from men), which had often been used to organise women's history, was now reappearing in serious disputes among feminists about appropriate strategies and about the very meaning of 'woman' and feminism. My intention in this volume is to make some sense of this theme, to understand the various ways in which it has been used, and to locate it historically.

The sameness/difference theme in feminism provides insights into many problems which confront feminists. It illustrates how feminists' views of the world are necessarily reactive at times. It shows also how the organising principles which feminists employ are sometimes borrowed from inappropriate analogies, and are sometimes foisted upon them by conventional political language. The constraints imposed by established institutions and conceptual systems figure largely in this study. The message is to interrogate more closely the terms employed in feminist political analysis and to remain sensitive to the cultural context of feminism. Perceiving issues in terms of women's sameness to or difference from men diverts attention from the inadequacy of social institutions. Focusing upon this question, therefore, is politically unwise.

Introduction

Are women and men the same or different? Or, importantly, as the question is more commonly put—are women the same as or different *from men*? It is, of course, possible to speak about the difference *between* one thing and another, but the usual meaning of difference is 'distance from a point of reference' (Guillaumin, 1987: 71). And, in Western conceptual systems, the feminine is always defined as a *difference from* a masculine norm (Schor, 1987: 100). Sameness also requires a point of reference and, in comparisons between the sexes, the point of reference is always 'man'.

The question of difference is a topical one. A good deal of psychological research investigates and compares the behaviour of the sexes both in the animal kingdom and in the human species, in an attempt to draw general conclusions about why we behave as we do (see, for example, Money and Ehrhardt, 1972; and Maccoby and Jacklin, 1974). These investigations often find their way into the popular media in the form of personality tests or androgyny scales or science programs comparing male and female behaviour.[1]

No one would dispute that most males and females have visible, physiological sex-specific characteristics.[2] As Jessie Bernard said in a recent interview, 'Men hardly ever get pregnant!' (Bernard interview, 17 February 1988). The problem is how we interpret these 'differences', or what implications flow from them. Generally, literature on 'sex differences' asks questions about whether physiological characteristics mean that women and men have particular roles in life, whether women are meant to mother, whether their hormones incline them to this task. Biological determinists and sociobiologists are keen to argue that 'there is an unbroken line between androgen binding sites in the brain, rough-and-tumble play in male infants, and the male domination of state, industry, and the nuclear family' (Rose, Kamin and Lewontin, 1984: 154).

The principal concern of this book is not to explore the natures of women and men, nor to ask whether anatomy is destiny. Rather, the book considers these questions at one remove: it considers how ideas about sexual difference have shaped the thoughts and arguments of various parts of the women's movement. The implication of the analysis, however, is that the question of difference has no meaningful answer. It is an inappropriate way of thinking about important social issues, such as how society is to reproduce itself and the kind of society in which we wish to live. Asking questions about women's sameness to or difference from men only serves to mystify these issues, which in turn may help to explain the ubiquity of the question in popular discourse. If these larger questions about how we should organise our lives can be obscured, they can also be conveniently ignored. The title of this volume is intended to suggest that, if society catered appropriately for all human needs, men and women included, discussions about women's sameness to or difference from men would be of little significance.

In the light of this hypothesis, this book sets out to examine just how feminists have engaged with the question of difference. According to some historians, the women's movement (referring here to the organised Anglo-Saxon women's movement of the last two centuries), has been divided from the outset by the question. Olive Banks puts this interpretation most clearly. She describes a movement with two 'faces', one looking towards the 'similarities between men and women', the other looking towards their differences (Banks, 1981: 102). Other histories (for example, Kraditor, 1971) describe continuous and separate 'justice' and 'expediency' traditions within the movement, the former insisting upon women's and men's common humanity (sameness), and the latter using appeals to women's mothering role (difference) to achieve some improvement in status. The unfortunate impression left by these histories is that feminists simply cannot decide if women are more like or unlike men. It is also implied, inadvertently perhaps, that these are the only two options available.[3]

This book challenges this interpretation. A more subtle approach to debates which use the language of 'sameness' or 'difference' (see Prologue to Part I) reveals that the organised movement has divided over the fundamental questions of women's and men's social roles or natures at *particular historical moments*. A close examination of these 'moments' is necessary to discover the causes of disagreement. Here we find that feminists use arguments from 'sameness' or 'difference' when political constraints suggest that these are the only means available to improve women's lives. They are influenced in this decision by available conceptual systems and the paucity of institutional alternatives. At issue in these debates, therefore, is not some ineluctable truth about woman's destiny, but competing political visions about appropriate ways to organise social relations.

The antithetical value systems, identified by Ferdinand Tonnies as *Gemeinschaft* and *Gesellschaft*, help to clarify the causes of division. These terms denote the changes in values which accompanied the 'movement of Western society from a hierarchical feudal society to market society'. In the *Gemeinschaft* type of social organisation, the emphasis is on law and regulation 'as expressing the will, internalized norms, and traditions of an *organic* community, within which every individual member is part of a *social family*' (Kamenka and Tay, 1986: 288—emphasis added). By contrast the *Gesellschaft* tradition, which arose out of the growth of individualism associated with modern bourgeois society, assumes '*atomic* individuals and *private* interests, each in principle equivalent to the other' (Kamenka and Tay, 1986: 292—emphasis added).

Gemeinschaft and *Gesellschaft* represent 'ideal types'[4] and no society exactly replicates these values. Liberal democracies, such as those which form the basis of this study (America, Britain, Australia), draw on both divergent theories of the relation of the individual to society. Stanley Benn and Gerard Gaus identify an individualist (*Gesellschaft*) and an organicist (*Gemeinschaft*) tradition within liberalism (1983: 31).[5] Although they find each to be internally consistent, the two traditions do not sit easily together. The historians Leonore Davidoff and Catherine Hall describe a tension at the heart of middle-class thinking, between a commitment to the values of a free market economy and a desire to maintain the ties of belonging to a social order (Davidoff and Hall, 1987).

Traditionally, women have played a key role in resolving this tension through their assumption of caring responsibilities in the family (Poole, 1984: 113). The *Gemeinschaft* model is status-based[6] and gender-based and explicitly assigns family responsibilities to women.[7] By contrast, *Gesellschaft* does not specify a particular role for women. However, as several feminist authors point out, the 'atomic individual', 'free and self-determined', is predicated upon the existence of a female support staff, usually a wife, to take care of the personal side of living arrangements (Smith, 1979: 165–166; Tapper, 1986: 38–42). *Gesellschaft* accommodates this contradiction by dividing the world into two parts. In the public sphere, the individual is assumed to be rational and self-contained. The private sphere, usually inhabited by women, is reserved for all our human 'differences', such as age and birth and the need for nurture. Katherine O'Donovan describes the family as the 'last outpost of *Gemeinschaft* values' (O'Donovan, 1985: 11). This bifurcation of human existence suits the needs of the market, which requires the 'standardization of labor as well as the standardization of products' (Wolff, 1985: 135).

The first clear division of the women's movement into 'sameness' and 'difference' camps occurred in the period between the two world wars. It was a result of the conflict produced when some women rejected their traditional role as 'guardians of the hearth', and sought to engage in free market competition alongside men. Most of these women endorsed *Gesellschaft* values and wanted women to have the opportunity to pursue *their* individual self-interest. They spoke in terms of women's 'sameness' to men. Since the *Gesellschaft* model assumed that women would take care of the personal side of life, including reproduction and childcare, 'sameness' advocates downplayed these activities. The majority of those who emphasised women's *differences* considered traditional sex roles the only means to promote community well-being, in the *Gemeinschaft* tradition. In the main they did not approve of married women working outside the home, and tried to find ways to increase women's economic independence and status within it.

'Sameness' and 'difference' therefore represented alternative strategies to improve women's lives, given the range of political options imposed by current ideology. Unfortunately, neither alternative worked well for most women. Those who wanted women to be free to pursue self-actualisation tended to be women who had the resources to hire others, often women, to assist with the day-to-day living arrangements which *Gesellschaft* disregarded. *Gemeinschaft* on the other hand ignored the fact that many married women had to or wanted to participate in paid labour, and that the social supports required to allow them to stay home were not forthcoming. Despite the fact that the existence of married women in the labour force exposed the contradiction at the heart of *Gesellschaft*, neither group challenged the assumption that somehow personal lives and work commitments could or should be kept separate.[8] The women who engaged in this dispute were constrained to think and argue in terms of 'sameness' or 'difference' by available conceptual systems and the absence of alternative models.[9]

While historical circumstance resolved the inter-war dispute (Chapter 4), there are lingering traces of this disagreement in the contemporary women's movement. At the policy level, there are debates such as the American equal treatment/special treatment debate over maternity leave (Chapter 5), and the British dispute over limitations on working hours for women (Chapter 6), which consider whether women should fit themselves to the market, or receive special consideration because they are mothers. At a more philosophical level, there exists a tension between those who eulogise the maternal ethic because of their dislike of the excessive individualism and competitiveness of the marketplace, and those who fear that this characterisation of women might be used to disadvantage those who wish to participate in the competition.

This brief description suggests that the tension between the values of *Gemeinschaft* and *Gesellschaft* remains relevant in contemporary sameness/difference debates.[10] Those who press for 'equal treatment' appear more enamoured of, or resigned to the competitive, individualistic model. They wish women to have the opportunity to participate as fully as possible in the public world of work. By contrast, some 'special treatment' advocates espouse more communitarian values, but identify these almost exclusively with women. Women are encouraged either to become as competitive as 'men', in order to succeed in a competitive world, or to remain passive and dependent, and on the side-lines.

In setting out the alternatives as being either like 'men' or different from 'men', the analysis stops short and fails to critique the system which encourages men to be a particular way—detached, competitive, individuated. The *Gesellschaft* model is premised on the hypothesis that individuals can operate independently of, or be abstracted from, the personal needs and commitments involved in living arrangements; *Gemeinschaft* portrays these as *women's* responsibilities. The argument to be developed in this book is that we need a new model which acknowledges the importance of living arrangements without assigning them on a gender basis. We have to challenge the model which says that men can ignore these arrangements.

There is no suggestion here that the movement divides neatly into two camps, nor that every feminist identifies with one or other of these positions. The point is that, *when* disputes which seem to be about women's sameness to or difference from men arise, it is important to show that the opposing positions represent conflicting political visions about how best to organise social relations, and that both approaches have limitations. Describing them as disputes about sameness or difference leaves the impression that feminists simply cannot decide whether women are more like men or different from them, and that women must choose one of these paths. Talking in these terms also implies an inevitability about the options available. It almost suggests that nature has created our options for us. These appear to be either joining the existing 'male' system, or opting out and constructing separate rules for women.

With this kind of analysis, we can easily lose sight of the fact that what is at issue are necessary social arrangements for humane living. As Christine Littleton suggests, 'Any particular way of thinking about sexual inequality defines not only what the problem is, but also the limits within which a solution can be sought' (Littleton, 1981: 487).[11] A sameness/difference framework places unacceptable boundaries on the possibilities for change.

Sameness/difference debates take a number of forms. Often the problem is described as whether women ought to seek 'equality' with men or to admit their 'difference'. Here, the question clearly hinges upon our understanding of the word 'equality'. The liberal model for equality is set in the *Gesellschaft* tradition. Ideally, people are to be abstracted from their particular circumstances and treated equally, meaning the same. Stuart Hall reminds us that the desire to create an ideal of 'equal treatment' for people, despite the possession of power and wealth, was a democratic ideal, opposed to the old order of feudal society where birth guaranteed privilege (Hall, 1986: 39–41). The notion, however, has been generalised to mean that to treat people equally in law you dissociate them from their 'contexts of family, religion, class or race' as if 'they had the same opportunities and experiences' (Minow, 1985b: 203).

A number of authors have drawn attention to the problems with this limited understanding of equality. Several have made the point that, if you ignore people's particular circumstances and treat them equally, you simply perpetuate inequalities (O'Donovan and Szyszczak, 1988: 4). Others show that the concept depends on the separation of public from private sphere mentioned earlier, so that all the 'differences' and 'inequalities' of life can be relegated to the private realm. This means, according to Robert Wolff, that 'traditional liberal political theory simply does not take seriously the dominant facts of human life, namely birth, childhood, aging and death' (Wolff, 1980: 133). As the mind is considered the measure of all 'men' in Western philosophy, and the body the repository of lesser animal instincts, it is not surprising that these 'messy' details of life, largely connected with bodies, are left outside the model (Tapper, 1986: 38).

Women experience the limitations in this conception of equality more often and more dramatically than men since they are given primary responsibility for the kinds of personal details the model disregards. Because the model also ignores existing inequalities of race and class, it also excludes many men. But, given conventional sex roles, men can more easily approximate the 'atomic' individual. Many men have also accepted that personal lives and living arrangements should not interfere with work commitments, and are content to assign these responsibilities to women. *This* is why demanding 'equality' has proven so problematic for women, and why 'difference' often appears to be the only viable option. The disputes among feminists described in this book—which take the form of sameness versus difference, equality versus difference, or equal treatment versus special treatment—are all attempts to reconcile this common understanding of equality and assumptions about traditional sex roles.

As in the inter-war period, then, the tendency to speak in terms of women's sameness to or difference from men is a consequence of the political models which shape our impression of what is possible. The question of difference, therefore, is a distraction from these large political questions such as whether we need a broader understanding of equality so that people's particular circumstances are acknowledged. The language of sameness and difference implies that women are the problem, whereas the problem here is the limited understanding of equality. The assumption also seems to be that, if we get an answer to the question of difference, everything else will fall into place. Men do not have to change, nor does the system, except to the extent that it must 'accommodate' women. The need for a more radical restructuring of relationships between home and paid work is thereby avoided. By posing some new questions about how we think and organise as a society, we open up the possibility of a new and better vision. The questions we must ask are: why should it matter if women are the same as or different from men? why is pregnancy constituted a disadvantage in our society? why does the economic system reward competition and penalise caring?

Several feminists have drawn attention to the limitations imposed upon analysis by talking about women's sameness to or difference from *men*.[12] The problem, I suggest, is not men *per se*, but their values and lifestyle. With 'man' as the standard for comparison, a claim to 'sameness' means aspiring to 'masculine' qualities—independence, autonomy, instrumental rationality—and denying one's culturally defined female identity as dependent, emotional and intuitive. At the policy level, asking for 'equal treatment' implies an acceptance of the conditions under which men live and work, and a desire to replicate them or to modify them only slightly. The 'difference' alternative leaves women with a male-defined identity and a limited sphere of activity. We need to challenge both sides of the equation, rather than playing with the balance between them.

One way to do this would be to construct a social model which *includes* women in the standards by which social rules are set. This would mean that speaking about women's sameness to, or difference from men would no longer make sense. The political agenda would simply include women's sex-specific needs. Since defining women as 'different' has provided the means for society to abrogate responsibility for a range of basic human needs, such as reproduction, including women in the standard has the potential to transform ways of thinking about the relationship between paid work and home, and social values generally.[13]

There are other problems with the sameness/difference framework which suggest that we ought to replace it with a new way of thinking about women's needs. As Black and socialist feminists have pointed out, contrasting 'men' and 'women' assumes that they form undifferentiated categories. This diverts attention from important 'differences' *among* women and *among* men. Bell Hooks asks pointedly, 'which men do women want to be equal to?' (Hooks, 1987: 18). Zillah Eisenstein put the same question (Eisenstein, 1981: 231). As Martha Minow explains, categories that take the form of dichotomies, such as 'same' and 'different', obscure 'the variety and range of characteristics that more aptly describe experience' (Minow, 1985b: 203). *Including* the range of women's diverse needs in the standard destroys the dichotomy and therefore makes it easier to talk about 'varieties and nuances rather than differences' (Finley, 1986: 1170). This is no small point given the concern in the contemporary women's movement to be responsive to women from a wide variety of backgrounds.

Talking about 'samenesses' and 'differences' also diverts attention from the problem of hierarchy, as Catharine MacKinnon observes (Du Bois et al., 1985: 20–21). If women are in fact 'different', the question becomes: why has this 'difference' been constructed as disadvantage? If women are in fact the 'same', the problem of their relative disadvantage and lack of power remains unresolved. There is a need therefore to shift the focus of analysis from the 'difference' to the structures which convert this 'difference' into disadvantage.

Language is important in these debates. The words 'sameness' and 'difference' can assume a variety of meanings, highlighting their indeterminacy and the urgency of using them with the utmost care. The problem is particularly acute in the case of 'difference'.[14] There is a stigma attached to the label (Minow, 1985b: 202–203). It implies deviance from a norm, and that the problem somehow inheres in the person so labelled. Because of the desire to challenge this representation of women, we need other terminology. I refer to women's 'sex-specific characteristics' when talking about pregnancy, for example. This is no conceptual sleight-of-hand. If women were *included* in the human standard, pregnancy would be neither a 'difference' nor a 'problem'. It would be one characteristic of some members of the human category 'women', a characteristic which must be recognised if our conception of humanity is to be accurate.

There is a tendency in some feminist literature to refer to women's disadvantage as women's 'difference'. Although there is no intention of saying anything more here than that women are disadvantaged *compared to men*, because of the meanings attached to 'difference' and the way legal language sets 'difference' against 'equality', it is probably wise to use more precise terminology. In fact, the number of occasions where women's disadvantage is deliberately referred to as women's 'difference' to imply that nothing can be done about the problem at hand (see the Sears case in Chapter 10), suggests that clarity in the use of these terms is of the essence. I use the phrase women's 'differential social location' to refer to the material reality of women's economic, political, and social inferiority.[15]

The purpose of the book therefore is to clarify what the sameness/difference framework obscures and to suggest its limited usefulness in feminist political analysis. Part I, the historical section, challenges the representation of the women's movement as perpetually riven into 'sameness' and 'difference' factions (Chapter 1). The conflicting political visions which produced division in the inter-war period are described in some detail, as are the institutional constraints which impelled feminists into 'sameness' and 'difference' camps (Chapters 2 and 3). Chapter 4 searches out the origins of contemporary sameness/difference disputes. Part I has a second agenda—to explain why the movement has been represented as continuously divided along sameness/difference lines when it is so important to recognise the historically specific circumstances which produced the disputes (Part I, Denouement).

Part II selects a number of contemporary controversies as case-studies to analyse the way in which a sameness/difference framework mystifies political issues. In some of these cases, some feminists use the framework. The purpose here will be to discover why they do so and how it affects their political analysis. These cases include the American equal treatment/special treatment debate (Chapter 5), the British dispute on hours limitation (Chapter 6), some divisions over custody and surrogacy (Chapter 8), the sexuality debates (Chapter 9), and the metaphysical debate about the meaning of 'Woman' (Chapter 10).

Other case-studies are introduced in which anti-feminists caricature feminist analysis to make it fit a sameness/difference framework. This happens in Chapter 7 on the relationship between antidiscrimination legislation and affirmative action, in Chapter 8 on divorce and in the Sears antidiscrimination case in Chapter 10. These examples illustrate the danger in allowing feminist arguments to be reduced to a sameness/difference formulation.

The case-studies together highlight the limitations in a sameness/difference analysis and the need to move beyond it. The suggestion is that it is preferable to bring to the surface the political disagreements which the framework subsumes. This could produce constructive critical analysis of the available political alternatives.

The scope of the study is large and therefore it lays no claim to comprehensiveness. It has selected individuals or groups who wrote or organised on behalf of women to represent the views of the women's movement. The term 'feminism' is used loosely. Linda Gordon's definition is helpful. Feminism, in her view, is a 'sharing in an impulse to increase the power and autonomy of women in their families, communities and/or society' (Gordon, 1977: xiv).

White, middle-class women dominate this particular study. Clearly, we also need to know how working-class and Black feminists dealt with the question of difference, but I will have to leave these projects to others. It is not that I have chosen to ignore these groups. In fact, Black and socialist feminists are largely responsible for drawing attention to the necessity for white middle-class feminists, of which I am one, to have a closer, more self-critical look at their intellectual tradition.[16]

A comparative analysis is employed in the book, but there is no intention to explore every issue in the same detail in each country. Since the focus is upon sameness/difference debates, countries and instances where these debates arise, attract most attention. Hence, many chapters deal primarily with America, where divisions are sharpest. Britain and Australia are often introduced by way of contrast. They allow us to hypothesise why sameness/difference debates among feminists do not appear there as often or not in the same form.

America, Britain and Australia were selected for several reasons. They share a common intellectual tradition and a common language, both of which are important in a study concerned largely with terminology and concepts. Yet, there are sufficient differences in their responses to women's issues to make comparison useful.

Part I, the historical section, contains no new body of literature. Rather, it is based upon a re-reading of well-known texts. The argument is that these texts need to be re-read to recapture the ambiguities which have been lost as a result of the tendency to slot feminists into sameness and difference camps. These ambiguities show that feminists have often had to manoeuvre among unattractive alternatives. They also help us to understand the constraining influence of available political language and conceptual systems.

Part II of the book is based upon a number of secondary sources and a series of interviews conducted with feminists in the three countries. Their names are listed in the Appendix. The interviewees are not intended to be a representative sample, although I tried to achieve a balance between feminists engaged in formulating policy and feminist academics. The categories, of course, are not exclusive. Also, where appropriate, I sought a balance between those overtly connected with a 'sameness' perspective and those who defend a 'difference' approach.

The interviews served two purposes. They supplemented existing literature and provided insights which seldom find their way into prose. There was, for example, a willingness to talk about the strengths and weaknesses of contending positions, instead of a defence of one side. The way in which political constraints set the terms of the debates was revealed. It also became clear that many feminists were aware of the limitations of a sameness/difference analysis and were looking for ways beyond it. *Same difference* is a contribution to this search.

I
The historical dilemma

Prologue

When did feminists divide into camps defending women's sameness to or difference from men? Over which issues? As mentioned in the Introduction some historians maintain that there has existed a constant tension in the movement between contending points of view. Two 'faces of feminism' have been described, one looking towards sameness with men, the other towards difference from them (Banks, 1981).

This section of the book offers a more subtle understanding of the ways in which some feminists engaged with the question of sexual difference. It suggests that, rather than treating any and all discussions about sameness or difference as if they were part of one ongoing debate, it is necessary to identify more precisely what the discussions were about. Some discussions, which I call 'metaphysical', concerned the fundamental nature and character of women and men. Others, 'functional' debates, questioned whether women and men had or should have distinct social roles or functions. Others, which I have labelled 'institutional' debates, asked whether women required specialised or separate institutions and legislation to deal with their particular needs. While there are obvious overlaps in these categories, identifying them reduces the possibility of talking about the movement in simple dichotomous terms which seriously misrepresents what the movement was about.

For example, using these categories, it becomes clear that, in the nineteenth century (Chapter 1), there was near unanimity *among feminists* about functional and metaphysical issues. The vast majority accepted that women had a sex-specific duty to be primary childcarers and that their maternal temperament suited them for this role. The major dispute in this period was institutional and was largely confined to Britain (Emily Davies versus Anne Jemima Clough, see pages 16–17). It had more to do with competing notions of educational reform than competing visions of woman's character or destiny. Divisions between romantic and rationalist interpretations of woman's nature, and between 'justice' and 'expediency' camps in the woman suffrage movement have also been overdrawn.

The first major division into identifiable 'sameness' and 'difference' factions (participants themselves occasionally used these labels), therefore, appears in the inter-war years, most clearly in Britain and America (Chapters 2 and 3). The question which caused the division was functional and concerned whether or not married women ought to engage in waged labour. The debate reflected competing political ideologies, *laissez faire* individualism (*Gesellschaft*) versus welfarism (*Gemeinschaft*), and competing strategies about how best to improve women's status and security. It was phrased in terms of women's sameness to or difference from men because models for sex roles were well established, and because political alternatives seemed to be restricted *either* to equal competition with men, foregoing provisions for family responsibilities, *or* accepting the traditional allocation of these responsibilities to women. Because both groups accepted that women were the natural mothers, the 'metaphysical' maternal mystique remained relatively uncontroversial in this period.

By the 1960s (Chapter 4) historical circumstances had more or less resolved the functional debate, at least as far as feminists were concerned. Married women were engaging in waged labour and in large numbers. Traces of this dispute remain in disagreements about the appropriate *institutional* arrangements to facilitate married women's workforce participation (equal treatment versus special treatment) and in the contemporary metaphysical debate about the desirability or danger of eulogising 'woman's' maternal character. In the latter the initial suggestion in early second-wave feminism (1960s–1970s) that, in order to succeed in a 'man-made' world, women had to overcome their conditioning as passive and dependent, produced a reaction to this proposition which elevated 'feminine' characteristics as the only hope for the world.

Feminism has not therefore always had a 'sameness' and a 'difference' face. These labels represent political responses to a world which seems to say either that women have to mimic the male lifestyle or create an alternative lifestyle for women. The circumstances in which the divisions appear make this clear.

Why then has the women's movement *been represented* by some historians as continuously divided over sameness and difference when it is so important to identify the historically specific issues which provoked dispute? In part, it is argued, the 'historical dilemma' is responsible. This is the tendency for contemporary 'sameness' and 'difference' groups to seek validating historical traditions. In the process, they impose their debates upon a past where there is at best an imperfect fit.

The dilemma is one faced by all historians and touches on those perennial questions of causality and historical explanation. Surely the task of a historian is to arrange the past in manageable categories, to make it 'make sense'. It is also generally acknowledged that these categories are frequently selected because of their current relevance. There is no single 'correct' history. E. H. Carr put it this way:

> Somewhere between these two poles—the north pole of valueless facts and the south pole of value judgements still struggling to transform themselves into facts—lies the realm of historical truth (Carr, 1976: 132).

This means that the various histories of feminism, this one included, are products of particular experiences. Those which identified 'justice' and 'expediency' traditions in the woman suffrage movement (Kraditor, 1971), for example, emerged at a time when pressing for equal rights seemed a workable strategy. My reinterpretation is in part due to a growing awareness of some of the problems with that strategy.

The objection here is to the way in which histories which use a justice/efficiency, equality(sameness)/difference framework oversimplify women's experience. We are left with the impression that the alternative strategies were clear and recognisable and that feminists selected between them. Rather it appears that the arguments were often mixed. A clearer division occurred in the inter-war years but even here particular arguments, invoking 'sameness' or 'difference' for example, were at times employed rhetorically for tactical reasons. The implication that there were two irreconcilable positions is also a misrepresentation when there was, as we will see, a good deal of common ground.

More disturbing is the tendency for histories in this tradition to set up a 'correct' and an 'incorrect' side and to imply that one of these views must prevail. This tends to freeze the debate and to discourage discussion of alternative formulations of the problem which, I feel, is very necessary. I agree with Anne Phillips here that '. . . there is no simple right or wrong. The disputes arise in contexts and a language we do not control, and they drag us into either/or choices where neither will do' (Phillips, 1986: 151).

The meaning of feminism has unfortunately become caught up in these disagreements about strategy, with each side claiming authenticity for its particular tradition. Instead of creating 'lesser' and 'greater' feminists, we ought to increase our sensitivity to the way in which feminist arguments reflect and are constrained by particular political, economic and social circumstances. We need to understand how feminism, in Anne Bottomley's words, has been built upon 'instances of the experience of power and lack of power' among women (Bottomley, Gibson and Meteyard, 1987: 47). A history which takes sides obscures this understanding.

1
The nineteenth century: equal but different

The ideology of the organised white, middle-class women's movement in nineteenth-century Britain, Australia, and America, was more of a piece than is often assumed. Concerning functional and metaphysical issues, feminists in this movement in the main shared a common vision. They believed that the maternal function was vitally important and that women were suited by nature for this role. They also believed that women were 'equal' to men in the sense that they shared a common human spirit. Women were equal, but different in their social function as childrearers and in their distinctive maternal character.

Divisions in the movement are sometimes overdrawn and sometimes misrepresented. Education, which seemed to divide British feminists into contending sameness and difference factions, was primarily an institutional dispute about which educational strategy to adopt to improve women's situation. At another level the identification of 'rationalist' and 'romantic' approaches to woman's nature underplays the consensus in these approaches about women's gender-specific function as childrearers. Similarly, historical analyses which differentiate between a 'justice' and an 'expediency' tradition within the suffrage movement ignore that most suffragists used both arguments: they argued 'sameness' to prove the justice of their cause; they appealed to women's 'differences' to convince men about the 'expediency' of enfranchising Christian, white, middle-class women. The reasons for the relative homogeneity of early feminist ideas and the implications for feminist political analysis form the substance of this chapter. The reasons some historians have underplayed this homogeneity in favour of a Janus-faced figure looking on the one hand to women's sameness to men and on the other hand to their difference from them are pursued in the denouement to Part I (see pages 97–101).

Feminists made frequent appeals to an abstract notion of equality in the late eighteenth and throughout the nineteenth century. The natural justice which ought to be accorded women on the basis of their common humanity with men seemed both a necessary point to raise and a logical one in the context of the times. It was necessary because women had not been granted full human status, and logical because of the currency of ideas like 'equality' and 'liberty'. As Juliet Mitchell explains, feminism arose 'as part of a revolutionary bourgeois tradition that had equality of mankind as its highest goal' (Mitchell, 1984: 63).

The intellectual origins of the first feminist tracts are well known but need to be rehearsed for the sake of the argument. Mary Wollstonecraft, commonly taken as the progenitor of the women's rights movement, was schooled in the company of radical Dissenters and inspired by the democratic impulse which found its outlet in the French Revolution (Charvet, 1982: 15). In *A Vindication of the Rights of Man* (1790), which preceded by two years her more famous tract, *A Vindication of the Rights of Woman* (1792), she used Lockeian arguments to demand full equal civil and political rights for *men* and the abolition of aristocratic privilege. As part of a middle-class ascendancy she had no difficulty reconciling these views with a continuation of class divisions. In fact, she assumed the existence of a servant class (Grimshaw, 1986: 11). Perhaps for this very reason the idea of equality was kept vague. As far as women were concerned her claim was simply that some women were as able as some men intellectually and ought to be given every opportunity to exercise their talents. Abstract equality meant little more than a declaration of common humanity. It certainly did not extend to social roles.

In Wollstonecraft's writings it was assumed that in the main women would remain the homemakers. She challenged the idea of innate sexual differences in intellectual capacity and attributed observable contrasts between men and women to their social environment. But she believed that the 'care of children in their infancy' was a 'grand' duty 'annexed to the female character by nature' (Wollstonecraft, 1983: 265). She also recognised that 'this duty would afford many forcible arguments for strengthening the female understanding', and used it well: '. . . make women rational creatures and free citizens, and they will quickly become good wives and mothers' (Wollstonecraft, 1983: 299). As Katherine O'Donovan and Erika Szyszczak explain, given the context of women's position when Wollstonecraft was writing, 'her view of equality was inevitably limited' (O'Donovan and Szyszczak, 1988: 2).

John Stuart Mill, whose booklet, *On the Subjection of Women* (1869), became the bible of the women's movement in Anglo-

Saxon countries had, like Wollstonecraft, a limited notion of democracy (Hall, 1986: 60). He believed that the world ought to be governed by an intellectual meritocracy. Some mode of 'plural voting' would assign to education 'the degree of superior influence due to it' (Mill, 1975: 287). Mill saw no reason why women ought to be excluded from this leadership. Status based upon merit would replace status based upon inherited title and wealth. Female emancipation meant 'the removal of women's disabilities', a turning free, almost in some sense a social counterpart to economic *laissez faire*. It did not mean altering the traditional division of labour within the family:

> . . . the common arrangement by which the man earns the income and the wife superintends the domestic expenditure, seems to me in general the most suitable division of labour between the two (Mill, 1929: 263).

Notions of natural justice were equally popular in the American States where the Revolution had heralded the end of British tyranny. At the Seneca Falls Convention in 1848, which is hailed as the beginning of the organised American women's movement, the women adapted the United States Declaration of Rights in this important way: 'We hold these truths to be self-evident: that all men *and women* are created equal. . .' (quoted in Charvet, 1982: 22—emphasis added). Many early American feminists had close links with the movement for the abolition of slavery which led them to ponder *women's* civic incapacity. Adroitly they marshalled slogans, such as 'no taxation without representation', likely to strike a sympathetic chord among republican rebels. In Australia similarly feminist demands were often '. . . couched in terms of a fundamental "natural" justice which worked persuasively among a ruling class with strong liberal origins. . .' (Magarey, 1985: 173).

In this vision of the future, laws which overtly restricted women were to be eliminated. These included laws denying them control over their property, laws barring their entry to certain educational institutions and professions, laws excluding them from voting privileges. The period is appropriately described as a period of 'lowering the barriers' and the victories were important ones. The new political ideas of liberty and equality proved very useful in these campaigns: 'theories of men's and citizens' rights made it possible to question the rights of women' (Browne, 1987: 9). With all this, the concepts 'liberty' and 'equality' remained ill-defined, and the functional differentiation between women and men based upon women's 'natural' responsibility for children was assumed. In the shift from hierarchical *Gemeinschaft* to democratic *Gesellschaft*, the home remained the repository of altruistic virtues and women remained its caretaker. 'Radical doctrines of equal rights', it seems, 'could easily coexist with highly conventional views about "true womanhood", about the proper work of women and men and about their heterosexual destiny' (Connell, 1987: 26). Men and women were 'equal' but 'different'.

The social critic, Alexis de Tocqueville, drew a distinction between feminists who demanded 'equality' and those who claimed 'identity'. In 1840 he praised Americans for raising women 'morally and intellectually to the level of a man', but expressed dismay at some Europeans who:

> confusing the divergent attributes of the sexes, claim to make of man and woman creatures who are, *not equal only, but actually similar*. They would attribute the same functions to both, impose the same duties, and grant the same rights; they would have them share everything—work, pleasure, public affairs (Tocqueville, 1966: 576–578—emphasis added).

As Leslie Goldstein points out, de Tocqueville probably had in mind the radical Utopian followers of Fourier and St Simon who were experimenting with communitarian solutions, including free love and the sharing of domestic work, to women's problems (Goldstein, 1987: 532). America had its radicals as well. The followers of Robert Owen set up model communities in which childcare, education and housekeeping were collective responsibilities, although most Owenites also upheld the popular notion that women had a unique moral mission. This early association between socialism and the suggestion that men and women should not be only 'equal but similar' probably made it difficult for more conventional feminists to consider a radical restructuring of sex roles (Taylor, 1983: 51–52, 30).

Among middle-class feminists there was a great deal of discussion about what 'women' could or could not do, but it centred mainly around single women. In their eyes these were the women most in need, single women waiting to be married as a result of the trend towards delayed marriage, single women who could find no husbands because of the decimation of the male population in the Napoleonic wars or the maldistribution of men in colonial societies. The 'woman question' referred specifically to the problems associated with finding appropriate occupations for middle-class women *until* they married. In Britain, in 1859, the 'ladies of Langham Place', Britain's first organised feminists, established a Society for Promoting the Employment of Women to find new respectable jobs for 'gentlewomen', for whom factory or domestic service was considered unsuitable (Hammerton, 1977: 54). *After* marriage, it was assumed that childrearing and homemaking would become full-time occupations. Married women and the domestic sphere were seen as coterminous. The *status* of married women vitally concerned feminist activists, however, as is demonstrated in the campaigns for property and custody rights. The goal in each instance was greater female autonomy.

The ideology of 'separate spheres' for women and men (Harrison, 1978) formed a backdrop to nineteenth-century feminist thought. Suffragists challenged this construction at one level with their demand for access to the public world of political decision-making. However the majority accepted a family–market divide which left women the homemakers and men the breadwinners.[1] References to women's 'sameness to' men as far as employment rights were concerned ignored this taken-for-granted functional differentiation. There is no suggestion here that things could have been otherwise. The project is to understand, not to second-guess, nineteenth-century feminist ideology.

At the metaphysical level a distinction between rationalist and romantic bases for feminism is commonly acknowledged. Rationalism emphasised the shared human capacity to reason. Romanticism allowed men and women to develop different faculties: man displayed hard reason, woman a softer intuition (Vogel, 1986: 17–18). Mill and Wollstonecraft represent the first of these traditions with their emphasis upon rationality and education as the keys to human liberation. The mid-nineteenth-century Englishwoman, Margaret Fuller, represents the second. Although Fuller insisted, 'There is no wholly masculine man, no purely female woman', she believed the faculties had been given 'in preponderance', the scientific to man, the poetic to woman. The goal was to bring these two forces into harmony: 'The growth of Man is two-fold, masculine and feminine...Energy and Harmony; Power and Beauty; Intellect and Love' (Fuller, 1972: 169). The 'especial genius of Woman' was 'electrical in movement, intuitive in function, spiritual in tendency' (Fuller, 1972: 115).

Too much can be made, however, of the rational/romantic distinction. People in both traditions actually endorsed a version of 'equal but different'. Fuller, for example, insisted that men and women were equal, meaning that they had equal value, despite their different roles. And, as far as functions were concerned, Fuller and Wollstonecraft would have been in complete agreement.

Fuller wanted all offices to be open to women, but assumed the majority would dedicate themselves to full-time mothering:

> Mothers will delight to make the nest soft and warm. Nature would take care of this; no need to clip the wings of any bird who wants to soar. . . The difference would be that *all* need not be constrained to employments for which *some* are unfit (Fuller, 1972: 175)

Therefore, although some feminists appealed to the notion of a common human rationality to justify changes in women's position, and others referred to a unique female essence, there was no sharp division into contending schools of thought. Most, as we will see, used both arguments to defend improvements in women's status. Only a few questioned their compatibility. The consensus about sex-specific functions, in particular the feeling that women were in some way defined by their capacity to give birth and their predilection for nurture, blurred the distinction between the two metaphysical traditions. Since rationalists agreed that *by nature* women were mothers, this carried over to an extent into characterisations of female mentality and psychology. Linda Gordon agrees that there has never been 'an acute shift' from one perspective to the other, from 'androgyny to female uniqueness' but that 'this duality exists within feminism' (Gordon, 1986: 27).

The mid-nineteenth-century education debate illustrates the types of ambiguity which surfaced in discussions about female character. It also indicates the variety of motives which produced appeals to either 'sameness' or 'difference', confirming the need to be careful in thinking about the movement in simple dichotomous terms. The subject of the appropriate form of education for women attracted some discussion in all Anglo-Saxon countries. At the most obvious level the question was an institutional one, though people could and did invoke functional and metaphysical arguments to support their case. Most of the disputes of this nature, however, were *between feminists and their opponents* rather than *among* feminists.

A whole range of essentialist[2] arguments were raised by antifeminists who wanted either to restrict or to shape female education. One of the most popular was that women's health could not stand the strain of excessive study. As the American, Dr Edward Clarke, explained in *Sex in Education*, 'The system never does two things well at the same time. The muscles and the brain cannot functionate [sic] in the best way at the same moment'. For young women going through puberty, intensive study had a disastrous effect in Clarke's view, 'the stream of vital and constructive force evolved within her was turned steadily to the brain, and away from the ovaries and their accessories' (Clarke, 1873: 40, 79–84). The result could be nervous collapse or perhaps, worse still, sterility. In Britain, Henry Maudsley used Clarke's book as the basis of his attack on women's educational aspirations. These views were widely supported, at times by 'reputable' authorities. The *British Medical Journal* reported, 'It is not merely her mind that is un-sexed, but her body loses much of that special charm that attracts men. In America the college woman when she does marry is often barren' (quoted in Edwards, 1985: 5).

Feminist educationists had to put their case within this framework. The American president of Bryn Mawr, M. Carey Thomas, explained in a 1908 address the kinds of pressures this placed upon educated women: 'I was terror-struck lest I, and every other woman with me, were doomed to live as pathological invalids in a universe merciless to women as a sex' (Cross, 1965: 160). In a world determined to construct women as different, arguments stressing the similar capacities and needs of the sexes appeared useful. In the same speech Carey Thomas insisted:

> . . . that women form one-half of the kindly race of normal,
> healthy human creatures in the world; that women, like men,
> are quickened and inspired by the same study of the great
> traditions of their race, by the same love of learning, the same
> love of science, the same love of abstract truth. . .

One might expect to find some tension between rationalists and romantics about whether women's education ought to develop the 'masculine' qualities of objectivity and detachment, or fine-tune 'feminine' intuition, and there is some evidence of this. In the *Englishwoman's Review*, a British journal associated with the same 'ladies of Langham Place', there was the occasional reference to the need for women to acquire 'manly qualities' to counter women's current character weaknesses:

> Women *are* weak, for want of use; excitable, for want of vent;
> unreasonable, for want of healthy motives for self-discipline;
> foolishly ambitious, for want of training to noble end, and
> power to calculate the distance between end and means
> (*Englishwoman's Review*, V, October, 1867: 277).

The remedy was an education comparable to men's.

This attitude was quite consistent, however, with a belief in woman's unique maternal qualities. A demanding education would simply 'bring out the best' in her. The first headmistress of

Adelaide's Advanced School for Girls justified women's higher education in these terms:

> Do we not rather long for one who, with *womanly tenderness and sympathy*, can unite the support of that strength which comes from knowledge, firmness, decision, and the ability to give wise counsel? The strengthening of the mental faculties will assist in developing *those very characteristics* (Dowdy, 1914: 10–11— emphasis added).

In a similar vein an 1880 article in the *Englishwoman's Review*, pleading for the 'Entire Freedom of Women Both in Education and Employment', asked: 'Does not the glory of true womanhood lie in the subtle power of a purifying moral influence over the strongest man?' (15 September 1880: 391). As Leslie Goldstein points out, the following quotation from the 'sexually conservative and emphatically Christian' Hannah More (*Strictures on the Modern System of Female Education*, 1794) could just as easily have come from the pen of the 'secular, sexual libertine Wollstonecraft'. Asking what a man needed in a wife, More replied:

> It is not merely a creature who can paint, and play, and sing, and draw, and dress, and dance; it is a being who can comfort and counsel him; one who can reason, and reflect, and feel and judge, and discourse and discriminate; one who can assist him in his affairs. . . strengthen his principles and educate his children (Goldstein, 1987: 534).

Alison Mackinnon also warns against exaggerating differences among the women activists interested in women's education (Mackinnon, 1984: 38).

The conviction that women needed 'mental discipline' was, in fact, as much a class message as a gender one. In part the desire was to spread the middle-class ideals of high moral tone, discipline and strength of character. A common complaint in the period was that young middle-class girls were 'flighty' and 'frivolous' because of the lack of intellectual demands placed upon them. There was near unanimity that the existing education offered to girls, based upon 'accomplishments' such as singing and piano playing, had to change. As one writer to the *Pall Mall Gazette* put it: 'All England is joining in one great cry against the frivolity of women' (reprinted in the *Englishwoman's Review*, January, 1869: 128).

A solid liberal education would 'brace the intellectual sinews', expand women's souls, give a woman 'mental culture'. The English suffragist, Millicent Garrett Fawcett, asked only that 'all, both men and women, have equal chances of maturing such intellect as

God has given them' (*Englishwoman's Journal*, VIII, July 1868: 492). This 'maturing' would better prepare women for their role as guardians of the young:

> Mothers are the prime educators for girls and boys alike, and the more we can raise the intellectual and moral standard among our women, the more we shall advance and ennoble our country (*Englishwoman's Review*, VI, January 1868: 358).

There was no dispute that most women would be mothers; there was also no dispute that single women and exceptional women needed some training in case they were forced to or decided to become self-supporting (*Englishwoman's Review*, July 1871: 216; October 1871: 262; April 1875: 147). You could also accept that women had a distinctive maternal character and a natural mothering role *while* suggesting they needed discipline in male-style educational institutions.

A few women openly challenged the rationalist–romantic dichotomy. One contributor to the *Englishwoman's Review* speculated on the outcome had 'the writers on metaphysics' been 'mostly women'. Assuming they would then have adopted 'the cultivated female intellect as the proper standard of comparison',

> ...it is by no means unlikely that they would have embodied the radical defects of the male intellect in such aphorisms as these:— Men generalise much too hastily. Men are deficient in the intuitive faculty... (*Englishwoman's Review*, XXX, October 1875: 445).

To men who used the argument that 'women lack aptitude to grasp broad principles' to justify the male monopoly of political power, she offered the 'female rejoinder': 'Men are too apt to exalt imperfect generalisations into principle, and to act thereupon without regarding the cases to which their principles apply'. Although this analysis rested upon male and female character stereotypes, the author offered a critique of the legal structure which many contemporary feminists would find appealing. In her view female legislators '...would never have exalted precedent into principle that a judge should be compelled to decide according to precedent in opposition to our sense of justice'.

An anonymous contributor to the suffrage debate went further and questioned the setting of reason *against* feeling, echoing some contemporary analyses (Midgley, 1981): 'It is not a question of reason against feeling, but of allying the two, instead of keeping them apart by an irreligious divorce' (Lewis, 1987: 211). The notion of a '*merely*' logical intellect, the cold-hearted amusement of arguing an important question without any real conviction', dismayed her. For some feminists then the encounter between rationalism and stereotypical notions of female character compelled 'the reconsideration of the whole set of principles on which much of our social legislation is built' (*Englishwoman's Review*, XXX, October 1875: 449). That such ideas were never taken up is due more to women's lack of power than to any lack of imagination!

The question of the actual content of the educational curriculum aroused some discussion among feminists, but even here the divisions were not as sharp as sometimes assumed. There was some debate about whether girls needed a domestic education to prepare them for their anticipated wifely role. If there was disagreement, however, it was usually about *when* not *if* domestic education should occur. Even Emily Davies, one of the strongest proponents of the need for an identical education for girls and boys, admitted that, as marriage was the 'profession' which 'absorbs the great majority of women', some 'technical preparation' was required for 'this calling'. She insisted only that, 'up to technical education', education be broad and humane: 'That the soul be without knowledge is not good' (Davies, 1910: 80).

The near unaniminity among middle-class white feminists about the desirability of domestic education had more to do with class than with gender issues. In Britain as the century advanced the idea that technical education was more necessary than liberal education gained some support among education reformers. The working classes became the principal objects of reform. The middle classes feared that the education of working-class children was 'too literary' and 'impractical' and that it tended to draw them 'away from manual work and into the blackcoated occupations which were traditionally middle-class preserves' (Holcombe, 1973: 30). There was also concern about increasing foreign competition and the need for a better-trained industrial workforce. Working-class girls had a different niche carved out for them—domestic service.

An early article in the *Englishwoman's Review* called it a 'public calamity, affecting the welfare of the upper and middle classes,' that so little had been said or written about the failure in the present system of national schools 'to prepare the lower classes for the confidential and responsible position of domestic servants' (*Englishwoman's Review*, VII, April 1868: 407). The author, Jane Luard, recommended industrial schools to rectify the situation. Emily Davies wished also to replenish the diminishing supply of domestics, 'one of the most precious civilising influences which modern society affords' (Davies, 1910: 98).

In the colonies the servant shortage became a problem sooner than in the mother country (Bacchi, 1986a: 407), forcing the South Australian educationist, Catherine Helen Spence, to modify slightly her vision for colonial women's education. Since 'all ranks had to dispense with hired domestics at times', she admitted that 'every woman was bound to know something about household work'. She therefore wished to have this very necessary labour accredited some dignity. A general liberal education would precede specialisation. Then those women of genius who had 'sufficient talent to carry them into special pursuits' could 'depute to others those domestic duties she has not time to discharge'. For the 'rank and file', those who had no 'special vocation', higher education would improve the quality of the work which 'ordinary middle-class women have to do' (Spence, 1878: 3), that is, housework.

Developments in Britain soon followed this trend. An 1890 article in the *Englishwoman's Review* greeted the establishment of a National Housewifery Training College as a development which would bestow 'true dignity' upon the 'domestic work of women', establishing 'its recognised place amongst the skilled trades, with its regular curriculum and certified teachers' (15 July 1890: 293). By the end of the century there was near consensus that every woman required some training for domestic duties.

In mid-nineteenth-century Britain feminists engaged in heated debate about whether girls' education ought to be the 'same as' or 'different from' boys' education. But the point at issue had little to do with conflicting views about either women's functions or their essential character. They all wished to produce a well-rounded cultured womanhood which in the main would assume its traditional responsibility for home and children. The debate was an institutional one and revolved around the question of university examinations. Emily Davies and the promoters of Girton College, Cambridge, campaigned to have the tests applied to university education for women exactly the same as for men. The promoters of Newnham College, Anne Jemima Clough (1820–1892) and Professor Henry Sidgwick, were willing to accept special exams in new subjects and special certificates.

Davies' motives were essentially pragmatic. She believed that women would not be accepted by entrenched interests unless women abided by their standards of measurement (Bryant, 1979: 84). Coming from an academic, Anglican and strictly orthodox educational background, Davies was also a traditionalist in educational matters.

By contrast, Clough and Sidgwick were reformers. Rebels against elitist structures, they promoted University Extension

Courses for women and men who could not gain entry to Oxford or Cambridge. They took higher education to 'women in their homes, to clerks at their desks, to artisans at their work, even to the princess in the palace.' The principle they adopted, according to Mrs Henry Fawcett (Millicent Garrett Fawcett), was 'If Mohammet cannot go to the mountain, the mountain must go to Mohammet' (Fawcett, *c.*1895: 13).

Some reformers who opposed identical examinations feared that the standard of teaching in girls schools would be too low to produce successful candidates. Another, Alice Zimmern, foreshadowed contemporary concerns that coeducation, the running of two separate schools under one structure, might actually disadvantage girls:

> The attempts recently made…to economize by teaching boys and girls together, abolishing the headmistress and putting a headmaster over boys and girls alike…letting the girls do the best they can with it, is only a revival, under a new guise, of the old idea, that girls are not entitled to the same consideration as boys.

'Under the pretext of equality' this could mean a 'subordination of the girls' interests' (Zimmern, 1898: 243–244, quoted in Delamont, 1980: 106–107).

When in 1868 Cambridge offered women a *special* Higher Local Exam, Davies opposed it on principle; Clough and Sidgwick accepted it as meeting a present need. A vigorous debate between the two groups lasted for several years, but in the end Davies accepted Newnham College as a valuable ally. Fawcett's characterisation of the dispute seems apt:

> I like to think of these two Colleges as sister stems of a beech tree, deriving their nourishment from the same root, but having an independent growth and differing from each other in some externals. The development of each presents some interesting examples of the inter-dependence or solidarité of the several parts of the women's movement (Fawcett, 1921).

As several historians have pointed out, this British controversy over the form of women's higher education 'is best characterized as part of a wider movement of middle-class reform' (Vicinus, 1985: 123; Bryant, 1979: 116). Mackinnon shows that even the debate between Miss Buss and Miss Beale about whether or not the competitive spirit ought to be encouraged in girls had a class component. It seems that Cheltenham, Miss Beale's school, and the North London Collegiate, Miss Buss's institution, drew upon different clienteles. The latter attracted the children of lesser professionals, smaller businessmen and artisans 'who needed competitive examinations to gain and validate a place in the growing service sector'. The former drew upon families of professional men, and 'gentlemen of independent means' who depended to a much larger degree 'on the older networks of patronage' (Mackinnon, 1984: 44). It seems inappropriate therefore to see these divisions as due to irreconcilable differences of opinion about either woman's character or her chief role in life.

In America education reformers were also debating the content of a liberal arts curriculum. As far as women were concerned, feminists did not divide publicly over the issue and, hence, for the purposes of this study the situation in America requires less attention. According to Barbara Solomon, the early women's colleges, lacking resources, proceeded cautiously with reform and 'were reluctant to dispense with the classical curriculum' (Solomon, 1985: 80). M. Carey Thomas, the President of Bryn Mawr, was a traditionalist like Davies on these issues. She objected strongly to the insertion of 'so-called practical courses' which would lower education's 'disciplinary quality' (Cross, 1965: 161). As more schools opened, innovations were introduced to attract enrolments. As a result women's academic options varied widely, accommodating most middle-class white women's needs. Similarly, in South Australia, a solidly middle-class state, the creation of an Advanced School for Girls in 1880 caused little discussion, let alone controversy. In Mackinnon's words, it provided 'for a group of bourgeois parents, from the professions and from commerce, whose needs for a serviceable education for their daughters at a reasonable cost were not being met' (Mackinnon, 1984: 74).

The education issue then was a very practical one. It concerned finding the best means to win acceptance for those women who would have to compete with men. In 1868 Emily Davies directly addressed the sameness/difference issue and indicated that, as far as she was concerned, these categories of thought were inappropriate:

> The controversy does not lie between those on the one hand who, believing men and women to be exactly alike, logically hold that all the conditions to which they may be subjected ought to be precisely similar, and those on the other who, regarding them as completely unlike, cannot believe that anything which is good for one sex can be anything but bad for the other. No rational person takes either of these clearly-defined views. . . . The abstract questions as to equality and identity may be quickly dismissed. The advocates of the

'common principle'—those who hold what may be called the
humane theory—altogether disclaim any ambition to assert
either (Davies, 1868: 3-4).

In a private moment Davies confessed that '...my feeling against
raising barriers between men and women has nothing to do with
the assertion of equality, or identity, in neither of which I believe...' (quoted in Mackinnon, 1984: 42). Nor did she feel that
women were 'a class apart' or that they should 'unite as a separate
movement' (Bryant, 1979: 84). Put simply, men had the advantages and Davies wished women to have access to them. In order
to do so, they had to compete on men's terms or at least on the
terms of the men against whom they wished to compete. As Bryant
puts it, Davies 'never claimed that women *ought* to do the same
as men but she was determined to demonstrate they *could* do
so...' (Bryant, 1979: 87).
    The education debate illustrates what will become a familiar
theme, the difficulties feminists face in choosing between short-
term solutions to immediate problems and long-term goals. In
another way the problem was how to contemplate reforming a
system without first gaining access to it. These were the issues
which lay subsumed beneath rhetorical appeals to sameness and
difference.

The woman suffrage campaign has also been presented by many
historians as fundamentally a battle over 'sameness' and 'difference'. Here the interpretation has been that the movement occurred in two phases, an earlier phase (1848-1890) concerned
mainly with asserting women's and men's common humanity (the
justice argument), followed by a later phase (1890-1920), which
emphasised women's differences (the expediency argument) (Kraditor, 1971; Bacchi, 1983).[3] This case rests largely upon the number of suffragists later in the century who publicly endorsed
women's maternal role and asked that women be enfranchised to
give public expression to their maternal qualities. While it is true
that it became a popular theme in late nineteenth and early
twentieth-century America, Britain, and Australia to speak in
terms of bringing the 'mother influence' into politics and of becoming the 'nation's housekeepers' (Summers, 1975; Holton,
1986), most suffragists claimed equal human status *at the same time*
as eliciting women's particular virtues. Sandra Holton's analysis of
the British movement applies to all three countries: 'early twentieth-century suffragists in Britain never completely abandoned

a humanist perspective' (Holton, 1986: 17). Any attempt to divide the movement into 'justice' or 'expediency' camps, therefore, 'oversimplifies the historical reality'.[4] The movement at this stage did not divide along sameness/difference lines. There was agreement that women had sex-specific functions, that they displayed unique maternal qualities, *and* that they were 'equal' to men.

This mix of arguments does not necessarily reflect ideological inconsistency. The ambiguity of the concept of equality[5] meant that feminists could give it any content they chose, and most chose *not* to equate it with identity. The American, Antoinette Brown Blackwell, for example, could agree that men and women had sex-specific functions—'females directly nurture offspring; males never do'—at the same time as she insisted that 'one sex is the equivalent of the other' (Schramm, 1979: 309–310). Anna Garlin Spencer, an American sociologist, spoke easily about women uniting 'on equal terms with men' and their 'distinctive role' as mothers (Spencer, 1923: 51). The American educationist, Gertrude Martin, enlisted democratic rhetoric, that '*men* were created free and equal' and 'had been endowed with certain inalienable rights', to support her view that woman was 'an independent human personality, capable of determining her own ends'. For most women she believed that this meant 'working at the mother task' (Martin, 1914: 42). The British suffragist, Helena Swanwick, defined 'equality' as 'equal opportunities to do the things they (women) feel able to do'. She wanted 'more help, more training, more expenditure of public money' to assist them in their 'peculiarly feminine work'.

'Equality' was not intended in a 'mathematical sense' (Swanwick, 1914: 159–160). Rather, it was reserved for legal citizenship rights: the 'demand for the recognition of human rights regardless of color, sex or previous condition of servitude' (Spencer, 1923: 291). There seemed no reason therefore for equality to mean identity of function. This allowed suffragists, as Nancy Cott explains, to ask for the right to vote because they were the 'same as' men and 'different from' them *in one and the same breath*, because they were citizens and because they had special qualities which were needed in the public world of politics (Cott, 1987: 19; Rendall, 1987: 15). The virtues which women were meant to bring with them were that familiar constellation associated with the feminine stereotype. Women would be more caring; they would ensure that policy reflected children's interests; they would be more honest, less acquisitive, less attached to party machines.

Even feminists like Charlotte Perkins Gilman, Olive Schreiner

and Helena Swanwick who advocated some sharing of roles between men and women continued to believe in a unique female
essence. The two sets of ideas did not always sit comfortably.
Gilman for example believed that 'Men are at present far more
human than women' but 'the women are more vitally human than
the men, by nature' (Gilman, 1911: 184). Olive Schreiner[6] downplayed observable character differences between men and women,
attributing 'such psychic differences' as do appear largely to 'artificial training'. But she insisted that *certain* psychic differences
remained which were 'inherent and not artificial' (Schreiner, 1911:
182, 185). Swanwick actually attacked the 'common feminist view'
that women had distinctive virtues, but still believed that women
were 'nearer to nature' and that men enjoyed fighting for its own
sake (Swanwick, 1914: 197, 49).

The shared belief that somehow woman's biological capacity to
give birth affected woman's character best explains these inconsistencies. For Gilman motherhood was a 'feminine function' more
akin to real 'human functions' which would bring into human life a
'more normal influence'. It was this which made them 'more vitally
human than the men'. From this starting point she could also
accept the standard suffragist argument that women would bring
special qualities to the governing process: 'Government by women,
as far as it is influenced by their sex, would be influenced by
motherhood; and that would mean care, nurture, provision, education' (Gilman, 1911: 189). Schreiner also attributed women's innate differences to their reproductive capacity:

> The relation of the female towards the production of human life
> influences undoubtedly even her relation towards animal and all
> life. 'It is a fine day, let us go out and kill something!' cries the
> typical male of certain races, instinctively. 'There is a living
> thing, it will die if it is not cared for', says the average woman,
> almost equally instinctively. It is true that the woman will
> sacrifice as mercilessly, as cruelly, the life of a hated rival or an
> enemy as any male, *but she always knows what she is doing and
> the value of the life she takes* (Schreiner, 1911: 178, emphasis in
> original).

Swanwick also asserted that men's and women's 'share in reproduction is different and produces differences of life, needs and
temperament'. On the other hand she attributed women's 'different' outlook to the material reality of their lives:

> We have only to consider the very different lives women lead,
> leaving out of account the debatable differences in nature, to
> see how impossible it is for a man to look on life with a

woman's eyes...Men are rich and women are poor. Men are
employers and women are employed. Wage-earning men think
mainly of wages, women are more concerned with prices.

Her conclusion, that '...in the main men will be more concerned
for property and women more concerned for the person...'
(Swanwick, 1914: 49), almost qualifies her as a 'feminist standpoint' theorist.[7]

In order to understand the feminist intellectual heritage we
need to recover the ambiguities in arguments like these instead
of wishing them away for our own theoretical purposes. We are
moving into a difficult interpretative area here. It seems clear from
the structure and content of suffragist arguments that there was
a conscious attempt to answer critics. And, since the historical
sources are predominantly public pronouncements, contradictions
may reflect the fact that speeches and books were tailored for
particular audiences (Uglow, 1983: 150). Contradictions might demonstrate simply the adroit management of political symbols.

At the same time contradictions and inconsistencies should be
anticipated. Contemporary political theorists readily concede the
ambivalent and shifting nature of political attitudes (Edelman,
1971: 3), and yet we are reluctant to admit such inconsistency in
historical personalities. This can only make it difficult if not impossible to understand either the past or the present. Cynthia
Cockburn's approach to her research for *Brothers* is exemplary
here:

> I tried to see contradictions not as problems to be ironed out
> but as the *goal* of the research. Such elaboration of paradox
> and confusion are painstaking and often painful. But it is
> precisely out of the process of bringing such contradictions to
> consciousness and facing up to illogicality or inconsistency that
> a person takes a grip on his or her own fate (Cockburn, 1983:
> 12).

At the very least we should try to empathise with the difficult task
early feminists faced. Social theorists are still struggling to explain
the relationship between the individual and society (Henriques,
et al., 1984). It ought not to be surprising therefore if some of
these ideas proved difficult to handle. Beyond this, the contradictions and inconsistencies may offer a *contribution* to that social
theory. Martha Minow makes the important point that 'the inconsistencies in the world we have made suggest that inconsistent
ideas may be less confused than consistent ones' (Minow, 1986:
911). The inconsistencies then might reveal not so much what is
wrong with thought processes as what is wrong with the world. If

women's lives are filled with contradictions, 'inconsistent' ideas may best describe them.

Interpretations of the women's movement which describe a shift from 'justice' to 'expediency' tend to present the later emphasis upon woman's traditional maternal role and character as an error that explains the decline of feminism after the vote was won (Babcock, Freedman, Norton and Ross, 1975: 39–40). The implication is that feminists would have done better to continue relying upon justice arguments. Since justice arguments were *never abandoned*, however, and since almost all suffragists accepted a traditional allocation of sex roles, it seems more relevant to understand the basis of this ideology than to suggest that some alternative might have been more successful.

Several factors contributed to the ubiquity of the maternal ethos.[8] The political climate of the late nineteenth and early twentieth centuries played an important part. The themes of 'national greatness' and 'national efficiency' filled the public press. The introduction of technical education and domestic science classes reflected the desire to increase national output and to improve the health of the population. The scientific community's discovery of evolution exacerbated these concerns. Eugenists applied theories of heredity to human samples, sometimes recommending segregation or sterilisation of those deemed unfit to breed (Pickens, 1968; Searle, 1976). I have already mentioned a few publications which lay out the implications of the scientific message for women (see page 11). There were many such texts.[9] Women had a duty to mother and to mother well. They were exhorted to reverse the decline in the birth rate, an obsession in Anglo-Saxon countries in those years, and to upgrade their mothering skills (Hyam, 1976; Searle, 1971; Bacchi, 1980a and b; Davin, 1978).

Feminists formulated their ideas within this framework. As Murray Edelman explains:

> . . . elite pronouncements feed into and partially create the language structures in terms of which people understand the world and psychologically defend their place in the world from contradiction. From this perspective, politics. . . [begins]. . . with conceptual structures into which people receive information and transform it into a world view from which action (or inaction) proceeds (Edelman, 1977: xxi).

People can and do manipulate these structures. Australian feminists for example placed greater emphasis upon environmental theories of evolution which gave women a more activist role than genetic theories which reduced them to 'mere breeders' (Bacchi, 1980b). Jane Lewis suggests that British women were equally adept at circumventing or reinterpreting scientific theories (Lewis, 1984: 88, 96). We should not underestimate however the extent to which feminists assimilated these ideas into their own 'world view'. Brophy and Smart note that 'the ideas and language of evolutionism formed part of the common sense of the period' (Brophy and Smart, 1985: 41). Charlotte Perkins Gilman, Olive Schreiner, Helena Swanwick, Anna Garlin Spencer, almost every feminist in the period, incorporated evolutionary ideas into their analysis. Many of them were eugenists. Women who claimed a right to self-actualisation were put on the defensive by these ideas and often themselves felt unsure about their priorities. One of the early histories of female education in America, by Willystine Goodsell, Associate Professor of Education, Columbia University, asked these questions:

> Are the higher education and the professional training of women unfitting them for marriage and motherhood? Is such education to result in the production of a type of woman more interested in her chosen life work than in giving life to a new generation? Is the maintenance of the race to be left more and more to the women of the laboring classes... (Goodsell, 1923: 30–31).

Feminists did not simply adopt the maternal ethos under duress, however. It also provided a popular and respectable image to women who had begun to feel a sense of sex solidarity. Martha Minow describes how Elizabeth Cady Stanton, the well-known American suffragist, constructed a conception of herself 'capacious enough to accommodate her commitments both to mothering and to social revolution' (Minow, 1985a: 1085).

Feminists who desired both a sense of identity and inclusion in political structures found that the maternal ethos served these functions better than available alternatives. They used it effectively for example in trying to convince their men to enfranchise them, arguing that good middle-class women could outvote the pauper and the foreigner (Kraditor, 1971: Chapter 6).[10] It also differentiated them from groups from which they wished to be distant. The asexual ideal, for example, which formed part of the ethos, set them apart from both the 'immoral' aristocracy and the 'brutish' masses (Bacchi, 1988: 44–45). In America, the cult of the 'true woman' distinguished white women from Black women and created a white middle-class model for Blacks to emulate (Hooks, 1981: 155). Some Black women lay claim to the ideal as an entrée to respectability. Anna Julia Cooper wrote an essay in 1892 advis-

ing Black women to serve their country by educating themselves
for motherhood:

> All I claim is that there is a feminine as well as a masculine side
> to truth; that these are related, not as inferior and superior, not
> as better and worse, not as weaker and stronger, but as
> complements—complements in one necessary and systematic
> whole. That as the man is more noble in reason, so the woman
> is more quick in sympathy. That as he is indefatigable in
> pursuit of abstract truth, so is she in caring for interests by the
> way...(Hooks, 1981: 167).

For most suffragists woman's maternal role then was assumed. It
formed a critical part of a middle-class world view which rested
upon the 'monogamic' family. The sociologist, Anna Garlin
Spencer, described the 'private family' as 'a priceless inheritance
from the past' which 'should be preserved' (Spencer, 1923: 5).
Middle-class commitment to the 'monogamic' family, however,
presented an almost insuperable barrier to women intent on self-
actualisation. To manoeuvre around this obstacle feminists developed a concept of liberty for women very different from that of
liberty for men. As Sarah Schramm explains, because 'restraint on
liberty is only warranted for self-preservation and perpetuating the
species' and because women were given responsibility for these
tasks, female liberty became tied to the 'path of duty' (Schramm,
1979: 183). Mackinnon discovered a similar attitude in that 'contradictory amalgamation' out of which women's higher education
was formed: 'to develop individuality, not for self-assertion, but
for better service' (Mackinnon, 1984: 50).

For the sake of community cohesion, therefore, women surrendered their claim to self-actualisation. To challenge the maternal
ethos would have meant striking at the heart of this political
framework. The anti-suffragist, Correa Moylan Walsh, understood
what was at stake. She worried that 'individualism is going over to
women' and then 'the family as well as the state is to break up into
its constituent atoms' (Walsh, 1917: 34).[11]

Many feminists meanwhile were critical of the rampant individualism and lack of compassion they observed in the world of
politics and in the marketplace. Their hope was that, given a voice,
women could temper this unfeeling world with the maternal influence which they would bring with them from the home. Men,
the *Englishwoman's Review* reported, had created a social economy
of 'elaborately arranged systems' that lacked 'the vitalizing warmth
of woman's work, and still more of woman's control—the *mother*
influence...' (Murray and Clark, 1985: xxi). The British

feminist, Josephine Butler, developed the idea in *Woman's Work and Woman's Culture* that women have certain 'ordering powers' based on a long tradition of care for individuals which were needed to alleviate the 'wholesale' impersonal nature of 'masculine' institutions (Uglow, 1983: 157). Elizabeth Cady Stanton condemned male 'indulgences, appetites and vices' which stood in the way of 'progress, harmony and social reconstruction of life'. She considered women more 'exalted than the men' because 'their moral feelings and political instincts' are 'not so much affected by selfishness, or business or party consideration' (quoted in Elshtain, 1985: 13–14).

There is some disagreement about how to assess this political analysis. Jean Grimshaw feels that it simply mirrored conventional attitudes towards men as corrupt and females as pure, and 'the sharp division between the harsh and immoral public world and the uncontaminated world of domesticity'. It did not, in her view, challenge the polarities (Grimshaw, 1986: 200). While in the main this interpretation is accurate, a few women did manage to challenge these polarities. Martha Minow feels that Elizabeth Cady Stanton managed to break free of the 'unsatisfying debate over sameness and difference', although her analysis was constrained by the available political framework in which 'men were the measure of rights and women the symbols of virtue' (Minow, 1985a: 1091). Another British feminist, Gertrude Martin, offered a different solution to woman's 'peculiar problem' which she identified as 'how to reconcile the conflicting claims of her own individuality and the race'. She believed that the time had come, not to lift the race burden, but to equalise it. 'What the race really needs', she declared, 'is not more mothering but more fathering' (Martin, 1914: 45–46).

Few feminists at the time were capable of these conceptual leaps given their intellectual and political heritage, and those who were, were ignored. By accepting that women had a sex-specific duty to care for the family in ways which men did not, two things happened. By implication men were released from these responsibilities. And, second, the kind of structural analysis which would bring together family and the market for men and women was left undone. Nonetheless the importance of the feminist critique of the existing political order should not be underestimated. The idea that politics was housekeeping on a grand scale drew attention to the role politics played in a range of 'domestic' affairs, education, health, consumer rights. In addition, the suggestion that public values needed to be changed and upgraded was in fact a challenge to the idea that 'public' morality did not have to measure up to the higher standards set for the 'private' sphere.

Susan Tenenbaum places the suffragists within a tradition of social critics who wished to 'salvage communitarian values from the ravages of economic liberalism' (Tenenbaum, 1982: 98). Rosalind Rosenberg makes the important point that feminists were not developing this challenge in isolation. With men like John Dewey, George Herbert Mead and Henry Hollingworth they were part of a major transformation in American intellectual life at the beginning of the twentieth century. These men also 'rejected the rugged, aggressive individualism that was so important an ingredient of Victorian manhood', and were drawn instead 'to the ideals of cooperation and social concern then thought to be particularly congenial to the female temperament' (Rosenberg, 1982: xvii). Progressivism in America, the New Liberalism in Australia and the egalitarian tradition of British and Australian Labour would provide fertile homes for some of these ideas. However, as will be seen, the dependence of the communitarian (*Gemeinschaft*) model upon a strict division of sex roles proved problematic for women in these traditions as well.

Consensus about the distribution of sex roles therefore carried over into mainstream feminist political analysis with unfortunate effects. Sex roles became 'role typologies', in Berger and Luckman's phrase, and for most people in this period they represented the 'integration of all institutions in a meaningful world' (Berger and Luckmann, 1979: 91–93). When roles were assigned in politics, they were assigned on a gender-specific basis. Here is the South Australian social reformer, Lillian Mead, writing in Adelaide in 1895:

> As a member of the home a man's special duty is for its advance, maintenance and defence; as a member of the State, his duty is also for the advance, maintenance, and defence of the State. A woman's special work at home is to promote its order, comfort and beauty. Her work in the State is to promote its order, comfort and beauty (Mead, 1895: 34–5).

Furthermore, because of the close association between women and the domestic sphere, 'womanhood' became almost a metaphor for domestic virtues. According to Murray Edelman, by intensifying selected perceptions and ignoring others, metaphors can give distorted perceptions: 'Each metaphor can be a subtle way of highlighting what one wants to believe and avoiding what one does not wish to face'. Because metaphors pervade our language, they need to be chosen carefully for 'appropriateness and potential fruitfulness' (Edelman, 1971: 67). The 'woman as superior' construct stopped short of the kind of political analysis which was needed. Instead of challenging the notion of the disembodied abstract individual and suggesting that men should share responsibility for living arrangements, women offered to continue their role as 'restrained' individuals.

The tension within feminism between 'sameness to' and 'difference from' men is then really an expression of the tension between a desire to share 'men's' individualistic lifestyle, to apply *Gesellschaft* values to women, and the feeling of responsibility for family and community well-being. This tension could be maintained in a 'functional ambiguity' (Cott, 1987a: 20) so long as feminists agreed that women would continue their traditional family role. Reforms to allow single women to work and to improve the status of married women could be accommodated within this view of social relations. When some feminists began to challenge the sexual division of labour, especially when some married middle-class women expressed their desire for careers, however, all of the philosophical problems of the relationship between the individual and the community, and the practical problem of how living arrangements were to be organised were opened up for debate. The organised feminist movement in Britain and America now divided into 'sameness' and 'difference' camps, depending upon their particular resolution of these problems. Chapters 2 and 3 explain how this happened.

2
The split (part I): 'equalitarian' versus 'reform' feminism

In the 1920s and 1930s serious divisions developed within the women's movement in both Britain and America. In part, these divisions were a result of the greater diversity of women from varying backgrounds who joined the movement and who brought with them conflicting priorities. A broader membership base, it seems, made it difficult to maintain the illusion of a single 'woman' movement (Cott, 1987: 6; Phillips, 1986: 93). The movement attracted larger numbers of working-class women and Black women and middle-class women with a variety of occupational backgrounds.

Put simply, tension arose between middle-class professional women who demanded a 'fair field and no favour' (the equal rights, equalitarian or ultra faction), and other middle-class women who were committed to a wider social reform movement (reform feminists). In America equalitarian feminists headed by Alice Paul, campaigned for an Equal Rights Amendment (ERA) and against protective legislation, such as minimum wages and maximum hours for women. Social reformers like Josephine Goldmark and Florence Kelley lined up on the opposing side. In Britain equal rights feminists, sometimes called 'ultras', formed two organisations, the Six Point Group and the Open Door Council. The social reformers were led by Eleanor Rathbone who claimed to speak for a 'New Feminism' which would give women 'real' equality. Australian feminists did not divide into sharply contending factions, although both equal rights and reform feminism had representatives.

The following collection of quotations confirms that feminists in this period identified a strategic and ideological tension within the

29

movement. A variety of labels, including 'sameness' and 'difference', were used to describe the contending positions. In 1914, for example, the American socialist, Charlotte Perkins Gilman, published an article in the *Forerunner Magazine* outlining the 'Conflict between "Human" and "Female" Feminism':

> The one holds that sex is a rumor department of life; that the main lines of human development have nothing to do with sex, and that what women need most is the development of human characteristics. The other considers sex as paramount, as underlying or covering all phases of life, and that what woman needs is an even fuller exercise, development and recognition of her sex (quoted in Cott, 1987: 49).

Gilman's 'human' feminists stressed the need to treat women and men equally; the 'female' feminists drew attention to women's 'special' requirements.

In 1925 Mary Anderson, head of the American Women's Bureau from 1920 to 1944, confirmed that there were two types of feminists, the 'ultra feminist', to whom '*legal* equality means almost everything', and the 'more moderate type' who will be the 'more practical woman, who sees and works with facts' (Anderson, 1925). In that same year the American social reformer and journalist, Crystal Eastman, reported from London that in every country where women had won the vote, 'Suffragists tend to separate into two distinct groups so far as their public activities go'. She described the 'humanitarians' who in her schema correspond to Gilman's 'female' feminists. These women devoted themselves to 'securing those measures of general human betterment for which enlightened women have always stood'. In contrast the 'pure feminists' or 'equalitarians', 'as long as any inequality exists between men and women, regard it as the chief object of organised women to remove it' (Cook, 1978: 154, 223, 224). She quoted Lady Rhondda (Margaret Thomas), one of the founders of England's Six Point Group, to the effect that the women in the woman's movement fell into two groups, 'the feminists, and the reformers who are not in the least feminists, who do not care two pence for equality for itself...' (Cook, 1978: 193).

Meanwhile, Eleanor Rathbone, the founder of the British Family Endowment Society, was laying claim to a 'New Feminism' which shifted the focus from equality with men to women's particular needs. Rathbone demanded 'what we want for women, not because it is what men have got, but because it is what women need...' (Stocks, 1949: 116). A 1917 collection of 'Essays in Feminism', edited by the Fabian, Victor Gollancz, contrasted

'New Feminism' and 'doctrinaire' feminism (Gollancz, 1917: passim, 173). Elizabeth Abbott, one of the founders of the British
Open Door Council, responded angrily to the charge that equal
rights feminists were doctrinaire: 'New feminism reads a dictionary definition, equality—sameness; men and women [in their opin-
ion] are not the same and therefore are not equal' (Lewis, 1984:
104). Finally Alice Henry, the Australian trade union organiser,
who moved to America to become active in the National Women's
Trade Union League, criticised 'radical feminists', another label
appended to equal rights feminism, for being willing, 'for what
they consider consistency', to scrap everything 'working women
have with such toil and suffering obtained' (Henry, 1971: 163–
164).

The argument developed in the following two chapters is that these
various labels, including references to 'sameness' and 'difference',
were rhetorical devices which hide more than they reveal. The
divisions among feminists in this period were due to an underlying
ideological tension between competing political ethics. The 'sameness' group (equalitarians, equal rights) accepted the values of
Gesellschaft and sought to apply them to women. The 'difference' or
reform feminist faction upheld the more communitarian *Gemeinschaft* vision which depended upon women's traditional homemaker role. Those who demanded equal rights accepted in the main
the ideology of liberal individualism. Those who upheld traditional
sex roles endorsed a more organic view of the social order based
solidly upon the nuclear family.

Chapter 2 begins with an examination of the background to this
conflict. It suggests that the underlying point of contention was
whether married women, particularly if they were mothers, ought
to engage in paid work. The debate was essentially then a functional one. Middle-class women in this period agonised over
woman's appropriate social function, trying to find a balance between the demands of paid work and family. 'Sameness' advocates
concentrated their efforts upon establishing all women's right to
compete in the marketplace. To this end they paid little attention
to the demands imposed by family obligations. 'Difference' reformers tried to find ways to increase women's autonomy within
traditional roles.

Chapter 2 concentrates upon divisions in Britain over protective
legislation in the nineteenth century, and the early twentieth-
century dispute between equal rights feminists and reform feminists in America. Chapter 3 follows up later developments in Britain and in Australia. Both chapters explain the combination of

influences which divided the movement into antagonistic camps. The types of issues which were raised remain dilemmas today— how to construct a reform program which addresses the diversity of women's needs, how to establish a balance between short-term objectives and long-term goals, and how to reconcile the desire or need for paid work with family commitments within a structure and ideology which continue to assume woman's primary responsibility for living arrangements.

Several kinds of changes in women's lifestyles brought the issue of women's workforce participation to public attention. It is of course critical to remember that different countries had different experiences (Tilly and Scott, 1978), but it is possible to generalise some of the factors at work. One of these was the trend towards marriage at a later age which meant that more women sought waged work for longer periods of their lives. Demographically women outnumbered men in most industrialised communities, creating a situation where many women would have to be self-supporting *throughout* their lives. Towards the end of the nineteenth century there were also important changes in the industrial composition of the female workforce. There was a steady decline in the proportion of employed women engaged in paid domestic service, relative stability in the manufacturing sector, and an increase in commercial and professional employment (Bacchi, 1986a: 407). Although married women constituted a relatively small proportion of the female workforce at this time (approximately 10%) the increasing availability of tertiary-sector occupations and the larger numbers of college-educated women seeking meaningful work outside their homes produced public concern about women's 'appropriate' social role.

The difficulty of combining marriage and paid work became 'The Problem' for women in the twentieth century. The daughters of the pioneers of the women's movement found themselves faced with this, the conundrum of women's lives. Many women in the previous century had resolved the dilemma by choosing spinsterhood and had campaigned to make that choice respectable (Vicinus, 1985). To counter the derogatory connotations associated with the term 'spinster', they worked to create a new image of 'lives of lonely and productive dedication' (M. Carey Thomas in Cross, 1965: 158). M. Carey Thomas made plain that in her generation to combine 'marriage and an academic career was impossible'. Her decision was an easy one: 'I knew myself well enough to realize that I could not give up my life's work...' (Dobkin, 1979: xv). For others, the choice was never so easy. By the turn of the century more and more women were asking why they should have to choose at all. Most of those who articulated this demand were middle-class; many were professionals. Working-class women frequently had to balance the demands of motherhood and a paid job.

There were really two questions. The first was whether a woman could continue working after marriage; the second was whether she could continue working after motherhood. The first seemed easier to resolve, at least as far as personal choice was concerned. Some of 'These Modern Women', seventeen women who contributed essays to the *Nation* in 1926–1927 with their views on feminism, declared that they preferred to follow their careers and remain single. Sue Shelton White (1887–1943), a southern leader of the American National Woman's Party (NWP), thought that 'marriage is too much of a compromise; it lops off a woman's life as an individual'. She admitted though that marriage had its attractions: 'Yet the renunciation too is a lopping-off. We choose between the frying-pan and the fire—both very uncomfortable' (Showalter, 1978: 17).

For those who decided to marry, remaining childless was one option. Amongst the seventeen contributors, only five had children. The artist, Wanda Gag, had no doubt that she would create *either* 'aesthetically' *or* 'physically'. She chose the former (Showalter, 1978: 127). Those who decided to 'have it all' most often had the resources to hire other women to assist them. Cornelia Bryce Pinchot (1881–1960), the wealthiest of the seventeen, believed that 'women can bear the children, charm her lovers, boss a business, swim the Channel, stand at Armegeddon [sic], and battle for the Lord—all in the day's work!' This was, as Elaine Showalter points out, a privileged view of feminism (Showalter, 1978: 120). An article in *Harper's Magazine* in the same period claimed that this option was available to *any* young woman determined to make a success of marriage and childrearing, and '*at the same time* [they are] moved by an inescapable inner compulsion to be individuals in their own right':

> . . . in this era of simplified housekeeping they see their
> opportunity, for it is obvious that a woman who plans
> intelligently can salvage some time for her own pursuits
> (Bromley, 1927: 552).

'If possible', of course, 'she will have a servant'. Young middle-class women were troubled by the dilemma. In 1919 a *Smith College Weekly* challenged the assumption that it was 'fixed in the nature of things that a woman must choose between a home and her work when a man may have both', and enjoined 'There must be a way out and it is the problem of our generation to find the way' (Solomon, 1985: 174).

'The Problem' was addressed at many levels. The women who wrote to the *Nation* seemed determined to confront the challenge as a personal one. Few examined the structural constraints which meant that they *had* to make a choice. They belonged to a tradition which asked only 'a fair field and no favour', even if this meant rejecting the opportunity to have children. They feared that *any* 'special pleading' would be counted against them. Elisabeth Kemper Adams warned 'aspiring professional women':

> They will have to learn not to ask or expect any concessions whatever on the grounds that they are women, nor even sometimes on the grounds that they are human, since any weakness is likely to be considered feminine. They will have to expect to be judged even more rigorously than young men of the same education doing similar work, and to breathe an atmosphere of being on trial (Showalter, 1978: 17).

The editor of the *Nation* series, Freda Kirchway, tried to live out this 'survival of the fittest' philosophy, painful though it proved to be. Kirchway, a keen journalist, felt it inappropriate to take more than the absolute minimum time off to have a child. In 1922, expecting her first child, she worked up to three days before the birth. She wrote to the publisher with reference to her motherhood: 'I'm not going to let it hurt the *Nation* if I can possibly avoid it and I'm sure I can'. Although a socialist, Kirchway had domestic help to assist her. She and her husband also believed that 'child-rearing was the province of child development professionals', according to Kirchway's biographer (Alpern, 1987: 68). It seems that later in her life Kirchway regretted taking off so little time to have her babies: 'I think that's silly. It is a strain that is fair neither to the woman nor the baby'. She admitted sadly that her generation had not discovered the means to achieve the tenuous balance between career and family: 'Though both ran smoothly, I always had a feeling of strain, of never being caught up with myself. That is true of a lot of my friends too' (Alpern, 1987: 97). Other women worked out other individual solutions. For example, Lucy Sprague Mitchell resolved the conflict by working from her home (Antler, 1987).

The subject was considered important enough to require systematic study. The Institute for the Coordination of Women's Interests, an organisation sponsored by Smith College, asked the psychologist, Lillian Gilbreth (1878–1972),[1] to investigate how college-educated women could better coordinate college training and career aspirations with marriage and family life. Gilbreth applied the principles of scientific management to housekeeping (Cott, 1987: 163). She concluded, like the contributor to *Harper's*, that women would simply have to become more efficient housekeepers. Research like Gilbreth's reinforced the notion that domestic work could become a 'science' and housewifery a 'profession'.

The same issue, how to meet 'the conflicting claims of the domestic and the independent life', attracted the attention of educationists. The British education reformer, Elinor Burns, showing remarkable if regrettable foresight, felt that a 'satisfactory settlement' of the 'rival claims of "the home" and of some kind of independent work' was a 'permanent problem by which the feminist movement will always be kept alive'. Although she believed that 'any particular adjustment' of the 'real conflict between the two kinds of life' could only be a 'temporary compromise', she hoped that 'wiser methods of education might do much to make the conflict less painful' (Burns, 1917: 160).

The educational curriculum itself, however, reflected a 'divided aim'. A contributor to Burstall's early history of *English High Schools for Girls* felt it would be comparatively easy to frame a curriculum and a course of school training which 'would fit a girl for the duties of home life'. Again, it would be comparatively easy to plan curricula which would give 'a sound preparation for professional and business life':

> But the difficulty lies in the fact that the future of so many of the girls is uncertain. They may not eventually decide or need to earn their own living in a professional calling. Their work may lie in domestic duties at home with their parents or in a home of their own. But during their school days it is necessary for a large number of cases to prepare them, so far as may be, for either event (Sadler in Burstall, 1907: 14).

Dolores Hayden describes in *The Grand Domestic Revolution* the efforts of a number of 'material feminists'[2] to develop new forms of neighbourhood organisations, including housewives' cooperatives, to help those who wanted to combine homemaking with paid work (Hayden, 1983: 1). Gilman had advocated cooperative kitchens. The British Labour woman, Marion Phillips, wanted national restaurant organisations, cooperative housing and nurseries (Mann, 1974: 30–34). Henrietta Rodman, one of the leaders of the radical Greenwich Village Feminist Alliance, called for centralisation of the 'four primitive industries', childcare, cooking, housework and laundry. She believed that childcare had to become the central issue for feminists:

> At the present time the care of the baby is the weak point in feminism. The care of children, particularly those under four

or five years of age, is the point at which feminism is most open to attack. We must have this apartment house before we can become honest feminists (Showalter, 1978: 18).

The 'material feminists' seem to have had a vision beyond that of the mainstream. In Hayden's words:

> They demanded both remuneration and honor for women's traditional sphere of work, while conceding that some women might wish to do other kinds of work. They were not prepared to let men argue that a woman's equality would ultimately rest on her ability to undertake 'man's' work in a factory or an office. Nor were they prepared to describe the state as the agency of their liberation... usually they stated clearly that women's work must be controlled by women—economically, socially, and environmentally (Hayden, 1983: 6).

These were some of the very issues which befuddled organised feminists and which caused the types of polarised positions evident in the collection of quotations at the beginning of the chapter. Why these divisions occurred reveals a great deal about the combination of influences which affects feminism and the types of arguments feminists use.

Since protective legislation was the most divisive issue in each of the countries under consideration during the period, it can be used as a starting place for unravelling the contenders in the debate and their points of view. The issue became contentious in Britain first for the simple reason that factory legislation was first introduced there. The 1842 Mines Regulation Act inaugurated sex-specific legislation. While the motives behind this Act were ambiguous, the next campaign for a ten-hour work limit for women was pursued by male unionists with the declared purpose of excluding women from certain kinds of work (Humphries, 1981: 28; Phillips, 1987: 83). The nascent feminist movement reacted hostilely.

Even at this stage, despite the consensus that the legislation disadvantaged women, there was a range of views. Emma Paterson of the Women's Protective and Provident League, which later became the Women's Trade Union League, opposed those parts of the legislation which affected women, but approved of the sanitary precautions and the restraint of children's employment (Hutchins, 1902: 91). Others, like the suffragist Millicent Garrett Fawcett, espoused the economic ideals of free trade and self-help and objected to all factory legislation as undue interference in the marketplace (Oakley, 1983: 191; Lewis, 1984: 104). Josephine Butler condemned the legislation on free enterprise grounds and because she objected to the implication that women needed protection because of their capacity to give birth: 'this doctrine of Reproduction is not the essential aim of existence for either half of the human race' (quoted in Lewis, 1983: 31).

By the turn of the century the debate had changed in certain ways. Principally, women active in the labour movement began to put their case that free, unregulated enterprise injured workers and that, because women were as yet poorly organised, 'special' legislation seemed the best way to secure improved working conditions for them. A conflict developed between these women and *laissez fairists* like Fawcett. The Fabian, Beatrice Webb, criticised those 'individualists, reinforced by a batch of excellent ladies (eager for the Right of Woman to work at all hours of the day and night with the minimum space and sanitation)' (quoted in Lewis, 1984: 91).

It is unwise to generalise about attitudes on the subject. Some working-class women such as the Lancashire textile workers and the 'pit brow' women opposed protective legislation as exclusionary; others, aligned with the Trades Union Congress and the Labour Party, supported it (Phillips, 1987: 88–90). The latter, who accepted traditional sex roles, were of the opinion that the best way to improve the conditions of working-class women was to raise the salaries of their husbands; therefore you needed legislation to stop women from undercutting male wages. Margaret MacDonald, the wife of Ramsay, declared that 'married women should not be earning money at all' (Mappen, 1986: 251).

These views affected the attitudes of middle-class women reformers closely aligned with the labour movement. Inquiries into the 'Sweating System', which paid women a low piece rate for home work, also mobilised middle-class reformers, male and female (Holton, 1986: 23–28). Protective legislation began to attract more supporters. One of these, Clementina Black, who founded the Women's Industrial Council, argued that legislation restricting night work for women produced in the end a higher piece rate so that 'the girls therefore were receiving practically the same pay—certainly no less—for a ten hours day as they had previously received for a day of sixteen to eighteen hours' (Black, 1902: 215). Black also believed that unregulated women's labour would simply 'oust men from employment', clearly an undesirable result in her view. Like many other labour sympathisers she accepted that there were 'fundamental differences' between men and women as industrial workers: women expected to remain wage earners only until marriage; they 'chose' occupations which required less training; and a good many did not care 'to earn a high wage at the expense of hard work'. They were inferior workers, of 'less value to the community generally' (Black, 1902: 204–210).

After Emma Paterson's death in 1890 the Women's Trade Union League, now headed by Lady Emilia Dilke, reversed its position and endorsed protective legislation. Like Black, Dilke accepted the sexual division of labour. She maintained that to argue that the Factory Acts

> . . . should under no circumstances take account of the differences of sex is to fight against indisputable facts which must, in the end, prove too strong for us. There is no danger to society in the recognising of *equal human rights* for both sexes, if we are also ready to recognise the divergence of their capabilities, for the relations of men and women to each other, *their functions in the family and the state*, must ultimately be determined—however ill it may please the most ardent female reformer—by the operation of *natural law* (quoted in Holton, 1986: 25, emphasis added).

She added: 'This principle lies at the bottom of all reasoned Trade Unionism which, insofar as it is concerned with the organisation of women's work, has for its ultimate object the restoration of as many as possible to their post of honour as queens of the hearth'. On another occasion Dilke explained why she opposed female labour:

> A well-known unionist has said, 'If women will not organise, for God's sake, boycott them out of their trade, so that the men can get a living wage for their families and for themselves'. She believed in that principle (Bondfield, 1940: 52).

Dilke has been quoted at length because it is important to realise that there were different strategies in the period for improving women's situation. The suggestion outlined above was to increase the family wage and to encourage women to remain home.

The Women's Cooperative Guild started in 1883 also decided to concentrate its efforts upon bettering women's position within the home by improving the economic position of the family (Davies, 1978: 16). It campaigned to have the 'neglected needs of married women' included in the 1911 National Insurance Act, secured a Maternity Benefit paid directly to the wife, and fought for protective legislation and a minimum wage for women workers (Davies, 1984: xiv).

As Anne Phillips explains, the changing composition of the women's movement shifted the central issue from 'too little work for women', the preoccupation of nineteenth-century, middle-class feminists, to 'too much work' for working-class mothers (Phillips,

1986: 93). Some feminists, middle and working-class,[3] declared their willingness to use state machinery to bolster women's place within the family. The strategy had problems. It assumed that women could and would want to stay home; and it ignored by default the large numbers of women who would end up inhabiting both spheres, the domestic sphere and the marketplace. Equal rights feminists on the other hand concentrated their efforts upon facilitating women's entry into the paid workforce, and underestimated the problems caused by family commitments. This set the backdrop for the renewed debates about protective legislation and family endowments in the 1920s and 1930s, taken up in the next chapter. One point needs to be emphasised at this time. A more communitarian spirit in Britain set its stamp upon feminism in a way which would continue to affect it throughout the twentieth century.

The background in America provides a dramatic contrast. America did not have a counterpart to the British Labour movement or the collectivist spirit which went with it (Hartz, 1986: 15–21). Organised labour almost never campaigned in support of hours laws for men. It was simply too weak and decided to use the mechanism of collective bargaining in preference to legislation (Ratner, 1980: 185–198).

The campaign for protective legislation for women was launched by turn-of-the-century reformers, often called progressives, who hoped to use it as the thin edge of the wedge to win the kind of factory legislation Britain had been experimenting with for more than half a century. In 1908, in *Muller v Oregon*, Louis D. Brandeis, a young lawyer later to become a Supreme Court Justice, presented a brief which argued that women needed legislation limiting their hours of labour because they were physically weaker than men, historically dependent upon men, and because their role in the creation of the next generation was a vital national interest which had to be protected (Goldstein, 1988: 20–25). Brandeis won the case. The decision in *Bunting v Oregon* (1917) to uphold a ten-hour statute *for men* seemed to suggest that the progressives' strategy had worked:

> They needed only to restrict their social welfare legislation at first to women, use the weaker-sex rationale to convince the Court to accept the protective legislation as 'reasonable' and then, having obtained this concession, enact the same reasonable measures to protect the men of the community (Goldstein, 1988: 24).

Subsequent court decisions which removed this legislation proved that their optimism had been premature.

Much of the material used by Brandeis had been collected by the prominent women reformers, Florence Kelley and Josephine Goldmark. Goldmark published the results of her research in a volume entitled *Fatigue and Efficiency* (Goldmark, 1913). Scientific management principles are very much in evidence in the work, as well as a genuine humanitarian concern to increase leisure for all working people. An underlying assumption, however, was that the protection of women's health was 'even more necessary than the protection of men's health' (Goldmark, 1913: 255). Goldmark rested her argument upon both basic biological 'differences'— 'women's physiological handicaps make them subject more than men to the new strain of industry'—and the material reality of women's lives: 'Women who work at night fare particularly ill. Those who are married cannot postpone the regular household necessities which await them in the morning...'

Fundamentally Goldmark's position assumed woman's responsibility for family management and that her role in this and in reproduction was important and necessary. She was distressed that, if women worked at night, 'Home life was totally lost':

> When the mother of a family spends the night or evening in work, disorder is almost unavoidable and the comfort of men as well as of the children dependent upon her ministrations is lost (Goldmark, 1913: 39, 267, 92).

The fear of disorder had moral undertones: 'Young women who work at night are deprived of all the restraining influences of home life'. Women who worked at night faced 'special "moral" dangers', 'peril of insult if not of attack'. The other threat was to the future of the race: '...industrial overstrain of women has commonly reacted in three visible ways: in a heightened infant mortality, a lowered birthrate, and an impaired second generation' (Goldmark, 1913: 86, 267, 90–91).

Goldmark spent a few pages discussing the opposition of the 'women's rights party' in Britain to factory laws. And while she conceded that 'superficially viewed', rights for women might appear inconsistent with the effort to protect one sex as contrasted with the other, she felt this attitude was based upon a 'fundamental misconception': 'it ignores the fact that protection of health has never been a bar to the efficiency of men as citizens' (Goldmark, 1913: 254–255). The implication was that citizenship rights could be separated from rights in other spheres. Florence Kelley accepted this separation: 'Sex is a biological fact. The political rights of citizens are not properly dependent upon sex but social and domestic and industrial relations are' (Kelley, 1922: 421). There is a conceptual insight here, limited only by the fact that both Kelley and Goldmark believed strongly in traditional sex roles and the strict separation of public and private spheres.

Kelley was the General Secretary of the National Consumer's League, one of the major American organisations to campaign for special protective legislation for women. She was a lawyer, had worked as a factory inspector in Chicago, and had been a resident for thirteen years in settlement houses, spending some time with Jane Addams at Hull House. She had campaigned hard for the introduction of laws limiting child labour, and believed that similar protection was needed for women, 'the weakest and most defenceless bread-winners in the state' (Kelley, 1905: 142). The Consumer's League insisted that, although women had the same rights as men, they were 'not identical in economic or social function or in physical capacity' (Babcock, Freedman, Norton and Ross, 1975: 257).

The types of arguments Kelley used were similar to Goldmark's. She endorsed the traditional allocation of sex roles: 'It is the commonly accepted division of labor throughout the Republic that men are occupied with business and professional duties and women take care of the children' (Kelley, 1905: 178). She was, moreover, particularly concerned to support that allocation of responsibility: 'A man who is in the position of the head of the family which is increasing ought to be held up by the community rigidly to his duty in supporting his wife and children'. If he would not do this, she remarked, 'I think he ought to go to the work house' (Lehrer, 1985: 197).

Kelley, it should be noted, was also a keen supporter of female enfranchisement. One of the main reasons she thought women should vote was that they could bring a more ethical approach to politics since they 'are less under the stress of competitive business'. She was not claiming here that women had a preserve on moral virtue—'Political corruption is not a matter of sex'—but that women had the benefit of being 'primarily interested in the nurture and safeguarding of the young' (Kelley, 1905: 202, 193).

In *Fatigue and Efficiency* Goldmark had expressed relief that America's equal suffrage societies had taken a 'logical stand' on protective legislation (Goldmark, 1913: 255). And indeed it is true that America's feminists had not yet openly divided on the issue of protective labour laws, though a few expressed concern at the implications of the *Muller* decision in 1908 (Sacks and Wilson,

1978: 115). The *effects* of this decision began however to attract
attention as the doctrine of sex differences enshrined in the case
was extended to obtain all kinds of protective and sometimes
excessively restrictive laws governing work conditions for women.
The argument that women needed to be safeguarded for the moral
and physical future of the nation was used to exclude women from
mines, iron mills, saloons, concert halls and other places where
'intoxicants were used'. Women were prohibited from operating
dangerous machinery, from working at night, from lifting heavy
weights, and from working a certain number of weeks before and
after pregnancy. Laws were passed limiting the number of hours a
woman could work and setting a minimum wage below which she
could not be paid (Kessler-Harris, 1984: 145).

A group of feminists led by Alice Paul, suffragists who had
picketed the White House in the course of the campaign for the
vote, reacted angrily to these restrictions. They formed the National Woman's Party (NWP) and, supported by several business and
professional women's organisations, prepared and introduced into
Congress in 1923 the Equal Rights Amendment. Reform feminists
like Kelley feared that such an amendment would make unconstitutional the legislation they had fought so hard to achieve. In the
first instance Paul tried to assure them that protective labour laws
would not be eliminated under the amendment, but legal advice
suggested otherwise (Cott, 1987: 121). According to Professor of
Law Felix Frankfurter, an amendment that asserted *equality with
men* could not simultaneously sustain *special class status for women*
(Kessler-Harris, 1984: 149). This kind of legal interpretation
which set 'equality' against 'difference' assured a schism in the
movement, with one group committed to the benefits of protective
labour laws and the other equally committed to establishing equal
opportunity. Conventional political ideas which set up these positions as alternatives impelled feminists to choose sides in the
debate.

The National Woman's Party has come in for harsh criticism
over the years. It has been called elitist, narrow and dogmatic.
Perhaps some of these labels are apt. In Rupp and Taylor's sympathetic treatment the NWP is described as 'A small exclusive
single-issue group, hardly popular even within the women's rights
movement' (Rupp and Taylor, 1987: 8). In the main the membership was solidly upper middle class, but it did contain a few
trade union women (Becker, 1981: 236; Lemons, 1973: 183). An
allied group, the Business and Professional Women, included
many clerks, typists and waitresses (Becker, 1981: 225). As Becker
suggests, these women faced real threats from legislation which
limited their work day.

The presence of trade union women in the NWP indicates that it is incorrect to assume that all working-class women supported protective legislation. The same types of divisions noted in Britain appeared in America. Most unions endorsed the legislation as part of a strategy to protect the male and hence the family wage. A representative of the American Women's Trade Union League, Rose Schneiderman, sounded like Dilke when she cautioned that those who 'want to work at the same hours of the day or night and receive the same pay might be putting their own brothers or sweethearts or husbands out of a job'. Women in the printing trade, however, started the Women's League for Equal Opportunity in 1915 to *oppose* protective laws (Babcock, Freedman, Norton and Ross, 1975: 257, 249). The position one took depended very much on where you were located in the sex-segregated labour market. If you were in a female-dominated industry, legislation limiting hours and setting minimum wages was sometimes useful. If you were in an occupation where there were men, such legislation could be a handicap. The conclusion Frances Olsen draws from this case is discerning: 'the effect of gender-specific labor legislation depends entirely upon the particular context in which it is enacted' (Olsen, 1986: 1534, 1540).

The division within the women's movement then, caused by protective legislation, reflected a division of opinion *within* the middle class and *within* the working class, rather than a conflict between the middle class and some other group. Both in Britain and America, the particular line a feminist[4] took in the debate depended upon the focus of her reform energies:

> Those feminists most concerned with women and industrial affairs (and this included a growing contingent of middle-class women) were re-examining their strategies; those claimed by other concerns (such as the battle for the vote) tended to stick by the old (Phillips, 1986: 86).

The NWP attracted women who had experienced discrimination in attempts to further their careers (Becker, 1981: 69); the reform feminists had, like Kelley, often worked closely with factory women and seen their conditions first hand. The impact of personal experience in shaping one's conceptual frameworks should not be ignored (White, 1986: 253). Political ideology, however, remained critical. While the leadership both among the reform feminists and among the equal rights feminists shared a middle-class view of the social order, the former tended to be more critical of existing industrial laws whereas the latter, in the main, were ardent exponents of *laissez faire* and self-help.

The spirit of American capitalism flowed through the veins of

the NWP leadership. Their rhetoric reflected a libertarian ideal—
'It is liberty we seek not repression'. They spoke about the 'free
and full development of woman' and demanded the opportunity to
'act and develop as freely as men' (Becker, 1978: 52–53). There is
a certain continuity here with the emphasis on liberty noted in
nineteenth-century American feminism, although the 'restrained'
version popular in that period seems to have disappeared among
these women at any rate (see Chapter 1).

As far as their politics were concerned, the majority had an
aversion to state intervention. One member, Mrs Hooker, said in
1923 that one of the NWP's most important functions would be 'to
bring before the American people the futility, the injustice and the
inadequacy of welfare law' and that 'no individual, man or woman,
can really be free while he or she eats out of another's hand'
(Becker, 1978: 145, 143). The NWP was allied with the National
Association of Manufacturers which denounced legislative interference in industry (Lemons, 1973: 193). In *Adkins v Children's
Hospital* (1923) the Counsel for Children's Hospital referred to the
NWP position on equal rights as part of their defence of 'freedom
of contract' for women and their opposition to minimum wage
laws, and won the case. In *West Coast Hotel v Parish* (1937) the
NWP filed a brief urging the correctness of this argument.

The social reformer and historian, Mary Beard, who took the
rather exceptional position of refusing to endorse either camp, was
concerned that supporters of the ERA ran the risk of 'positively
strengthening anachronistic competitive industrial processes' (Bad-
cock, Freedman, Norton and Ross, 1975: 256). She agreed with
the NWP that protective legislation 'embodies the objectionable
idea of dependence'. But on the other hand she felt that seeking
liberty to compete on equal terms with men implied 'satisfaction
with the fight over the crumbs which fall from Dives' table'
(Sealander, 1983: 81–82).

It is too simple, however, to see all supporters of the equal rights
line as *laissez faire* ideologues. The NWP always insisted that
its preference was to extend protective legislation to men and
women;[5] they objected only to women being singled out in a way
which had the effect of making them less competitive. NWP
membership also included women like Crystal Eastman who were
closer to socialism than *laissez-faire* liberalism.

Eastman distinguished between different kinds of protective
legislation. She thought that minimum wage and maximum hour
laws were 'not so indefensible', because 'woman's labor is the
least adapted to organization'. But she condemned laws which
prohibited certain trades to women 'on the ground of their physical

inferiority'. On balance she concluded that the greater danger was that the principle of sex prohibition once admitted in the law would be used by powerful unions 'to keep women out of trades for which they are manifestly fit', and joined the ERA campaign (Cook, 1978: 157–158).

The inflexibility of political and industrial institutions, therefore, convinced equal rights feminists that they would have to work within the system as it existed. As a result they displayed almost a paranoia about admitting vulnerability, echoing Elizabeth Kemper Adams' fear that 'any weakness is likely to be considered feminine' (see page 34). In their rhetoric the self-made man found his female counterpart. Harriet Stanton Blatch criticised the portrayal of industrial women as 'spavined, broken-backed creatures'. Doris Stevens said it was unfair to ask women to 'set their pace with the weakest members of their sex'. The NWP accused advocates of protective legislation of holding a pathological view of the female sex and made a guarded reference to menstruation: '. . .maternity, of course, accentuates the malady but even in the unmarried it is there, obstinately recurring as does the moon at regular intervals' (Becker, 1981: 51, 143). These attitudes were not confined to America. In Britain the League for Freedom of Labour Defence opposed laws for the special protection of women as 'unjustifiable and injudicious tutelage'. In the *Freewoman*, edited by Dora Marsden and Mary Gawthorpe, women were asked to choose between 'the comforts of protection and the harsh responsibilities of freedom' (Walsh, 1917: 210–211).

Protective legislation took on a symbolic meaning for equal rights feminists. In a world where women were excluded from certain activities because they were women, it seemed to reinforce the idea of a crucial difference. This symbolic import made it difficult to consider the benefits of particular pieces of legislation or the usefulness of legislation for selected occupations.

Given this fear of identifying women as 'different', one might have expected a committed equal rights feminist to disclaim any idea of female uniqueness. Alice Paul, however, actually invoked an image close to the nineteenth-century maternal ethos:

> Women are certainly made as the peace-loving half of the world and the homemaking half of the world, the temperate half of the world. The more power they have, the better world we are going to have (Rupp and Taylor, 1987: 55).

Perhaps, as Drude Dahlerup suggests, instead of two sharply divided approaches to the question of identity, each individual feminist experiences a tension during her own lifecycle between showing that '"we women are able to do what men can do" and a search for the femininity of our foremothers' (Dahlerup, 1986: 23). Perhaps equal rights feminists felt little conflict between their insistence that women were the 'same as' men and their invocation of a maternal mystique because they always assumed that women were primarily responsible for childrearing. Few, however, discussed the social supports such as childcare centres, which would be needed to facilitate women's workforce participation, or a more serious restructuring of home–work relations (Becker, 1981: 235). Wealthy themselves and with domestic labour to assist them, they pursued their analysis no further than a demand for equal access. Their *laissez fairist* ideology also impeded them from considering collectivist solutions. At the same time however they campaigned to improve the economic status of housewives.

Feminists in both camps agreed upon the desirability of gaining recognition for women's domestic labour. The NWP assured reform feminists that maternity legislation like the Sheppard-Towner Act would not be invalidated by the ERA.[6] Mothers were a special category, according to NWP member Doris Stevens, like 'invalided soldiers', and you could therefore provide special protections for them. The proviso was that this special protection would be restricted to the domestic sphere and not be carried over into the marketplace where it would affect all women by making them less competitive (Stevens, 1984: B-28). The proviso meant that laws such as those sponsored by the Consumers' League requiring employers to give women paid leave before and after childbirth could not be countenanced.

Jennifer Hochschild has found that most Americans today hold different notions of equality for different spheres. In the political domain and in the socialising domain (family), they use a strict meaning of the word equality—all people may make the same claims on social resources. In the economic domain by contrast they invoke a principle of differentiation—'people may legitimately make varying claims on social resources' depending on their talents or their merit (Hochschild, 1981). Most American feminists in this period worked within a similar ideological framework. As long as women remained at home, they could be protected. If they entered the marketplace, it was 'no holds barred'.

Many reform feminists, especially those in America, actually shared this world view but saw workers as *single* women who could compete on these terms. They hoped all *married* women would remain within the homemaker category. They had no difficulty in cooperating with the NWP in a number of campaigns, for women's right to sit on juries, to retain their maiden names, to have equal inheritance and guardianship claims (Becker, 1981: 8). The problem arose when considering the relationship between married women, or more precisely mothers, and the marketplace. Protective legislation was really an expression of the reform belief that, faced with this choice, women belonged at home.

Reform feminists were not unthinking exponents of separate spheres ideology, however. They often advanced sound structural reasons for women's 'special' needs. Mary Anderson, head of the Women's Bureau which campaigned for protective legislation throughout this period, saw restrictions on night work as essential simply because of the reality of most women's lives: 'A woman at work in a factory, or anywhere outside her home, does not give up her household tasks. If she is married she has literally two full-time jobs. . . .' (Anderson, 1925: 50) Another keen supporter of protective legislation, Professor of Industrial Law, Alice Hamilton, agreed that as things stood a man who worked at night could still have his sleep during the day and have his meals prepared and his children cared for. In contrast, the mother of a family could not, even if the husband were there. She hoped that perhaps in the future men might come to accept some of these responsibilities (Hamilton, 1984: B-29).

Hamilton was a pragmatist and had had numerous disappointments trying to get the government to accept a more responsible attitude to workers in general. She found that the American legislator could not be aroused to much indignation over descriptions of 'poisonous, dusty, heavy, hot, and filthy work' if it is done by men. The same 'hard-boiled legislator', however, had a soft spot when it came to women. As in the Brandeis case, arguments from difference were useful strategically to improve the working conditions of at least some workers. Hamilton resolved to take what she could get and be thankful (Hamilton, 1984: B-29).

The industrial reformer, Mary Van Kleeck, was exceptional among reform feminists in her conviction that, married or unmarried, women should be given the opportunity to engage in all the occupations open to men (Van Kleeck, 1919: 6). Her ultimate goal was lower hours for all workers. For practical reasons, however, she was willing to deal with women as a separate case. According to Van Kleeck, women needed 'special' legislation because they were the lowest-paid and most exploited workers, not because they were women. She admitted that some protective legislation discriminated against women, but believed that women's industrial weakness made a piece-by-piece approach to the removal of these particular laws preferable to a blanket amendment like the ERA. Van Kleeck's pragmatism surfaced in a 1928 Women's Bureau study into labour laws which she directed towards women-dominated industries on the grounds that discrimination was keeping women out of other industries anyway (Babcock, Freedman, Norton and Ross, 1975: 251; Technical and Advisory Committee, *c.*1927: 10). This approach threatened, of course, to become a self-fulfilling prophecy, illustrating the practical difficulties involved in designing a single program for all women and in formulating a policy to meet the immediate needs of some women without enshrining the status quo.

The reform feminists also believed firmly in the principle of equal pay. The Women's Bureau campaigned throughout the inter-war period to secure equal pay legislation. It has been suggested that the 'advocacy of special conditions and special legislation for women' contradicted and hence weakened the advocacy of equal pay (Sealander, 1983: 103). This is true, of course, only if you accept the model of equality described by Hochschild which in the economic sphere distributes reward on the basis of merit. Since the reformers did not challenge this model, they can be seen as inconsistent. But this may be one of those places where inconsistency reflected what was wrong with the world rather than what was wrong with the argument. (See page 22.)[7] Women at the time required *both* certain industrial protections *and* equal pay.

Feminists had to operate within institutional as well as ideological constraints. If progressive labour laws had existed for all workers, there would have been no need to campaign for women alone. Alice Henry who had participated in labour organisations in both Australia and America pointed out that in Australia, where minimum wage laws covered both women and men, that area had been eliminated from contention. Such laws would be more difficult to obtain in America, according to Henry, because of the rigidity of the Constitution, the commitment to 'freedom of contract', and the different role played by the unions. Ideally the legislation would be extended to men but this was unlikely to happen, Henry explained, because American trade union men 'are not yet willing to ask for general limitation of hours for men, still holding to the position from which they have departed in Great Britain, that organisation is the only channel through which men should obtain advance of hour or wage standards' (Henry, 1971: 144, 147, 165). Mary Anderson was also keenly aware that any attempt to broaden the legislation to cover men would antagonise the unions (Anderson, 1925: 51).

So while at one level the factions were separated by a fundamental ideological disagreement about woman's sex-specific role, with the reformers emphasising her motherhood and the NWP supporting her right to work unfettered, the positions were taken up because the political ideology, the institutions within which they had to work, and the complexity of women's lives made it difficult to see alternatives. Unfortunately, instead of questioning why women had to face such choices, the debate became frozen as a disagreement about whether women were the 'same as' or 'different from' men. In part the women were forced to use these categories of thought by their opponents. Oliver Wendell Holmes said it would need more than a Nineteenth Amendment to convince him that there were no differences between men and women (Lemons, 1973: 239). In part the women accepted societal assumptions about innate differences and role assignations without questioning why some roles were more constrained than others. In part the women used the categories as debating ploys. The women often had to put their case in open meetings or in brief newspaper articles. Labelling opponents as believing simply in 'sameness' or 'difference' or as 'doctrinaire' seemed to strengthen one's own case. In such a spirit Florence Kelley remarked, 'the cry Equality, Equality where Nature has created Inequality, is as stupid and deadly as the cry Peace, Peace, where there is no Peace' (quoted in Cott, 1987b: 56).

The women had become committed to winning a case rather than solving a dilemma. Arguments became heated and personalised, deteriorating at times into name-calling. Mary Anderson branded the NWP 'a kind of hysterical feminism with a slogan for a program'. Florence Kelley claimed that they were financed by 'powerfully organized exploiting employers of men' (Babcock, Freedman, Norton and Ross, 1975: 250). On the one side the reformers' persistent references to women's duty as mothers rankled equal rights feminists determined to downplay the physical side of being a woman because it seemed to confirm that women were less employable under existing work rules. On the other side the equal rights program threatened reforms for which women like Kelley and Anderson had battled for years.[8] The nature of debate itself resulted in the issues being oversimplified. 'Sameness' and 'difference' became catch-cries, precluding more thoughtful discussion of the social structures which made it necessary for women to advocate one of these alternatives.

The way in which existing political institutions and ideas impelled the women to adopt irreconcilable positions is nicely demonstrated in a 1927 confrontation between Mary Van Kleeck and Alice Paul. Ostensibly the clash was about which American states and which industries to study in a planned Women's Bureau investigation into labour laws. Paul was suspicious about the whole enterprise, given the Women's Bureau's consistent support of protective legislation. There seems little doubt that Van Kleeck was constrained by her organisational links to the Bureau.[9] As feminists became a part of the public administration their presentation of women's issues necessarily reflected these ties. Paul was determined to thwart the Bureau and adopted an obstructionist stance.

The language used in the confrontation reflected a dependence upon conventional conceptual systems which in turn reflected the political culture. Van Kleeck had studied as a social scientist and was committed to the principles of scientific management. Repeatedly, some ten to fifteen times within the space of the meeting, she referred to the need to employ appropriate social science methodology. She objected to Paul's suggestion that public hearings on the subject be organised: 'It simply gives a chance to explode. But a really serious investigator gets facts'. The investigation would be conducted by 'experts'. It would be a 'really scientific thorough study of where women are standing in industry', using 'fair sampling'. 'There is no other way in science' (Technical and Advisory Committee, *c.*1927: 4, 15, 18, 23, 25).

On the other side Paul wanted industries to be selected which would illustrate the point she wanted to make, that they restricted women's opportunities. She admitted that 'a great many of these special laws do not in their effect injure women *except as setting up a wrong principle*' (emphasis added). She wanted samples to be chosen 'where the law was extreme enough to make a difference ...'. As mentioned previously Van Kleeck had decided to concentrate upon women-dominated industries (see page 47). Paul wished to examine only 'occupations closed to women'. She saw the investigation as the 'trial of a theory', a fight for a principle (Technical and Advisory Committee, *c.*1927: 21, 31, 32, 40).

Both Paul and Van Kleeck tried to fit women's diverse experiences into the straitjacket of a single rule instead of challenging the feasibility of doing so. Women would *either* compete on the same terms as men, *or* they would be singled out for 'special' treatment. They would *either* ignore the fact that they had children and children needed care, *or* they would accept that children were their responsibility. Social attitudes and social arrangements constituted these as either/or options. Unfortunately neither position addressed the situation of women who had to or who wanted to engage in paid work, but who did not wish to be penalised because they had families. Nor did either position recognise that men too had families but that social institutions refused to deal with this reality. The drawing of battle-lines in the movement foreclosed discussion of these issues. The meeting was adjourned.

3

The split (part II): 'ultra' versus 'new' feminism

Chapter 3 introduces Britain's 'New Feminists' and describes the basis of the conflict between these women (and some men) and those labelled 'ultras', the equivalent of America's 'equalitarians'. The fundamental point of contention, whether married women ought to engage in paid labour, was the same as in America. A partial resolution to the problem presented itself in the post-World War II Beveridge reforms which provided basic maternity leave support. Following these reforms, the equality/difference dispute over this particular issue disappeared *among feminists*. The case supports the book's central thesis that, when feminists resort to arguments about women's sameness or difference, the problem is actually inadequate institutional arrangements for family mainten-ance and human needs more generally. The way in which Austra-lian feminists were spared the sameness/difference debate over wages because minimum wages existed for *all* workers illustrates the same point (see page 48). When all people are treated as fully 'human' beings with family attachments and decent working con-ditions the debate dissolves.

This resolution became possible in Britain and in Australia be-cause of the existence of a more collectivist political culture. The values of *Gemeinschaft* were retained in the maternity leave and minimum wage cases, even while it was acknowledged that tra-ditional sex roles had changed. This is not to suggest that the problem of reconciling paid work and home commitments has been resolved in these countries. As we will see, faced with a government committed to deregulation, British feminists become ambivalent about whether it is preferable to encourage women into the labour force or to support them at home. The maternity leave and minimum wage cases simply illustrate the direction which reform should take and that sameness/difference debates disappear once human needs are addressed. The terms 'sameness'/ 'difference' and the debate itself are political constructs shaped by circumstance.

As in America in the years following World War I, the organised women's movement in Britain experienced heated disputation and divided into contending 'equal rights' and 'reform' factions. Britain's Labour heritage meant that the latter dominated developments there. Britain's *reform feminists* came from a variety of backgrounds. Politically they ranged from Fabian socialists to moderate liberal reformers. There was no single formula for reform. Even the Fabians did not agree among themselves. All were influenced, however, by Britain's more collectivist political ideology which showed in the willingness to use the state to improve women's situation. Most reflected the conviction that married women ought to remain at home and dedicated their efforts to helping working-class mothers.

Eleanor Rathbone, a leading reform feminist, used the phrase 'New Feminism' in her 1918 inaugural speech as leader of the National Union of Societies for Equal Citizenship (NUSEC), the successor organisation to the National Union of Women's Suffrage Societies (NUWSS). She declared that the time had come to provide women with 'real' equality. To achieve this goal, NUSEC eventually included in its program demands for family allowances (family endowment) and free access to birth control information (Lewis, 1980: 169).

Rathbone was not a Labour Party member. She refused to commit herself to any political party and remained an independent throughout her parliamentary career. Her political ideology has been described as 'vague liberal reformism' (Macnicol, 1980: 19). At first committed to the 'punitive charity' principles of the Charity Organisation Society[1] her personal contact with working-class poverty while she researched *How the Casual Labourer Lives* (1909) caused her to develop a more sympathetic attitude towards the poor. Her interest in family endowment emerged out of her investigation into the financial circumstances of Poor Law widows and their children in Liverpool. The dependence of housewives on the whim of their husbands particularly disturbed her:

> . . . whether he expends the wages so received upon the family or upon his own 'menus plaisiers' depends, of course, entirely upon his goodwill, since the State, though it recognizes in theory the rights of wife and children to maintenance, does practically nothing to enforce it (quoted in Macnicol, 1980: 21).

A family endowment, consisting of a set amount per child, would constitute payment to the wife by the state in recognition of her service to the family and her role in creating new citizens. Such a payment would also enable women to stay home, a trend Rathbone hoped to encourage.

The Fabians had been discussing some form of 'mother's pension' from the beginning of the century. H. G. Wells had proposed State Endowment in 1912 (Garner, 1984: 70). A Fabian Women's Group, founded with the principal object of studying ways to increase women's financial independence, included among its members Beatrice Webb, Marion Phillips and the Labour MP Margaret Bondfield. Sally Alexander calls the 'distinctive quality' of Fabian feminism in this period 'economic individualism', since it emphasised that women ought to gain economic independence. There were several means to this end. Some looked to women's 'full and equal participation in the workforce'; others preferred 'some sort of State support for maternity' (Reeves, 1979: xv).

Victor Gollancz, who edited the 'Oxford Essays' setting out the views of the 'New Feminists', was a Fabian. So were A. Maude Royden and Elinor Burns who contributed essays to the collection. Rathbone also had an essay in the volume. Gollancz claimed that the book was an attempt to produce a 'unified feminist policy'. It began with a critique of the 'old formula' which, he claimed, had erred by concentrating on the 'humanity of women', and their 'similarity with men', coming to the hasty conclusion that 'women could achieve freedom and happiness simply by approximating the conditions of their life to those of a man's as it is at present lived'. Sounding much like 1970s socialist feminists who campaigned for wages for housework,[2] Gollancz emphasised that 'few men' in fact are 'free and happy' under a 'capitalist regime' where labour means something 'very like slavery' (Gollancz, 1917: 28).

A second problem was that the emphasis on women's similarity to men had diverted attention from the necessity to create 'special conditions for women to suit their special characteristics as a sex'. This referred of course to their maternal function. While Gollancz had a number of recommendations for alleviating the isolation and 'drudgery' of full-time homemaking, his eugenic beliefs resulted in a firm commitment to the conventional distribution of sex roles. He hoped that the endowment of motherhood would mean that working-class mothers would no longer be 'forced' into industry, whether they wished it or not (Gollancz, 1917: 31). Gollancz ended his introduction, however, with a description of a different kind of future, where women and men shared domestic responsibilities:

> If the dignity of labour were a fact and not a myth, if the work
> of the world, being neither soul destroying in character nor
> unduly prolonged, gave men the happiness for which they
> should look to it, if women desiring work away from their
> home did not have to face a complete withdrawal, and men,
> released from the absolute absorption in bread-winning, could
> take their share in domestic interests, then would a satisfactory
> adjustment be possible between the competing claims of the
> active and the domestic life...(Gollancz, 1917: 178)

This conclusion can only mean that he did not think that the
endowment proposal achieved such an adjustment but that for the
time being it was expedient.

The non-militant suffragist, A. Maude Royden, developed these
ideas in a direction that sounds in some ways like the ideas of
cultural feminism discussed in the next chapter, though there are
critical differences. Her major point was that feminists had erred
in measuring women against a male 'norm'—'women have been
obliged to seek to prove that they were not only equal to men, but
so exactly like them as to be able to do their best work and develop
their best capacities under like conditions'. Women as a result had
become 'round pegs' in 'square holes':

> This is...the crux. The assumption that man was the norm
> inclined women to show that they could be as square as
> he...But it would be more useful and comfortable in a round
> one unless it is ashamed of its roundness (Royden, 1917a:
> 129–132).

The world, she proclaimed, must cease to be 'virocentric'. It must
cease to suppose that 'the way in which men work is necessarily
the "right way"...'

Instead of undertaking a critique of the way in which men
worked, however, Royden set women up in their own work environment, the home. Women would make the care of children the
first claim on them during a major part of their lives which would
mean, inevitably, withdrawal from any other occupation for a
'considerable period'. For this, women would pay a price: 'it is less
likely that women will reach the top of a tree than a man' (Royden,
1917a: 143). Special treatment meant separate development.

It is too easy, however, to dismiss reform feminists as mouth-
pieces for patriarchal ideology because of their willingness to surrender part of women's development for the sake of the race. In a
1917 volume, *Women and the Sovereign State*, Royden criticised the
'halo' cast around motherhood and the implication that women had
only two duties, the bearing of children and the satisfaction of

men's sexual desire. She objected to the way in which the state saw women as 'just a sex' and never admitted her existence as a human being. In this volume she constructed a *political* rather than an essentialist identity for women:

> Women, it will be said, are not a class. They reply that this is true; but exploitation has made of them a class and assigned to them a status which is not theirs and which they find injurious (Royden, 1917b: 139).

Nor did Royden revel in some uncritical celebration of difference. In a scathing and witty review of the scientific literature on the subject of sex differences, Royden attacked the supposed standard of scientific objectivity:

> To read the arguments (?) adduced by scientific men to show that women are at all important points the inferiors of men, is to be startled indeed at the havoc which the fundamental falsity of a preconceived idea can work in the brains of scientific men (Royden, 1917b: 128).

The ultimate goal of reformers like Royden and Gollancz was to increase women's autonomy. Family endowment was to be paid to the wife as a means of releasing her from the 'demoralising dependency' on her husband. It was also considered just reward for her labour. Royden objected strenuously to the notion that a man 'supported' his wife (Royden, 1917b: 75). The reform feminists started from the rather reasonable premise that someone had to care for the children and found the available structural alternatives to one-on-one childcare unappealing. 'Is a child less than a work of art?' Royden asked. And 'can any cooperative system of nurseries do what the individual mother did for us?' The demands of motherhood meant that, in the final analysis, 'The average woman must choose between being a typist or a mother' (Royden, 1917c: 56–57).

Another Fabian feminist, Mabel Atkinson, needs to be looked at, as much for the differences as for the similarities in her analysis. Like so many other feminists in the period she identified the conundrum of women's lives—'to secure for women freedom and independence, the right to control their own destinies and yet to make it possible for the same women to be wives and mothers' (Atkinson, 1914: 20). The modern professional woman was forced to reconcile 'two needs of her nature' which 'the present constitution of society make irreconcilable'. She wants work, she wants control of her own financial position, she wants education and the right to take part in the human activities of the state, 'but at the same time she is no longer willing to be shut out from marriage and motherhood'. The problem with the present organisation of society was that for most women 'the two are alternatives':

> Women do not want either love or work, but both; and the full meaning of the feminist movement will not develop until this demand becomes conscious and articulate among the rank and file of the movement.

Atkinson recognised that the solution to this problem would not be easy, but she was certain of one thing. Neither an approach through 'sameness' nor 'difference' was an answer. She rejected both methods 'advocated by either of the schools of thought that now hold the field': 'the feminists of the more old fashioned sort...who simply demand for women the same rights as men possess, ignoring all the inevitable differences of sex' and 'those who believe that sex is the only characteristic of women that matters'. In her view, 'Neither independence alone nor protection alone will meet the case'. And she warned that 'the whole problem is still so new that it is perhaps best to be cautious in dealing with it' (Atkinson, 1914: 20).

Atkinson considered Gilman's crèches as a possible solution, but thought they would help only a few 'exceptional women' who possessed sufficient ability to earn large incomes and who had enough energy not to break down under 'the twofold strain of working for a living and bringing children into the world'. She felt that it was obvious that women could not work on exactly the same terms as men, especially during the six months of the pre-natal and post-natal life of a child. She was however uncertain about the principle involved either in acquiring half the husband's salary, which she considered 'legalized dependence', or in state endowment. With other Fabians, she agreed that state endowment of motherhood was both necessary and justified—'No act of citizenship is more fundamental than the act of bringing into the world and protecting in his helpless infancy a new citizen'—but she warned feminists to be wary of developments which intensified 'the dependence of women outside the child-bearing years'. Eugenists were a danger here, she explained, with their endorsement of a woman's 'absolute dependence' on a husband.

Atkinson is unusual in following through her analysis to the point of the mother's return to waged labour. Realistically she anticipated that, 'under the existing state of competition in business', a woman who dropped out for the childbearing period could hardly expect to be reinstated. But she wanted the government to *impose* on private industry rules which would make this feasible.

Her commonsense is appealing: 'the absence and subsequent return of the married women to their work will no doubt be incon-
venient, but the inconvenience must be faced, and the women as
far as possible be placed at no disadvantage...' (Atkinson, 1914:
23). Atkinson's vision went far beyond Rathbone's who hoped
simply to remove women from the labour force (Rathbone, 1917:
112, 116, 127).

Family endowment did not cause a schism in the women's
movement, but it had its opponents. Millicent Garrett Fawcett, the
founder of NUWSS, left NUSEC, the successor organisation,
when it accepted family endowment as a plank in its platform in
1925. A classic nineteenth-century liberal, Fawcett's 'radical individualism' could not accommodate the degree of government intervention involved in the proposal. She felt that the cash benefit
would undermine paternal responsibility, as she explained in a
letter to *The Times*: 'I am one of many who regard the responsibility of parents for the maintenance of their young children as an
invaluable part of the education of the average man or woman. To
take it away would dangerously weaken the inducements for steady
industry and self control.' Her comments are reminiscent of the
NWP's Mrs Hooker (see page 44): 'Are we going to work for and
promote an independent and self-supporting industrial population,
or a spoon-fed subservient working class?...These socialistic
schemes are all founded on the ruins of personal independence'
(Mann, 1974: 26). Equal rights feminists tended to be *laissez
fairists*. The request for 'a fair field and no favour' simply applied
these principles to women.

The equal rights claim to equal pay, for example, rested upon an
acceptance of the free market mechanism. Fawcett had no doubt
that in present circumstances many women would not be able to
compete against men because of lack of physical strength or training. She asked no more than 'to secure for women a fair field of
competition with men, their work being accepted or rejected on its
merits'. 'Equal pay for equal work' in her terms meant 'equal pay
for equal results' and if, as she assumed, women could not quite
make the grade in some occupations, they ought to be paid less
(Fawcett, 1918: 3–4). Similarly, the British peeress, Lady
Rhondda, who founded the equal rights Six Point Group in 1918,
allowed that, 'by the ordinary rules of economy', women would be
excluded from work where they proved to be less efficient than men
(Rhondda to Prime Minister, 5 December 1918, Fawcett Collection). This was indeed equality with a vengeance, especially given
the common presumption that women were inferior workers.

Fawcett had no reason to fear that Rathbone had converted to socialism, however, nor that she sought to undermine the family. Like American reform feminists, Rathbone placed a high value upon the family as a social institution. These words could easily have been spoken by Florence Kelley, for example: 'A man with a wife and family may talk revolution but he is much less likely to act it than one who has given society no such hostages' (Rathbone, 1927a: 12). 'A few shillings a week for each child', she was convinced, would not deter either 'paternal or maternal self-sacrifice' (Rathbone, 1927b: 57). But Rathbone's research experience had made her suspicious of 'paternal responsibility' and in a sense she considered mothers the key to family and social stability. She endorsed a more 'organic' view of society than equal rights feminists, with each member of the body politic 'having a claim on the whole body' (Rathbone, 1927b: 8). Her ideas fit comfortably within the organicist liberal tradition identified by Benn and Gaus (see page xii).

Political ideology, therefore, played a critical role in the sameness/difference debate. In some ways it set the terms within which the question was discussed. Nowhere is this demonstrated more forcefully than in the response of American feminists to family endowment.

The writings of the American sociologist, Anna Garlin Spencer, provide an example. Like British reform feminists, when it came to adjusting women's 'new freedom' with the 'ancient family claim', Spencer ended up accepting the traditional sexual division of labour: 'the whole arrangement of society. . . is based upon the economic leadership of the husband and father in the home partnership' (Spencer, 1923: 279). As with the Fabians, eugenic ideas influenced this decision. Spencer, it seems, was concerned that the 'best' women were not breeding enough. She also felt, like Gollancz, that the 'housemother' had advantages over a 'woman factory hand' in 'matters of health and work-time', though she insisted that marriage had to become more democratic (Spencer, 1923: 142).

The idea of family endowment, however, did not sit comfortably with Spencer's political ideology. Although she clearly reflected the more collectivistic spirit of the period—she made reference to the functions of the 'Father and Mother State'—she could not tolerate this degree of intrusion into the family. She felt it preferable to find some means of making 'the father's care in the share of children more definite and better rewarded, less often shirked or incompetent' to 'any scheme for state subsidy for the care of the children' (Spencer, 1923: 175). Any and all references to the kind of welfare spending which was becoming a part of the British way of life at this time were greeted with the same response: 'Is this sound American doctrine?' (Spencer, 1972: 45). Spencer had a vision for the future where men and women alike could 'serve the generations in family devotion to the sort of work fathers and mothers have to do' and yet 'cherish some personal and ideal vocational effort which may sweeten and enrich their lives'. For the time being she could only advise 'women in ordinary circumstances', who could not earn enough to hire help, to 'stay home' (Spencer, 1923: 150).

In large part, as the British suffragist Helena Swanwick said, the decision women faced in the period was whether they would develop the family along individualist or socialist lines (Swanwick, 1914: 86), involving the state in the support of living arrangements or leaving people, usually women, to sort these out. The alternative selected depended upon historically and culturally specific circumstances. Spencer illustrates the American free enterprise model. The fact that the political mood in the 1920s was hostile to social experimentation would have influenced her stand as well. The 'red-baiting' of reform feminists, which Lemons talks about, would have deterred consideration of 'radical' social options.[3] Discussions about sameness and difference, both the content of the terms and the options to move beyond them, were always in context.

The case of Australia makes a useful contrast here. As mentioned previously, Australia had initiated a number of progressive reforms in the early years of the twentieth century, winning the title of 'Social Laboratory of the World'. The minimum wage laws mentioned by Alice Henry were among these reforms (see page 48). Another was the idea of a 'basic family wage' of 7 shillings per day, endorsed in 1907 by Justice Higgins. The wage was meant to support a man, his wife and three children. A 1919 Federal Basic Wage Commission headed by Justice Piddington found that the basic wage was inadequate in several ways. It paid the single man more than he needed and could not respond to differences in family size. Since employers were loath to boost wages, Piddington recommended as an alternative, a separate basic wage adjusted to the needs of a man and wife, supplemented by family allowances for such dependent children as actually existed (Cass, 1983: 54–58). Australia did not introduce federal child allowances until 1941, but Rathbone and others acknowledged the country's contribution to the development of the reform (Rathbone, 1927a: 31; Stocks, 1949: 94–95).

Australian feminists saw a great deal to recommend in the idea of family endowment. It seemed most obviously the key to separating woman as individual from woman as mother. Mary Gilmore wrote to Justice Higgins in 1909 that the state has 'a perpetual covenant with the family (which reproduces itself to create and maintain the state and therefore has a claim against the state)'. 'Brief labour covenants' on the other hand were simply a matter 'of individual unit to individual unit'. The two were separate and could not be successfully covered by any 'law made to cover both' (Mary Gilmore to Justice Higgins, 17 July 1909. MS 1057 Item 156 Australian National Library). The problem with the separation was that it assumed that women would fit into either one category, as individuals seeking 'brief labour covenants', or the other, as servants of the state through their family role. Not only did both options have disadvantages, but the framework failed to deal with the reality that most women would overlap the categories. It also assumed that men could always seek 'brief labour covenants', even if they had families, since women would be caring for them. Nonetheless, given the political climate, it seemed an attractive and feasible alternative to the traditional model which allowed women *no* status as individuals in their own right.

The idea of endowment, for example, made it possible to defend 'equal pay for equal work'. Since, hypothetically at least, men received a higher wage because of the assumption that they were responsible for the family's financial support, removing children from the equation seemed to remove the justification for paying women less. Using this logic, one of South Australia's leading feminist groups, the Women's Non-Party Association, described child endowment as 'the corollary to equal pay for equal work' (Nicholson, 1983: 21). Rathbone, who believed in the principle of a family wage (Rathbone, 1927a: 35) and who thought that equal pay in present circumstances would 'weigh the scales against the woman', also saw family endowment as a way out of this dilemma (Rathbone, 1917).

British feminist attitudes on equal pay were complicated by the political allegiance of many to the labour cause. Traditionally the British Labour movement endorsed the division between home and marketplace, and traditional sex roles. Henry Broadhurst, the parliamentary secretary of the TUC, made this clear in his declaration that 'the factory was an unsuitable place for women and that wives should be in their proper place—the home' (Caine, 1987: 38). The union movement had built its wage strategy upon the idea of a family wage and, as mentioned previously, many feminists believed that the best way to improve working-class women's lives was to increase that wage, not to reduce it. You could, with this attitude, either oppose equal pay and guaranteed minimum wages for women outright, or support them on the assumption that women would not be able to compete under these conditions and would be driven from the trade altogether. Dilke, introduced in the preceding chapter, welcomed minimum wage legislation for women because it would 'both stop women dragging down wages and raise male incomes, thus making the work of married women unnecessary' (Lewis, 1984: 201). Beatrice Webb, in her Minority Report to the War Cabinet in 1919, defended equal pay on similar grounds. She believed it would lead to female unemployment because women were less efficient workers, but this was no bad thing since women could always return to the home (Lewis, 1984: 203).

Some Labour supporters, like A. Maude Royden, hoped that family endowment would strengthen traditional family roles since, while it made equal pay a realistic possibility, it also 'would withdraw a large number of women from the labour market' (Royden, 1917a: 143). Others feared that endowments might be used to attack existing wage rates. Very few challenged the idea that the ultimate purpose of any legislation ought to be to bolster the family.[4] An anonymous Appendix to the 'Oxford Essays' put the favoured position that the real interest of working women was not in their own wages but 'in the general wage and more particularly in the wages of their men folk' (Gollancz, 1917: 217).

Family endowment seemed then to its advocates to resolve the dilemma facing women in these years. It offered a degree of economic independence, accredited the value of domestic labour, and allowed women without family ties to compete on an equal basis with men. The reform had two weaknesses. As already mentioned, it falsely assumed that women would fit into an either/ or categorisation. It also, as Sylvia Mann explains, overvalued what would simply become an additional contribution to family budgets (Mann, 1974: 80).

The second part of the 'New Feminist' package, free access to birth control information, was more controversial, given the generally prudish attitude to sexuality in the period. The reform gained respectability by being placed successfully within the context of maternal health. This was one area where the paranoia about racial improvement in these years could be used to advantage, if used properly. Some feminists cleverly appealed to the importance of the quality rather than the quantity of population to justify the use of contraceptives. The Australian suffragist and health reformer, Brettena Smyth (1842–1898), lectured publicly on the 'Limitation of Offspring', defending artificial contraception on the grounds that, if women had fewer children, they would produce a healthier and stronger type of humanity (Smyth, 1894).[5]

Rathbone needed to make both family endowment and birth

control acceptable. To those who feared that giving money for each child might encourage the 'unfit' to breed, Rathbone answered that on the contrary the endowment would lead to an increase in standard of living which, in turn, would encourage thrift and provide an inducement to curtail family size (Mann, 1974: 14). Birth control information provided the means to that end. To those who blamed the 'differential birth rate'[6] on the loss of the maternal instinct among middle-class women preoccupied with education and politics, Rathbone used Smyth's argument that women now had more regard for their own health and the health of their offspring than in the past. Rathbone supported birth control for reasons other than national efficiency. She also felt that women wanted something more than motherhood in their lives (Rathbone, 1927a: 113). NUSEC came out in support of birth control in 1925, the same year that it officially endorsed family endowment. One of its executive members, Mary Stocks, considered the reform an essential complement to allowances, since, if women were to fully control their lives, they had to control fertility.

The birth control issue illustrates the difficulty in trying to understand the women's movement in these years and particularly in trying to understand how lines were drawn between contending factions. NUSEC successfully maintained an appearance of unity until 1927, largely according to Crystal Eastman because it was still engaged in the campaign to extend the suffrage to women on the same terms as men (the 1918 Act had enfranchised only women aged 30 and above). In that year eleven members of the executive resigned, leaving Rathbone President of the remainder of the organisation. Those who had resigned—the equal rights faction—became aligned with either Rhondda's Six Point Group, founded in 1918, or with the new Open Door Council, headed by Elizabeth Abbott. Crystal Eastman was in London at the time of the split and reported the incident to the American movement through the newspaper *Equal Rights*. A supporter of the ERA and a member of the NWP, Eastman still provides useful insights into the schism. In her view, the issues were 'Protection versus equality for women in industry, birth control and family endowment versus "straight" feminism' (Cook, 1978: 226).

It is certainly curious to any feminist who has lived through the 1960s to see feminists of any persuasion giving low priority to birth control, but more especially to see this position upheld by a faction identified as 'strong equal rights'. This indicates again the need to locate feminism historically. At this time birth control was associated primarily with maternal health; the equal rights group were suspicious of anything associated with women's reproductive capacity which they thought would be used to hold women back. Their stance reflected a principle, insisting on women's similarity to men, which they felt compelled to adopt by the options available to women at the time. While a member of the equal rights faction herself, Eastman, who thought that a good deal could be said for birth control 'from a Feminist standpoint', expressed disappointment with the 'pure Feminist' whom she called 'a bit of a doctrinaire': 'She likes to advocate something that can be stated literally in terms of equality' (Cook, 1978: 230).

Here in fact is the crux of the matter. Why did equal rights feminists feel compelled to advocate something that could be stated 'literally in terms of equality'? Because the common understanding of equality made it necessary to take such a stand. Felix Frankfurter had laid down the ground rules when he told supporters of the ERA that an amendment proclaiming equality with men could not simultaneously sustain special class status for women (Kessler-Harris, 1984: 149) (see page 42). The law made it necessary, therefore, to choose *between* 'equal treatment' *and* 'special' consideration, regardless of the circumstances. Women were told that they could either accept existing standards or opt out of them.

Some women were so afraid of the implications of this interpretation that they even refused *political* rights. The anti-suffragist, Correa Moylan Walsh, explained that, if women were granted political rights equal to men, then women must be treated exactly like men. But since women were 'periodically enfeebled' by childbearing and by child nurture, 'which no man, as a rule, can or will perform' (Walsh, 1917: 224), she did not feel that women dared assert this degree of independence:

> There is the alternative: female independence, without children, and then a certain end to civilization; or female dependence, with children, and then the possibility of the continuance of civilization (Walsh, 1917: 227).

Like many right-wing women today, Walsh feared that by demanding equality women would lose their 'privileges', such as the husband's obligation to support them or to pay alimony upon divorce (Walsh, 1917: 233). She thought that the claim to equality in effect discriminated against some women, 'the marrying and child-bearing kind of women, by discriminating against their husbands'. If women tried to invade men's work, they would lessen men's ability to support them (Walsh, 1917: 220, 233). The alternative to *direct* dependence on men, state support, Moylan considered a 'disguised dependence on men' and a form of socialism

(Walsh, 1917: 118). Again, political ideology constructed the parameters within which strategies were devised.

As far as rights were concerned, Walsh identified some that were
human, some that were distinctively male and some distinctively
for women, 'as when they are maids, wives and mothers' (Walsh,
1917: 31). Their principal 'right' was support by some man. In
exchange Walsh agreed to surrender the right to vote, equal pay,
property rights, equal access to divorce, and equal custody rights.
If this is where an acknowledgement of 'difference' could lead, it
is little wonder that the equal rights feminist became a 'bit of a
doctrinaire' about equality, though no suffragist would have agreed
that *political equality* was threatened by an assertion of difference
(see pages 20, 40).

Walsh identified two kinds of feminists: those she called 'consistent' and those who were aware of the problematic outcomes of
their argument. The latter admitted the necessity of protective
legislation because of women's biological and functional 'differences'. The former were committed to 'equal rights' at all costs.
Walsh correctly observed that even these, the 'consistent feminists', admitted one exception—that men are not to bear and tend
children (Walsh, 1917: 222)—which, given their emphasis on
women's 'equal' ability to compete, necessitated reducing pregnancy and child nurture to a 'temporary indisposition'. Neither
group disputed the sexual division of labour nor the assumption
that it was appropriate for labour regulations to ignore family
commitments. In a society where individuality and dependency
were set up as alternatives, one chose to emphasise the former, the
other tried to justify the latter.

As in America, protective legislation was the issue which produced
open confrontation. In 1925 NUSEC had declared itself completely opposed to legislation specifically directed at women. Labour
women, like Marion Phillips and Margaret Bondfield, then began
to defend the legislation publicly. At a 1927 conference on the
subject hosted by NUSEC several women's trades unions were
represented and most of their delegates spoke against the resolu-
tions condemning protective legislation. They argued that the
'Feminists' could have spent their time better in trying to *increase*
the safeguards in the Factory Bill (Cook, 1978: 217). Combined
Labour and union pressure produced a new 'Object of the society'
in that year:

> To obtain all such reforms as are necessary to secure a *real
> equality* of liberties, status and opportunities between men and
> women and also such reforms as are necessary to make it

possible for women adequately to discharge their functions as
citizens (Cook, 1978: 223, emphasis added).

The resolution was passed by a narrow majority and the eleven
executive members walked out.

The Labour influence in shifting the debate towards women's
'special' needs was critical. The victory of this faction in NUSEC
indicated the direction British feminism would follow from this
point. The decision according to Eastman was whether to 'level up'
or 'level down'—whether feminists would insist that men workers
be brought under the safety and health regulations which applied
to women or, if this seemed unlikely for the present, whether they
would remove those regulations. Eastman correctly deduced that
'the British Feminists will favour the "levelling up" form of
amendment' (Cook, 1978: 218). Jennifer Dale and Peggy Foster
call this approach, which gave priority to the immediate material
needs of women over and above abstract notions of equal rights,
'welfare' feminism (Dale and Foster, 1986: 7–8), an approach
which has dominated British feminism since. This is not to say
that equal rights feminism disappeared, but neither the Six Point
Group nor the Open Door Council ever attracted the equivalent
attention given to the NWP in America, due largely to the ERA
campaign there. Corresponding British legislation, drafted by
Dorothy Evans of the Six Point Group, died with its originator in
1945 (Six Point Group, 1945: 24–25).

American equal rights feminists actually played a vital role in
mobilising their British counterparts. In 1925, Alice Paul co-
ordinated the establishment of a British Advisory Group to the
NWP. It included in its membership Rhondda, Dorothy Evans
and the former militant suffragist, Mrs Emmeline Pethick-
Lawrence (Cook, 1978: 167). This group proved helpful in Paul's
efforts to influence the direction of international feminism. It
lacked the power, however, to prevent the rejection of the NWP's
application for membership in the International Suffrage Alliance
in 1926 (Cook, 1978: 186). Although the Alliance claimed that
rejection had nothing to do with the Party's stand on protective
legislation, the NWP's arch-opponent, the American League of
Women Voters, was already a member, and it was clear that the
two groups could not work together because of this very issue
(Cook, 1978: 203). Rhondda retaliated by removing the Six Point
Group's application for membership. Elizabeth Abbott proceeded
to enlist equal rights activists in an Open Door International (ODI),
established in 1929 (ODI, 1935). International feminism now had a
reform faction and an equal rights faction.

The object of the Open Door International was identical to that of its British parent group:

> To secure that a woman shall be free to work and protected as a worker *on the same terms as a man*, and that legislation dealing with conditions and hours, payment, entry and training shall be based upon the nature of the work and not upon the sex of the worker; and to secure for a woman, irrespective of marriage or childbirth, the right at all times to decide whether or not she shall engage in paid work, and to ensure that no legislation or regulations shall deprive her of this right (Open Door International, 1935—emphasis added).

Rathbone told equal rights feminists: 'If you set yourselves to work for pure equality between the sexes and nothing else you are following an arid, barren and obsessing idea' (Cook, 1978: 231). Abbott responded: 'New feminism reads a dictionary definition, equality—sameness; men and women are not the same [in their opinion] and therefore are not equal' (Lewis, 1984: 104). The complex subject of appropriate and humane working conditions had been reduced in debate to a sameness/difference formulation of the problem.

Despite the sharp division over protective legislation, there was a considerable amount of common ground among British feminists, as among American feminists (see page 46). The British were united not only by the campaign to extend the franchise. They worked together for the Sex Disqualification Removal Bill (1919) and against the marriage bar which allowed women in certain occupations to be fired on marriage (Lewis, 1984: 102). They united behind the 1925 Guardianship of Infants Act (Macnicol, 1980: 25). They were also equally insistent upon the need to have the value of women's domestic labour acknowledged.

As in America equal rights feminists in Britain supported moves to upgrade the homemaker's status. Although Millicent Fawcett could not endorse family endowment, she wanted to find a way to recognise the wife's work in her household and suggested either a definite sum as wages or a proportion of her husband's wage (Holton, 1986: 26). From its inauguration the Six Point Group included among its demands, alongside equal pay, that 'The economic value of the work of women in the home must be recognised' (Cook, 1978: 146). One of the offspring of the Group was the Married Women's Association, otherwise known as the Housewives' Trade Union, formed because 'If any section of people need a trade union to protect them from overwork and underpay it is the housewives. They are omitted from all labour legislation, even from health insurance' (Six Point Group, 1945: 8).

Rhondda took on the well-known social critic, G. K. Chesterton, in debate on the value of 'homework'. Chesterton put forward a classic defence of the home as haven. 'Home', he said, 'is the only place where there is any liberty left, any chance for creative imagination, any room for the development of personality'. The only place where a man can call his soul his own in modern capitalist society, said Chesterton, is in that 'self-willed, self-chosen group of the home'. A man can have some fun in his home. 'He can do as he likes, say what he likes, even like as he likes. Why should women want to get out of it into the slavery of the commercial world?'

In response, Rhondda made the simple point, repeated by many contemporary feminists, that 'for women there is no such thing as home in this sense'. For the person who stays at home and whose business it is to maintain it, claimed Rhondda, the home can be no 'island of liberty', no oasis of comfort or relaxation. The feminist, she insisted, did not want to destroy the home. Rather, she wanted to find a man to share in the burden and joy of homemaking so that she could share in the burden and joy of earning the living. 'Home for women too' could be 'the new feminist slogan' (Cook, 1978: 105).

Many reform feminists, certainly Fabians like Royden and Atkinson, would have cheered Rhondda's position. Feminists agreed that women should have the chance to develop their individuality; they also agreed that women's domestic labour was undervalued. They disagreed only about the possibility of combining the two roles. Some reform feminists like Royden felt that for the sake of the race the commitment to motherhood had to preclude other commitments. Others like Dora Russell, sounding a little like Betty Friedan in *The Second Stage*, pondered if perhaps the pursuit of economic independence was worth the cost—'Life isn't all earning your living' (Cook, 1978: 118). The equal rights feminists, without paying much attention to how it was to be arranged, insisted upon women's right to compete in every sphere.

The equal rights view was often ferociously individualistic. These feminists had absorbed the message of industrial capitalism and were prepared to play by the established rules. Rhondda distinguished between 'reformers' and 'feminists'. She criticised the former for being motivated by the 'passion to look after your fellow man', and praised the latter for their 'desire to put into every one's hand the power to look after themselves' (Cook, 1978: 193). In the domestic sphere roles could be differentiated, and 'differences' accommodated. Equality at home meant equal value.

In the marketplace, in contrast, equality meant equal access only, the distribution of resources to be dependent solely upon merit (Hochschild, 1981: Chapter 3). There was certainly no room for 'special pleading'. In her endorsement of the Open Door Council, the suffragist, Cicely Hamilton, reflected that reluctance to admit vulnerability, discussed in the previous chapter (see page 45):

> ...its aim was to correct the tendency of our legislators to be overkind to women who earn their livelihood; to treat them from youth to age as if they were permanently pregnant, and forbid them all manner of trades and callings in case they might injure their health (Lewis, 1983: 31).

An acceptance of the value of unrestricted competition led many equal rights feminists to condemn any attempt to make employers respond to the specific needs of female workers.

In this spirit the Open Door International protested against three International Labour Organization Conventions (ILO): the 1919 Night Work Convention, the 1919 Childbirth Convention, and the 1921 White Lead (Painting) Convention (ODI, 1935: 11). The first, ratified by Britain, imposed restrictions on women's ability to work at night. Crystal Eastman spoke for all equal rights feminists when she condemned the law for being based on false moralism—a concern that women might succumb to the dangers of the midnight streets. Eastman expressed defiance in the face of such paternalism: '*I am not a child*. I will have none of your protection' (Cook, 1978: 157, emphasis in original).

The White Lead (Painting) Convention resulted in the introduction of a Lead Paint Bill in 1927 which proposed prohibiting altogether the employment 'of women and young persons in painting any part of a building with lead paint' (Cook, 1978: 212). The debate on the Bill raised a number of arguments which are still being used today (see Chapter 6). Lord Balfour of Burleigh protested that there was no medical proof of women's greater susceptibility to lead poisoning, nor of the contention that the evils were transmitted more through a poisoned mother than a poisoned father. Elizabeth Abbott found herself defending Beatrice Webb's Minority Report on Women in Industry which stated that what was needed was neither the exclusion from work of all persons of one sex, nor even the subjecting of them to special restrictions, but 'the minute, careful and persistent observation, by the medical officer...of the individual worker irrespective of sex' (Abbott, 1924: 3). Given the unlikelihood of that happening, however, Abbott and the ODI were content for the moment to 'level down'. They demanded:

...the right to work by day or night, above ground or underground, and in particular *the right to undertake heavy or dangerous work*, or work in dangerous materials such as lead, subject to no greater restrictions on herself or her employer in the interest of health, welfare or morals, than those to which a man or his employer is subject (ODI, 1935: 65, emphasis added).

In a society where protection for all workers was inadequate, it seemed necessary to insist upon women's 'sameness' in order to prevent their exclusion from the marketplace.

The critical issue, which could have been anticipated, was how to deal with maternity in the workplace. Both groups would have been happier to ignore it. Reform feminists felt that ideally women would remain at home, but women inconveniently refused to do so. Equal rights feminists wanted women to work on equal terms with men and avoided the subjects of maternity and childcare which seemed to pose impediments to this objective. Consistently, their fear was that, if employers were required to pick up additional costs for employing women, they would not hire them or would pay them less (which seemed fair to people who accepted that 'you should only get what you are worth', estimated in purely economic terms). On these grounds, Elizabeth Abbott condemned any attempt to get employers to provide crèches for women employees (ODI, 1935: 30). The same argument was used to reject the ILO's 1919 Childbirth Convention (otherwise known as the Washington Convention) which gave a woman a right to six weeks' maternity leave before confinement, prohibited work during the six weeks after confinement, and guaranteed that her job would be kept open for her (Abbott, 1924). Recall that the NWP also opposed the idea of paid leave before and after childbirth (see page 46).

The history of maternity legislation, specifically paid maternity leave, demonstrates that positions in the sameness/difference debate are historically specific and politically determined. The following discussion of what occurred in Britain in this early period should be carefully compared to current American debates on the subject (see Chapter 5).

In Britain, the National Health Insurance Act of 1911–1912 made no allowance specifically to cover interruption of earnings due to pregnancy. It provided a sickness benefit for all insured persons who had paid the minimum required contributions. But it was uncertain if maternity fell within the definition of 'sickness'. Some argued that pregnancy was a natural process, not an illness. Others said it was an illness only if there were complications (Brown and Small, 1875: 8ff.). Seeking assistance from the

Approved Friendly Societies, private insurance companies, proved no more satisfactory. According to Margaret Bondfield, nearly all the Approved Societies refused sickness benefit to women who were pregnant, even if they were certified as incapable of work. This action was defended on the grounds that, if these claims were met in full, it would lead to insolvency (Bondfield, 1940: 131). Since Britain did not ratify the 1919 ILO Childbirth Convention (Brown and Small, 1985: 9), this was the situation facing equal rights feminists like Abbott. The subject was debated at the Fourth Conference of the Open Door International held in Copenhagen in 1934. The various positions illustrate the importance of cultural context and the rather sad range of options available.

Strange as it may seem for a vigorous defender of liberal egalitarianism, Abbott became enamoured of the Russian example where all incapacitated workers received full pay when absent from work. The solution to the maternity problem was, in her opinion, to apply this model to pregnant women, who were similarly unable to work. Pregnancy should be treated like other incapacities (ODI, 1935: 30–31). The French representative objected to such an analogy since in France childbearing was considered a 'social service', not an illness. She wanted absence due to maternity to be put on a par with absence due to military service, and supported on those grounds. The Honorary Secretary, Winifred Le Sueur, protested against the assimilation of childbirth and conscription, because the idea 'savoured too much of the production and destruction of cannon-fodder'. A letter from a French member of the Board drew attention to the dangers of the 'military service' analogy. It deserves to be quoted at length because of the popularity of this argument today[7]:

> It follows that if the rights of the mother are to be based on services rendered, these rights will cease to exist the day when the service ceases to be considered as such, either on account of over-population, or because the woman is deemed to be unfitted to bring into the world a strong, healthy child, useful for the prosperity of society.
>
> By basing the right of the mother on service to society, we tend to return to the mistake we are combatting; that is, we tend to subordinate the right of the woman to the public interest and to make of her a means and not an end (ODI, 1935: 34).

'Conscription' to motherhood or pleading incapacity—one dangerous and the other unsatisfactory—were the choices open to women so long as they were considered solely responsible for the family and so long as women were defined in terms of their childbearing capacity. For the future the ODI recommended treating pregnancy like incapacities brought on by accident or illness, 'and where a medical certificate is required in the one case, it should also be required in the other' (ODI, 1935: 60). Just beneath this resolution the text carried a paragraph which hinted at a broader understanding:

> The two parents of each child, the mother and the father, are equally responsible for its birth. They are equally responsible morally for providing the money and other assistance needed in connection with such incapacity of the mother, and the birth and extreme youth of the child. Public authorities which provide such assistance as, for example, money, doctors, midwives, crêches, etc., help both the mother and the father to carry out these responsibilities. . . They are relieving both parents of part of their responsibilities.

The ODI did not object to the provision of these services so long as they were financed by the community and did not therefore impose a competitive handicap upon women employees. But the group saw this as, for the moment, outside its brief, which was securing 'the same rights as a man for the woman a worker for pay'. When some of these services were provided as part of the post-World War II reforms which emerged from the Beveridge report, the debate shifted to another set of concerns.

Beveridge's 1941 Social Security arrangements offered a mixed bag to married women. The Married Woman's Option 'allowed' a married woman to exempt herself from paying insurance contributions on the understanding that the husband would probably support her. In compensation married women were offered the right to widows' pensions based on their late husbands' insurance and a special maternity benefit including *an allowance during work interruption due to pregnancy* (Brown and Small, 1985: 15). Elizabeth Abbott and Katherine Bompass of the Open Door Council immediately launched a campaign condemning the proposal which allowed married women to opt out of the insurance scheme, on the grounds that it created the married woman worker as a class of 'pin-money worker' (Abbott and Bompass, 1943: 20). They also demanded that, despite the difficulties involved, housewives ought to be covered by insurance benefits. The issue of paid maternity leave, however, dropped from the debate since Abbott and Bompass seemed to be satisfied that the problem was now dealt with under national insurance. They continued to make the important conceptual point that

> Maternity Grant and Benefit and Guardian Benefit should be acknowledged for what they are: not individual benefits, but Family Benefits, designed to safeguard the bearing, rearing, sustenance, health, home life and general well-being of children (Abbott and Bompass, 1943: 20).

While it might seem with hindsight that equal rights feminists had been too eager to reject benefits for working mothers, it should be remembered that the inter-war years in Britain were characterised by extreme pro-natalism. And, while such a climate allowed women's labour organisations to further their claims to improve conditions for working-class mothers (Riley, 1983: 182), it was a climate fraught with danger for women—shades of Le Sueur's 'conscription' fears (see page 70). Feminists were justifiably cautious about drawing too much attention to women's maternal requirements since maternity was often offered as justification for *controlling* women and their childbearing capacity for the sake of the race. The possibility of achieving some social responsibility for reproduction without turning it into national service seemed remote.

With no institutional supports for pregnant employed women, feminists had had little option to claiming either that women could function like men or insisting that they could not. Once society acknowledged a degree of responsibility for children, by granting working women minimal paid pregnancy leave, British feminists ceased arguing in these terms over this particular issue. The example illustrates that the problem is not whether women are the same as or different from men, but the inadequacy of institutional arrangements for basic human needs.

As mentioned at the outset, there is evidence that Australian feminists were not of one mind on protective legislation and related issues, but the movement does not appear to have experienced a schism comparable to Britain or America. While some of the positions are identifiable as reform feminist or equal rights feminist, they sometimes combined in rather unusual patterns. The South Australian Women's Non-Party Association (WNPA) consistently opposed protective legislation on the grounds that the demand for equality could not be an 'advocacy for favours' (Nicholson, 1983: 29). Like other opponents of protective legislation the Association added that equally humane hours and conditions should apply to all workers. But the group was not typically equal rights in any sense. The WNPA campaigned vigorously for family endowment, a reform more closely associated with reform feminism. Perhaps, as Alice Henry had observed, the progressive climate in Australia, which meant that the desire to 'level up' was more than a fond wish, allowed equal rights and reform feminism to move closer together.

Jessie Street, President of the United Associations of Women (UA), is a good representative of Australian equal rights feminism. A middle-class group, the UA in its constitution called for 'freedom and equality of status and opportunity for men and women' (Ranald, 1982: 276). Like other equal rights feminists, Street also wanted to raise the status of women's domestic labour by securing for them a portion of their husbands' wages. She was ambivalent, however, about the benefits of equal pay. She feared it would force employers out of business, causing unemployment for both women and men. Her priority remained the maintenance of the family and of social order.

Muriel Heagney, President of the Council of Action for Equal Pay, represented the views of Australia's labour feminists. She believed that equal pay was a matter of social justice. At the same time she expressed the opinion that the family wage was sadly inadequate and ought to be supplemented by a family endowment. Heagney took issue with Street's proposal that some of the husband's wage be set aside for the wife, on the grounds that the average working-class wage was simply not large enough. She would have agreed however with the desirability of improving the status of the housewife. Heagney saw women as the 'custodians of the race' and felt that the average woman in industry had to be regarded as a 'potential mother' (Bremner, 1982: 295).

Australian feminism seemed to coalesce in a position closer to reform than equal rights feminism. According to Crystal Eastman, in the 1923 Rome Congress debate, Australia lined up with the 'humanitarians' (Cook, 1978: 155–156). And, although Australia was represented at the 1934 ODI Conference, delegate Linda Littlejohn explained that she had no mandate to say that Australian women were for or against 'protection' (ODI, 1935: 46). The fact that in Australia the positions do not appear to have been as clear-cut suggests again the danger in generalising the experience of feminism, and in supposing that 'sameness' or 'difference' referred to abstract states rather than to historically specific circumstances.

A legacy of the inter-war period was the construction of the meaning of 'feminism'. Fluid in its initial usage,[8] in America it became almost equated with the NWP style and program. 'Feminists', according to the NWP, put 'women' first; they demanded 'equal', meaning 'the same', treatment as men. If you deviated from this line, if you so much as mentioned 'difference', you were no feminist.

Reform feminists tried for a time to retain the title. In 1925 Mary Anderson called herself a 'good feminist', and in 1924 Alice Hamilton declared the goal of all feminists to be the same, 'the securing for women of as great a degree of self-determination as can be enjoyed in complex community life without detriment to others' (Anderson, 1925; Hamilton, 1984: B-29). But the way in which the debate evolved made it difficult to continue this attempt. In press coverage the term came to be associated with the ERA and so women who opposed the amendment were less likely to use the word. By the years of the New Deal, women interested in Roosevelt's legislative innovations declared that they were social reformers rather than feminists (Rupp and Taylor, 1987: 53; Ware, 1981: 16).

Equal rights, as we have seen, was never such a powerful catch-cry in Britain and the strength of the labour movement there gave feminism a different history. Rathbone refused to abrogate the title 'feminist', and in fact insisted that it was time to revamp its meaning. The term remained sufficiently ambiguous for left-wing women to use it. In fact the close association between socialism and feminism in Britain has meant that strong equal rights advocates occasionally shy away from the label.[9] This brief review of the way in which the term evolved in just two countries should warn feminist historians today about the difficulty and perhaps the inappropriateness of searching for a single feminist tradition.

It may seem somewhat paradoxical that, while feminists debated whether married women ought to stay home or enter the market-place, the question of woman's essential maternal character was not seriously disputed during this period. Perhaps this was because both groups ultimately accepted women's responsibility for children. Perhaps also the maternal image continued to provide a respectable and inspiring identity. Perhaps feminists were simply too preoccupied with the question of whether or not married women should join the labour force to consider how women's character fitted into the equation. The social theory drawing out the impact of socialisation on behaviour was just entering public parlance. In any event, concern about the symbolism of the maternal mystique and the feeling that it did not sit comfortably with a claim to equality did not emerge until the 1960s. Chapter 4 takes up this story.

4

The 1960s resurgence: from equal rights to post-feminism

By the 1960s it had become clear that, despite ideological preference, most married women were engaging in paid labour. Feminists therefore united behind a social program which invited men to share family responsibilities, and asked the government to provide social supports such as childcare. An underlying tension remained, however, about whether it was preferable for women to compete *on the same terms as men*, or whether women needed 'special' assistance, a tension which surfaces today in institutional debates about equal versus special treatment (Chapter 5).

This chapter begins with a description of the historical circumstances which led to the resolution of the functional debate, which had characterised the inter-war period, about whether or not married women belonged at home. It then turns to the complex and heated contemporary controversy about women's and men's character 'differences'. The origins of this metaphysical debate are traced to the heavy reliance of much early second-wave feminism (1960s/1970s) upon socialisation theory which suggested that, for women to succeed in the world of paid work, they had to overcome their conditioning as 'women', and develop 'male-style' aggressiveness and independence. The image of women as naturally maternal and morally superior to men, which had been accepted by most feminists until this time, came under attack. Now, to be 'equal', women had to abandon or minimise their mothering role *and* the characteristics associated with that role. A good deal of the literature accentuated the desirability of a forceful and competitive personality. Instead of focusing upon the way in which the economic system rewarded these characteristics, there was a tendency to essentialise the style as 'masculine' and 'male'.

The renewed 'equal rights' emphasis produced two reactions.

First, women who were convinced that women inevitably lost in any attempt to compete on 'men's' terms gave their support to a right-wing backlash which attempted to revive the traditional nuclear family and clear-cut sex roles. Second, a number of feminists, increasingly critical of the public world of work and the public politics of environmental pollution and the war machine, revived 'maternalism', but more as a symbol than as a recommended role option. In revulsion against aspects of competition and individualism, they offered 'women' as the purveyors of a countervailing and humanitarian ethic. In this way complex political realities were reduced to gender metaphors, heavily dependent on a rhetoric of 'sameness' and 'difference'.

As far as men's and women's assumed *social functions* were concerned, feminists now faced anti-feminists. Some feminists faced each other in *institutional* and *metaphysical* disputes. In each instance, the tendency to reduce the analysis to discussions about women's sameness to or difference from men distracted attention from deeper political issues, such as the relationship between personal life and work commitments and the way in which Western industrial societies privilege competition and downgrade caring.

Second-wave feminism has been accompanied by significant theoretical developments. As inadequate as they are, the traditional labels—liberal, socialist and radical—will be used to identify major traditions. To these will be added cultural feminism, pro-family feminism, poststructural analysis and post-feminism, which will be explained as they arise. The purpose of this chapter is not to provide an overview of feminist theoretical contributions but to see the ways in which feminists have engaged with the question of difference.

The story of feminism from the 1960s to the present is closely linked to developments in America. For Britain and Australia at least the ties are critical. These countries often took (and take) their lead from the American example and, though they produce their own literature, American texts form an important part of the collective wisdom (Curthoys, 1988: 2). This may in some ways be unfortunate, for part of the message of this book is that it is useful to be aware of precise historical and institutional circumstances in order to understand the forms feminism takes in any particular country. Some of America's debates simply cannot be transposed. More will be said about the distinctive characters of British, Australian and American feminism in this and subsequent chapters.

On one level, by the 1960s changes in women's workforce participation seemed to resolve the debate about women's roles. In America (and the pattern is similar elsewhere[1]) many more women were working for wages. In 1920 one in four women engaged in paid labour; by the mid-1960s 40% of women participated in the labour force. More significant still was the marital status of this new female workforce. As of 1970, 63% of the female labour force was married, compared to 23% in 1920. For the first time the number of married women in waged labour exceeded the number of single women (Sealander, 1983: 161; Showalter, 1978: 25). Jane Lewis confirms that in post-war Britain, the 'most startling development' was the increase in the number of married women working for wages (Lewis, 1984: 218).

A combination of factors affected the pattern of women's workforce participation. After World War II, the tertiary sector expanded, opening up job opportunities for women. Fertility continued to decline, and improved public health reduced the fragility of infants. More energy was now invested in the social and economic future of children than in their physical survival. The needs of children required 'additional expenditures of money and less of a mother's household time' (Tilly and Scott, 1978: 221, 229).

These changes called into question the appropriateness and feasibility of the traditional domestic ideal of 'Mum at home' and 'Dad at work'. The open rift between America's reform and equal rights feminists was healed as a result. Long-time campaigner for protective legislation and director of the Women's Bureau in 1961, Esther Peterson, explained that 'rapid changes in the economic and cultural climate in this country' had changed her mind on the ERA (Peterson, c.1976: 20–21). A dedicated humanitarian, Peterson felt that the extensions of the 1939 Fair Labor Standards Act, and the Civil Rights Bill of 1964 now made it possible to broaden the protection campaign to 'extending good labor standards to both men and women' (Rupp and Taylor, 1987: 62).

The resolution of conflict did not occur overnight. The President's Commission on the Status of Women, established in 1961 by John F. Kennedy, played an important role in bringing together the competing factions but, as Cynthia Harrison points out, the Commission itself had difficulty balancing the ideals of equal opportunity and traditional motherhood. On the one hand, the Commission recommended education for motherhood, accepted the view of women as dependants, and left final responsibility for children with mothers (Harrison, 1988: Chapter 9). The buoyant economic conditions of the 1960s meant, however, that one of the key motivations of the Kennedy Commission was a concern for *womanpower* (Rossi, 1982: 15–16). As a result the Commission found itself endorsing childcare and equal pay for equal work (the Equal Pay Act was passed in 1963).

The Women's Bureau continued to fear that an insistence on

equal rights would deprive women of hard-won protections and so opposed the addition of 'sex' to Title VII of the 1964 Civil Rights Act. Some, including Peterson, hesitated to support the amendment because they feared that it might lead to the Bill's defeat and that this was the 'Negro's hour' (Harrison, 1988: 177–178).[2] In the event, the Bill passed. Reform feminists proceeded to pressure the newly-established Equal Employment Opportunity Commission (EEOC) not to use Title VII against protective labour laws. Equal rights feminists mobilised, formed a new national organisation, the National Organisation for Women (NOW), in 1966, and lobbied the EEOC to declare protective legislation incompatible with equal opportunity. This it did in 1969, marking the victory of equal rights feminism.

It is easy to misrepresent the character of equal rights feminism, which has often been done. The group has been caricatured as anti-motherhood and uncaring of the needs of mothers (Hewlett, 1986: 143; Riley, 1987a: 179–180). This image, as will be seen (Chapter 8), has been used to 'blame' feminists for the loss of alimony payments and for the phenomenon described as the 'feminization of poverty' (Weitzman, 1985: 363). The media is partly responsible for the misrepresentation. It preferred more extreme statements to the careful analysis produced by groups like the Citizens' Advisory Council which consistently reported on such issues as job-related maternity benefits and mechanisms for guaranteeing child support (East, 1986: 18; Citizens' Advisory Council on the Status of Women, 1971, 1972, 1973). The *Spirit of Houston*, the report of the First National Women's Conference in 1977, included as one of its planks the needs of homemakers, and looked at the low status and lack of security accompanying the role (National Women's Conference, 1978: 57). The needs of married women were a concern of equal rights groups throughout the century. Their *priority*, however, remained gaining access to opportunities 'enjoyed' by men.

The testimony to the 1970 Senate Subcommittee hearings on the ERA contains a sampling of their views. The Hon. Florence P. Dwyer, a representative in Congress from New Jersey, said that women wanted to be treated as 'whole citizens': they have 'the right to earn a living and obtain an education. . .to receive the job and promotional opportunities commensurate with their talent' (Stimpson, 1972: 21). The representative from Massachusetts, Margaret M. Heckler, caught the mood of the period: 'The old saying "you can't keep a good man down" might well serve as a warning. . .women are unlikely to stay down and out of the field of competition for much longer' (Stimpson, 1972: 28).

Labour representatives at the hearings were divided. On one side the United Automobile Workers and the League for American Working Women supported the ERA since it would eliminate restrictive laws and practices (Stimpson, 1972: 202). On the other the AFL-CIO representative, Mortimer Furay, presented slides to demonstrate women's physical incapacity and greater susceptibility to fatigue. Another AFL-CIO member, Myra Wolfgang, drew attention to some of the problems identified by reformers like Mary Van Kleeck and Alice Hamilton earlier in the century. Women, she said, were poorly organised, and held down not one, but two jobs. Emancipation had released women *for* work but had not released them *from* home and family responsibilities (Stimpson, 1972: 54, 92–96). Wolfgang asked, 'Who will take care of the children, the home, cleaning, the laundry and the cooking?'

The equal rights response was that these roles would be shared by men and women. NOW's major theoretical contribution was that sex roles were not immutable. Its 'Statement of Purpose' read:

> We reject the current assumption that a man must carry the sole burden of supporting himself, his wife and family...or that marriage, home and family are primarily woman's world and responsibility—hers, to dominate—his to support. We believe that a true partnership between the sexes demands a different concept of marriage, an equitable sharing of the responsibilities of home and children and of the economic burdens of their support.

The vision of joint responsibility meant, according to Cynthia Harrison, that equal rights feminists presented a coherent and logical program for the first time: 'Women could insist upon equal treatment in the workplace now because fathers, too, had the responsibility to take care of children' (Harrison, 1988: 199–200). What used to be seen as women's 'difference' would now be shared.

This solution of the dilemma facing women could only be partial, however, while the social supports, such as childcare, which facilitated role-sharing did not exist. Nor did it address adequately the needs or desires of many working-class women who would have preferred to have been liberated *from* rather than *for* work. Black feminists were quick to point out that they had always worked and it had not liberated them (Brill, 1987: 97). Gayatri Spivak added another dimension to the criticism by reminding 'bourgeois feminists' that entry to the workforce could make them part of a multinational complex that exploits other (Third World) women (Spivak, 1985: 138).

The search for the kind of self-actualisation promoted by equal rights feminists, therefore, was predominantly a search undertaken by Anglo-Saxon middle-class women. Emphasis was placed not on structural supports, but upon a free market opportunity to compete. The economic buoyancy of the 1960s made everything seem possible so that practicalities occasionally received low priority. Although NOW and its representatives demanded childcare, it ranked fourteenth of NOW's fourteen planks. Rhetorically the group downplayed the 'differences' which seemed to handicap women in economic competition and one of these was motherhood. Wilma Scott Heide, Chairperson, Board of Directors of NOW, declared that 'biology is not relevant to human equity'. The written submission from the Commission on the Status of Women, Iowa State House to the ERA Senate hearings, put the case that 'If women were meant to be maternity machines, they would not have been given minds'. Jean Witter of NOW wanted motherhood to be recognised as a 'temporary condition' and to encourage young mothers to realise that they can expect to do other things in addition to being a parent, 'just as men do' (Stimpson, 1972: 192, 238, 245).

Like 'These Modern Women' of the 1920s, freedom to compete had to mean 'freedom' to be as much like 'men' as possible. The solution to the conundrum of women's lives seemed to be to allow them to explore the individual development available to men. Of course, in a free enterprise state like America, where the President vetoed national childcare legislation on the grounds of its 'communal' (read communist) implications (Wallis, 1987: 58), most women are left trying to find a precarious balance between family and paid work. The tension between individual self-actualisation and community cohesion (see page xii) is unresolved.

Britain's equal rights feminists expressed some of the same ambivalence about women's traditional homemaking role. The Six Point Group continued to be active into the 1960s. Writing on behalf of that group in 1968 Hazel Hunkins-Hallinan criticised the over-concentration on domesticity in women's lives, the creeping 'home sweet home' idea which must be shorn of its 'saccharin sentimentality'. Domesticity, she felt, denied the wholeness of a personality, and restricted activity to a biological function which 'when all is said and done, is usually a small part of life' (Six Point Group, 1968: 9). The veteran campaigner for equality legislation, Margherita Rendel, also made a case for women moving outside the domestic domain, which many found 'boring, frustrating and lonely'. Echoing Friedan's identification of the 'problem that has no name' (see Betty Friedan, *The Feminine Mystique*), Rendel claimed that many housewives felt cut off from the world, 'lacking the identity which our society bestows on members of an occupational group, and completely dependent on their husbands' (Rendel, 1968: 21).

Still, the distinctive characteristic of the British movement continued to be the close links between Marxism and feminism, forged as a result of the strength of the trade unions and the Labour Party which had no parallel in the United States (Wilson and Weir, 1986: 96–97). (It is largely due to these links that, as we will see in Chapter 6, the debate on protective legislation continued into the 1980s.) As a result of Britain's welfare heritage some feminists, echoing some of the disputes in the 1920s and 1930s, remain uncertain about whether to concentrate upon women's needs in the home or to assist them into the workforce (Phillips, 1986: 187). The problem is that feminists have to deal with a historical reality not an ideal state and, in present circumstances, some reforms, such as dependent spouse allowances, which help one group (dependent wives) disadvantage the other group (women in paid work). The degree of institutional reform required so that traditional caring roles are accepted as social responsibilities and so that people who fill these roles are not penalised, is so daunting in Thatcher's Britain that feminists continue to be forced into either/ or choices when neither will do. The lack of welfare options in America made it easier and perhaps necessary for feminists there to agree upon an equal access campaign.

Some British socialist feminists display a somewhat ambivalent attitude towards equal rights feminism, an ambivalence Anne Phillips attributes to a 'skeptical questioning' of socialism's claim that capitalism is chiefly responsible for women's subordination (Phillips, 1987: 11). Michèle Barrett, for example, while in sympathy with Marx's critique of liberalism, refuses to dismiss 'mere' political emancipation. Juliet Mitchell also wants to 'rescue equal rights as worthy' despite its limitations.

British feminism has been less affected by the American campaign for equality, however, than by the radical feminist literature of women like Kate Millett and Shulamith Firestone (Wilson and Weir, 1986: 98). Radical feminism was a development within the younger branch of the 1960s resurgence, a branch sometimes called 'women's liberation'. These women were also predominantly middle-class and white. Many had participated in student radicalism, anti-Vietnam war protests and the civil rights battles of the 1960s. 'Women's liberation' encompassed 'politicos', who emphasised the role of capitalism in perpetuating women's subordination, and radical feminists, who identified men rather than the system as the main enemy (Hole and Levine, 1971: X). Radical feminism posed real problems for a tradition built upon the solidarity of working-class men and women. Although at the outset disagreements did not produce antagonistic factions, the British women's movement has since been plagued by disputes between radical feminists and socialist feminists. Moves to heal the rift will be discussed later.

American feminism can therefore be characterised as predominantly equal rights in character and British feminism as welfare-oriented. Australia meanwhile inherited both traditions. There is a strong equal rights lobby which has succeeded in making women's issues a visible and legitimate government concern. The success is marked by the number of administrators in public service positions ('femocrats') committed to feminism (Summers, 1986: 60). Simultaneously, Australia has maintained an active socialist feminist community. Legislatively, as will be seen (Chapter 7), there is an attempt to balance welfare and equality legislation. Although it is not so clear-cut whether the equal rights or welfare tradition predominates (Curthoys, 1988: Parts IV & V), Australian feminism continues to coalesce in a position closer to reform feminism (see page 73).

The theoretical foundation of 1960s/1970s feminism, socialisation or sex role theory, was particularly strong within the equal rights branch of the movement. Socialisation theory challenged the idea that women possessed innate character differences based upon a maternal instinct which had run as a sub-theme throughout the women's movement to that time. Sex role theory explained these differences and then explained them away. It told women that perhaps they were softer and more nurturant than men, but that these characteristics were a product of their upbringing. If girls were treated and educated in the same way as boys, it was suggested they would develop the strength and assertiveness needed to succeed in a system which demanded these qualities. The term 'androgyny' was used to represent a blending of stereotypical masculine and feminine character traits. At this time, however, it usually implied that women needed to become more like 'men', that an increase in aggressiveness and competitiveness needed to complement access in order to guarantee success.

There was obviously a similarity between these ideas and the demand made centuries earlier by Wollstonecraft for an education which would encourage women to become rational, tough-minded and resolute (see page 7). The historical circumstances however were different, as was the content of the analysis. Wollstonecraft spoke to a generation of women who had little opportunity for serious intellectual pursuits. And the mental discipline she wished women to develop was to be directed ultimately to childrearing and homemaking tasks. Contemporary socialisation theory was premised on a *challenge* to traditional sex roles. It also encompassed a broader list of desirable character traits than mental discipline.

Bob Connell traces the concept of 'sex roles' to the 1930s (Connell, 1987: 47). Basically role theory describes male and female character as the outcome of responses to social stereotypes about desirable behaviour. Women become 'feminine' and men become 'masculine' because society defines these behaviours as appropriate and threatens sanctions, such as social ostracism, if people do not conform. Men and women therefore 'become' different though, as Connell suggests, the theory builds upon an assumed substratum of biological difference (Connell, 1987: 50). When Simone de Beauvoir proclaimed in 1949 that 'One is not born, but rather becomes, a woman', she was using sex role theory. Neither biology nor psychology nor economy, but civilisation produced 'woman' as we know her (de Beauvoir, 1961: 249).

The character of 'this creature, intermediate between male and eunuch' was not an appealing one, according to de Beauvoir who was particularly hard on the women of her age. She described 'woman' as revelling 'in immanence', in contrast to the higher human goal of 'transcendence':

> ...she is contrary, she is prudent and petty, she has no sense of fact or accuracy, she lacks morality, she is contemptibly utilitarian, she is false, theatrical, self-seeking and so on (de Beauvoir, 1961: 562).

The fact that neither her hormones nor her brain was responsible did nothing to soften this negative characterisation. De Beauvoir's answer to 'the woman question' was 'the adoption by women of male habits and values' (Evans, 1985: xi). According to Janet Sayers, de Beauvoir identified with the masculinity embodied by her father (Sayers, 1986: 171).

Friedan's 'average woman' in *The Feminine Mystique* is also portrayed as unable to attain full human development. Partly to blame are women's childrearing and domestic work which are described as intrinsically infantilising:

> They (women) have learned to 'adjust' to their biological role. They have become dependent, passive, childlike; they have given up their adult frame of reference to live at the lower human level of food and things. The work they do does

not require adult capabilities; it is endless, monotonous, unrewarding (Friedan, 1965: 266).

The concept of self which Friedan wished women to develop was that 'pursuit of self-actualisation', that 'attempt to free oneself from dependence on others' which equal rights feminists had seen as critical to autonomy from the beginning of the century (Grimshaw, 1986: 160).

In role theory, change depends upon altering the 'stereotyped customary expectations' fed to women by families, schools, mass media, and other 'agencies of socialisation' (Connell, 1987: 34). Britain's Six Point Group called upon women to overcome their conditioning which restricted their development, 'until they have no vision of anything before them' (Six Point Group, 1968: 9). The Group deliberately dissociated itself from the old suffragist notion of woman's essential goodness, which was now seen as a debilitating rather than an empowering image.

Since radical feminists focused upon male power as the key to women's subordination, they were unlikely to become enthusiastic about liberal 'reformist' attempts to alter women's character. There were, however, some important similarities in their analysis. Kate Millett, for example, saw conditioning as decisive in 'assuring the maintenance of the temperamental differences between the sexes' (Millett, 1971: 31). Mary Daly's picture of women under patriarchy, moreover, closely resembles de Beauvoir's: they have become 'domesticated, controlled, docile, submissive, dull, insipid' (quoted in Grimshaw, 1986: 125). 'Femaleness' was a handicap, something to overcome.

Some radical feminists saw women's biology as even more restricting than their character. Shulamith Firestone, for example, believed that the basis of women's subordination was the ability to become pregnant. She anticipated enthusiastically the cybernetic society and test-tube babies. 'Only with this radical erasure of our most radical difference from men' could Firestone envision a 'feminist revolution' (Eisenstein and Jardine, 1980: xvi). Women would have to become like 'men'. De Beauvoir had also been somewhat ambivalent about female biology which in one place was described as limited by its social construction, but which in another became 'the iron grasp of the species' (Mackenzie, 1986: 147).

Together the message of much 1960s feminism was that women should leave home to 'work', that maternal tasks were undemanding as well as unrewarding, and that to find fulfilment women had to engage in the public world of men. Equal rights feminists had been saying some of this throughout the inter-war period. The critical new departures were the insistence that men had to share the responsibility for childrearing and that women had to reject the characteristics associated with the maternal identity which had inspired and united them. These messages produced dramatic reactions within and without the movement. Within, we see the evolution of a new cultural feminism and without, a powerful right-wing backlash.

Because of its links to fundamentalist Christianity, the right-wing backlash reached a scale in America not experienced elsewhere (Wilson and Weir, 1986: 98). To the embarrassment of the feminist movement, women were in its vanguard. In order to understand women on the right, it is necessary to grasp the same complex mix of political ideology and personal experience which produces the feminist. Rebecca Klatch describes two types of right-wing women, the 'social conservative' rooted in religious belief, and the '*laissez faire* conservative' who measures the world in terms of the political and economic liberty of the individual (Klatch, 1987: Introduction). The social conservative considers the family to be a sacred unit and views feminism as an anti-family force because of the attack on sex roles. The *laissez-faire* conservative believes that the primary constituent of society is the rational, self-interested individual and actually endorses the woman's right to compete, though she has no sympathy with efforts to help her do so. The groups are united by their opposition to communism and to government intervention to aid the disadvantaged.

A large number of the social conservatives are housewives. Their fears, legitimate in some ways, are that in a world which insisted upon women earning their keep, they would lose out. Barbara Ehrenreich sees women divided into two groups. There are those who 'facing the age old insecurity of the family system' decide to fight for equality, and those who decide to fight for more security in the home (Ehrenreich, 1984: 151). The options must by now be sounding familiar. For some women, Ehrenreich explains, dependency in marriage is preferable to modest self-sustenance as a single woman (Ehrenreich, 1986: 100). (The types of jobs in which women congregate tend to be low status and low paying.) These are the women who oppose abortion reform because it seems to undercut male responsibility towards women and children, by making pregnancy 'a woman's choice' (English, 1984). A feminism which demanded equal access appealed, according to Ehrenreich, only to the 'slender, the intelligent and the upwardly mobile' (Ehrenreich, 1981: 98). Catharine MacKinnon put the point tersely:

'Only women who are most *like* the male norm are advanced or advantaged by this notion of equality' (Du Bois et al., 1985: 24).

The invitation to compete in the world of waged work as it is presently constructed presents women with 'Hard Choices', to use Kathleen Gerson's phrase (Gerson, 1985). Given the continuing unresponsiveness of social institutions to the demands imposed upon people by family commitments, and the continuing assumption that these are women's responsibility, women face a tension in their lives between the pull of the market and that of the home. Feminists have the difficult task of moulding a political message which will resolve the contradictions in women's experiences. In a sense, 'Feminism inhabits the same household as "femininity"', as Beatrix Campbell says in her study of the *Iron Ladies*; 'it is about naming the contradictions of "feminine experience" and it seeks to transform aspects of that experience into feminist strength' (Campbell, 1987: 298).

Cultural feminism emerged as one attempt to transform 'aspects of that experience into feminist strength'. This development in feminist theory arose in part as a reaction to the unflattering portrayal of women as mindless and weak in early second-wave feminism. A second influence was the countercultural revolution against bigness (the 'small is beautiful' movement) and competition (the 'rat-race'), which made some women begin to question the values of the system to which they were demanding access. Cultural feminism spoke about the existence of a separate female or woman's culture based upon distinctively female characteristics such as nurturance, care and the ability to relate to others. These were the characteristics traditionally assigned to women but now they were to be valued not denigrated.

Radical feminism contributed to the revaluing upwards of women's stereotypical character traits in several ways. Most importantly, it encouraged women to feel positively about their experience together and to think critically about aspects of male behaviour. Lesbian feminists had played a leading role in radical feminist theorising from the outset. They now broadened their analysis in ways which appealed to a wider audience (Echols, 1984a: 64). The writing of women like Andrea Dworkin and Susan Brownmiller drew attention to male violence and aggressive sexual behaviour. Adrienne Rich created an image of a 'lesbian continuum' among women, a wide range of woman-identified experience. Rich also offered a reassessment of motherhood, portraying it as the source of powerful affective emotions rather than as limiting or infantilising. Female physiology and female psychology became sources of strength, not of incapacity (Dworkin, 1981; Brownmiller, 1975; Rich, 1976).[3]

The 'female as superior' construct was re-activated. There were several versions of the origins of this superiority. Essentialists traced it to women's biology, either to their hormonal makeup or to their life-giving capacity (O'Brien, 1981). Men were seen as 'hormonally' deficient or as less connected with life. The belief that women were natural pacifists and men likely war-mongers was a logical extension of these ideas (Bacchi, 1986b: 62).

Others adapted socialisation theory to serve cultural feminist purposes. Jean Baker Miller (*Towards a New Psychology of Women*) argued that, as a result of their subordination, women had developed a capacity to express vulnerability and to cultivate cooperativeness. In the past, says Miller, these characteristics had been devalued in Western rationalist thought which tends to valorise objectivity and detachment. But in fact they were important skills and more desirable than the aggressiveness and egocentricity displayed by the 'dominants' (males) in our society (Miller, 1976). Women's role as primary parents could also be seen as contributing to the development of a more caring, other-related personality type (Ruddick, 1980).

Some feminist psychoanalytic theories have also affirmed women's 'differences' as positive. Nancy Chodorow, for example, uses object relations theory to explain that women are more 're-lational' because of connections with their same-sex mothers, while men become more 'individuated' in an effort to establish an identity separate from their mothers (Chodorow, 1978). There is no doubt that being 'relational' is considered more admirable than being 'individuated'.

Some studies are more concerned with the *fact* rather than the *cause* of woman's projected distinctive approach to life and others. Carol Gilligan's widely-read psychological study, *In a Different Voice*, posits the existence of an ethic of caring and responsibility which contrasts with the dominant ethic in contemporary society which stresses rights and the benefits of individuation. Although Gilligan insists that the ethic of care is not unique to women, she found that women used this moral 'voice' more often (Gilligan, 1982; Kerber et al., 1986). In contrast, the feminist philosopher, Nel Noddings (*Caring*) suggests that women have a head-start in acquiring an ethic of caring through their biological capacity to give birth (Noddings, 1984). Both Gilligan and Noddings found Chodorow useful.

Some parts of French feminist theory suited cultural feminism and began, as a result, to be incorporated into the argument. For example, Luce Irigarey's emphasis upon the distinctive way in which women experience their bodies and pleasure was useful. In Irigarey, woman's pleasure is seen as fluid and diffuse: *'woman has sex organs just about everywhere*. She experiences pleasure almost everywhere' (Marks and de Courtivron, 1981: 103—emphasis in original). This is contrasted with the masculine model which is portrayed as penis-fixated and goal-oriented.

Some feminists revelled in the creation of a new positive identity for women. Others were suspicious of a message which seemed to enshrine those very characteristics—nurturance and caring—which had been used in the past to typecast women in particular roles. The French journal, *Questions Féministes*, challenged the essentialist line in a 1977 editorial: 'In the present context, since oppression is not over, to demand the right to Difference without analyzing its social character is to give back to the enemy an effective weapon' (Marks and de Courtivron, 1981: 219). Colette Guillaumin thinks we need to distinguish between the ethereal notion of 'femininity' which is not necessarily the way we are, but the way men tell us we are, and the empirical reality of 'difference': 'Women are not milk cows (females) but a specifically determined social group ("women") whose main characteristic is that they are owned by others' (Duchen, 1987: 65).

Simone de Beauvoir expressed similar reservations. In a 1972 interview she acknowledged that women have developed particular 'feminine qualities', as a result of their oppression, which ought to be retained and which men should acquire. But she warned against going to the other extreme and claiming that 'woman has special ties to the earth', which played into the hands of men 'who will be better able to oppress them'. De Beauvoir thought it a good thing that women were no longer ashamed of their bodies, and she agreed that work, meaning waged work, was not a panacea: 'women often have to choose between two forms of dehumanization: being a housewife or working in a factory'. Nonetheless, paid work remained the first condition for independence. De Beauvoir also rejected the notion of 'a distinct woman's language' speaking a 'woman's desire'. Like Guillaumin, she emphasised the importance of a political identity for women based upon their experience of oppression (Marks and de Courtivron, 1981: 153, 35).

Some liberal feminists are converts to cultural feminism. Betty Friedan wants more books like Carol Gilligan's. True equality, she argues, is not possible 'unless those differences between men and women are affirmed' and 'until values based on female sensitivities to life begin to be voiced in every discipline and profession' (Friedan, 1985: 13). Some are fearful. 'If men are judged more rational, aggressive, etc.', warns Kathleen Gerson, 'then women's subordinate position is justified in certain ways' (Gerson, 1985: xiii). Some are disdainful. Janet Sayers quips: 'Woman's supposed "complicated, pain-enduring, multipleasured physicality" hardly seems a very hopeful basis on which to build resistance to their subordination' (Sayers, 1986: 42). Some, like Janet Radcliffe Richards and Ellen Du Bois, equate a defence of women's special virtues with an acceptance, albeit inadvertent, of separate spheres which in their view is 'incompatible with the pursuit of equal rights' (Richards, 1983; Du Bois et al., 1980: 26–30). A few, like Judith Lorber, who have a gender-neutral Utopia as their vision of the future, are willing to utilise the new 'feminine' identity to mobilise women: 'By flaunting their differences as marks of superiority, not inferiority, the underclass might begin to impose its view of the world on that of the dominant group' (Lorber, 1981: 65; Lorber, 1986). An assertion of 'difference' can sometimes be a means to an end, rather than an end in itself.

One of the chief concerns about a notion of 'essential womanhood' is its 'false universalism'. Hester Eisenstein explains the origins and the limitations of the idea:

> To some extent, this habit of thought grew inevitably from the need to establish gender as a legitimate intellectual category. But too often it gave rise to analysis that, in spite of its narrow base of white, middle-class experience, purported to speak about and on behalf of all women, black or white, poor or rich (Eisenstein, 1984: 132).

The diversity of the types of women involved in contemporary feminism meant that some would resist a development which seemed to subsume the 'differences among women'. Black feminists like Bell Hooks objected to the 'mystification of women's experience' on these grounds (Hooks, 1987: 86). Audré Lorde addressed an 'Open Letter to Mary Daly' on the subject: 'Within the community of women, racism is a reality force in my life as it is not in yours. . . .' (Lorde quoted in Fowlkes, 1987: 3).

Hooks also condemned the kind of theorising which lay behind a celebration of women's 'difference' for producing ultimately a weak political analysis. She objected to the equation of oppression with 'maleness'. Black feminists have good reason to seek solidarity with their men as a strategic necessity in the battle against racism. Mis-identifying the enemy who, according to Hooks, is 'Imperialism and not patriarchy', would make it difficult to develop 'viable resistance strategies and solutions' (Hooks, 1987: 86, 128–130).

Socialist feminists share many of these reservations. They reject reductionist arguments which attribute women's oppression to patriarchy *or* capitalism (Jaggar, 1983). As mentioned previously, radical feminism which appeared to give the nod to patriarchy caused dissension in socialist ranks. Recent theorising about an essentially benevolent womanhood has raised these issues anew.

Lynne Segal has launched the socialist attack against what she calls 'maternal revivalism', which is in her opinion mainly an American product, but one which is having a serious impact on British feminism. Her book *Is the Future Female?* rejects both biological essentialism, such as that found in Andrea Dworkin's 'analysis of the timeless nature of male power and male violence', and 'psychic' or psychological essentialism in which category she places Carol Gilligan's *In a Different Voice* (Segal, 1987: 211, 215, 146–148). Gilligan's work worries her because of the exaggerated focus on difference between women and men, the 'minimal interest' in conflicts and contradictions within the female identity, and the 'false universalising' of gender categories. Some of Segal's reactions can be anticipated, coming as they do from a good socialist who believes that women should 'generalise' their politics and 'didn't need to work only within a separate sphere of women's politics' (Segal, 1987: 209).[4] The theorising of women's consciousness or 'subjectivity' has, she feels, become disconnected from the 'immediate political priorities of most women'. Further, it increases the polarisation between women and men, limiting 'the scope of political struggle' and distracting attention from major questions about the nature of human needs and how work is organised (Segal, 1987: 213–214, 217).

The radical/revolutionary feminist critique of heterosexuality also concerns Segal. If political separatism is a danger to socialist politics, lesbian separatism is even more threatening since the basis of separation becomes biology. Lesbian separatism has also in Segal's opinion placed women 'at odds with one another', since heterosexual women stand accused of 'consorting with the enemy'. Segal is reluctant to identify 'the sphere of the sexual and the problem of male violence as the root of women's oppression' (Segal, 1987: 208).

In a recent article in *Marxism Today* Cynthia Cockburn warily explores the middle-ground between radical feminism and socialist feminism (Cockburn, 1988a: 19). In this and other work Cockburn insists, at the risk of being no longer a 'credible comrade', that sexual politics must be a part of the socialist agenda (Cockburn, 1981, 1983, 1988a, 1988b). Cockburn even treads into the controversial area of *biological* difference with her proposal for a

'politics of physical power'. But more important than inborn discrepancies in size, strength and reproductive function is the way in
which these small *differences* are transformed into *advantages* for
men (Cockburn, 1981: 44).

Cockburn's handling of the question of woman's essential character is a bit of a balancing act. On the one hand she recognises the
use Fascism has made of an appeal to woman's 'essential motherli-
ness'; on the other she enjoys the radical feminist 'affirmation of
woman'. Not surprisingly, given her politics, any 'difference' she
admits to is more likely to be due to women's lived experience than
to hormones: 'somehow women's long march through history has
given us, broadly speaking, a gender-specific set of values' (Cockburn, 1988a: 21, 23). An emphasis upon the 'objective conditions
of the lives of women' simply extends the material base of Marxist
theory beyond the purely economic to encompass the *socio-political*
and the *physical* (Cockburn, 1981: 43).

Other socialist feminists have used an expanded version of the
material base in their exploration of 'woman's culture'. Nancy
Hartsock, for example, argues that material life structures consciousness, that we are what we do, and since women 'do' reproduction and domestic labour, these activities shape their world
view. Reluctantly Hartsock lays aside 'important differences
among women across race and class boundaries' to uncover 'things
common to all women's lives in Western class societies' (Hartsock,
1983: 290). In the end her analysis, which she calls 'feminist
standpoint', sits comfortably within the broader category of cultural feminism because of the positive characterisation of women's
experience. Women, we are told, have a 'unity with nature'
through reproduction; they 'define and experience themselves re-
lationally and men do not'. In contrast, the male construction of
identity as differentiation from the other 'sets a hostile and combative dualism at the heart of both the community men construct and
the masculinist world view' (Hartsock, 1983: 296). In work like
Hartsock's, socialism and a feminism premised on female uniqueness seem to have found a 'happy marriage', but I have no doubt
that Segal and others would have difficulty accepting an analysis
which sets men up as 'hostile' and 'combative'.

The other problem cultural feminism poses for socialist feminists is its inadvertent acceptance of the traditional family through
the emphasis on woman's mothering role. This certainly seems
to disturb Lynne Segal. She lays claim both to classical Marxist
theory, which identified the family as the source of women's
oppression (Engels, 1968), and to earlier feminist writings, when
she makes the point that 'women's caring work in our society is

often stressful, isolating and undermining of personal confidence' (Segal, 1987: 215). Part of the socialist message has consistently been the need to broaden the boundaries of isolated 'nucleated' existence to embrace others. Segal continues to relay this message: 'We belong to more than our "families" (however sacred they may be to conservative thought)' (Segal, 1987: 238). Other socialist feminists disagree that the family is the cause of women's oppression (Curthoys, 1988: 102; Humphries, 1982).

The family or, more generally, living arrangements, remain problematic for every feminist because of the obvious need to provide for people's personal needs and the popular assumption that women have a particular responsibility in this area. It lay behind the functional debates of the 1920s and 1930s. It appears again in the metaphysical debate about the meaning of womanhood (see above). Early twentieth-century equal rights feminists promised to develop themselves *and* to take care of the home. Later 1960s/ 1970s equal rights feminists tried to make men accept some responsibility for the family. Some working-class women experience home as a prison. Others and some Black women identify it as their powerbase (Humphries, 1982). According to Bell Hooks, 'many black women find the family the least oppressive institution' (Hooks, 1987: 37). The anti-feminist backlash, which includes the writings of those Judith Stacey calls 'conservative pro-family feminists', and of 'post-feminists' concerns ultimately the same problem which has plagued feminism since the turn of the century—how to reconcile *women's* responsibility for the family with the desire for individual development outside that sphere (Stacey, 1986). 'Sameness to' and 'difference from' men continue to be used in this context.

Two of the leaders of the 1960s feminist resurgence, Betty Friedan and Germaine Greer, have been accused of recanting feminism in their recent publications, *The Second Stage* and *Sex and Destiny* respectively (Friedan, 1981; Greer, 1985). They have rejected this accusation, but there certainly is a shift in emphasis in their work. In the 1960s, Friedan felt that it was necessary to free women from compulsory domesticity, the 'feminine mystique'; she now feels it is critical to save women from compulsory careerism, which she labels the 'feminist mystique'. Greer is more consistent. In *The Female Eunuch*, her controversial exploration of women's sexual needs, she was looking for an alternative to the stifling, soul-destroying nuclear family (Greer, 1971). She is still looking and is having some success in the extended 'Family' of Italy's peasant culture. Both women now emphasise the positive side of homemaking and childrearing in reaction against the sterility of the corporate world. To Friedan, the family has become

> ...the symbol of that last area where one has any hope
> of individual control over one's destiny, of meeting one's
> most basic human needs, of nourishing that core of
> personhood threatened now by vast impersonal institutions and
> uncontrollable corporate and government
> bureaucracies...(Friedan, 1982: 235).

Janet Radcliffe Richards expressed the fear that cultural feminism would reinforce the existence of separate spheres (see page 89). Friedan's and Greer's new work seems to justify these fears. Cultural feminists are happier at home since they are rebelling against the whole set of values associated with the public world of work. Like the suffragists at the turn of the century, they see these values as 'male', and equate womanhood with the intimacy and warmth associated with a domestic ideal. Friedan wants women to be able to work outside the home but also hopes to retain the kind of sanctuary she believes the home should be. Zillah Eisenstein makes the point that this fond desire for women to have the best of both worlds is illusory in the existing system. It has not happened, and it will not happen until we understand why social relations have been constructed so that women are given responsibility for living arrangments, until we explore the basis of the relationship between home and market, and until we cease equating women with one side of this dichotomy (Eisenstein, 1984).

Friedan's anxiety about 'uncontrollable government bureaucracies' is critical to understanding her retreat to the home. Liberal feminists have faced the same quandary throughout the century. They wish to secure the social supports which are required to free women for the individual development they see as desirable, without creating an interventionist state which to them is politically anathema. Where socialist feminists are willing to use the state to resolve women's dilemma and are fearful of the family, liberal feminists like Friedan are willing to use the family and are fearful of the state. Political attitudes structure responses to women's needs.

Another example is the political philosopher and feminist[5], Jean Bethke Elshtain. Stacey correctly identifies Elshtain as a 'disenchanted democratic socialist' who in company with other disenchanted democratic socialists, like Christopher Lasch, have abandoned the liberal welfare state because of its intrusiveness and are seeking instead a democratic 'ethical polity' based upon the family (Stacey, 1986: 227). Here we have some socialists reconciled to using the family, though I would maintain that their starting place is not the needs of women but their conception of a workable public order. Both Lasch and Elshtain are most concerned with rediscovering the importance of family ties in order to counteract the drug culture and sexual promiscuity, the effects of the 'me generation'. In each case women will be the ones who resume responsibility for those family ties.

Lasch correctly indicts the present organisation of the workplace for forcing some women to choose between paid work and family, but he sees children as 'her' children and families as 'their', meaning women's, families. He condemns feminists for not answering the argument that day care provides no substitute for the family, but offers no alternative himself, other than the traditional family formation (Lasch, 1979: xv). Elshtain is more forthright in her allocation to women of the role of 'guardian of the prerogatives of the *oikos*, preserver of familial duty and honor, protector of children'. She seems content to allow women to 'sacrifice individual goals' in order to preserve 'a particular type of public good' (Elshtain, 1982: 51, 55). Elshtain makes the important point that feminism has been trapped within other political narratives such as Marxism and liberalism, and asks why it should wish to remain there. She does not seem to realise that she is offering another variation on another narrative, a dichotomous public order based upon ascribed gender roles (Elshtain, 1985: 39).

The sad thing about Elshtain, Greer and Friedan is, as Judith Stacey remarks, that one senses in their work a 'despair of alternatives' (Stacey, 1986: 231). Feminists have tried for a generation to conceive of new ways to resolve the tension between work and home commitments, but their efforts have not yet resolved the problem identified by the *Smith College Weekly* in 1919, why 'a woman must choose between a home and her work when a man may have both' (see page 33). It is little wonder they are frustrated. The label 'post-feminism' is reserved for those who have given up trying. Terri Apter is a case in point (Apter, 1985). She considers 'women's rights and women's hopes' a 'casualty of the recession'. Positive discrimination for women who interrupt their working lives to care for their children is, in her view, 'highly unlikely'. And without it, the woman who takes time off for childcare will be held back. Given the lack of options, Apter defends women's 'special suitability as mothers'. This reassertion of 'differences' between men and women she sees as 'feminism's only hope of salvation' (Apter, 1985: 150). The pendulum swing back to 'difference' provides no real answer to the social problems at issue, however. In fact, describing it as a viable alternative undermines the political analysis of social arrangements which is necessary.

Apter's conclusion is not a necessary outcome of cultural feminist analysis. But the tendency to invest hope in 'woman', conceptualised as a single pan-cultural, transhistorical identity clearly creates political problems. The chief concerns are the way in which it homogenises women's diverse experiences and the fact that it offers no clear program for change.

Feminist scholars schooled in deconstructionism and poststructuralist theory criticise the focus upon a unitary concept of 'woman'. Deconstructionism, poststructuralism and postmodernism are all labels for the recent philosophical challenge to Enlightenment epistemology.[6] Put simply, poststructuralists reject the attempt to find an 'absolute grounding for knowledge' and embrace instead the 'fractured identities modern life creates' (Hekman, 1987: 66; Harding, 1986: 28). As a consequence they insist upon recognising the differences *among* women, or the 'differences within women', as Teresa de Lauretis puts it (de Lauretis, 1987: 2). Deconstructionism therefore resists 'an essentialist freezing of the concepts of gender, race and class' (Spivak, 1987: 129). Rather, it encourages feminists to 'celebrate their hyphens'—Blackfeminist, socialist-feminist, Asian-American-feminist, lesbianfeminist (Harding, 1987: 7–8).

Postmodernist theories produce another problem for feminism, however. The question becomes how to reconcile the recognition of women's diverse experiences with a political ideology which claims to speak on behalf of all women. Sandra Harding asks pointedly if we can afford to give up the necessity of trying to provide 'one, true, feminist story of reality' (Harding, 1986: 28). More will be said about this problem in Chapter 10.

There are important links between the metaphysical debate about what it means to be a woman and the other kinds of sameness/difference debates which have engaged and which continue to engage some feminists. To an extent the positions reflect competing political visions. Those who insist upon women's ability to compete in the marketplace accept individualism as a guiding ethic. Those who rejoice in the idea of a maternal character have a more communitarian vision but, as in the case of the inter-war reform feminists, they see women as responsible for community values. In both cases, women are offered either assimilation to the status quo or segregation from it. Neither alternative is workable and both leave many women disadvantaged.

A way has to be found to challenge and change the structures and values of a system which ignores people's interdependency. A sameness/difference framework distracts attention from the level of political change which is necessary. Part II of the book uses six contemporary case-studies to illustrate further the limitations of reducing social problems to discussions about women's 'sameness to' or 'difference from' men.

Denouement

The story has come full circle. It began by challenging the idea that feminists have *always* divided into two camps, one endorsing 'sameness to' men, the other accepting 'difference from' men. When women were willing to accept responsibility for the domestic domain, as in the nineteenth century, debates within feminism were more tactical than substantive. The education debate in Britain is an example. The schism within feminism along sameness/difference lines occurred when some women insisted upon their equal right to individual self-actualisation. The battles over protective legislation, the ERA and family endowment were battles over whether it was possible for women to reconcile this 'right' with *their* family responsibilities. One group chose to try to strengthen women's position within the home; the other decided to pursue the self-actualising goal. Neither alternative worked well for most women and the problem of reconciling work commitments with living arrangements was left unresolved.

Similar tensions arose in the 1960s feminist resurgence, though they had a distinctive cast due to changing historical circumstances. As far as social functions were concerned, the majority of feminists now accepted that most married women would engage in paid labour, and demanded a restructuring of family roles to facilitate this fact. The 'equal' versus 'special' treatment debate, taken up in the next chapter, shows that feminists are still struggling to construct an institutional framework which accepts women as both mothers and paid workers.

The development of cultural feminism raised the debate to a metaphysical level. Feminists determined to follow the career road rejected an identity closely associated with the maternal role. Other feminists reasserted that identity as a statement of *their* rejection of the values associated with the public world of waged labour.

As a denouement to this chapter, I would like to consider *why* some feminist historians portray the movement as continuously riven by the question of difference, when the historical specificity of the debate is critical to understanding why feminists divided along sameness/difference lines. Part of the reason has been the tendency to impose contemporary controversies upon the past. Feminist historians who were a product of the 1960s resurgence sought a validating tradition for their particular approach to women's problems. The most important works were Aileen Kraditor's *Ideas of the Woman Suffrage Movement* (1971) and William O'Neill's *Everyone Was Brave* (1969).[1] The belief that autonomy and freedom depended upon access to the labour market made it difficult to understand or respond sympathetically to the powerful maternal ethos in much of the suffragist literature. These women seemed to have 'let the side down' by resigning themselves to traditional sex roles. There was a tendency to blame them and their 'erroneous' analysis for the subsequent 'failure of feminism' after the vote was won. The acknowledgement of women's 'difference' was held responsible for the retreat to domesticity after World War I. Other strong supporters of the equal rights tradition, for example, Babcock, Freedman, Norton and Ross, whose book *Sex Discrimination and the Law* is an *apologia* for the ERA, use Kraditor and O'Neill to support this conclusion:

> . . . the suffragists themselves had lost much of the sense of the justice of the women's cause as the rationale for their efforts, and were therefore in no position to unify women around a radical feminist banner (Babcock, Freedman, Norton and Ross, 1975: 57, 58).

All these authors claim that progenitors of the equal rights perspective existed in the period *before* 1890. They are identified by their appeal to a common humanity, or to justice and equality, ideas which fit the equal rights version of the issues at stake. These ideas are then set up as a separate and radical tradition, overcome temporarily by the pragmatism of 'maternal feminists' who were willing to promise the continuation of traditional roles in exchange for enfranchisement. The admission of 'difference' is then linked to the introduction of protective legislation which is presented as an inappropriate strategy to advance women's interests:

> The change from justice to expediency had more profound implications than the suffragists realized. The argument that women should have the vote because of the good they would do implied that women were fundamentally different from men— otherwise, why would they vote differently? The argument made by social reformers that women workers were different and needed 'special protection' was thus perfectly consistent with the suffragist view of women in the last decades before the vote was won (Babcock, Freedman, Norton and Ross, 1975: 40–41).[2]

While it is true that each history, if read carefully, will talk about inconsistencies and contradictions (Cott, 1987a: 290–291, fn. 10), the impression remains that feminism consists of two continuous traditions, a 'sameness' tradition which spoke in terms of justice for women and 'genuine equality', and a 'difference' tradition which is portrayed as accommodating, 'respectable', and co-opted. The implication is that now fortunately the 'radical' tradition is being revived by 1960s equal rights feminists.

This interpretation is both ahistorical and misleading. It is ahistorical mainly because it ignores the fact that almost every feminist in the nineteenth century accepted the sexual division of labour and that there was therefore no separate tradition which led directly to contemporary liberal feminism.[3] In fact, 'feminism' in the contemporary liberal sense of the word, meaning a demand for entry into the workforce for all women, including married women, on the same terms as men, did not really emerge until World War I or thereabouts. The interpretation is misleading because it implies that the 'failure of feminism' was due to an admission of 'difference' and that an insistence on 'sameness', whatever that might mean, would have made the feminist vision a reality.

It was not the fact that feminists ceased demanding justice, however, which led to the 'demise' of feminism after the vote was won. Feminists never stopped demanding justice! Most suffragists combined justice and expediency arguments (see pages 19–20). Nor is it at all clear which approach, equal rights or protection, best advanced 'women's' interests. These comments are intended more as observation than criticism. To quote E. H. Carr again: '. . . we can view the past and achieve our understanding of the past, only through the eyes of the present' (Carr, 1976: 24). The point is that we are now operating from a different present than the 1960s and yet women face very similar options—paid work, family, or some version of the double burden. Simply demanding an end to sex roles does not seem to have had much effect. Until we radically rethink the relationship between home and paid work for women and for men, women will remain bedevilled by either/or choices and dual workloads.

Just as equal rights feminists produced their own history, so too did cultural feminism beget a historical counterpart. Their writing explored the historical experience of women interacting with women. The new trend was labelled 'women's culture'.

Debates about the meaning and value of 'women's culture' parallel concerns about the tendency among cultural feminists to essentialise womanhood. Ellen Du Bois tends to equate the idea of a 'woman's culture' with the 'cult of true womanhood' since both focus upon women's traditional role and stereotypical characteristics. As a result she considers it restricting and dislikes history which tends to romanticise it (Du Bois et al., 1980: 26). Carroll Smith-Rosenberg, a strong believer in the virtues of female solidarity, insists on the other hand that feminism is intricately rooted in women's experience of their separateness from men and in their primary identification as women (Du Bois et al., 1980: 56). There seems to be some ambiguity about just what the term, 'women's culture', implies, an ambiguity which, it will be suggested later (Chapter 10), needs to be clarified for practical political reasons.

An unfortunate side effect of the way in which contemporary debates have been transposed onto the past has been that the very meaning of feminism has become contested ground. Much of women's history has become obsessed with finding worthy banner-carriers for the cause. To those who believe that feminism necessarily involves a challenge to traditional sex roles, first-wave feminists who accepted the primacy of woman's mothering and domestic obligations (and they were the overwhelming majority), prove something of an embarrassment. Some historians therefore apply qualifiers such as 'maternal' or 'social' to this feminism, implying a diminished commitment or a misguided perspective. Some declare simply that 'they were not feminists' (Babcock, Freedman, Norton and Ross, 1975: 40). Feminists who empathise with the suffragists' emphasis upon women's gender-specific role as mothers have no difficulty portraying them as feminists, without qualification. The representation of the past becomes a restatement of present theories.

It makes no sense to judge the views of women at the turn of the century by contemporary standards. Many people have pointed to the danger of judging history retrospectively. Many feminists have been at pains to draw attention to the historical specificity of women's experience (Barrett, 1980). The material conditions of life for most women in the early stages of industrialisation were dramatically different from post-World War II conditions. This needs to be taken into account.

At the same time academics have been accused, perhaps fairly, of ignoring or refusing to understand that 'feminism covers an enormous range of diverse theoretical positions' (Bottomley et al., 1987: 47). This involves more than simply recognising a liberal, a Marxist, and a radical feminist tradition. It means trying to understand the difficulty of being a woman pressing for change in particular historical circumstances and in particular political cultures. It means seeing that feminism emerges in different guises and with different emphases in different lives. Our class background, our intellectual heritage, our particular biography will affect the position we take on a range of issues. The tendency to create and impose categories of thought where there is an imperfect fit ignores the ambiguity in the debates on these questions and more importantly the reasons for the ambiguity.

How then do we *identify* feminists? In sum, the task is futile, unless we use the term in a very general way. We almost invariably seek echoes of our own views (since an echo can only occur after the initial cry, it makes my point nicely). The task instead should be to understand how women who expressed disquiet at women's position in society negotiated new positions which they thought would be improvements. If they ended up not being improvements, it becomes important to ask why not.

There are no heroes or villains in this story. There are only groups of women and individual women using available political language and working within existing political systems to rescue for themselves an analysis which seems to make sense of their lives. If their analysis appears inconsistent or inadequate, this simply reflects the limitations of that language and the inflexibility of those systems. Neither the idea of 'sameness', whether expressed as equality or humanity, nor the vocabulary of 'difference' addresses the diversity of women's needs. They represent rather the alternatives facing women in a society which says that either they or no one will take responsibility for living arrangements and the 'human' side of existence. In effect then they obscure the socially irresponsible behaviour of employers and government. The conceptualisation is one, therefore, which feminists ought to approach warily. We need to explore its inadequacies, not to accept unquestioningly or reinforce this construction of the way things are. Part II of the book takes up this project.

II
Current controversies

Prologue

In the first part of the book it was argued that the women's movement did not divide into contending sameness/difference factions until after the turn of the century. The divisions which appeared at that time among the leadership of the organised movement were a result of differences of opinion about the most appropriate strategy to improve women's situation. The disagreement about strategies reflected political differences of opinion about the way in which society ought to be organised. The labels 'sameness'/'difference', 'equality'/'difference' came to represent these contending philosophies.

The issue which caused the division was whether or not married women ought to engage in waged labour. The 'difference' group accepted parts of a traditional (*Gemeinschaft*) view of social relations. They believed that women had a sex-specific responsibility to take care of day-to-day living arrangements, and that this involved a full-time commitment. Their hope was to increase women's autonomy and status within the domestic sphere.

Those who insisted that women aspire to 'equality' with men adopted the *Gesellschaft* model of free, competing individuals. They demanded that women too be treated as independent and self-actualising. Because they wanted women to be free to pursue interests outside the home, they paid little attention to the requirements imposed by family commitments.

At the deepest level the conflict was due to the fact that these options were offered as either/or alternatives. It was presented as a debate about women's 'sameness to' or 'difference from' *men* because it was generally accepted that the *Gesellschaft* model suited men. Reducing the debate to a sameness/difference framework diverted attention from the larger political question about how work and home commitments ought to be reconciled.

Once it became clear that the feudal ideal based upon a stay-at-home wife had outlived its usefulness, the schism among feminists in its original form ended. The suggestion that men share parenting responsibilities seemed to free women for self-actualisation while providing for the basic necessities of day-to-day living. The resolution, however, failed to work. Men in the majority did not share nurturing duties, not because they were necessarily selfish or uncaring, but because the system penalised men who departed from the expectation that they were free, unfettered, abstracted from the messy details of life. The few men who took time off for childcare, for example, were unlikely to be the men who received promotions. Most women were left with the practical difficulty of reconciling home and work demands. As a direct result, the 'liberation' of women into 'self-actualisation' did not proceed as smoothly as anticipated. Despite increases in retention rates at school and attendance rates at university, women remained clustered in low-paying, low-status jobs and the goal of 'equal pay' remained elusive.[1]

Feminists investigated the reasons for the failure of their program and much of the analysis came back to the family. The proposed solutions to the reconciliation of community/family and individual needs quite clearly were not working. The simple proclamation of 'equality of opportunity' had failed. A deeper probing into the causes of inequality and how to resolve them uncovered tensions in the women's movement which had never really gone away. Many were still uncertain about whether women could or should, or would even want to replicate the 'male' model. These tensions appear in the American equal treatment/special treatment debate, in the 'conflicting perspectives' in the British movement about whether to place greater emphasis upon 'improving women's position in the labour market' or securing for women an 'income from the State for the work they do at home' (Dale and Foster, 1986: 124), and in the larger metaphysical debate about women's essential character.

Catharine Stimpson categorises contemporary feminists as either 'minimalists' or 'maximalists'. The minimalists, who have dominated the post-1960s revival, support a strategy of assimilation to the existing 'male' norm and consequently minimise 'differences' between women and men, attributing them largely to 'historical forces and the processes of socialization'. Maximalists on the other hand emphasise women's biological and psychological 'differences' and insist that these be recognised. In Stimpson's words they use 'sex dissimilarities as a theoretical basis for a double task: recognizing what might be "special" about women and simultaneously claiming that they ought to have the opportunities and rights of men' (Stimpson, 1988: 23; see also McFadden, 1984).

Katherine O'Donovan identifies a similar tension within contemporary feminism. Early second-wave (1960s/1970s) feminists aimed in her view 'to eliminate women's differences as a source of sub-ordination as far as possible by opening up the public sphere and assimilating women to men...' To this end, they challenged gender-based classifications. A later woman-centred analysis cele-brated women's virtues and 'women's private existence' (O'Dono-van, 1985: 17).

While O'Donovan and Stimpson have identified a real and im-portant disagreement among some contemporary feminists, de-scribing the division too simply could lead people to conclude falsely that all feminists fall into one or other of the perspectives they identify. As mentioned earlier, the disagreement surfaces in *certain* debates. Also, the terms 'minimalist' and 'maximalist', like the terms 'sameness' and 'difference', could leave the impression that feminists simply cannot decide whether they are more like men or different from them, whereas the disagreement, when it surfaces, reflects different strategic responses to the perceived range of political alternatives. Finally and most disturbingly, pre-senting the movement as divided in this way could also create the impression that there are only two alternatives available to women. While the terms provide useful 'shorthands', it may be more important to bring the underlying political differences of opinion to the surface.

Once this is done it becomes possible to identify the limitations in either perspective. As O'Donovan says, the problem is that neither strategy is adequate because neither challenges the 'dicho-tomy between public and private'. Similar in some ways to the inter-war disputes, one vision encourages women to live as much like men as possible; the other encourages them not to. Neither seriously challenges the feasibility or appropriateness of the male lifestyle. Setting out the alternatives as assimilation or separation diverts attention from the important political question about whether anyone can or should live as if they have no personal side to their lives.

Case-studies are used in this section of the book to explore the limitations of a sameness/difference framework. In some cases the framework is invoked by feminists. In others it is employed by anti-feminists to caricature feminist positions. Chapters 5 to 8 deal mainly with policy and institutional debates. Chapters 9 and 10 concentrate upon the contemporary metaphysical/philosophical debate. Links between the two areas are drawn where they are relevant. Each chapter develops the argument presented in Part I—that the sameness/difference framework mystifies political issues which should be brought to the surface of the debate; that feminists are constrained to argue in sameness/difference terms by language, conceptual systems and the range of perceived political alternatives; and that genuine reform involves challenging the norm against which women are compared.

As mentioned in the Introduction, each of the following chapters begins with a series of quotations mainly from interviews conducted in late 1987, early 1988 with activist and academic feminists (the categories are not necessarily exclusive) in Britain, America and Australia.[2] The intent is not to present any one side of the various debates as correct, but to show the remarkable consistency with which the same problems are identified and similar solutions proposed, although different language may be used at times. The quotations show that a large number of feminists are aware of the way in which particular institutional arrangements force them into adopting 'sameness' or 'difference' postures. They also show that the vast majority are aware of the limitations of this construction and are identifying ways of getting beyond it. They therefore contain an important body of evidence supporting the book's central hypothesis that the sameness/difference framework is a limited way of conceptualising social problems.

5
'Equal' versus 'special' treatment

Feminists based in America:

Now, there's a way out of this argument but it's a hard way out. The way out is to construct a humane society in which social legislation is available for the needs of whichever individual needs it.

Alice Kessler-Harris

Our vision of humanity has to take into account that half of it reproduces this way.

Wendy Chavkin

We give so much lip-service to motherhood and childhood and no support whatsoever. Having children is not something women do for their amusement.

Judy Goldsmith

Maternity leave isn't to be seen as a concession you give women. It's an overdue acknowledgement of their reproduction of the workforce.

Veena Oldenburg

What we do not have is the acceptance of women as full workers.

Mary Jean Collins

Men and women live in different worlds and you can't even think of them in identical positions. They have been in different worlds from the time of Adam and Eve...Men hardly ever get pregnant! Things cost men differently.

Jessie Bernard

The system here is just lunacy compared to what we (Australians) are used to...Stuff we just take for granted they think is Utopia.

Anne Summers

I don't think we want a 'lesser life'. I think we want a balance between work and family.

Shirley Dennis

Feminists based in Britain:

We should go on the offensive and not be defensive about the need for society to provide for women to be pregnant without disadvantage.

Tess Gill

The way I would look at it is men and women together have babies. No woman ever had a baby on her own. Therefore, it's important that both parents should be involved in the bringing up of children because that is the next generation of the country.

Lady Platt

I don't see it (pregnancy) as necessarily something which distinguishes between men and women on the basis that women will get pregnant and give birth, and men won't. That's not 'special'. It is only 'special' if we define the man as being the man at work and obviously we don't want to do that.

Paddy Stamp

It's striking in view of the amount of time people spend talking about biological sex differences that in the one area in which it needs to be taken into account in social policy terms— maternity rights and legislation—it isn't.

Ann Oakley

There is a difference here in classical liberal societies in which children are seen as a matter of choice and private pleasure, and societies where children are seen as some kind of public investment. Insofar as we've been a classically liberal society, then I think public policy has got to pay attention to the fact that for the time being childrearing is seen primarily as the responsibility of women.

Elizabeth Meehan

One of the problems of producing crèches at mother's place of work is that people will always produce crèches at mother's work. This underwrites the idea that it's women's responsibility to look after children. Sometimes you are in a situation where you have to make choices between evils. You've got to say—is it better that that happens and there actually is the facility or do we stick out for there not even being the facility and actually screw it up for a lot of women?

Elizabeth Vallance

It is a question of language and of what you are used to. If in England you turned it (maternity leave) around and called it a disability, that would be seen as a major setback because the language of disability is that you are only a half-person; there is something really wrong with you. Maternity leave, I mean, employers grumble about it but it's part of everyday life. Women have it. . . The notion of the 'welfare package' has until this year been so strongly embedded in Conservative and Labour governments that free teeth, free eyes, and free maternity leave are all seen as the same.

Lisanne Radici

Feminists based in Australia:

The lack of general job security and protection for the health of the mother. . . must surely rank as one of the longest standing areas of discrimination which remain in Australia.

Jan Marsh, quoted in Niland, *1979*

I think it is absolutely crucial that legislation be concerned with the needs of all employees as parents. . . We don't want to see women and children in some sort of national service but of course in the end both for business and for government there is important work being done. . . I think that there is too much enshrined of a male concept of full time, full year, forty-nine years of work.

Bettina Cass

I really believe that many men would not be able to hold down their jobs at a very senior level if they did not have somebody who looked after the family, who organised them for their frequent overseas visits, who held things together.

Valerie Pratt

The 'equal' versus 'special' treatment debate concerns primarily how pregnancy ought to be treated in the workplace. Some American feminists are sharply divided over the issue. Broadly, the debate is between those who want legislation directed specifically at maternity requirements (the special treatment or positive action approach), and those who feel it is wiser and more ethical to set maternity rights within the wider context of gender-neutral disability or nurturing leave legislation (the equal treatment approach).[1]

In neither Australia nor Britain do feminists divide into contending camps over this particular issue, although feminists in all Western countries are concerned about the degree to which they should single women out for 'special treatment', given the traditional understanding of the principle of equality that 'all workers should be protected in accordance with their individual needs' (Women's Bureau, 1985: 39). The particular institutional arrangements in a country determine the extent to which *feminists* are divided on the approach to take to reform in this area. The intensity of the debate in America is due to the fact that as a rule women there have no guaranteed maternity leave, *paid* or *unpaid*. In contrast, in Britain, maternity leave is covered, if only minimally,[2] by national insurance, and in Australia an industrial award guarantees unpaid leave. A few American states have maternity policies, but most women rely upon their employers to provide some form of insurance, and employers are under no obligation to do this.[3] Feminists therefore are very cautious about how they frame demands. Equal treatment advocates fear that, if employers have to make provision for maternity, they might decide not to employ women. Special treatment supporters insist that employers acknowledge women's 'difference'.

This chapter describes the genesis of this debate, and explains why feminists seem unable to compromise. Emphasis is placed upon the way in which the law, the American individualist political culture, and the resultant inability to involve the state in providing a solution have set the terms of the debate in America. At the same time it is argued that both positions, as articulated, are inadequate. As in the inter-war years in Britain, the equal treatment option caters inadequately for the demands of family and personal life while special treatment implies that these duties are women's. A model is needed which acknowledges social responsibility for reproduction without converting that responsibility into a justification to control procreation and hence women. Including women's sex-specific needs in the standard by which social rules are set achieves these ends.

The genesis of the equal treatment/special treatment debate lies in the history of American equal rights feminism. The first campaigns in the area of pregnancy and maternity leave had to do with challenging *compulsory* maternity leave provisions. Before the 1960s many companies and public institutions had rules allowing them to compel a pregnant woman to leave her job at a set time and forbidding her to recommence work before a set date. These rules promised neither monetary compensation nor reinstatement. The experience of the feminist lawyers who fought for and won the removal of these arbitrary restrictions on a pregnant woman's right to work led them to endorse an equal treatment approach to maternity leave.

The fundamental antidiscrimination principle that *likes should be treated alike* (Fiss, 1977: 85) set the parameters within which these women had to shape their arguments.[4] This principle was interpreted to mean that people who were 'similarly situated' should be treated the 'same'. If people were judged not to be similarly situated, they could be treated 'differently' and this treatment did not constitute discrimination (O'Donovan and Szyszczak, 1988: 87). Pregnancy was commonly recognised as women's 'difference', with unfortunate effects for women.

In 1973 Susan Cohen challenged the rule of the Chesterfield County School Board which specified that she *had* to go on leave at the end of the fifth month of pregnancy (Babcock, Freedman, Norton and Ross, 1975: 308–311). Cohen won her case at the District Court level on the grounds that pregnancy, although unique to women, was *like other medical conditions* and therefore failure to treat it as such violated the equal protection clause of the Fourteenth Amendment.[5] The decision was repealed in the Court of Appeals where it was argued that pregnancy was *not* like other medical disabilities *because it was natural*. It was, the court said, also usually voluntary and could therefore be planned for. As to whether the treatment was an 'invidious discrimination based upon sex', the court ruled that such invidious discriminations are found only 'in situations in which the sexes are in actual or potential competition' (that is, similarly situated), and the fact that only women experienced pregnancy and motherhood removed all possibility of competition between the sexes in this area:

> No man-made law or regulation excludes males from those experiences, and no such laws or regulations can relieve females from all of the burdens which naturally accompany the joys and blessings of motherhood (Babcock, Freedman, Norton and Ross, 1975: 309).

The Supreme Court consolidated this case with another challenge to mandatory leave, handing down the decision in *Cleveland Board of Education v La Fleur*, 414 US 632 (1974) that such policies were an infringement of freedom of personal choice, a liberty protected by the Due Process Clause of the Fourteenth Amendment (Goldstein, 1988: 456).

American feminists involved in this case decided that the best way to advance women's interests and to gain some protection for pregnant workers was to downplay the uniqueness of pregnancy and anything else which seemed to suggest that women could not compete on the same terms as men. Jacqueline Gutwillig, Chairperson of the Citizens' Advisory Council on the Status of Women, encouraged perhaps by the District Court's ruling in the Cohen case, decided that all that women had to do was to emphasise the *similarities* between pregnancy and other physical conditions and in that way prevent women from being singled out for treatment which disadvantaged them. To defend this position she had to argue *against* the idea that pregnancy was 'a *special* condition warranting *special* arrangements' (Babcock, Freedman, Norton, and Ross, 1975: 314, emphasis in original). As a corollary, this meant de-emphasising the 'roles, behaviour patterns and mythologies' surrounding pregnancy (Wendy Williams in Kamerman, Kahn, and Kingston, 1983: 38). Produced in this climate, EEOC (Equal Employment Opportunity Commission) guidelines stated that all disabilities relating to pregnancy and childbirth should be treated *like any other temporary disabilities* (Baer, 1978: 160).

Subsequent court decisions demonstrated that feminists would have to battle to have this interpretation accepted. *Geduldig v Aiello* (1974) sustained California's disability insurance program which at that time *excluded* all disabilities arising from normal pregnancy. The court ruled that the state had a 'legitimate interest' in maintaining the self-supporting nature of its insurance program and, if pregnancy were included, it would be too expensive. As to whether such a policy discriminated against women, the decision stated simply that, 'Normal pregnancy is no risk from which men are protected and women are not. Likewise, there is no risk from which women are protected and men are not' (Goldstein, 1988: 467). Expanding upon this intriguing logic the court explained that, while it was true that only women could become pregnant, it did not follow that every legislative classification concerning pregnancy was a sex-based classification. The disability program, it argued, divided potential recipients into two groups—pregnant women and nonpregnant persons—and while the first group was exclusively female, the second included women and hence treatment had not been sex-based.

An attempt by Martha Gilbert to use Title VII to claim sex discrimination because of her exclusion from General Electric Company's employee disability plan proved no more successful. The grounds for the decision (1976) were similar to those in *Geduldig*. Justice Rehnquist, writing for the majority, declared that pregnancy-related disabilities constituted an '*additional* risk, unique to women' and 'the failure to compensate them for this risk does not destroy the presumed parity of the benefits, accruing to men and women alike' (Goldstein, 1988: 472). As far as pregnancy was concerned, you simply could not compare women and men.

As a result of the *Gilbert* decision, feminists organised a concerted effort to secure an amendment to Title VII of the Civil Rights Act, stipulating that discrimination against pregnancy was indeed sex discrimination. The Pregnancy Disability Amendment (PDA) to Title VII was passed in 1978. It stated that:

> The terms 'because of sex' or 'on the basis of sex' include, but are not limited to, because of or on the basis of pregnancy, childbirth, or related medical conditions; and women affected by pregnancy, childbirth, or related medical conditions shall be treated *the same for all employment-related purposes*...as other persons not so affected but *similar in their ability or inability to work* (Kamerman, Kahn, and Kingston, 1983: 41–42, emphasis added).

American women now had the right to require that employers treat pregnancy and maternity *the same as* or *no less favourably than* any other illness or disability. The result was a logical outcome of an approach designed in the first instance to stop employers from disadvantaging women on the grounds that pregnancy made them a special case. It emerged logically also out of a decision to try to extend existing disability coverage, limited as it was, to include pregnancy. The lack of commitment of the government to the health and welfare of the people and the unlikelihood of securing nationally-funded maternity leave compelled feminists to try to use the existing law to gain for women the minimal protection which was available. The commonsense understanding of discrimination as 'treating likes unlike' meant that the most successful strategy involved claiming that women were *like men*, that pregnancy was a disability like other disabilities. Whenever women had been singled out as 'different', it had been used against them, as in the mandatory leave laws.

The victory, and there is no doubt that it was a victory, had clear limitations however. It did not require employers to set up disability insurance policies which under the PDA would now have to include pregnancy. It has also been suggested that it persuaded some employers who had been thinking about introducing maternity leave to abandon the idea (Finley, 1986: 1150). Viewing maternity as an illness has also meant that, as soon as a woman is physically capable of returning to work, she is compelled to do so. Kamerman, Kahn and Kingston (1983: 145) conclude that

> US employment practices with regard to pregnancy and childbirth seem to reflect the most niggardly approach of any advanced industrialized country, and defining maternity as a disability seems only to reinforce this.

Feminist groups had united in their campaign for the PDA. Divisions among them appeared only in the next stage of the evolution of maternity policy which concerned whether or not laws guaranteeing pregnant women certain rights and/or privileges ought to be allowed or encouraged. The dispute revolved around two cases. In the first (1979) the Miller-Wohl Company of Great Falls, Montana, appealed against a judgment that the company had violated Montana's Maternity Leave Act (MMLA) by firing a recently-hired sales clerk who discovered that she was pregnant and missed a few days of work due to morning sickness. The Miller-Wohl Company had a policy which denied sick leave to any employee for the first year of employment. Montana meanwhile was one of those few states which had a policy providing that it was unlawful to terminate a woman's employment because of pregnancy. Miller-Wohl claimed that Montana's MLA violated Title VII by discriminating *against men*. In a second similar case (1983) the California Federal Savings Association (Cal. Fed.) appealed against California's Fair Employment and Housing Act which requires a reasonable period of leave, not to exceed four months, for employees disabled by pregnancy or childbirth-related medical conditions (Krieger, 1987: 58 fn. 1).

These were the cases which sparked the equal treatment/special treatment debate, although there are hints that divisions in the feminist legal community appeared earlier.[6] A number of feminist groups including the National Organization for Women, the Legal Defense and Education Fund, the League of Women Voters and others, as *amici curae*, urged that the MMLA should be either *extended*, by guaranteeing other workers short-term disability leave, *or abandoned* (Williams, 1984: 371). An opposing contingent of Californian feminist lawyers strongly defended the MMLA in its original form. The dispute produced a series of conferences in 1982 and 1983 (Krieger and Cooney, 1983: 515 fn. 11). The Cal. Fed. case brought the disagreement to the awareness of a broader public (Hacker, 1986: 28).

The most obvious difference between the PDA and laws like the MMLA is that the former guaranteed that pregnant women should be treated no *less favourably* than men while the latter singled out pregnant women for favourable attention (Taub, 1982: 170). This is important, as is the fact that the grounds for that favourable consideration was the very characteristic, pregnancy, which had been invoked previously to rationalise discrimination *against* women. It is little wonder that feminists schooled in campaigns to overturn mandatory leave laws were suspicious of a policy which now said that indeed pregnancy *was* a *unique* condition, requiring *special* treatment. It is equally understandable, of course, why any group of feminists would want to secure maternity benefits which women in other countries, even in Thatcher's Britain, could take for granted (see page 110; quotation from Lisanne Radici).

At one level the basis of the disagreement is tactical. The equal treatment group argue fairly consistently that, if employers were required to subsidise maternity leave either by direct payment or by restructuring and planning around pregnant absentees, they would have a financial incentive *not* to hire women (Babcock, Freedman, Norton and Ross, 1975: 315; Goodman and Taub, 1986: 23; Williams, 1982: 175).[7] The alternative of state support, as in the British model, is politically anathema to many free enterprise Americans. As a result, few feminists consider it politically feasible. The other practical argument is that providing leave only for women would antagonise fellow workers, men, and women who chose not to get pregnant.

On the other side special treatment advocates claim that comprehensive short-term disability programs will be a long time coming and that coverage for maternity will be easier to obtain since it requires a less radical restructuring of workplace rights (Goodman and Taub, 1986: 23). They also point out that the disability approach is plainly inadequate. Women are required to produce medical certificates attesting to their inability to work, and doctors are reluctant to provide these for 'normal' pregnancies. Moreover, insurance companies have to be satisfied that the disability is real (Chavkin interview, 18 March 1988). This means that it is difficult to get coverage and whatever coverage one does obtain is for a limited time (Chavkin, 1986: 470–471).[8]

Tactically the equal treatment group fear that any identification of pregnancy as unique will encourage courts to re-invoke the *Geduldig* and *Gilbert* standard which allowed pregnancy to be treated *less* favourably on those very grounds (Krieger and Cooney, 1983: 533). Wendy Williams, a strong and articulate equal treatment proponent, feels that a doctrinal approach which will permit the state constitutional freedom to create 'special *benefits*' for pregnant women is the same approach which allows 'pregnancy to be treated *worse* than other disabilities'. 'If we can't have it both ways', she cautions, 'we need to think carefully about which way we want to have it' (Williams, 1982: 196).

Special treatment advocates are convinced that women will never achieve equal opportunities in the workplace *until* pregnancy is taken into account. Mary Segers insists that 'employers must regard sex as relevant if it is to become irrelevant'. In order for 'arbitrary discrimination' on the basis of sex to be removed from the workplace, 'reasonable discriminations' on behalf of the female sex need to be made in the areas of pregnancy, maternity leaves, and childcare assistance (Segers, 1979: 323).

Contenders in the debate admit that the divisions between them are ideological as well as tactical (Goodman and Taub, 1986: 23), indicating important links between developments in feminist theory and policy positions. 'Equal treatment' women are from the 'early Friedan' era. Inspired by *The Feminine Mystique*, they oppose 'trapping women in their homes' (Collins interview, 18 February 1988). Special treatment theorists on the other hand represent that later development (mid-1970s and subsequently) within feminist theory, loosely labelled 'cultural feminism' or the woman-centred approach (see page 86ff). Rebelling against the 'system' and the values of the marketplace, they extol maternity and motherhood which embody, in their view, a countervailing ethic of caring and cooperation, values which the world sorely needs.

These ideological differences begin to show through in the ways in which the two groups perceive and describe pregnancy. The special treatment lobby has no hesitation in claiming that pregnancy is 'unique' and 'special', and in stating their desire that motherhood be a 'profoundly human and enriching' experience (Finley, 1986: 1139; Law, 1984: 1007; Scales, 1981: 437). The equal treatment group prefer to see pregnancy as just one more human experience. Williams describes it is as a 'purely physical event' (Williams, 1984: 355). Nadine Taub wants it to be considered as 'the generative component to other creative abilities' (Taub, 1984: 382 fn. 5). Jacqueline Gutwillig readily accepted the analogy between childbirth and disability because 'for employment purposes' they shared similar characteristics—'loss of income due to temporary inability to perform normal job duties' and 'medical expenses'. To those who claimed it was a 'normal physiological condition', she replied that she was certain that 'medical care, hospitalization, and death are not normally associated with this phrase' (Babcock, Freedman, Norton, and Ross, 1975: 314). The medicalisation of pregnancy is something to which special treatment supporters object strongly. Pregnancy is 'special', but it is certainly *not* an illness (Chavkin interview, 18 March 1988).

The equal treatment commitment to counter the idea of 'pregnancy as unique' proceeds logically from their analysis of discrimination. Taub and Williams describe how, once feminist litigators in the 1970s realised that discrimination was due not simply to a 'miscalculation' of women's abilities, but to deeply entrenched notions of women and men as 'fundamentally different kinds of human being' with different roles and separate spheres of activity, they set out to dismantle these stereotypes. They belong to that group of 1960s feminists (see page 82) who argued that psychological differences between women and men were socially constructed rather than innate, and that physical differences were 'average rather than absolute'. Invoking a political ideology which rested upon the principle of individual capacity, they insisted that women be judged *as individuals* rather than be categorised by their membership in a class or group of 'women' (Taub and Williams, 1985: 825–827).

Since attitudes towards pregnancy were seen as 'central to the sex role mystique', pregnancy had to be 'demythologised' (Babcock, Freedman, Norton, and Ross, 1975: 315). This meant challenging the traditional notion that 'women have a special place in the scheme of human existence when it comes to maternity' and diffusing 'the narrow focus on motherhood, which has limited women's social participation to date' (Williams, 1982: 195; Taub, 1984: 382). Taub feared that special maternity leave laws might put pressure on women to become mothers. Williams is afraid that they might reinforce the 'traditional asymmetrical family model, with father as chief breadwinner and mother as childtender and housekeeper' (Taub, 1982: 170; Williams, 1984: 377).[9] Reluctant to think of homemaking as a career, equal treatment proponents place a priority upon facilitating women's engagement in paid labour. Special leave laws are opposed because symbolically they reinforce the idea of women as marginal workers. According to Goodman and Taub, women who made use of them only 'confirm this stereotype' (Goodman and Taub, 1986: 23).

Equal treatment theorists also have a trepidation, born of experience, that admitting that women need special consideration because they get pregnant will lead to them being typecast as lesser workers. Catharine MacKinnon suggests that the impulse behind the equal treatment approach is 'Whatever you can do, we can do. Just let us do it' (Du Bois et al., 1985: 22), invoking memories of earlier equal rights feminists who feared admitting to any 'female' weakness (see pages 45, 68). Wendy Chavkin, a 'special treatment' advocate, cautiously hypothesised that equal treatment theorists ascribed, to an extent, to a 'Superwoman' model and felt 'profoundly threatened by the vulnerability that has been associated with pregnancy and reproduction' (Chavkin interview, 18 March 1988). In the cut and thrust of the marketplace, admitting vulnerability is tantamount to admitting failure.

Equal treatment theorists claim higher principles for their position. Goodman and Taub declare that it is unfair to single out pregnant women for 'special privilege' when other workers' needs for leave and work flexibility are often as 'great as those of pregnant and post-partum women'. Equal treatment advocates, they say, will wait and fight for laws that 'accommodate the needs of *all* workers', even if this results in 'immediate losses for some women' who might have taken maternity leave. They endorse a 'philosophical structure that joins them (women) with, rather than isolates them from, humanity as a whole' (Goodman and Taub, 1986: 23).

Unfortunately, the willingness to sacrifice some women now for all women in the future would not be class-neutral in its impact. Self-critically, Alice Kessler-Harris admitted that women like herself, 'relatively well-off professional women', have tended to dismiss the 'dropping the barriers is not enough' argument by saying there are ways around it or that individual solutions can suffice. This excludes women, however, who cannot afford to create their own solutions. She expressed reservations about legislation currently before the House of Representatives, the Family Medical and Parenting Leave Act, which, if passed, would provide for gender-neutral *unpaid* leave, on the grounds that it will benefit those who need it least—'women and men who could in any event take the time off' (Kessler-Harris interview, 17 March 1988). The hope of course is that the legislation will provide an opening wedge for *paid* leave but, given American aversion to state intervention, for the time being they will take what they can get.

On the other side special treatment theorists claim to represent a new political vision. They portray equal treatment as part of classic liberalism which 'dissociates the individual person from any context of family, religion or class'. In contrast to an analysis of abstracted *individuals*, they say that they are willing to identify the needs of women *as a group*, and to suggest that the goal ought to be 'equality of effect' rather than 'equal treatment' (Krieger and Cooney, 1983: 551–554). They claim that they are proposing a 'dialectical materialist' rather than an abstract legalistic formula for change.

The attack upon the abstract liberal individual is timely and necessary, and is fully supported in this text. Yet much special treatment literature stops short in this analysis, and tends to identify women as those responsible for living arrangements and/or caring values, much in the way the traditional *Gemeinschaft* model for social organisation allocated home responsibilities to women. Some, in fact, talk about women's *distinctive social function* in the way reform feminists did in the inter-war dispute.

The philosopher, Elizabeth Wolgast, a strong special treatment advocate, for example, insists that the 'differences' between men and women are substantial, and that 'sexual equality will be achieved only if society deals with those differences respectfully and fairly by developing accommodating institutions'. Women, she argues, need both 'equal rights' and 'special rights' (Krieger, 1987: 56). She describes 'parental roles' as 'asymmetrical', and asserts that 'having sex roles is natural to us'. Married women become an 'anomaly' within individualistic capitalism and, to make them fit, another model is needed but only, in Wolgast's schema, *for them*. The model for men remains unchallenged:

> . . . individualism obscures, that one of society's chief and rudimentary concerns is that the children in it, and the families who care for the children, and *the mothers who are their primary parents*, have the best support it can provide (Wolgast, 1980: 22, 32, 158, emphasis added).

This position is not very far from that of the anti-suffragist Correa Moylan Walsh (see page 63) and resurrects the idea that, in the tension between individual rights and community needs, women will take care of the latter. On the other hand, as Lucinda Finley says, the equal treatment approach is 'tilted much too far towards the solitary end of the individual–community continuum' (Finley, 1986: 1167). It seems women are still the ones trying to reconcile the conflict within middle-class thinking produced by an acceptance of the free market and the desire for a sense of community (see page xii).

Krieger and Cooney admit that Wolgast's theory has problems, that without a 'limiting principle', it could place women on the 'slippery slope of judicial stereotyping'. As a result they invoke Ann Scales' 'incorporationist' model which specified that 'women should be regarded as having rights *different* from men *only* with respect to sex-specific conditions which are *unique* to women, namely pregnancy and breast feeding' (Krieger and Cooney, 1983: 562–563, emphasis added). According to special treatment theorists a comparison approach, which underlies traditional discrimination theory, is simply inadequate since the biological functions of men and women are not comparable. Any attempt to compare them leads to strained analogies, asking for example if 'a man who is nauseous with a hangover and misses work is "similarly situated" with a woman who has morning sickness'. Men are the norm in such a construction, they argue, and women try to fit themselves to that norm (Krieger and Cooney, 1983: 552, 539, 545; see also Scales, 1981: 428). Williams defends the equal treatment approach against this charge. She insists that, by getting the Supreme Court to recognise pregnancy as a disabling condition, she is undermining a male norm which excluded that condition: 'It sought to overcome the definition of the prototypical worker as male and to promote an integrated—and androgynous—prototype' (Williams, 1984: 363).

Given their objections to analogies between pregnancy and illness, paradoxically Krieger and Cooney proceed to endorse Wolgast's 'reasonable accommodation' model which builds upon the provision in Title VII compelling employers to 'reasonably accommodate' an employee's religious beliefs or *physical handicaps*. Wolgast uses the example of a handicapped person's 'special right' to have a ramp to gain access to a building in order to exercise their 'equal right' to employment. Similarly, says Wolgast, women have a 'special right' to maternity leave which facilitates their 'equal right' to compete. The model is deceptively attractive, but the whole construction of women as needing 'special rights' still assumes that they have an unequal and a greater responsibility for reproduction of the next generation. There is no reason why the biological 'fact' of pregnancy should require this. Women have a right to maternity leave not because they are 'different', but because society has a responsibility to create humane conditions for its own reproduction. Williams adds the practical point that the 'Supreme Court has interpreted accommodation requirements very narrowly' (Williams, 1984: 367). Women, it seems, will be short-changed under either model.

There are important nuances in this debate which get lost when people are slotted into 'special treatment' and 'equal treatment' categories. In contrast to Wolgast, for example, some special treatment theorists insist that their goal is not to *exclude* women from the labour force, but to *include* them 'by removing barriers to their full participation' (Segers, 1979: 333). Still, identifying women as 'different' or pregnancy as women's 'difference' implies that pregnancy is their problem. This could easily lead to exclusionary policies. It also makes it difficult to argue that workplace rules for men need to be changed and should be designed for people with children. The long-range goal, to make the workplace responsive to the 'private' side of people's lives, will require 'different' treatment for both women and men. The word 'different' would then of course make no sense.

The problem here is primarily conceptual since most special treatment and equal treatment advocates agree that, following the leave women require around the actual birth, parental leave should be shared by women and men (Taub, 1984: 383). Pregnancy

remains the problem. Rather than labelling it 'difference', however, it should be described as a sex-specificity which workplace
rules must acknowledge.

On the other side, it is unfair to represent all equal treatment
proponents as American-style rugged individualists. I met very few
who would endorse San Francisco's Mayor Dianne Feinstein's
much-quoted remark: 'What we have been saying all along is we
want to be treated equally. I don't think the work market has
to accommodate itself to women having children' (Hacker, 1986:
28). One would hardly place Nadine Taub's recommendation for
paid nurturing leave within classical liberal economic theory. And
Wendy Williams, who is a lawyer and a pragmatist, supports equal
treatment largely because she is convinced that the courts will do
no more than measure women against 'white male middle-class
interests and values'. Personally, she has a larger vision (although
she slips it into a footnote): 'Imagining a world set to the dimensions of women might generate desirable changes' (Williams, 1984:
364 fn. 146). To this extent Krieger typecasts equal treatment
theorists much too simply (see page 123; Krieger, 1987: 57–58),
though it remains true that they are more enamoured of political
liberalism and the public world of work, and less attracted to
idealised domesticity.

Both groups, however, have been influenced by recent 'woman-
centred' theory. Carol Gilligan finds her way into the footnotes of
equal treatment and special treatment theorists alike, though the
former emphasise that any character differences between men and
women are cultural rather than natural (Freedman, 1983: 965 fn.
277, 967 fn. 285; Law, 1984: 967). Using Catharine Stimpson's
terminology, many institutional 'minimalists', who downplay the
need for gender-specific legislation, flirt with metaphysical 'maximalism', which sees women as having special insights. Not that the
flirtation is unproblematic. The characteristics associated with the
cultural feminist reconstruction (see Chapter 4), dependency, pas-
sivity and maternity, are the same stereotypical female characteristics equal treatment supporters are intent on challenging because
they seem to impede women's success as competitors. The suggestion of a group identity also sits uncomfortably with their individualistic model. The ideas certainly have given them pause to
think, however. Wendy Williams asks: 'If we gain equality, will
we lose the special sense of kinship that grows out of experiences
central to our lives and not shared by the other sex?' (Williams,
1982: 200). Nadine Taub puzzles if 'the valuable aspects of
womanhood require a separate women's culture to survive' (Taub,
1980: 1695). Together they ask, 'are we doomed forever to oscillate

between dualities—group vs. individual equality, assimilation vs. accommodation, "formal" vs. "real" equality?' (Taub and Williams, 1985: 835). It could even be suggested that cultural feminism with its emphasis upon women as a category has shifted equal treatment theory in a direction where there is now at least a willingness to talk about *group* needs and the state's role in addressing them.

Taub and Williams, for example, suggest that the doctrine of 'disparate effects' could provide a way out of the equal treatment/ special treatment stalemate. A corollary to discrimination theory, it states that, if an apparently neutral policy has a disparate impact on either men or women, it is in effect discrimination, albeit indirect discrimination.[10] 'Disparate effects' is, as they say, sensitive to group inequality. It also provides a tool to use in securing maternity and other leaves, since it could be argued that a no-leave or a short-leave policy has a disparate impact upon women. The company would then be compelled to broaden the leave package (Williams, 1984: 373). Here, special treatment and equal treatment supporters find themselves on common ground, though Williams insists that, as far as she is concerned, the result would have to be 'disability and health insurance for all', rather than 'special protection' for pregnant women. She is also aware of the limitations of the theory. As discrimination law now works, disparate impact, which involves a comparison between men and women, would be of little use in a markedly sex-segregated labour market. Full 'incorporation' will require substantive legislation (Williams, 1984: 365–366; 1982: 175).

Special treatment advocates take cultural feminism a stage further. They tend in effect to *identify* women with caring values. Summarising Gilligan in a fashion I suspect Gilligan might not approve, Krieger starts from the premise that 'women adhere to a different system of moral reasoning than do men' (Krieger, 1987: 47). She goes on to suggest that equality jurisprudence is in the throes of a Kuhnian 'paradigm' crisis and that a woman-inspired 'ethic of care' paradigm needs to replace the older male-styled 'ethic of rights'. She locates the equal treatment theory within the latter and describes the special treatment view, called here 'bivalent or incorporationist' from Wolgast and Scales respectively, as 'more contextual, more willing to make exceptions to "the rules", and more willing to compromise the equal treatment principle to achieve equality of effect': 'In short this approach reflects the ethic of care identified by Gilligan as being more characteristic of women than men' (Krieger, 1987: 57–58). We can only hope that Krieger is right about the paradigm crisis in jurisprudence but, in company with Catharine MacKinnon, I wonder about the accuracy and wisdom of presenting the new-style 'ethic of care' as female in origin.[11] Leaving women responsible for *Gemeinschaft* values reinforces the bifurcation of human existence into public and private spheres.

A number of feminists have contributed to the task of pushing the analysis beyond an equal treatment/special treatment or sameness/difference formulation. MacKinnon places both the equal treatment and the special treatment approaches within a single 'differences' model of equality since both, despite their claims to challenge the male norm, assess women's needs *in comparison to men's*. But, as she explains, the basis of gender is not 'difference' but inequality, and this should be the starting place for laws. That is, laws should be designed to remove the inequalities between women and men, not to fit them into categories which can then be compared. Power and hierarchy are the issues which need to be addressed, illustrated for MacKinnon most disturbingly by male violence towards women. Pointedly she asks why male violence is not considered an equality issue. Why indeed? Since the threat of male violence constrains women's participation in certain activities, it is an impediment to equal participation and hence to equal opportunity (Du Bois et al., 1985: 27; MacKinnon, 1979: 4).

MacKinnon's 'inequality' model has great appeal, especially given most women's experience of overt male domination at some stage in their lives. Ann Scales found her argument convincing and modified her 'incorporationist' interpretation accordingly.[12] Now Scales says:

> Law must embrace a version of equality that focuses on the real issues—domination, disadvantage and disempowerment—instead of on the interminable and diseased issue of differences between the sexes (Scales, 1986: 1394).

Sylvia Law offers a narrower and, she feels, more achievable version of MacKinnon's anti-hierarchy doctrine. She wants laws which classify on the basis of gender to be distinguished from laws governing reproduction. The former would always be subjected to 'strict scrutiny'.[13] The latter would be subjected to such scrutiny only after they had passed MacKinnon's 'inequality' test, that is, after it had been determined whether or not they contributed to women's subordination (Law, 1984: 962, 1005–1012). This would allow laws which did not contribute to that subordination, which may in fact be alleviating that subordination, to stand unchallenged.

MacKinnon might have been surprised to find her 'inequality' approach treated by Nadine Taub as another version, albeit philosophically more expansive, of special treatment. It does, does it not, envisage the use at least at times 'of separate standards for judging women and men'. Part of the problem here is the way in which the commitment of equal treatment theorists to assimilation can lead to downplaying what I have described as 'women's differential location' (see Introduction). In a model based upon abstracted 'equals', 'differences' get collapsed into a single category which must be ignored.

Taub is also concerned, as is Sylvia Law, that MacKinnon's approach depends upon the present judiciary first recognising that something disadvantages women and then being willing to do something about it. Such an expectation could clearly backfire. Those old restrictive categories singling women out for disadvantageous treatment could be resurrected. Like Law again, however, Taub finds the 'inequality' approach useful in the identification of truly neutral rules (Taub, 1980: 1690, 1691, 1694).

Herma Hill Kay constructs an 'episodic' model which suggests that 'we take account of biological sex differences and treat them as significant only when they are being utilised for reproductive purposes'. Kay makes a nice point when she suggests that in the *Geduldig* decision the court used overly broad classifications when it compared pregnant and nonpregnant persons. It should have been comparing persons of the opposite sex who engaged in reproductive behaviour and who wished to continue working. She fails to see, as I fail to see, why the consequential disadvantages of reproductive conduct should fall solely upon women (Kay, 1985: 22, 23 fn. 125, 26, 30).

Lucinda Finley expands upon Kay's insight and makes, I feel, a significant breakthrough. Although pregnancy is a 'difference' between men and women, explains Finley, this does not mean that 'pregnancy and its consequences affect only women'. *It almost invariably affects men and other people.*[14] Therefore policies labelled 'special treatment' for women are not in any sense a hand-out for women since they benefit men and children as well. Framed in this way women do not need *special* treatment; parents require appropriate consideration (Finley, 1986: 1169, 1137, 1174). Georgina Ashworth suggested using the word 'specific' rather than 'special' to remove some of that sense of women as petitioners or beggars (Ashworth interview, 12 April 1988). This reconceptualisation can be used effectively against employer complaints that 'women' are unreliable because *they* go off to have babies, and court rulings that a disability policy cannot include pregnant women because it is too expensive to do so (see page 113).

To obviate the danger that this approach might freeze sex roles, it ought to apply only to the contested area of accouchement or pregnancy leave. Efforts to obtain leave beyond the period surrounding the birth must continue to be pressed in gender-neutral terms. 'Parental' leave should then be long enough to achieve an appropriate balance between work and family. By implication, these reforms will require rethinking the traditional career pattern and the meaning of 'work' and 'leisure'.

There are two things at stake here. One is getting the function of reproduction accepted as a *social responsibility*. The other is challenging the assumption that people's public working lives have nothing to do with their private personal lives, and that their personal lives should not be allowed to interfere with their jobs. We need to expose the lie behind the public/private conceptualisation so that both women and men can achieve a better balance in their lives between the demands and rewards of paid labour, and the demands and rewards of home-life.

Finley accuses both equal treatment and special treatment theorists of being insufficiently critical of workplace values and of accepting in the end a continuation of the split between public and private spheres (Finley, 1986: 1143, 1145, 1156).[15] Whether you talk about pregnancy as women's 'special' need, or draw analogies between pregnancy and other 'disabilities' so that women can compete even though they get pregnant, you are still conceptualising this part of life as women's responsibility. *The problem is not whether women ought to be treated the same as or different from men but what sort of institutions will resolve the tension between individual self-actualisation and family/community life without leaving women responsible for one side of this equation.* The debate is an incarnation of the either/or choice which has plagued women from the turn of the century. To move beyond it we have to insist that men no longer be allowed to approximate the neutered automatons of liberal theory serviced by a support staff of surrogates—women. This is not only because such a structure disadvantages women in obvious ways, although that would be reason enough to justify change. It also has detrimental effects for men and through them for all of society, as subsequent chapters will explain. In the place of a sameness/difference analysis we need a view of the world which demands the integration of home and paid work in new ways for women and men (Finley, 1986: 1160, 1165; see also Weinzweig, 1986: 86). The fiction that these parts of our lives are or can be kept separate has to be disclosed.

Allow me to hypothesise how, in the best of all possible worlds, this reconceptualisation might work. Take the case of a single parent with two young children applying for a job and getting knocked back on the grounds that he/she will be less dedicated or less efficient. The company should be charged with discrimination, not because it applied a stereotype which might *not* be accurate in this particular case, but because it should accept that the applicant might indeed need specific social supports.

Clearly, there are dangers in insisting upon *social responsibility* for reproduction. In a sense Finley's argument seems to suggest that women deserve justice *only* when men are also affected. Women are collapsed into the family (Ehrenreich, 1988) in a way which could be used to control women's fertility. We need to remain ever-watchful since countries which provide the most extensive maternity benefits invariably have pronatalist motivations which constrain women in other ways (Kamerman, Kahn and Kingston, 1983: 30–32; Jancar, 1978: 51–56; Riley, 1981 and 1983). Insisting that women's sex-specific needs, including social supports for their offspring *and* control over their fertility, be included in the standards by which social rules are set obviates this danger.

The American equal treatment/special treatment test-case illustrates that the issue at stake in sameness/difference debates is not whether women are the same as or different from men but the general working and living conditions of women and of men. It shows that feminists themselves are impelled to adopt these oppositional stances when government and employers refuse to accept social responsibility for basic human needs such as childbearing and child nurture. This becomes even clearer when we ask why this particular debate is not replicated in this form in either Britain or Australia.

In the interviews which formed part of the research for this project, a clear contrast emerged between the way in which American activist feminists, and those in Britain and Australia responded to a question asking if women and men were different. In America I was immediately immersed in the equal treatment/ special treatment debate. In Australia and Britain responses tended to raise the metaphysical question about woman's character. When asked directly if legislation ought to take women's biological needs into account, Australian and British respondents tended to ask what I meant. When I volunteered maternity leave as a starting place, they replied 'Of course!' Australian and British feminists also found NOW's position in the Cal. Fed. case incomprehensible. How could any feminist oppose maternity leave? Worse still, how could she describe pregnancy as a disability? The availability of maternity leave in these countries frees feminists from this particular agonising debate.

The history of the introduction of maternity leave in Britain suggests, however, that feminists there ought not to be too sanguine in their comments. As Chapter 3 related, the plea prior to the post-World War II social security reforms which introduced paid leave was that maternity be treated 'just like any other disability'. The very arguments Americans are using today were rehearsed in Britain six decades ago. The issue was settled then because of historical circumstances and the evolution in Britain of a more activist welfare state which meant that feminists could present maternity leave as 'family need'. Once humane working arrangements exist for male and female employees, feminists no longer have to puzzle over how to present demands for those arrangements without penalising women. They no longer have to insist that women are 'different'. Nor do they have to claim 'sameness' because of the fear that admission of difference might be used against women.

The fragility of the construction and its susceptibility to changing economic and political climates, however, is illustrated in some recent court cases. While British women have statutory maternity leave, they are protected against unfair dismissal due to pregnancy only if they have been with an employer for two years. Since the Thatcher government came to power the qualifying period for protection has increased from six months in 1975 to one year in 1979, and in 1980 to the present two-year term (Maternity Alliance, 1987: 8). Some cases have been brought to court under the 1975 Sex Discrimination Act which makes discrimination on the grounds of sex, but not pregnancy, unlawful (Coussins, Durward and Evans, 1987: 6; Kenney, 1986: 401). The most successful have been those cases which used an analogy to sickness. An EOC (Equal Opportunities Commission) News Release praised these decisions as an important victory:

> If pregnant women can show that male employees who take time off work, e.g. for sickness, would not be sacked, then they can claim sex discrimination. This must make employers think twice about sacking women out-of-hand when they become pregnant (EOC, 1987: 1).

In 1980 Britain also had its own *Geduldig* (see page 113). In *Turley v Allders Department Stores*, the Employment Appeal Tribunal held that under the Sex Discrimination Act a woman could be lawfully dismissed for pregnancy because a pregnant woman was a 'woman with child' and therefore had no male equivalent. Hence, it could not be said that the woman was treated less favourably (McGinley, 1986: 418).

Britain has also recently dragged its heels on a number of equality issues. Several times it has been hauled before the European Court and told to get its house in order.[16] Most recently, the UK was the only member state to refuse to endorse an EC Directive on Parental and Family Leave (EOC, 1985: 2). In this climate it is not surprising that many feminists now wonder whether to 'press for the proper appreciation of women's work and responsibilities for the family, and for the revaluing of non-aggressive "feminine" principles' or to 'press for equality *tout court*' (Barrett and McIntosh, 1982: 19). The more a government is committed to reducing its responsibility for basic human needs, the more feminists are constrained to think in terms of either/or, sameness/difference strategies. Still, American feminists would have been saved much anguish and much internecine strife had they National Insurance and a Sex Discrimination Act like Britain's which contained a proviso that discrimination *in favour* of women connected with childbirth or pregnancy was allowed (McGinley, 1986: 415). This of course was both possible and necessary only because of the existence of maternity leave legislation.

Similarly in Australia maternity is accepted as a condition requiring specific action,[17] although the amount of action is inadequate and sporadic. Australia has no general maternity leave legislation. Benefits have usually been secured through industrial awards and legislation. The breakthrough came in 1979 when the Australian Conciliation and Arbitration Commission granted a period of up to 52 weeks unpaid leave 'including a six week compulsory period after the birth, to both full- and part-time employees with at least 12 months continuous service with the employer before taking leave' (Wulff, 1987: 14). Paid maternity leave is available only to some female public servants.[18] The Women's Electoral Lobby (WEL), Australia's largest feminist lobby group, feels that Australian maternity provisions are 'the "pits" compared with any European country EXCEPT Britain' (WEL [SA] Newsletter, October, 1986: 11).

Australia faces conceptual as well as practical problems, because of the way in which leave was first introduced. Sue Brooks, past Director of the Office of the Status of Women, feels that Australian women created a 'classic mistake' in opting for a test case in *maternity* leave instead of *parental* leave: 'It seemed to me that what we have done is imposed even greater responsibility on women instead of trying to shift the debate' (Brooks interview, 24 November 1987). The fears of some American equal treatment feminists about reinforcing sex roles appear then to be well-founded. The preamble to the ACTU (Australian Council of Trade Unions) Working Women's Charter (1983) shows a sensitivity to the need to broaden this conceptualisation, so that women are no longer typecast as solely responsible for domestic duties:

> It is recognized that some policies supported by the ACTU to achieve equality also apply to male workers. However, until such time that male and female workers have equal responsibility for domestic duties and child rearing, many of these policies must be directed principally towards female workers.
>
> Congress believes that in order to achieve equality an increasing emphasis must be placed on policies which provide for men and women to share domestic responsibilities. This means that policy initiatives called for in this Charter reflect this aim and that these provisions must be increasingly directed to all workers (ACTU Congress, 1983).

Currently the ACTU is campaigning for twelve weeks' paid maternity leave and up to two years' unpaid leave for either or both parents (*Advertiser*, 12 September 1987).

The recent role of some Australian trade unions in advancing women's interests is due largely to the growing numbers of union-ised women and to the increasing influence of white-collar unions where women are well represented.[19] British Labour has a some-what different heritage which has heightened the tension between feminists and unionists. Beatrix Campbell believes that British men's belief in their role as breadwinner has subordinated 'all other dimensions of their workplace politics to the politics of pay—their own pay' (Campbell, 1984: 147). This causes problems given some women's different workplace priorities such as hours and other working conditions. According to Georgina Ashworth, for women, 'equality of time use' is vital to accomplishing 'equality of access', otherwise women continue to create men's time to be politically active (Ashworth interview, 12 April 1988). Perhaps Australia's centralised wage-fixing system has made it easier for Australian women unionists to get issues other than pay onto the agenda. Recent debates about comparable worth (see page 171), however, show that working through male-dominated institutions is always problematic (*Financial Review*, 17 October 1988: 13).

A major battle in Australia today is over how issues like matern-ity or parental leave will be described in 'popular discourses'. On one side unions, feminist academics, male and female, feminist bureaucrats, and progressives like Dr Don Edgar, Director of the Australian Institute of Family Studies, feel that managers must 'acknowledge that workers have families and that families are more important to people than the job that provides an income' (*Women at Work*, July/August, 1987, vol. 7, no. 2, 10). On the other side are reactionary employers who persist in arguing that 'If female candidates are more likely to take leave, then it is clearly in the firm's interest to give preference to males over females' (*Financial Review*, 13 July 1987), and women like Professor Dame Leonie Kramer, a former Chairman [sic] of the Australian Broadcasting Corporation, who does not feel that 'because you are a woman and *you may have family responsibilities—which are of your own choosing*—you should have compensating advantages' (*Scope*, vol. 2, August 1987, 21, emphasis added). Feminists in Australia may not have to debate each other in terms of sameness or difference over maternity leave, but people who wish to minimise government intervention and hence governmental responsibility for basic human needs are keen to reduce the issue to this framework.

There are lessons in a comparative study of maternity leave. Critically important is the way in which institutional constraints affect feminist arguments. A recent volume by Sylvia Hewlett, in the post-feminist tradition (see page 94),[20] castigates American feminists for being unwilling to consider women's maternity needs seriously and for clinging to an egalitarian ideology which quite simply does not meet women's requirements (Hewlett, 1986: 143). Upon reflection, it does seem a little shortsighted to blame *feminists* for America's lack of progressive social legislation.

Every equal treatment feminist to whom I spoke was vitally aware that the American political culture with its emphasis upon privacy and the 'self-sufficient family' (Kamerman, Kahn and Kingston, 1983: 253) posed an almost insuperable barrier to necessary reform in the area of maternity (Taub interview, 11 March 1988; Kessler-Harris interview, 17 March 1988; East interview, 18 February 1988). Alice Kessler-Harris agreed with me that the equal treatment/special treatment debate would dissolve if America had the equivalent of British National Insurance.[21] Hewlett, in her opinion, began with the right perspective, but then blamed it all on the women's movement instead of saying 'Hey, wait a minute. *There's a structure within which this movement exists* and against which it struggles...' (Kessler-Harris interview, 17 March 1988—emphasis added). Basic human needs such as health insurance or creches or paid maternity leave are not only *not conceived of* in America, Kessler-Harris informs us, 'they are seen as contrary to the American spirit of free enterprise'.

Borrowing Hester Eisenstein's analogy of a river, the women's

movement 'As it shapes the landscape. . .in its turn is also shaped'.
As Eisenstein says:

> A historical and political self-consciousness about the dialectic
> between the women's movement and the social and political
> institutions of the countries in which it is active is crucial. . .for
> any discussion both of achievements and of future objectives
> (Eisenstein, 1985 and forthcoming).

Whether a welfare structure exists, whether trade unions are
strong or responsive to women's claims, whether one lives in a
country where it is easier to achieve change through litigation
or legislation, whether social policy is a state or federal matter,
whether one can use the party system to extract promises, these
and many other factors are vital to understanding why feminists
have had to argue for particular reforms in particular ways.

The fact that pregnancy leave is controversial *among* American
feminists and not *among* Australian or British feminists highlights
the point that feminists do not divide over whether women are
the 'same as' or 'different from' men. They never have! They
divide in this instance over how to conceptualise reproduction in a
particular political culture. In the absence of public recognition of
society's responsibility to grant and fund maternity leave, one
group struggles to downplay this function while the other is prepared to elevate it. The former risks insufficient provision; the
latter risks an inadequate and possibly dangerous solution, since
identifying women as 'special' makes it difficult to challenge the
model of work for men and leaves the door open to equating
women with family and domestic life. This is not to say that
Australian and British feminists have not had to be careful about
how they have formulated their arguments but, in a political
system which provided some room for state-endorsed solutions,
they have not had to fight *with each other* about whether they
should draw analogies between pregnancy and some other disability or claim 'special' status. When the standards are different, the
debate dissolves, at least at the institutional level.

The argument in this chapter is that feminists should work to
shift the standard to *include* women, which goes beyond either
'assimilating' them or constructing a parallel system for women
only. Inclusion does not mean *adding* women to existing standards;
it means reformulating standards with women as active participants in the process. The result will be a *transformation* of existing
rules and practices. It leads to a reconceptualisation of social
arrangements whereby '. . .all individuals are regarded as active
interrelated participants in a cohesive community involved in com-

mon social undertakings' (Weinzweig, 1987: 87). And it does this without subsuming women in that community.

The fact that one form of the sameness/difference debate can be historically and culturally specific confirms that the terms in themselves are empty. The problem has never been 'difference' but 'difference which matters', in the sense that it is the cause of disadvantage. Pregnancy becomes a 'difference which matters' when groups in power make it matter by leaving it as women's responsibility. It can also be included in the formulation of work rules so that it is in fact no longer a 'difference', since it no longer matters. This means also that there is no single 'male norm'. It is a political construct and can be either very narrow or broader and more humane. There is an American 'male norm' and it is causing problems for American feminists. As Wendy Chavkin put it:

> In a society like the United States men are so deprived of so many basic human rights that fighting for equality with them is a short-sighted and stupid goal. So, what we're really after is a restructuring of political systems to accommodate human needs. We really need to expand a whole panoply of rights for both (Chavkin interview, 18 March 1988).

The conflict over 'equal' versus 'special' treatment needs to be resolved. It is more than unfortunate when feminists work to defeat each other's legislation. This chapter is intended to facilitate a resolution. The main point is that, while it may appear that there is a fundamental ideological contest here over 'sameness' and 'difference', these terms have no absolute meaning. Therefore, it becomes critically important to expose the political issues underlying the formulation rather than to allow these issues to be presented as a case of 'equality' versus 'difference'. In practical terms, accouchement or pregnancy leave should be supported, with fathers or partners having some leave as well, around the time of birth. And, most importantly, the language to express the demand must be chosen carefully: women need 'specific' legislation in this case, not because women are 'different', but because the system must acknowledge that people have children.

6
Protective legislation and industrial health hazards

Feminists based in America:

Now a job may be dangerous for men and women in different
ways. The specific danger may break down by gender. What is
important is that the zone of danger transcends gender...
In the area of reproduction and in certain health areas there
is a clear difference that legislation has to take account of.

Catharine Stimpson

I don't want these damaged sperm producing babies.

Leslie Wolfe

It is crucial that we identify what the real problems are because
if we don't, if we focus only on the woman when she is
pregnant and her capacity for pregnancy, the solution will be
to exclude women and we won't clean up the workplace.

Nadine Taub

There are some problems which affect pregnant women...
Obviously if they are known and a women is known to be
pregnant, she should not be exposed to them.

Anne Summers

...if something is a reproductive hazard, the workplace should
be cleaned up rather than telling women they can't work there.

Judy Goldsmith

Feminists based in Britain:

I go along with those who say what we should be seeking to do
is to restrict unsocial working hours for both sexes as far
as possible. It's a retrograde step just to extend these to
everybody. If we do have a more advantageous position we
ought to stick to it and try to bring men up to that level rather
than have a general deterioration.

Tess Gill

Every health hazard has to be looked at for its effect on men
and on women as different biological entities...There must be
radiating things that affect testicles as well as ovaries.

Georgina Ashworth

On balance I think it is a matter of tactics rather than
principles. Although it would be very nice to get 20% of your
workload removed when you were pregnant, I think it probably
would be a more dangerous strategy to adopt. In a different
culture it would be a reasonable thing to do.

Michèle Barrett

The question shouldn't be how you fit the worker to the work,
but how you change the work to fit the worker.

Ann Oakley

I see no reason why men should be subjected to hazardous,
unsocial, unpleasant, overdone working hours any more than
women should....We should be working towards the day
when nobody, man or woman, has to crawl along the coalface.

Jo Richardson

Feminists based in Australia:

There is a responsibility and an onus on the employer to create
an environment in the workplace which is healthy, which is
non-hostile, which is not necessarily nurturing but which
allows an employee to do an honest day's work for an honest
day's pay. And when you take that kind of philosophy, which
is once again taking an aspect of the American dream and
writing it in a different way, you can run the sexual harassment
argument, you can run a whole lot of other arguments.

Carmel Niland

Women are more in danger of being attacked in the streets.
Our current social situation does mean that women need a
particular type of protection.

Ann Curthoys

The issue of protective legislation which seriously divided the
women's movement in the inter-war years has not gone away.
Some remnants of the old legislation remain. The question of the
impact of industrial health hazards upon the fetus and the pregnant woman has become even more controversial than earlier in
the century. Some companies in America, Britain and elsewhere
are excluding women of childbearing age from work processes
where there is a known danger to the fetus, unless they can prove
themselves sterile (Owen and Shaw, 1979: 62; Williams, 1981:
641; O'Donovan, 1984: 82). An increased sensitivity to ergonomics

and occupational health and safety has raised the suggestion that pregnant women and women in general require sex-specific regulations. Feminists continue to be torn between the desire to meet women's needs and to avoid confirming stereotypes which can then be exploited to women's disadvantage. The situation has been complicated by the introduction of equality legislation which says that you must treat women and men the same, not differently, since antidiscrimination means treating likes alike (see page 112).[1]

The way in which these topics have been addressed in the United States, Britain and Australia highlights the role that institutional factors, political culture and legal doctrine play in setting the parameters for feminist arguments. It also supports the idea that approaching these questions using a simple sameness/difference analysis—are women more the same as or different from men?— can divert attention from vitally important social needs. Labelling women 'different' is often used by employers to avoid introducing adequate safety standards and humane working conditions for women and for men, while the offer of 'equality' or 'sameness' frequently means access to equally demeaning conditions. A more optimistic message is that resolving the conflict between 'sameness' and 'difference' by insisting that women's sex-specific needs be included in the standard by which work rules are set, transforms and broadens current understandings of suitable working conditions.

While American feminists experienced the most agonised confrontation over protective legislation, in the end they achieved the least painful resolution. Chapter 4 (see page 77) describes how the EEOC declared in 1969 that state protective laws tended to discriminate against women rather than to protect them, and hence were illegal under Title VII of the Civil Rights Act. The Commission ruled that 'although originally promulgated for the purpose of protecting females', such laws and regulations 'have ceased to be relevant to our technology or to the expanding role of the female worker in our economy' (Spritzer, 1972: 591).

The issue was complicated by the several varieties of protective legislation. Broadly, the laws fell into two categories: those which offered some benefit or positive working conditions for females but not for males, such as minimum wage laws or mandatory rest periods, and those which imposed certain restrictions on the employment of females but not on males. The latter included restrictions on hours of employment, prohibition of nightwork, weight-lifting limits and prohibition of employment in specific occupations or industries (Spritzer, 1972: 568). Categories however are seldom exclusive. It is a moot point, for example, whether minimum wages were more restrictive than beneficial since they might lead an employer not to hire women, or whether restrictions on hours of employment might not be more beneficial than restrictive because they prevented employers from demanding overtime.

The EEOC ruled that *restrictions* should be removed and, where possible, *benefits* extended to include men. The latter happened on very few occasions. A number of minimum wage laws were extended in this fashion. More generally the laws were struck down. As a result America has no general weight-lifting limit or nightwork limitation or limitation on daily or weekly hours (Brown, Emerson, Falk and Freedman, 1971: 927, 934).[2]

Removal of maximum hours legislation proved to be one of the most contentious issues. Some union representatives put the case made by reform feminists earlier in the century that 'all overtime should be optional for both men and women', but that it was 'absolutely mandatory that overtime for women be regulated because of her [sic] double role in society' (Babcock, Freedman, Norton and Ross, 1975: 279). The Women's Bureau also emphasised that 'long hours and arbitrary scheduling' would make it difficult for women to meet the 'dual obligations' of work and family (US Department of Labor, 1976: 17).

Those who opposed the laws started from the assumption that they could not possibly be extended to men since 'employers must be able to schedule overtime work'. Under equal treatment rules, protection therefore had to be removed from women, although this might cause hardship. Otherwise an employer would be able to 'bar women from any job or promotion which he defined as requiring overtime work' (Babcock, Freedman, Norton, and Ross, 1975: 272). The point was also made that, since under the Fair Labor Standards Act, overtime work was often paid at one and a half times the regular rate, overtime was necessary for workers, male or female, to maintain their standard of living (Brown, Emerson, Falk and Freedman, 1971: 934). The option of increasing wages to allow reasonable living standards without overtime was not considered.

The idea that employers should have an absolute right to set hours to suit themselves fitted comfortably into the American free enterprise ethic, with its 'fetish of individualism' and 'anemic sense of communal responsibility' (Robinson, 1988: 9). Women who absorbed this ethic and who wished to prove that women could be like 'men' took on a commitment to demonstrate *equal* self-sufficiency and independence. America's 'self-made man', rather than man in some abstract sense, became their role-model.

Women, like men, would stand alone, without social supports. Offered the 'choice' between 'equality' and 'difference', which implied exclusion, they 'chose' 'equality'. The impossibility of and, in some cases, the aversion to calling upon the government to create reasonable working conditions for all workers set up these unattractive alternatives as the only available 'choices'.

In Britain the debate took a different direction. Whereas British feminists stood solidly behind guaranteed maternity leave since the post-World War II welfare reforms, protective legislation caused serious divisions within the movement. On one side, the Equal Opportunities Commission (EOC) undertook the task of dismantling those parts of protective legislation which conflicted with its brief, to treat every person equally 'without differentiation by sex' (EOC, 1988: 5). On the other side, unionists and the Women's Rights Unit of the National Council for Civil Liberties (NCCL), representatives of that tradition within British feminism which concentrated upon the health and welfare of working-class mothers, pledged themselves to 'levelling up' rather than 'equalising down'. In a sense this is Britain's version of the equal treatment/special treatment debate, though the categories are inexact and, as we will see, some in the special treatment category pushed well beyond the notion that women were a separate group with special needs. The question they addressed is at any rate the same: should women fit into existing work regulations, or should separate provisions be set up for them because of 'their' family duties and/or 'different' physical characteristics?

As in America, the subject of protective laws was debated in the 1960s largely as a result of the buoyant economic conditions which produced an increased demand for labour. Women had to be 'freed' from 'restrictive' labour laws because their labour was needed. That Britain did not follow America's path in removing most protective laws was due largely to the role played by the British Trade Union Congress (TUC). The Department of Employment set up a Working Party to examine the issue in 1969, but business and union representatives could not agree. The Council of Business Industry (CBI) favoured abolition of protection; the TUC favoured retention, particularly of the nightwork clauses which prohibited labour for women between 10 pm and 7 am. In 1973 the Conservative Government issued a Consultative Document pressing for repeal of limited hours legislation on the grounds that such legislation could not coexist with equal rights policies (Meehan, 1985: 77). The following year the Labour Government responded with a White Paper which recommended retaining hours laws for the present and which asked the newly formed EOC to inquire into their operation (EOC, 1979: 21–22).

In 1979 the EOC presented its Report, entitled *Health and Safety Legislation: Should we distinguish between men and women?* In short, the answer was 'No, we should not'. As far as hours were concerned, the EOC decided that:

> ...the hours of work legislation constitutes a barrier—often an artificial one—to equal pay and job opportunities for women. So long as this legislation remains as it is at present, women as workers will be disadvantaged (EOC, 1979: 92).

The Commission considered the possibility of extending hours limitation to men but decided that this was not feasible, given the 'likely economic consequences'. The Report contained a number of qualifications referring to the need to assist parents with scheduling shifts to accommodate parenting duties, but these unfortunately were lost in the general message that, for the sake of equal opportunity, women should be free to 'choose' to work when they wished (EOC, 1979: 128, 74; Gregory, 1987: 18).

The TUC condemned the proposals as 'muddled...thinking' which would have the effect of inflicting upon women 'all the bad practices which are forced on men at work'. The only equality it promised was 'equality of misery'. The TUC's position on women's labour was reminiscent of those reform feminists who had argued earlier in the century that women ought *not* to work for the sake of the family. It reflected a Labour tradition which saw the man as breadwinner and which wished to reduce competition from women for jobs. Boosting the family wage was considered the most useful way to improve the living standards of working-class families. Women were identified as having a 'multiplicity of jobs'. Nightwork for women was condemned because of the 'serious effects' it could have on the 'well being of the family' (Coyle, 1980: 7–8). According to W. B. Creighton, the TUC was simply following another sound trade union principle, 'not to give anything away without receiving something in return' (Creighton, 1979: 35). Angela Coyle suspected that in their new enthusiasm for collective bargaining, the unions saw protective legislation as a concealed wage demand (Coyle, 1980: 10).

The NCCL put forward some similar arguments but went beyond them in important ways. Anna Coote agreed that as a rule women held two jobs and that therefore repealing the hours laws would not reduce discrimination but 'merely increase the pressures on women with families—and on the families themselves, particularly the children' (Coote, 1972: 5). Jean Coussins supported the view that the equality the EOC offered was a 'spurious kind of equality', a 'superficial and dangerous' equality, making women 'equally vulnerable with men to the pressures of working long and unsocial hours to gain a decent wage'. Similarly, the 'freedom of choice' offered to women was considered a false choice since it put employers in the position where *they* made the choices about how long people should work (Coussins, 1979: 9, 18).

Therefore the NCCL was willing to endorse 'different but not discriminatory treatment of men and women'. But the 'difference' they recognised was not based upon assumptions about woman's 'natural' role, as was some of the TUC literature, nor upon generalisations about physical incapacities. As will be seen shortly, the NCCL was committed to keeping legislation addressed specifically to women's biological needs to a minimum. The 'difference' identified was a *structural* one based upon recognition of women's differential social location. 'Different treatment' was justified because, 'Past sex discrimination and current domestic or family responsibilities are, on the whole, still borne by women in our society' (National Council for Civil Liberties, 1988: 16)

Even more importantly, the NCCL insisted upon the *absolute necessity of extending the laws to include men* so that the recommendations did not simply reinforce traditional sex roles. Whereas restrictions on nightwork only for women supported the idea that women were responsible for family maintenance, in addition to whatever else they might do, extending the laws to include men represented a first step towards recognising that 'the achievement of formal equality in the public sphere' must be accompanied by 'material equality' in private, or the integration of the two spheres. As long as legislation ignored the sexual division of labour and women had to seek jobs which fitted in with home responsibilities, equality of opportunity was a myth (O'Donovan, 1984: 87; Shimmin, 1984: 515).

The NCCL added that the shift system was an 'unsatisfactory way of working for women *and* men', that rotating shifts were bad for the health, and that nightwork was socially disruptive (Coote, 1972: 5). Coussins accused the EOC of ignoring the fact that men were 'rounded human beings, with families, likes and dislikes, a personal or political life'. She wanted to achieve equality for women without 'deterioration of their working conditions', without 'equalising "down"' (Coussins, 1979: 5, 9).

Jeanne Gregory is correct that 'Protective legislation did not create the sexual division of labour at work and at home: it was a reaction to it'. She is also correct that 'Repealing the legislation will not of itself break down the barriers to sex equality, but neither will its retention'. *Its extension to men could, however, begin a process of healing the rift between the family and the market* (Gregory, 1987: 20).

The significance of this challenge to conventional labour standards should not be underestimated. In contention here are two conflicting social visions, one which says that we should be 'allowed' to work as long and as hard as we want to, and the other which says that this is a false choice and that we often work long hours either to retain a job or to meet the expenses of an over-consumerist lifestyle. The debate is not about whether women are the same as or different from men, but about the sorts of lives we want to lead.

Britain's tradition of state intervention allowed some feminists to formulate a policy proposal which moved beyond the alternatives of either leaving women responsible for living arrangements or turning them loose to compete in a social structure which denied that people had families. Unfortunately, the proposal to extend hours limitation did not come to pass. The 1986 revised Sex Discrimination Act repealed most of the hours laws, illustrating the vulnerability of any reform program to the whim of the government in power (Kenney, 1986: 395). The NCCL pointedly complained that the EOC, a 'quango' subject to ministerial supervision of funds and appointments, seemed more concerned with the Conservative Government's objective of *deregulation*, of 'Building Businesses...not Barriers', as a 1986 Government White Paper put it, than with meeting women's needs (NCCL, 1988: 4; Gregory, 1987: 109).

The political lesson in all this is that, instead of viewing 'standards applied to women as a "concession" to be given up when equality arrives', they should become guidelines to acceptable working conditions for all (NCCL in Chesterman, 1981: 265). According to Angela Coyle, women are sometimes better able to see what is at issue because they are the ones most often required to shoulder the dual responsibility of family and waged labour. She quotes Audrey Wise who puts the case simply: 'if the economy wants me to work night shifts, then I want a different economy' (Wise in Coyle, 1980: 10).[3] There are precedents for extending hours limitations to men. In Scandinavia neither men nor women are allowed to work night shifts (Coyle, 1980: 5). Equally progressive is a recent EEC Report which recommends a generalisation of hours limitations to include men and ideally a ban on all nightwork (EEC, 1987: 19).

In Australia the issue of hours is on the union agenda but is a sensitive subject because of the importance of overtime in the male wage packet. In 1979 Melbourne's Working Women's Centre discussed the impact of shiftwork on family and social life, and emphasised that the absence of a father is just as disruptive as the absence of a mother (Owen and Shaw, 1979: 46). A 1986 ACTU *Action Program for Women Workers* calls for a general reduction in overtime which would also 'assist in reducing the discrepancies in earnings between males and females' (ACTU, 1986: 10). A recent tripartite Conference on Legislative and Award Restrictions, with representatives from government, industry and unions, heard a paper which concluded that the 'adverse occupational health and safety effects of shiftwork affected men and women equally' and called for a national code of practice on forward rotation and maximum number of continuous night shifts and workload. The ACTU and the CAI (Confederation of Australian Industry) agreed, however, *only* to the '*removal of outdated restrictions on the hours of employment for women*' (Conference, 1986: 14, 27—emphasis added).

Australia is having more success with the modification of restrictive weight-lifting standards for women. A recent New South Wales Sex Discrimination case drew attention to the discriminatory effects of such legislation, which exists in five Australian states. Thirty Port Kembla women, who were denied employment at Australian Iron and Steel on the grounds that the company had to abide by Section 36 of the *NSW Factories, Shops and Industries Act* which sets a sixteen kilogram lifting limit for women, registered an appeal. A Report prepared by Chloe Refshauge revealed that management used the weight-lifting limitation in a cavalier fashion to keep women in certain tasks and to bar them from others and from promotion (Refshauge, 1984: 73–75; Burvill, 1985: 27–29). Refshauge recommended substituting legislation sufficiently flexible to take account of individual variation in workplace requirements. The ACTU has endorsed a 'preferred standard' on manual handling which advocates a limit of sixteen kilograms on unaided lifting for *both* men and women. The larger goal, as declared, is to 'reduce the burden for workers' and to 'secure safe work practices that apply regardless of sex'.

It is misleading, therefore, to present sex-based specification of occupational safety standards as incompatible with the pursuit of equal opportunity. The solution to this 'conflict of principles' is to make so-called 'women's standards' effective standards for all. Protective legislation should be reviewed, according to an ACTU Working Women's Charter, with one aim in mind—'protecting both male and female workers' health' (ACTU, 1985: 5). As Chloe Refshauge says, 'When adequate health and safety standards have been achieved for all workers, then all workers will have the protection they need' (Refshauge, 1984: 83).

The recommendation to 'level up' may appear to be more difficult to adopt in cases to do with women's 'unique' reproductive functions, or at least this would be the claim made by those companies who have excluded women of childbearing years from certain occupations because of threats to the fetus. The most notorious case is that of the American Cyanamid Company where five women underwent sterilisation in order to win back their jobs (Williams, 1981: 642). Although there may well be other motivations such as restricting female competition, the employers have defended their policy on two grounds: first, that they have a moral responsibility and would probably be held liable under America's Occupational Safety and Health Act (1970)[4] to protect the health of the next generation, and second, that the injured offspring of workers could file suit against negligent employers. Their defence against a charge of sex discrimination is that women are *unique* in their susceptibility in this area. Hence they are 'unlike' men and 'different' treatment is not discrimination. To justify their use of a sex classification, the employers argued that it is a vital 'business necessity' to fulfil their obligations under federal health standards and to protect themselves against litigation.

Wendy Williams feels that the 'comparisons' or equal treatment model of American antidiscrimination legislation is adequate to prevent the type of discrimination evident in so-called 'fetal protection' policies. She would like to see the courts enforce Title VII strictly, and refuse to accept *any defence* to a policy which excluded women of childbearing age from employment. This would force the company to develop a gender-neutral policy directed to the reproductive health of all workers, if it chose to develop any policy at all. Williams admits the vital importance of the Occupational Safety and Health Act without which employers could simply decide to expose all employees to hazards 'equally' (Williams, 1981: 701–703).

Under this strict interpretation of Title VII employers would not be able simply to use the argument that female workers were subject to *unique* risks. They would have to *prove* this fact and prove also that there was no adequate alternative with a less discriminatory effect to exclusion from the workplace (Williams, 1981: 667). While this approach would force employers to undertake the required scientific research to prove their case and to consider such alternatives as temporary job transfer, however, it would still leave open the option of firing women where there is 'clear evidence of unequal jeopardy' (Williams, 1981: 664, 667; Law, 1984: 1030). To eliminate this possibility it seems that an amendment to Title VII *defining* exclusionary policies as discriminatory would be necessary. This would make it compulsory for employers to meet *all* health-related employment needs on a non-discriminatory basis and hence would remove the incentive to identify any workers as 'hypersusceptible'. As to the employer's concern regarding litigation, as Joan Bertin says, 'an employer's best protection is to prevent foreseeable injury' (Bertin, 1989).

Britain has also had to address the 'fetal protection' problem. In *Page v Freight Hire* the Employment Appeal Tribunal held that women could be excluded from certain jobs if the employer 'thinks it right not to allow an employee for his (or her) safety, to do the particular job' (McGinley, 1986: 435; O'Donovan, 1985: 168). The EOC responded by recommending that provisions relating to lead and ionising radiation, the two most discussed hazards, should require men and women to be treated equally, 'except in so far as it may be necessary to protect the fetus'. As far as ionising radiation is concerned, the Commission recommended narrowing the category from all women of childbearing age to 'women of reproductive capacity', in the hope that this would exclude fewer women (EOC, 1979: 220–221).

The NCCL criticised the EOC for treating the question of reproductive hazards in the workplace 'as if reproduction were an exclusively female preserve'. The Council objected both to the assumption that all women will bear children and to the lack of attention directed towards the male reproductive system. On the grounds that there is adequate evidence to suggest that men are also vulnerable to the effects of certain toxic substances and that 'the children fathered by these men are more likely to be damaged than other children', the NCCL recommended that the standards set for pregnant women be *extended* to include men (NCCL, 1988: 9, 11–12; Coussins, 1979: 15). The Council in other words is prepared to enforce higher standards of protection for all, removing the possibility that employers might argue women's greater susceptibility. This proposal states in different words the proposition in this book that women's sex-specific needs be included in the standard.

In the comparison between the EOC's and the NCCL's approaches to protective legislation, a paradox emerges. As we have seen, the NCCL has fought for years to retain a ban on nightwork for women. Using the categories suggested by Catharine Stimpson in the Prologue to this section of the book, the group appears to be 'maximalist' because of this willingness to identify women's 'special' needs. However, as far as reproduction is concerned, it does not wish women to be singled out, and appears to be 'minimalist'. The 1988 report reads:

> Only in a small minority of cases, however, and each case viewed on its own particular merits, should protective legislation distinguish between men and women. In most instances, special health and safety measures will be required for women only during pregnancy. On no account should women be automatically excluded from employment by virtue of supposedly different physical factors (NCCL, 1988: 16).

In contrast, the EOC clearly endorses an equal treatment ('minimalist') approach to protective legislation, seen in the opposition to hours laws, and yet holds out for 'special treatment' ('maximalism') in the one area of women's reproductive capacity. This seems to suggest not only that the categories overlap but, more significantly, that the reasons for adopting a position have less to do with whether one thinks a woman is more the 'same as' or 'different from' a man than with other political goals. The EOC's motives seem to be a mix of a desire to deregulate and a nationalist concern for the health of the nation. The NCCL places a priority upon addressing the immediate needs of women and challenging stereotypes which have been used against women in the past.

Australian feminists in the main are closer to the NCCL position. There is no obvious split between those prepared to remove protection laws and those wanting to extend them to men. Almost all agree on the latter policy. Valerie Pratt, Director of the recently-formed Affirmative Action Agency, wants to apply 'commonsense attitudes' and go by the scientific evidence which reveals the chromosomal damage men suffer on exposure to certain compounds (Pratt interview, 24 August 1987). Carmel Niland, former President of the New South Wales Anti-Discrimination Board, states simply that 'there is a responsibility and onus on the employer to create an environment in the workplace which is healthy....' (Niland interview, 26 August 1987). Diana Wyndham of the University of New South Wales Social Welfare Research Centre makes the same point: 'A woman should not have to have herself sterilised to keep a hazardous job, neither should men nor women have to risk their health or that of their unborn children by working in toxic environments' (Wyndham, 1981: 273). The ACTU's safety representative's handbook emphasises that many fetotoxic agents are also toxic to the male reproductive system. The policy of excluding women, therefore, is logically absurd since, 'if a policy of excluding workers is to prevail, then it should apply to men as well as women—that would leave few eligible workers—in fact only the neutered and the sterilised' (Matthews, 1985: 429–430).

These ideas were brought home to the Australian government at the recent tripartite Conference on Legislative and Award Restrictions, referred to earlier, when Josephine Tiddy, the South Australian Commissioner for Equal Opportunity, pressed for a national code of practice on hazardous substances. The suggestion received support from the ACTU, CAI and participating state governments (Conference, 1986: 11–12). While Australia seems prepared to extend certain parts of protective legislation to men, Australian feminists need to remember the union stance on hours legislation and that the situation could be very different under a different government (Johnson and Wajcman, 1986: 91). For the purposes of this study what is important is that, where the government seems prepared to accept responsibility for improving working conditions across the board, feminists are not forced to divide into contending 'sameness' and 'differences' factions. The situation in Australia also confirms that there is no necessary contradiction between safe working conditions and equal opportunities (Wyndham, 1981: 273).

The suggestion that 'women's' protections be extended to men raises another important theoretical point. On first appearances the fact that some women were forced to undergo sterilisation to save their jobs, to 'sacrifice their "femaleness"' in Joan Bertin's words, seems a prime example of women being compelled to fit into a workplace designed for men. But Bertin also makes the point that 'hazards are often ignored or minimised, except when they involve female aspects of reproduction' and that men are wrongly presumed invulnerable 'to the effects of chemical exposures until conclusive and undeniable evidence of hazard has been amassed' (Bertin, 1989). The assumption that women and reproduction are coterminous has meant that scientific enquiry almost completely ignores the male reproductive system (Kenney, 1986: 398). Women have been constructed as *vulnerable* for a multitude of political and economic reasons—to keep them in certain jobs and out of others, and to keep them reproducing—but men have been constructed as *invulnerable* for economic and political reasons as well, mainly to obviate the necessity of creating genuinely healthy working conditions. This may be a 'male norm', but it is probably a norm many men would now prefer to reject. Putting reproduction onto the political agenda has revealed that neither men nor women are the neutered automatons of liberal theory, although the sexual division of labour has made it easier for men to approximate this model. Katherine O'Donovan drives the same point home forcefully:

Is it possible to promote a free labour market which all persons enter devoid of personal aspects concerning their reproductive capacities and their family responsibilities? At present all women are assumed to carry with them their personal baggage, and no men are. The classification is not only over-inclusive, but also wrong (O'Donovan, 1985: 168).

The parallel, though apparently paradoxical, conceptual break-through is that, once it is acknowledged that the marketplace has to accommodate human beings rather than automatons, it becomes possible to press for women's *specific* needs. Surely the recognition of the importance of human attributes in the employment environment means the recognition of heterogeneous attributes. The problem with the model constructed so far is that it has assumed that, in order to address *women's* problems, they have to be shown to be *men's* problems as well. That is, if it could be established that male reproductive systems were *also* affected by toxic compounds, then maybe the hazard would be eliminated. The claim which should be made is that, even if there is concrete evidence that *only* the fetus is affected and *only* through the mother, this is sufficient evidence to demand that the threat to fetal health, rather than the woman, be removed. Women have to be *included* in the standards, not asked to live up to existing standards or set aside as a special case. As Frances Olsen says:

Men should be neither a model nor a contrast. Women should not have to claim to be just like men to get decent treatment, nor should they have to focus on *their* differences *from men* to justify themselves whenever they demand a policy different from the present treatment afforded to men (Olsen, 1986: 1541).[5]

Sally Kenney has some useful insights on this point. She shows that there are good strategic reasons to press the case that women and men are probably equally vulnerable to toxic substances. For one, given the way in which antidiscrimination law is currently interpreted, arguing equal vulnerability of women and men fore-closes the possibility that women will be excluded from the work on the grounds that they are 'different'. The 'equal vulnerability' argument is also likely to win many male trade union support-ers who are concerned about male workers' health (Kenney, 1986: 411). However, as Kenney says, there are dangers in this approach. In cases where it is difficult to prove equal vulnerability or in cases where it is clear that the fetus is affected only through the woman, the door to exclusion reopens. As in the pregnancy example, therefore, while it is useful to show that men are also disadvantaged by work rules which treat employees like childless people, it is vital to keep women as primary actors.

The demand that women's sex-specific needs be included in the standard by which work rules are set achieves this goal. This proposal restates Catharine MacKinnon's 'inequality' approach to sex discrimination under which any 'difference' between women and men would never be allowed to justify differential treatment which disadvantaged women (MacKinnon, 1979: 106). To make this demand more realisable and to capitalise on some of the strategic advantages of the 'equal vulnerability' argument, one could 'marry' the two approaches, using the European Parliament's Directive on Lead as a model. The Parliament demanded that the directive set a 'single low standard' of exposure for women and men, 'not only because men's reproductive health was at risk by the higher standard but because to set a dual standard would be discriminatory' (Kenney, 1986: 408).

Putting this case is clearly more difficult in some contexts than in others. It is particularly difficult in America where the possibility of 'levelling up' seems remote. Many feminists there fear that *any* acknowledgement of women's *particular* needs will be used against them. These fears lie behind the equal treatment/special treatment debate regarding maternity leave. The same tension surfaces predictably over any suggestion that pregnant women may require other types of 'special' consideration.

In 1984 Wendy Chavkin, an acknowledged exponent of 'special treatment', edited a book entitled *Double Exposure: Women's Health Hazards on the Job and at Home*. Chavkin insists upon putting gender squarely on the occupation health and safety agenda for three reasons:

1 Women work in ghettoized jobs and therefore face the hazards particular to those jobs.
2 Women's physical role in reproduction means women have specific health needs at work.
3 The work women do in the home is not acknowledged to be work, so that hazardous conditions there and on the community level are not taken seriously.

Chavkin mentions that exposure to toxic substances can affect men's reproduction as well as women's, but her focus is upon the 'workers' "femaleness" per se' (Chavkin, 1984: 4–5). In another publication Chavkin insists that work rules accommodate pregnant women, that employers facilitate breastfeeding and that, although the results differ when race and class factors are taken into account, pregnant women be relieved of physically fatiguing job activities which cause premature delivery and which could affect fetal outcome (Chavkin, 1986: 467–469).

The almost deliberate reference to 'femaleness per se' sparked a predictable reaction from the equal treatment lobby. In a review of *Double Exposure* Joan Bertin criticised the 'glorification of motherhood' and the representation of women 'as a class' 'always more vulnerable, more susceptible or more disabled by the unique characteristics associated with their gender than men are' (Bertin, 1986: 92–93). In an interview Chavkin claimed that the equal treatment group just do not think that 'pregnancy is a big deal', though she also admitted the tactical limitations of both sides: 'I see where mine is vulnerable and I see where theirs doesn't get us very far' (Chavkin interview, 18 March 1988). The problem for women in America is simply 'Damned If You Do, Damned If You Don't' (Chavkin, 1984: viii).

Both Chavkin and Bertin were sensitive to the fact that their personal experience produced different emphases in their analyses. Chavkin is an obstetrician and gynecologist, currently Director of the Bureau of Maternity Services and Family Planning, New York City Department of Health. Bertin is an attorney with the Women's Rights Project of the American Civil Liberties Union. Bertin noted perceptively:

> What may be lacking in her experience is precisely what is overwhelming in mine: knowledge of the ways in which women's 'uniqueness' has been turned against them in the competition for education, employment, dignity, and status (Bertin, 1986: 93).

She did not note, however, that what was lacking in her experience was overwhelming in Chavkin's—the particular difficulties faced by pregnant women in waged work.

In Britain similarly personal experience affects whether one chooses to emphasise or to downplay women's specific requirements. The Maternity Alliance, which deals daily with the concrete problems facing pregnant women, follows NCCL's policy on 'levelling up' as far as protection from hazardous substances is concerned, but is also prepared to propose that guidelines take account of the fact that pregnant women are 'particularly susceptible to back injury'. The Alliance also proposes that the period in which employers are *prohibited* from employing women after child-birth be extended from four to six weeks (Maternity Alliance, 1988: 3–5).

In contrast, while insisting upon different treatment for structural reasons such as women's domestic responsibilities, the NCCL, as we have seen (see page 144), is reluctant to draw attention to biological 'differences'. Paddy Stamp told me that '...the kinds of additional needs that pregnant women have are comparatively few'. She drew analogies between pregnancy and other disabilities. In her opinion transferring pregnant women to less arduous work bore 'an obvious parallel with the man who just had a hernia operation or an operation on his prostate...that's basic health and safety legislation but I don't think it's specific to pregnancy'. Stamp, like Bertin, is probably more familiar, because of her NCCL experience, with the ways in which women's 'differences' have been used against them. Institutional constraints force feminists to choose between unattractive alternatives.

In Australia it no longer seems quite so necessary to avoid references to women's *specific* needs. The National Occupational Health and Safety Commission has an Advisory Group on Women's Issues which among other things has been set up to 'identify the particular occupational health and safety problems faced by women' (Conference, 1986: 30). The ACTU safety representative's handbook has a section on the 'Specific physical and physiological needs of women'. These include the need to fit the job to the woman ergonomically, the possibility that 'women have a different hormonal response to stress than men', and the possibility that 'forced retention of urine' is more of a problem for women because 'their bladders are smaller than those of men'. The handbook even dares to raise the sensitive subjects of menstruation and pre-menstrual tension. On the latter it concludes that the 'evidence for PMT does not stand up', besides which '...it would open the door to employers using PMT to exclude women from certain jobs'. On the former it resolves that:

> ...menstruation does not normally incapacitate a woman, and that work will not normally make menstruation more painful or uncomfortable provided work is organised with women's comfort in mind (Matthews, 1985: 424).

Where it becomes feasible to demand reasonable working conditions for all workers, women need neither to emphasise their particular vulnerability nor deny their sex-specific needs.

While it may seem reasonable to ask that work be organised 'with women's comfort in mind', once the full implications of the proposition are explored, it becomes clear how truly radical it is and hence why it is so resisted. Fully extended, *including* women in the standards reveals the hidden gender bias which has permitted employers to ignore certain problems; it threatens to increase employer responsibility in ways which are bound to prove costly, at least in initial calculations; and, most radical of all, it challenges the sharp division between paid work and family life which facilitates worker (unpaid and paid) exploitation.

In America, as Graham Wilson and Virginia Sapiro explain, occupational health and safety standards contain a gender bias because of the focus upon accidents rather than upon diseases, while women are more likely to be found in industries 'where health risks appear to be more important problems than accidents' (Wilson and Sapiro, 1985: 141). Gender 'neutrality' also ignores the structural impact of the sex-segregated labour market which means that women congregate in certain kinds of jobs with particular problems. For example, since women are concentrated in labour-intensive, repetitive jobs, such as assembly or clerical work, they display a higher incidence of repetitive strain injury (Matthews, 1985: 419). Women's differential location has effects which need to be addressed.

Another occupational health 'discovery' is that the major health problem for women workers 'involves their having *two jobs*, as worker and housewife' (Owen and Shaw, 1979: 53). The fatigue which may then lead to accidents is often attributable to the double burden. Normal work stress is also frequently compounded by anxiety about childcare. Any serious attempt to remedy problems in the workplace can therefore no longer ignore the intimate relationship between home and paid work. Nor can society persist in disregarding the occupational health problems of houseworkers, and these are considerable, by pretending that what women do at home is not really work (Wilson and Sapiro, 1985: 142. See also Darroch, 1981; Rosenberg, 1984; and Broom, 1986).

Extrapolating in the other direction, from the 'private' to the 'public', the 'discovery' of sexual harassment has revealed the extent to which 'private' attitudes can create work problems. Sexual harassment presents a threat to women's health since it produces stress and stress-related illnesses. It therefore not only affects 'the quality of the lives of the women themselves, but the quality of the work they can offer' (Wilson and Sapiro, 1985: 153).

Sex discrimination legislation has been forced to recognise this fact, at least to the extent that it is possible to claim sexual harassment as an illegal form of sex discrimination when it affects an individual's employment, retention, promotion or job performance (Koziara, 1987: 389; Gregory, 1987: 102–104; Mc-Ginley, 1986: 425–426). Australia's Sex Discrimination Act also covers harassment in educational institutions (Ronalds, 1987: 118). In South Australia sexual harassment is unlawful even if it has no clear impact on employment; it is adequate that the person 'should feel offended, humiliated or intimidated by the conduct' (*S.A. Equal Opportunity Act, 1984*, Part VI, Section 87: 35). And, while the degree of employer liability varies widely, the mere suggestion that employers have a responsibility to ensure that workplace environments impair employees neither psychologically nor physically is significant indeed.

Drawing attention to women's sex-specific biological characteristics also highlights the need to revise many general workplace standards, challenging the idea that workers can be dealt with as disembodied, and exposing the myth of the 'male norm'. According to June Redgrove:

> Most jobs have been designed for the average man, who by some peculiar quirk of fate, tends to be a white male undergraduate aged 18 to 23. This means that many jobs are unsuitable for most men and women (Redgrove, 1984: 470).

This insight should help overcome the paranoia among some feminists caused by any mention of women's physiology. It is never physiology per se which is the problem, but whether or not the workplace is responsive to the needs of its workers. And therefore if specific provisions are necessary, even desirable in some situations, it is, as Martha Fineman says, 'not because of women's inherently different internal quality but because of the discriminating qualities of the institutions with which they must deal' (Fineman, 1983: 818). If the workplace provided safe and healthy conditions for all workers, women's sex-specific needs would simply be catered for. They are labelled women's 'difference' in order to avoid this responsibility.

Finally, perhaps the greatest threat to the status quo posed by the demand that women be fully recognised as workers is the implied condemnation of the traditional work ethic. Since women are usually the ones required to juggle the double burden of waged labour and living arrangements, some have displayed less work-achievement motivation than most men. A redistribution of family responsibilities would in all likelihood require a diminution in *male* work-achievement motivation. According to June Redgrove, a new balance would 'enable men and women to fulfil themselves in more areas of life' (Redgrove, 1984: 471). Little wonder including women in the standards is perceived as threatening by those determined to increase, not to diminish, worker motivation!

Talking in terms of women's 'sameness to' or 'difference from' men can therefore be misleading and removes attention from the general inadequacy of workplace rules. Insisting that women be *included* rather than assimilated or segregated or even accepted (Littleton, 1987)[6] and examining why that inclusion is resisted highlights those inadequacies.

If a workplace is not safe for pregnant workers, therefore, it is not safe. If a workplace does not provide leave and job protection for pregnant workers, it is denying part of its workforce necessary guarantees. If pregnant workers require some consideration, the workplace should respond to the needs of these workers. If women have specific requirements and disadvantages, the workplace should respond to the needs of these workers. Now, if only men will extrapolate from these propositions to their own situation, we may begin to see the beginning of real and vital reform.

7

Sex discrimination and affirmative action

Feminists based in America:

> Legislation is inevitably abstract and therefore you tend toward
> generalisations that don't always serve the purpose that they are
> intended for...When I work with legislation I feel reduced by
> the necessary process of rules to a simplicity that, I feel, is not
> reality. All that aside, we need the legislation.
>
> *Charlotte Bunch*

> Somewhere along the way the struggle over equality becomes a
> struggle over definition.
>
> *Shirley Dennis*

> Regarding Title VII of the Civil Rights Act (1964), 'it gave a
> floor, not a ceiling to equality' (with reference to a State law
> that provides for pregnancy disability leave).
>
> *Ruth Shinn*

> The will to enforce the law is weaker than the law itself and
> that is a terrible limitation.
>
> *Leslie Wolfe*

> It is not sufficient to say what we need is equality. What we
> need is to reorganise services and supports so that we're not
> just reflecting the old-fashioned norm of men doing one thing
> and women doing the other. Much legislation that actually
> takes account of women's needs, that you are not going to get
> through an equality approach, is necessary.
>
> *Nadine Taub*

> In a society like the United States men are so deprived of so
> many basic human rights that fighting for equality with them is
> a short-sighted and stupid goal.
>
> *Wendy Chavkin*

> When you are talking about differences you always have to
> separate out the differences that sexist history has created, that

legislation can be used to rectify, and the differences that our reproductive capacities have created—in which case we have to create laws that don't perpetuate inequalities but do recognise them.

Catharine Stimpson

Feminists based in Britain:

What we are on about is moving the dialectic along, changing the language, changing the terms of the debate. We started off in this country talking about the whole question of equality in terms of discrimination. It became very clear after quite a short time that direct discrimination scarcely matters...The real difficulties are about the way the whole social fabric works.

Elizabeth Vallance

Equality of opportunity is actually about removing barriers and obstacles whether they are a result of inherent biological differences or whether they are a result of different social conditioning or different opportunities in the past or whatever.

Paddy Stamp

Regarding affirmative action, 'When people say it's unfair I do get very angry. When you think of how unfair men have been to us all these years!'

Mary Stott

You have to somehow transcend both the difference and the non-difference, the equality and the non-equality by actually looking for a situation which basically reflects women's political needs.

...Equality without demands about the way the organisation works and the nature of power is a dangerous demand.

Cynthia Cockburn

Equality is a relevant concept but an extremely difficult one. On the one hand it could mean the same treatment or the same outcomes, and on the other hand it could mean different treatment and possibly different outcomes. I prefer concepts like justice and autonomy because I think it is an open question whether that would require different treatment for men and women or whether it would require the same. Perhaps in our particular society, you need policies which do both.

Elizabeth Meehan

Feminists based in Australia:

The men can actually vaguely grasp what you are talking about when you are talking about not discriminating against women.

But after a little while they look at you with little eyes and say, but you seem to be saying that you should discriminate in favour of women, because they have children.

Denise Bradley

Equality means equality of opportunity given also the biological role that we play.

Valerie Pratt

When we are dealing with equality legislation we have to write into it a series of provisions. Firstly, equality legislation is based on the premise of comparing the genders in the same or similar circumstances and working out if one gender suffers a disadvantage or a detriment when they are not treated equally. We then have to write into that legislation provisions to protect pregnancy because that is not a comparable thing. There is no way you can compare a pregnancy with a prostate. That's in equality legislation. You then have to write in special provisions to protect affirmative action in employment and in other areas, or the minor affirmative action provisions which protect and nurture human difference so that the move is not to androgyny...

Carmel Niland

Feminists operate within specific political and historical contexts. This theme has been raised several times previously. It means that feminists work with inherited legal structures and ideas which constrain their analyses in some ways. The inheritance includes nebulous concepts like equality and liberty which form part of our commonsense understanding of socially desirable goals. It also includes more concrete and cumbersome collections of rules enshrined in constitutions or legislative precedent. The debates among some feminists over maternity leave and protective legislation (Chapters 5 and 6 respectively) are largely a result of attempts to fit women's diverse experiences to established and inflexible rules, and to political structures unwilling to accept responsibility for human needs.

One of the chief problems feminists encounter in both these cases is the nature of sex discrimination legislation and in particular, as mentioned previously, the fundamental antidiscrimination principle, that *likes should be treated alike* (Fiss, 1977: 85). This principle lies behind American, British and Australian sex discrimination legislation. As far as maternity leave in America is concerned, it creates the possibility that men could claim discrimination if women were judged to be treated more favourably. In weight-lifting and foetal protection cases, it permits women to be excluded from certain jobs on the grounds that they are 'different', and hence could be treated 'differently'. Both constructions allow employers and governments to evade social responsibility, in the first case for the reproduction of citizens and in the second for safe working conditions for all employees. In both cases, as Martha Minow notes, feminists have been compelled to resort to sameness and difference arguments 'simply to be heard within a judicial or legislative forum' (Minow, 1985a: 1093). While the task is daunting, it is clear that to break out of the dichotomy it is necessary to challenge the terms of analysis.

This chapter begins this process. It traces the evolution of sex discrimination legislation, examines the basic confusion over the meaning of 'discrimination' and the way in which it has become linked with 'difference', and shows how this has created problems for feminists seeking to use existing laws to instigate needed reforms. The common understanding of antidiscrimination, for example, has caused a few feminists to fear and condemn affirmative action. More frequently, *anti-feminists* accuse feminists who endorse both equal opportunity and affirmative action of inconsistency on the grounds that you cannot have both 'equal treatment' and 'different treatment'. The purpose of this chapter is to demonstrate that it is inappropriate to set equal treatment against different treatment in this way. Like other cases where a sameness/difference framework is used, setting up an opposition between these principles has the effect of averting necessary social change.

America has no single Sex Discrimination Act, but rather a collection of pieces of legislation at the federal and state levels which covers particular aspects of discrimination, such as access to credit or educational facilities.[1] The difficulty in achieving quick and comprehensive change in this setting has led feminists there to concentrate their efforts upon judicial interpretation of both Title VII of the Civil Rights Act and of the Equal Protection Clause of the Fourteenth Amendment of the Constitution (see page 277 fn.5). This amendment was introduced in 1868 to enable the federal government to strike down the ignominious Black Codes or Slave Codes which denied Blacks the opportunity to own property, attend schools, or enter certain occupations. Despite the anomalies of the separate-but-equal decisions over the next 100 years which illustrate the susceptibility of the clause to the vagaries of judicial interpretation, 'equal protection' was interpreted to mean that 'those who are similarly situated be similarly treated'. And after 1964 it was more or less accepted that 'people of different races are always similarly situated' (Goldstein, 1988: 88; Babcock, Freedman, Norton and Ross, 1975: 71; Freedman, 1983: 928). Race discrimination became the model for sex discrimination in America (seen again in Title VII) and in Australia and Britain,[2] with the result that discrimination came to mean 'different treatment' of 'similarly situated people'.

The problem in applying the Equal Protection Clause and anti-discrimination legislation to women was that most judges were convinced that innate *differences* between women and men prevented them from being 'similarly situated' and therefore justified treating them 'differently'. In a classic case in 1873 Myra Bradwell was denied access to the bar to practise as a lawyer on the grounds that she was a married woman and that '... the civil law, as well as nature herself, has always recognised a wide difference in the respective spheres and destinies of man and woman' (Goldstein, 1988: 71). The famous Brandeis brief which produced hours limitations for employed women in 1908 used an elaborate differences argument to justify different treatment. The court in the end conceded:

> ... that her (woman's) physical structure and a proper
> discharge of her maternal functions—having in view not
> merely her own health, but the well-being of the race—justify
> legislation to protect her from the greed as well as the passion
> of man (Goldstein, 1988: 22).

Brandeis had to argue 'difference' to obviate an equal protection challenge from men that they too needed protection against inhuman work conditions, a challenge employers would have fought strenuously.

In subsequent years an appeal to women's differences was used to exclude them from all sorts of activities. It became in effect the grounds upon which courts upheld nearly all cases of sex discrimination (Baer, 1978: 66). The merest suggestion of 'difference' seemed adequate in some cases to treat women unfairly. In 1948, when Ms Goesaert challenged a Michigan statute that prohibited a woman from serving liquor as a bartender unless she was 'the wife or daughter of the male owner', Justice Frankfurter dismissed the case in an almost cavalier fashion:

> The fact that women may now have achieved the virtues that
> men have long claimed as their prerogatives and now indulge in
> vices that men have long practiced, does not preclude the States
> from drawing a sharp line between the sexes, certainly in such
> matters as the regulation of the liquor traffic (Goldstein, 1988:
> 102).

Feminist reformers became convinced that, in order for women to be treated fairly, they had to stop the courts from using arguments from difference to discriminate against women. They wanted 'sex' therefore to be made a 'suspect' classification under the Fourteenth Amendment. This would mean that, as with race, reference to group characteristics would be 'suspected (or assumed) to be "invidious" (based on unreasoning group antagonisms) until proven to be justified by a "compelling legislative purpose"' (Goldstein, 1988: 89). Because of the way in which references to women's 'differences' had been used against them, feminist lawyers concluded that 'Our legal structure will continue to support and command an inferior status for women so long as it permits any differentiation in legal treatment on the basis of sex' (Brown, Emerson, Falk and Freedman, 1971: 873). Those who felt that the Equal Protection Clause would never adequately protect women against this form of discrimination promoted a new Constitutional Amendment, the Equal Rights Amendment, which would 'obliterate sex as a functional classification within the law' (Babcock, Freedman, Norton and Ross, 1975: 256). In short, the history of antidiscrimination jurisprudence made 'difference' a dirty word in the feminist vocabulary.

Judges, however, were not easily convinced that 'different treatment' disadvantaged women. Common beliefs about women's social duties produced the conviction that the court had a role to play in protecting women, or perhaps more precisely, in protecting their function as reproducers of the race and mainstays of the family. In 1961, in *Hoyt v Florida*, the Supreme Court upheld a statute which excluded women from jury service unless they volunteered, on the grounds that 'woman is still regarded as the center of home and family life'. She should therefore 'be relieved of the civic duty of jury service unless she herself determines that such service is consistent with her own responsibilities' (Goldstein, 1988: 107–108). The presumption here was that 'women's' homemaking role precluded them from certain citizenship responsibilities unless they insisted upon being included.

The courts have proved susceptible to changing social standards, however. In a landmark 1971 case (*Reed v Reed*) the Supreme Court struck down an Idaho statute creating an automatic preference for men over women of the same entitlement class to administer estates. With respect to such activities, it was decided, women and men were 'similarly situated' and hence there was no justification for treating them differently (Scales, 1986: 1374). The same year a California Supreme Court, in a case similar to *Goesaert v Cleary* (1948) (see above), ruled that a state statute excluding women from bartending violated equal protection and that the 'pedestal upon which women have been placed has... upon closer inspection, been revealed as a cage' (Goldstein, 1988: 511). Two years later, in *Frontiero v Richardson*, the Supreme Court ruled that it constituted discrimination for Sharron Frontiero, a lieutenant in the US Air Force, to receive fewer benefits towards the support of her dependent husband than male members of the 'uniformed services' who had dependent wives (Goldstein, 1988: 116).

The feminist lawyer, Ruth Ginsburg, used male litigants in a series of cases to press further upon the judiciary the injustice of outmoded stereotypes. Her strategy, to prove that 'discrimination by gender cuts with two edges', that in fact men could be disadvantaged by laws which singled women out for different treatment, proved very successful (the cynic might add, perhaps not surprisingly). In *Craig v Boren* (1976) the Supreme Court struck down an Oklahoma law which permitted girls to buy beer at age eighteen, three years younger than the legal age for boys. And in *Califano v Goldfarb* (1977) the court recognised the justice of equal social security provisions for widows and widowers, whereas previously widows had been favoured (Ginsburg, 1978: 145).

According to Wendy Williams these and similar decisions simply reflected the fact that the Supreme Court now recognised that the real world outside the courtroom had changed, and that the breadwinner–homemaker stereotype no longer applied in many families (Williams, 1982: 179). Equal access cases could also be appreciated by judges schooled in the civil rights era. In the words of Kenneth Karst, 'The Justices easily recognize the stereotypical construct of woman when it directly hinders access to the ladder' (Karst, 1984: 470).

The decision about when 'differences' are relevant or irrelevant, about when the court ought to acknowledge or ignore them, however, remains highly controversial. Ann Freedman identifies two separate approaches to legislative sex classifications in the courts since the mid-1970s. One, the Rehnquist-Stewart approach, focuses upon the identification of 'real' differences, and led to the infamous *Gilbert* decision (see page 113) which concluded that, since men could not get pregnant, men and women could not be 'similarly situated' with regard to a company's disability insurance policy. Hence pregnant women could be treated differently, that is, excluded from coverage. In the Title VII case of *Dothard v. Rawlinson* (1977) the Rehnquist-Stewart interpretation was applied to an Alabama rule that restricted women's employment as prison guards. The court decided that the restriction was not discriminatory because the 'employee's very womanhood' was a 'real' difference which would make her more susceptible to sexual assault and 'would thus directly undermine her capacity to provide the security that is the essence of a correctional counsellor's responsibility' (Freedman, 1983: 930–937; Goldstein, 1988: 509).

The second approach, the Brennan-Marshall approach, permits the use of sex-based classifications only if they are 'substantially related' to an 'important' governmental goal. Freedman grants that the Brennan-Marshall presumption is in favour of sex-neutral rules but feels that it runs into trouble in the 'hard' cases identified by Wendy Williams. These are cases such as the exclusion of women from the military draft, and the imposition of criminal penalties for statutory rape only on males, cases where it remains unclear if the different treatment is due to 'outmoded' stereotypes (Freedman, 1983: 953; see also Williams, 1982).

The American background has been traced in some detail in order to explain the strong commitment of America's equal treatment feminists to denying any identification of woman as different. If judges start from the presumption that women and men are *not* similarly situated in the way in which the peoples of all races are, feminists are automatically involved in the task of trying to prove that women *are* similarly situated. The judges' assumption that all distinctions between races are odious, but that some sex classifications are indeed beneficent also impels feminists to emphasise 'sameness'. As Richard Wasserstrom says, sexism in our society is a 'deeper' phenomenon than racism because the identification of women as 'different' is built into commonsense understanding of the way the world runs. It is so deeply embedded in ideological assumptions that we are inclined 'to take as appropriate even overt instances of sexist laws, e.g., that it is appropriately a part of the definition of rape that a man cannot rape his wife' (Wasserstrom, 1977: 602). The judiciary, aptly described as in the main a 'monopoly of elderly, white men from privileged backgrounds' (Gregory, 1987: 153), is more rather than less likely to hold these views, making the task of reform through the courts particularly difficult.

To say this is not to deny the racism of those judges nor to suggest that the effects of sexism are worse than the effects of racism. I tend to agree with Ruth Ginsburg that white women 'have not been impeded to the extent ghettoized minorities have', nor do most non-minority females encounter a 'formidable risk of "death at an early age"' (Ginsburg, 1978: 147). As Bell Hooks points out, one of the main problems with the race/sex analogy is that it makes Black women disappear from the analysis (Hooks,

1981: 141). The analogy is strained. We are using 'borrowed language' which can work only in cases closely modelled on racial civil rights cases (Finley, 1986: 1164 fn. 197; 1142, fn. 108).

The notion of discrimination which emerged from 1960s civil rights battles has, in point of fact, proved inadequate *both* for Blacks and for women. In the first instance discrimination seemed obviously to be a result of malice or evil motive, and there were doubtless many cases which displayed this character. In an attempt to get a better understanding of the phenomenon, sociologists transformed 'malice' into 'prejudice', interpreted as an irrational reaction to 'difference'. This had several effects, according to Julian Henriques. It reduced racism to individual aberration and suppressed recognition of institutional and structural racism. It also seemed to suggest that, since racism was due to a mistaken belief that people are 'different', 'differences' do not exist, making it difficult to address the 'differences' which resulted from social and economic causes, that is, from differential social location. It had another effect on policy by shifting the focus from the perpetrator to the 'objects' of prejudice, in this case Blacks, to see just what it was about them which caused others to perceive them as different. It also implied that the problem would go away if we launched a consciousness-raising campaign to draw attention to the shared humanity of Blacks and the rest of 'us' (Henriques et al., 1984: 64–74). Similar difficulties have arisen in the reaction to sexism.

Feminists who encountered 'women's bald exclusion from opportunities open to men' initially attributed discriminatory behaviour to an inaccurate assessment of women's abilities. They soon realised, however, that the problem went deeper than misunderstanding, and that judgments about women were based upon sex stereotypes shaped and reinforced by 'a powerful informing ideology, inherited from the nineteenth century, about the proper allocation of the tasks of the sexes' (Taub and Williams, 1985: 825–826). Since these stereotypes formed the basis of the conclusion that women were 'different', which was subsequently used against them, the strategy became to raise the consciousness of the judges to recognise the inaccuracy of those stereotypes.

As in the case of racism therefore the idea developed that the cause of discrimination was predominantly the behaviour of ill-informed people operating with outmoded ideas about the sexes. The argument ran that individuals should not be judged by unsubstantiated generalisations, but by their personal abilities. The model is an individualistic one. Within this tradition the Equal

Rights Amendment calls for the elimination of 'rigid sex role determinism' and the recognition of 'individual potential' and 'individual self-fulfillment'. Classification by sex is considered wrong because it is over-inclusive and ignores the extent to which *some persons* break free of stereotypes: 'Such a result is in direct conflict with the basic concern of our society with the individual, and with the rights of each individual to develop his or her own potentiality' (Brown, Emerson, Falk and Freedman, 1971: 885, 890). Stereotypes are indeed 'damaging', and Nadine Taub's suggestion that their use be automatically labelled discrimination is a progressive one (Taub, 1985), but this strategy leaves many problems unresolved.

By focusing upon the individual, this approach underestimates the structural problems which prevent people from 'measuring up' to the established criteria of success.[3] Therefore only those individuals who manage to free themselves from those structural disadvantages will succeed. And their success will no doubt leave the impression that the system is working. The types of structural disadvantages which affect women, such as those associated with the sexual division of labour, cannot be addressed using this model.

Nor will a challenge to stereotypes help women in situations where the stereotypes may be 'true' to an extent. The most 'intractable' problems arise where stereotypes are so strong that they have become some women's reality (Cole, 1984: 56). As Christine Littleton says:

> ...a focus on 'inaccuracy' ignores the possibility that the very women most damaged by an unequal social structure may be those about whom conventional assumptions are accurate, that is, those who have internalised society's limitations on their interests, abilities and social roles (Littleton, 1981: 488).

The focus upon stereotypes also perpetuates the feeling that lying behind discriminatory activity is either ignorance or malicious intent. This is the most basic understanding of discrimination and is written into our laws. Although 'malicious' motives are no longer necessary, the court's interpretation of direct discrimination under Title VII necessitates that there be an 'intent' to treat the sexes differently:

> 'Disparate treatment'....is the most easily understood type of discrimination. The employer simply treats some people less favorably than others because of their race, color, religion, sex, or national origin. Proof of discriminatory motive is critical,

> although it can in some situations be inferred from the mere
> fact of differences in treatment...(in Williams, 1981: 670).

There is a growing consensus about the need to move away from
this fault-based approach to discrimination, due partly to a new
awareness of the 'sociocultural patterns' which produce discrimination and hence disadvantage. It is impossible to compress these
problems within the 'constraints of a Nineteenth Century liberal
conception of an individualised harm giving rise to a civil action'
(Thornton, 1985: 33–34; Broom, 1984: xx). There is also a greater
concern with the *effects* rather than with the *cause* of the behaviour.
As Nadine Taub says, 'there seems to be little reason to distinguish
conscious from unconscious gender bias' (Taub, 1985: 105; see
also Wallace, 1985: 18), if harm is the result.

The idea of indirect discrimination is one important outgrowth
of experience with the inadequacy of the 'facial discrimination'
model.[4] Broadly, indirect discrimination occurs when an apparently neutral policy has a disproportionately adverse effect on a group
protected under discrimination legislation, and the employer can
produce no evidence that the rule is a pressing business necessity.
The Supreme Court recognises 'disparate impact' claims and does
not generally require proof of discriminatory motive (Williams,
1981: 670). In a key case, *Griggs v. Duke Power Company*, (1971),
a unanimous court found that a requirement for educational qualifications which were unrelated to job performance but which
effectively ruled out Blacks was discriminatory. The absence of
discriminatory intent did not '...redeem employment procedures
or testing mechanisms that operate as "built-in headwinds" for
minority groups and are unrelated to measuring job capability'
(Gregory, 1987: 34–35). Both the British and Australian governments have written 'indirect discrimination' clauses into their Sex
Discrimination legislation.[5] In an important British case, the Employment Appeal Tribunal upheld the complaint of Ms Price
against the Civil Service Commission that the upper age limit of 28
years for new applicants had a disproportionately adverse impact
on women, 'as fewer women could comply with such a requirement than men, since many in their twenties were otherwise engaged in bearing or bringing up children' (EOC, 1982: 63).

The Price case indicates the potential of disparate impact theory,
a potential feminists have been quick to recognise (O'Donovan
and Szyszczak, 1988: 97). Equal treatment and special treatment
feminists agree that it offers a way around the pregnancy dilemma.
Simply by pointing out that a short-leave or no-leave policy has a
disproportionate impact on women, the mechanism for change

may be set in place (see page 123). Expressed as a generality, that 'the way the employer organises the work might be challenged as having a disparate impact on women', the rule seems ultimately flexible. This after all is the very point to which feminists have been trying to draw attention—that the way in which the world of work is organised disadvantages many women! It is innovative both in shifting the focus from the individual to the needs of the group, and in taking some account of the reality of many women's lives (O'Donovan, 1985: 167).

The limitations are significant, however. Cases are difficult to prove, especially in Britain where courts are unaccustomed to the presentation of sociological and statistical evidence which is necessary to prove disproportionate impact. Moreover, an element of evaluation is involved at two levels, first in deciding when a woman can or cannot comply with a regulation, and then in deciding if it is justified by business necessity. In Britain the employer needs only to 'advance good grounds' 'acceptable to right thinking people'. B. A. Hepple is convinced that such a test is not rigorous enough in an area where decisions will clearly have a dramatic impact on employment practices. Hepple in fact concludes that the structure of the judicial process is not suited to the kind of 'purposive social engineering' implied in discrimination cases of this sort, and that perhaps there is a need for 'new forms of public arbitration' (Hepple, 1983: 82–85; see also Gregory, 1987: 45–46).

At a theoretical level disparate impact leaves unresolved the tension between the desire for self-actualisation and the needs of the family. It takes a step in the right direction by recognising that women's traditional domestic obligations have an effect on their workforce participation, but it does little more than recognise this. It does nothing to resolve the dilemma, and in fact seems to imply that, if domestic roles are taken into account in getting women *into* the workforce, as in the Price case, all that needs to be done has been done. Katherine O'Donovan makes the point nicely:

> The concept of indirect discrimination attempts to modify
> market requirements to meet the needs of a considerable
> number of women who cannot conform to the male model. Yet
> the dilemma for these women continues. Should they try to
> adapt to the market or will the market meet them?

So long as work rules ignore the 'claims of the private' both for women *and for men*, women will remain the ones responsible for these claims (O'Donovan, 1985: 173,179).

Disparate impact theory shares yet another limitation with other antidiscrimination legislation. As constructed, it necessitates a comparison with a comparator in order to prove less favourable treatment or disproportionate impact, and the comparator has to be a man. However, one of the largest problems facing women workers is the fact that they congregate in a few low-status, low-paying occupations. This 'sex segregation' of the workforce then creates a serious problem. In the words of Catharine MacKinnon, 'There are no men around to compare with' (Du Bois et al., 1985: 23). The example illustrates the unworkability of a model which asks only that 'likes be treated alike' (see also Kahn, 1985: 90; Thornton, 1986: 10).

Positive or affirmative action is a response to some of the obvious inadequacies in antidiscrimination legislation. It appears as several models. In America in the 1960s Presidents Kennedy and Johnson issued Executive Orders which obliged government departments and firms holding government contracts to produce written affirmative action plans under threat of contract cancellation. Under these Orders institutions conduct an analysis of their workforce and set targets for increasing the representation of women. Federal courts have at times imposed mandatory targets or quotas upon employers found guilty of discrimination (Sawer, 1985: 6). British Sex Discrimination legislation contains some modest positive action provisions which permit training schemes to be targeted at underrepresented groups. Jeanne Gregory calls the provisions 'little more than a goodwill gesture...within which people and organisations already committed to the fight against discrimination can develop programmes for action' (Gregory, 1987: 52–53). In 1986 the Australian Parliament passed the Affirmative Action (Equal Employment Opportunity) Act which required all higher education institutions and all private sector employers with 100 or more employees to produce affirmative action programs. Separate legislation requires government departments and statutory authorities to introduce Equal Employment Opportunity programs. These programs follow an eight-step model including the requirement to analyse the institution's employment profile, to consult with unions and employees, and to set objectives and forward estimates (Ronalds, 1987: 28–29).

The idea of positive or affirmative action has, perhaps not surprisingly, caused some difficulty for *strict* equal treatment feminists. Since they insist that sex 'should be a prohibited basis for official line-drawing', that is, that sex as a category should be *ignored*, it becomes difficult to ask that sex become the *grounds* for certain policies (Ginsburg, 1978: 143). The conviction that any identification of women as 'different' will be used against them has led some to conclude that they dare not run the risk of asking for any 'special treatment'. One ERA supporter warned that the 'concept of benign discrimination' was 'fraught with danger if applied to women': 'Any permitted difference in treatment as between men and women is likely to protect away women's liberties' (Eastwood in Gregory, 1987: 16). (Whether or not the ERA would prohibit such legislation is unclear [Flowers, 1977: 36; Brown, Emerson, Falk, and Freedman, 1971: 904].) Another equal treatment supporter openly condemned a recent much-publicised Supreme Court decision in favour of affirmative action (see Goldstein, 1988: 563 for details). She saw it as an attempt to revive protective legislation which in her opinion does more to harm than to help women:

> In my view, the women's movement was aimed at allowing women to compete on an equal footing without regard to their sex, and I think what this decision does is return us to the nineteenth-century concept that says women are the weaker sex and need special protections in order to compete (*New York Times*, 29 March 1987).

As argued in the preceding two chapters, there are obvious problems with accepting the designation of women as 'different'. Women are not 'different'. Quite simply, their sex-specific characteristics have been disadvantaged because society has been organised in such a way that pregnancy and childrearing are ignored. Feminists who accept or fear that these processes will continue to be ignored downplay them for strategic reasons. The determination to present women as the 'same' as men leads some to fear affirmative action because it singles women out as a disadvantaged group. Their fear of 'difference' produces a reluctance to admit the sex-specific disadvantages produced by women's differential social location. Instead of challenging the adequacy of a rule which says simply that likes be treated alike, they have taken it to an extreme.

Not all in the equal treatment camp are this negative in their reaction to affirmative action. Ginsburg is willing to accept 'transitional' programs which attempt to 'redress long-standing disadvantageous treatment' (Ginsburg, 1978: 146). Wendy Williams states explicitly that she is not 'one of those who believe that affirmative action, properly conceived and limited, is more harmful than helpful to women and minorities' (Williams, 1982: 180). But she and Nadine Taub are hesitant in their endorsement. They remain concerned that affirmative action contains 'one of the dangers of group treatment—re-enforcement of stereotypes', but they are satisfied that the danger is 'minimized by the under-lying rationale':

> Affirmative action, in theory at least, self-destructs when the group is brought up to the starting line with everyone else. It is thus an adjunct to the equal treatment, rather than a manifestation of the group treatment, approach (Taub and Williams, 1985: 830 fn. 23).

Catharine MacKinnon is not surprised that affirmative action re-mains problematic in the equal treatment approach. After all, she says, 'A differentiation still looks like a differentiation' (MacKin-non, 1979: 118).

The point is that the current understanding of antidiscrimination as treating likes alike has meant that equal treatment and the kind of 'different treatment' implied in affirmative action have been set up in opposition. Working within a framework which stipulates that you cannot expect a government to be both 'sex blind', that is, treat-ing 'sex' as a suspect category, and 'sex conscious' in affirming women's need for specific legislative assistance, feminists who for good historical reasons fear the sex conscious approach tend to opt for sex blindness. Options are artificially constrained by a narrow understanding of what constitutes discrimination.

On the other side, although special treatment theorists tend to use the language of 'positive action' to defend their approach to maternity leave (Krieger and Cooney, 1983: 513–514), not all in this group are willing to accept other forms of affirmative action. Mary Segers, who approves of special conditions for working mothers 'in order to make equal opportunity a reality', is suspi-cious of what she calls 'reverse discrimination', which in her opin-ion '. . . might well confirm and perpetuate a view of women as second-class beneficiaries of "tokenism"' (Segers, 1979: 337). The lines between the two camps are not always clearly drawn, and in some ways there are important similarities between them. Neither group in this instance seems willing to use government machinery to radically restructure workplace rules. The notion of positive action is limited on either side in America.

One might have expected a more enthusiastic reception for positive action in Britain, given the closer ideological fit between the idea of assisting specific groups and welfare capitalism (Gregory, 1987: 163). In the interviews I found nothing akin to the reluctance among some American feminists to endorse this degree of govern-ment intervention. The limited nature of the British provisions, however, and the fact that they are unlikely to be broadened by the present government has alienated those on the left in the movement. Jennifer Dale and Peggy Foster expect the Equal Opportunity Commission to have little impact on the economic position of the majority of women (Dale and Foster, 1986: 123). Gillian Pascall agrees that legislation for equal pay and against sex discrimination makes 'a small ripple on a deep pool':

> There is no legislation about who does the housework and cares for old and young; no Act of Parliament that will put women in top jobs or give them places in the public world. Where domestic work, paid work, and political work are so profoundly gender-divided, legislation about equality can touch only that minority of situations where women's lives are like men's; it leaves out those more important areas where men's and women's lives divide (Pascall, 1986: 33).

Similarly in Australia while the majority in the movement seem to be prepared to 'give the new legislation a go', those on the left expect it to produce little real change. The Australian legislation was designed with the American experience in mind. With a determination to avoid the controversy associated with quotas, the government settled for 'objectives and forward estimates'.[6] The requirement to produce an affirmative action program is at this stage voluntary and carries, for non-compliance, only the threat of being named in Parliament. Those close to the operation of the legislation, Valerie Pratt, the Director of the Affirmative Action Agency, and Hester Eisenstein, former Chief Education Officer of the Equal Employment Opportunity Unit of the NSW Department of Education, however, are optimistic. Eisenstein, with a solid background in the American women's movement, is, in her own words, 'astonished at the power of legislation in Australia' (Eisenstein interview, 25 August 1987).

Affirmative action, as it is presently conceived, however, goes no further than either direct or indirect discrimination legislation in resolving the conflict between individual and family needs. Despite its obvious importance, it has the same blind spot as antidiscrimination legislation since it does not address directly the impact of living arrangements upon workers' lives. The suggestion is not that the legislation will not work, but that it *will* work only for a few, those who are best able to approximate the male profile or, more precisely, the profile of white, middle-class males. Margaret Thornton sees affirmative action as consistent with the ideology of equal opportunity since the theory permits 'limited affirmative measures to allow women to be brought up to a point where they may compete equally with men for education and jobs'. But since it will likely benefit only those women 'who are most like their male comparators', and since it in no way confronts 'the inequities of the private sphere', Thornton has serious doubts about its effectiveness. She warns women to be wary of 'fine-sounding rhetoric and anaemic legislation' (Thornton, 1986: 9–10; 1985: 35–40; see also Rosewarne, 1988: 78). Margaret Wallace describes affirmative action as fitting comfortably into the liberal 'rat-race' model for society. It only 'takes some notice of the condition of the "runners" and of the "track"' (Wallace, 1985: 28–29) The American, Frances Olsen, offers an even more stinging condemnation in her suggestion that affirmative action hurts rather than helps women, since it creates 'another reason for women to blame themselves when they fail in the marketplace' (Olsen, 1983: 1555).

There are other problems with the principle, or at least with the way in which it is presently being implemented. In America, for example, women are being made to compete *against* minority-group men for a 10% 'set-aside' quota of highway contracts (*New York Times*, 5 March 1988). In another case, Sally Hacker followed up the impact of the requirement that A.T. & T. produce affirmative action plans and found that, while some women moved up, more moved out. In the end affirmative action 'placed thousands more men in traditionally women's work than it placed women in traditionally men's work' (Hacker, 1982: 248–255). Nor does the legislation address directly the problems faced by women in sex-segregated areas of the labour market (Game and Pringle, 1986: 290). Rather, affirmative action programs mostly benefit women already working in relatively well paid and high status jobs (Sharp and Broomhill, 1988: 84).

There are no easy answers, it seems. As feminists increase their understanding of the complexities and intractable nature of discrimination, approaches which at one time appeared sound now come up for re-examination. The growing awareness of the subtle and not-so-subtle interaction of class, race and gender variables requires the subjection of strategies to increasingly 'strict scrutiny'. The need to fit these strategies to particular institutional contexts adds to the complexity of the task.

For example, comparative or comparable worth has evolved as one tactic to deal with sex segregation in the labour force. Comparable worth cases are intended, not to alter the distribution of women and men across jobs, but to increase the value of jobs which have traditionally been female. Starting from the assumption that women's work is poorly paid, not because it is low-skilled but in fact because it is women's work, those in favour of comparable worth ask courts to employ job evaluation schedules and to set wage rates accordingly (McGinley, 1986: 440). The argument on one side is that many women are happy in their jobs and there would be no reason for them to shift if they received the wages they deserved. On the other side some feminists fear that comparable worth will reinforce sex stereotypes, lock women into traditional occupations, and impede 'genuine' affirmative action (Weinzweig, 1987: 72, 78).

The issue in Australia has been complicated by the fact that comparable worth has been pursued in the industrial arena rather than as an issue of discrimination (O'Donnell and Golder, 1986: 60). Since the idea is considered a serious challenge to traditional wage-fixing principles, some Labor feminists are disinclined to pursue it. In an introduction to a study of job evaluation in Australia, Edna Ryan warned Australian feminists not to be swayed by the slogan 'comparable worth' because of its origin in free enterprise America which ought not to provide a model for wage earners in Australia. She drew attention to the 'perceived threat to central wage fixing', the 'vital difference in the definition of work value between the American and Australian practice', and the hidden gender bias in comparable worth methods, the major point raised in the volume she was introducing. Ryan concluded that Australian women ought to settle for the existing wage settlement system: 'We delay by seeking to change the system which has served the male workforce so well. The male standard is our immediate objective' (Burton, Hag and Thompson, 1987: vii, viii). Other feminists are convinced that, because of the union commitment to traditional wage-fixing principles, they may in fact be an impediment to change (Rosewarne, 1988: 76–77; *Financial Review*, 17 October 1988: 13).

In the area of education, feminists campaigned long and hard historically to gain access to higher education, to coeducation, and to elite male educational institutions. While they are of one mind that *all-male* educational institutions ought not to be allowed to exist, however, there is less agreement about the desirability of *all-female* institutions. Those who participated in the campaigns to unlock the doors of male institutions tend to maintain a commitment to coeducation (Brown, Emerson, Falk and Freedman, 1971: 906,881; Freedman, 1983: 951; Harman, 1978: 29). But even they have been influenced by the kind of research produced by Dale Spender and others which highlights the disadvantages for girls in mixed education. Boys, for example, tend to monopolise both physical and linguistic space, and the teachers' attention (Spender and Sarah, 1980; Spender, 1978). Sexual harassment in the classroom, verbal abuse and 'put downs' become the normal experience of many girls in mixed classes (Mahoney, 1983). Segregated classes on the other hand can mean more confidence for girls in subjects like mathematics, while the boys appear to be no worse off. Girls from single-sex schools also seem to have the 'academic lead' on their coeducational sisters (*Canberra Times*, 22 March 1988).

Some of this evidence, admittedly, is debatable. It has been suggested both in Britain and in Australia that some of the comparisons have been skewed by setting single-sex *private* schools against mixed *government* institutions (Scorer and Sedley, 1983: 29; *Canberra Times*, 22 March 1988). And even if it might be true that girls perform better academically in single-sex schools, other questions need to be asked. There are questions, for example, about the gender and class relations of single-sex schooling. Single-sex schools were maintained longest by middle-class parents who wished to cultivate particular images of appropriate male and female ('lady-like') behaviour, images which need to be interrogated before they are endorsed (Adams and Arnot, 1986: 29). There are also warnings about the effects of single-sex schooling upon boys, that it produces a kind of male bonding 'which accentuates male difference from (and feelings of superiority towards) women' (Blackburn, 1984: 12). Finally tension exists between those who feel that single-sex groupings are 'tantamount to creating a cocoon', and those who feel that 'girl-centred school organisation' is the best way to train girls to encounter the male hierarchy (Inner London Education Authority, 1987: 9; Weiner, 1985: 11–12).

There are more than two sides on the question though it may sometimes appear that the debate is polarised. There is rather an increased sensitivity to the mix of influences upon attitudes and roles, and a heightened commitment to interrogate all evidence. Almost every woman I interviewed expressed ambivalence about the direction for the future. Personal factors such as their own schooling (many had come from single-sex schools), or whether they had sons to educate weighed heavily in their preference for 'equal' treatment or 'special' education. Even ardent ERA supporters seemed to hope that there might be room to manoeuvre on this particular issue: it has been suggested that the ERA might make single-sex education unconstitutional (Brown, Emerson, Falk, and Freedman, 1971: 906). For the time being it seems advisable to proceed cautiously and use a case-by-case approach.[7] The Australian education reformer, Jean Blackburn, recommends concentrating upon the sexual dynamics within coeducational schools, the provision of separate classes for girls in some subjects, and simultaneous structured experimentation with some single-sex schools for girls (Blackburn, 1984: 12).

Nor ought feminists to allow themselves to be distracted from the larger question of general curriculum reform by debating whether girls ought to be integrated into the existing system or set up in parallel institutions. Blackburn warns against uncritically underwriting existing curricular content which might well only make girls more competitive and aggressive. 'Asserting that the care of dependants is more valuable than missile building', she says, 'is a prior issue' (Blackburn, 1984: 10, 15). In a similar vein the American educational philosopher, J. Martin, argues that education should develop the qualities associated with both the 'public world of production' and the 'home world of reproduction and childrearing', in order to produce 'caring, empathetic, responsive, intellectual, and technically skilled well-rounded human beings' (Finley, 1986: 1168, fn. 202).[8] It is inadequate either to make women like 'men' or to let them be 'women'. There is a need to challenge both sides of the equation.

Feminists have learnt a great deal from their experience of discrimination and discrimination law over the past twenty years. One of the clearest lessons at this time appears to be the inadequacy of abstract rules. For example, the fundamental antidiscrimination principle, that likes be treated alike, has been found to be useful at one level but positively destructive of the possibility of real reform at another. The fact that the principle has been used to avoid social responsibility for maternity and safe working conditions illustrates how the supposedly neutral rule can serve conservative purposes.

The problem which Katherine O'Donovan and Erika Szyszczak have identified is that, while the principle is rational and we would certainly not wish to return to a situation where people could discriminate at will, it 'begs the question of the level of abstraction from personal characteristics at which the comparison is to be made' (O'Donovan and Szyszczak, 1988: 55). Therefore, when feminists were informed that it was impossible to discriminate against pregnant women because, as far as pregnancy was concerned, women and men were not 'similarly situated', they decided to 'raise' the level of abstraction to the notion of common disability. As mentioned in the Introduction, the individual conceptualised in the theory which informs the antidiscrimination principle is the abstract individual, detached from race, gender or class, from the body, and from the messy details of life. It is little wonder, therefore, that the theory has difficulty coping with pregnancy and with a whole range of structural problems, such as the impact of domestic living arrangements.

Women are offered the alternative *either* of being treated 'like' individuals (men) who are not considered to have responsibility for living arrangements, *or* of taking care of those arrangements themselves. As in the other cases where a sameness/difference formulation is used, the antidiscrimination principle as presently conceived offers, as alternatives, assimilation to an existing standard or opting out of that standard, instead of questioning the standard (when in effect the existing standard may be the key to the problem). In other words, it is seen as discriminatory to treat any outgroup unlike the ingroup. The treatment of the ingroup becomes the norm and is unquestioned. In fact, it is the very treatment of the ingroup (men) which in this case causes the problems for the outgroup (women). By treating men as automatons, ignoring their human characteristics, women are left responsible for the personal side of life which then causes them to be disadvantaged. To quote Lucinda Finley:

> We could move further toward the goal of responding to social problems such as gender hierarchy if we focused not on sameness and differences, but on the conditions that have produced the problem, such as the separation of home and work and the consequent barriers for women and strictures for men (Finley, 1986: 1169).

Peter Westen demonstrates that the slogan, treating likes alike, is tautological and that it can be manoeuvred to argue any case, depending upon the criteria selected to identify 'likes' and/or the 'like treatment' they ought to be accorded. For example I could argue simply that women and men are 'alike' in their human potential for development and that therefore they should be treated 'alike' in giving them the opportunity to develop that potential. Of course, the specifics of that treatment might be 'different'. The particular rule behind the slogan is everything; the slogan on its own means nothing. Westen concludes that, on these grounds, 'Equality is an empty vessel with no substantive moral content of its own' and it should therefore 'be banished from moral and legal discourse as an explanatory norm' (Westen, 1982: 547, 542).

Given its important place in our intellectual heritage I would prefer to emphasise the broader, commonsense understanding of equality. Karst describes the historical meaning of the word in America as 'the presumptive right of each person to be treated by society as a respected, responsible, participating member, regardless of the differences between persons' (in Weinzweig, 1987: 83). Ronald Dworkin's notion that the right to treatment *as an equal* ought to be anterior to the right to *equal* treatment expresses similar sentiments (Dworkin, 1978: 227). This is really very close to the idea of equal respect which nineteenth-century feminists advanced in defence of women's citizenship rights (see pages 20–21). As we have just seen, even the narrow rule of 'likes being treated alike' can be interpreted to embrace any substantive right including the right to be free of certain kinds of injuries (Weinzweig, 1987: 83). This is the meaning of equality which needs to be recaptured.

Westen uses the example of affirmative action in race relations to illustrate the tragic consequences of applying the abstract rule, 'likes must be treated alike', while ignoring the substantive issues at stake. In *Sweatt v. Painter* (1950) the Supreme Court found that it was unconstitutional to exclude Blacks from a Texas law school on the basis of race. In *De Funis v. Odegaard* (1976) the court ruled that the University of Washington Law School could not deny admission to an otherwise qualified applicant solely because he was white, overthrowing the University's affirmative action policy. There was, the court said, a common principle: 'race is not a difference that is constitutionally allowed to make a difference'. This decision loses sight of one critical factor, however, that 'Texas sought to perpetuate racial segregation whereas Washington sought to end it'. Westen calls this the 'fallacy of equivalences' by which he means the tendency to 'confuse equivalences in mathematics with equivalences in law and morals'. The erroneous assumption is that 'if two parties are morally or legally equivalent for one purpose, they must be morally or legally equivalent for all purposes' (Westen, 1982: 582–583).

Cynthia Cockburn related an incident in a recent interview (6 April 1988) which, I believe, illustrates the same fallacy at work, this time for women. She is studying the history of affirmative action in a British polytechnic. One man complained with irritation that affirmative action guidelines precluded him asking women job candidates in interview whether they have children. Yet, no sooner do the women arrive in the job (says the man), but they claim that they cannot attend lectures at 9 pm because they have children. What, he wants to know, do the women want? To be the same or different?

As in other cases in this book, setting forth 'sameness' and 'difference' as separate and alternative choices misrepresents the complexity of the social situation. Women clearly do not wish to be discriminated against and to this extent desire 'equal' treatment.

But those who assume the primary childrearing role, who are most often women, need to have the social disadvantages caused by assuming this role addressed. This may involve *specific* provisions to assist primary childrearers. The attempt to turn social responsibility for childrearing into women's 'difference' which is then set in opposition to equality is an attempt to deny the need to do something about it. The same point is made again in Chapter 10.

The choice between equal treatment and different treatment is a false choice. It is another example of the 'fallacy of equivalences'. Because women and men are or should be considered equivalent in their ability to fill a job, it does not mean they are (as things stand) equivalent in their particular requirements. People are not algebraic symbols and cannot simply be slotted into an equation. As Katherine O'Donovan says, 'If equality is to be more than merely formal, if it is to be taken seriously, then we must look at individuals in their particular situations' (O'Donovan, 1985: 208).

The problem then in traditional equality legislation is that the focus has been upon classification rather than upon conditions (Littleton, 1987: 1282 fn. 21). That is, the employment of a gender or racial category triggers the analysis, ignoring whether the category has been invoked to the *benefit* of or to the *detriment* of the person affected by the behaviour. Intuitively we know that this is not as it should be. The professed purpose of antidiscrimination legislation is to prevent people from being treated in a fashion which is unfair and which harms them. One way of treating someone unfairly is to single them out because of their race or sex, and to use this as a rationalisation for unfavourable treatment. Surely, however, it is the unfavourable treatment and the harm which we wish to eliminate, not the singling out. It is the fact that the treatment is injurious, not that it is 'different', which forms the basis of the complaint. The word 'different' in this context seems entirely inappropriate.

The problem then is not that there exists some inherent philosophical contradiction in supporting antidiscrimination and affirmative action at the same time, but that the policies have been reduced to an equal treatment/different treatment formula which is made to appear contradictory. The 'equal treatment' which is offered and which is clearly intended to eliminate discriminatory behaviour is reduced to some notion of identical treatment regardless of circumstances. 'Different treatment' which was meant to describe discriminatory behaviour is now extended to include affirmative action which grew out of attempts to compensate for past discrimination and current social injustice. Affirmative action, strictly speaking, is not 'different treatment', though its opponents will persist in calling it this so that they can neatly counterpoise it to the 'equal treatment' of antidiscrimination theory. While affirmative action obviously involves gender-specific policies, it is, as Lesley Caust has recently said, a 'dynamic process' aimed at improving working and living arrangements generally (Caust, 1989: 28).

Given the ambiguity attached to the word 'difference' and the way in which it is so often set, albeit inappropriately, against equality, it may be wise to find more accurate and more precise language. In discrimination cases it is not 'different' treament to which women object, but 'discriminatory' and 'injurious' treatment. Women do not require 'different treatment'; they require affirmative or positive action. Women are not 'different'; they are disadvantaged. Removing the focus from the 'differences' between men and women will then make it easier to theorise the 'differences' among women. Here I take Lucinda Finley's point that talking about varieties and nuances will 'make it easier to see the necessity and desirability of many human distinctions' (Finley, 1986: 1170).

The important point in this debate is that in contention are competing social visions, one which acknowledges social responsibility for a wide range of human needs, and the other which feels it adequate to prevent one individual from infringing on the rights of another. Any attempt to present the problem as fundamental inconsistency between equal opportunity and affirmative action needs to be seen in this light. Wojciech Sadurski makes this important point:

> ...we had better realize that our opinions about equality in law
> are unavoidably determined by our opinions about what law is
> *just*...and not by some objective properties of the law...
> The controversies about different purposes of law (and their
> different relative weight) should be openly formulated in terms
> of competing social philosophies and the substantive social
> ideals that they endorse, rather than apparelled in guise of
> the problem of 'equality in law' (Sadurski, 1986: 138).[9]

The social vision presented in this text follows the lead of many other feminists from a wide range of political backgrounds (see, for example, Weinzweig, 1987; Finley, 1986; Hooks, 1987). It requests that human interdependency be recognised and that a degree of social responsibility for basic human needs be accepted. With Sandra Harding I see the feminist project as the identification of 'distinctive aspects of women's experience which can provide resources for the construction of more representatively human understanding' (Harding and Hintikka, 1983: x).

The vision has far-reaching structural and philosophical implications. Structurally, the challenge to the home/work divide will have to mean more eventually than flexible work hours, and more and better day care centres, although these are necessary reforms. Ultimately, a complete rethinking of the meanings of 'work' and 'leisure', and an analysis of the reasons for the constructed separation between the two is necessary.

Philosophically the analysis implies a fundamental challenge to rights-based justice. The dominant tradition in liberalism, which Stuart Hall calls 'establishment liberalism', privileges liberty, meaning freedom from constraint, over equality which means 'primarily that all individuals are equal because they are born with the same *rights*' (Hall, 1986: 40–41, 55). Rights in this model are interpreted as 'zones of non-interference' (Jennett, 1987: 366; Karst, 1984: 487). Minority groups have long been aware that the freedom which is offered is useful only to a select group of predominantly white middle-class men. Now a majority group (women constitute a numerical majority in most Western industrialised countries) is being made aware of this truth.

New models are necessary. One possibility would be to broaden the notion of rights to encompass the right to be 'free from injury'. Karst talks about organised society's responsibility for 'preventing or alleviating harms which are dehumanising' (Karst, 1984: 494). Another alternative might be to incorporate a reciprocal listing of responsibilities into the traditional rights regimen. Carol Gilligan's 'inclusion solution' which integrates caring and justice offers an attractive ethical alternative to a narrowly-based rights model (Du Bois et al., 1985: 73–75).

A first practical step towards achieving some of these visionary goals might be, as Karst suggests, for the courts to redefine the idea of discrimination, 'abandoning the requirement of a showing of discriminatory purpose in favor of a principle recognising a law's discriminatory *impact* as a constitutional harm requiring justification by the state' (Karst, 1984: 488). The 'different' treatment model of discrimination should also be replaced with a model based upon the identification of injury or disadvantage. Disparate impact theory goes some way towards examining regulations which have injurious effects, but it needs to go further. The requirement to provide a male comparator should, for example, be eliminated.

It follows that, if we focus upon the intent of legislation, there is no conflict between demanding on the one hand that group characteristics be *ignored* and on the other that they be *considered*. In the first case people should not be treated in an injurious fashion because they belong to a particular subset of humanity. In the second, legislation *should* take account of the realities of people's lives. On the one hand employers will need to *cease* certain activities, such as preferring male to female employees because of assumptions about women's character or domestic responsibilities. On the other hand employers will be obliged to *undertake* certain activities, to encourage women where encouragement is appropriate, and to consider their particular requirements, given the distribution of domestic responsibilities in most families. This is the motive-force behind affirmative action but it should be interpreted more broadly. In order to be effective, programs must ultimately include measures which will encourage the redistribution of domestic responsibilities to men. For example, parental leave laws could stipulate that, in dual-parent families, a certain amount of leave is allocated to each parent. Sweden's Social Democratic Party has been promoting such a policy for a number of years on the grounds that:

> You can't just wait for change. You must change attitudes. If fathers were *required* to take part of the leave, there would be no question about employers discouraging them (Scott, 1982: 75).

It is heartening that a substantial portion of Swedish union members favour the idea of a 'father's quota, since it offered their only real option for claiming a portion of the leave!' (Stoiber, 1989: 55).

In all this, there is a need to remain theoretically flexible and to design policies to respond to immediate contingencies, instead of trying to fit them to some over-arching abstract principle. In the words of Frances Olsen, 'Principled decision-making' must mean more 'than being able to come up with an abstract, general rule that will achieve the desired result in most cases' (Olsen, 1986: 1522 fn. 16). I am reminded of Martha Minow's point that 'inconsistent ideas may be less confused than consistent ones' (Minow, 1986: 910). The attempts by some feminists to fit women's diverse needs into the straitjacket of existing law and language have produced many of their disagreements. If disputes caused by the ambiguity and inadequacy of certain political ideas were recognised for what they are, the door could open to constructive brainstorming either to find the best way to approach and use the existing system, or to suggest necessary changes to that system.

8
Divorce, custody, and Baby 'M'

Feminists based in America:

No-fault divorce didn't do away with alimony....Feminists never backed no-fault divorce. They did back greater economic protection for women.

Catherine East

Our society has not generally conditioned men to regard fatherhood as being associated with any kind of responsibility.

Judy Goldsmith

The women's movement recognised the incredible fragility of women in the economic system, that we were very dependent and that, without having really given women more opportunities in the workplace, to take away their only means of income and support would have been absurd. It wasn't us who did it!

Mary Jean Collins

You should have consciousness-raising for domestic court judges.

Catharine Stimpson

Joint custody is not always a happy resolution.

Ruth Mandel

Feminists based in Britain:

It is not enough for the advocates of divorce to say that the state will enforce the maintenance of the children; they must show by what means this can by done.

Englishwoman's Review, *October 1870*

You need to make a tactical political decision about whether you want women to be a) more dependent on men, b) more dependent on the state, c) more economically independent. The last thing we'd choose is to be dependent on men since that is the one we're busy escaping from.

Cynthia Cockburn

It's a miserable life to have to continue to be dependent on the person you once married and now hate.

Tess Gill

I think you would have a much more peaceful world if men got to know the next generation, got to love it.

Georgina Ashworth

In surrogacy cases you have to ask why was this woman in a situation where she would do something which is going to be so painful for her.

Michèle Barrett

Feminists based in Australia:

Our legal system is simply not designed to deal with the affective side of human relations. It is just a failure in this regard. It can only deal in clumsy and crass generalities.

Margaret Thornton

It is not just the question of equitable treatment, or maintenance for children, and proper allocation of assets; it is also a question of how women are going to take up their position in society again.

Sue Brooks

Regarding the division of property, we need to take account of the way in which the woman has contributed in kind to the capacity of the man to build up property.

Helen Campbell

Custody should be awarded to the parent who is most capable of nurturing the child.

Susan Ryan

Anti-feminists sometimes caricature feminist analysis to make it fit a sameness/difference framework. In the divorce test-case which follows, social conservatives typecast feminists as upholders of a narrow understanding of 'equality', meaning the assimilation of women to men. Women are then advised to recognise that they are indeed 'different', need special protection, and ought to return to their 'natural' dependency upon a male supporter. 'Sameness' and 'difference' are offered as the only available alternatives. The first part of this chapter examines the political motivations which lie behind this argument. It also shows how feminist analysis has been oversimplified in order to blame feminists for the unresponsiveness of social institutions to the vulnerability of dependent spouses and children.

On the highly sensitive issues of custody and surrogacy, parts of a sameness/difference formulation of the problems sometimes surface in feminist arguments. This tendency is more marked in America. Why does this happen? What does it mean? And is it a useful contribution to political analysis?

The second part of this chapter takes up these questions. It suggests that, as in the maternity leave debate (Chapter 5), the lack of social supports for reproduction and day-to-day living arrangements such as childrearing inclines those feminists who wish to encourage women to compete in the market to downplay pregnancy and mothering. Other feminists cling to these as women's only available sources of power. It would be more profitable, I suggest, to discuss the political conditions which produce these unattractive alternatives rather than to allow the problem to appear to be whether women are more the same as or different from men.

Divorce has become controversial within the last decade or so as a result of the discovery of the phenomenon which has been labelled the 'feminization of poverty'. Although Britain has not adopted the phrase with the same enthusiasm as America and Australia, figures in all three countries support the generalisation that poverty wears a female face (Cass, 1985: 67–89; Thurow, 1987: 26–33; Pascall, 1986: 203–206). Women dominate several categories of the poor. Their greater longevity and their inadequate access to pension plans or superannuation produces more elderly poor women than elderly poor men (Women's Bureau, Australia, May 1984). Women also comprise a larger proportion of the non-aged single poor, partly due to their higher unemployment rates and partly to their relatively low pay when in work.[1] Women in poor families, with a male breadwinner present, are obviously also poor. And then there is the hidden poverty of female dependants, 'where the breadwinner has adequate income but does not distribute it equitably within the family unit' (Cass, 1985: 73).[2]

None of these patterns of poverty has attracted the amount of attention directed at poor single mothers, for several reasons. Poor single mothers have poor children and poor children have always touched a sensitive nerve in the public conscience. In addition, the growth rate in this category is significant and observable.[3] Finally, many in this category have had to fall back on public resources, clearly a problem for governments trying to cut budget deficits.

Figures reveal that, despite the claims of some moralists, these poor single mothers are not the product of a sudden surge in illegitimacy. Rather they are part of the 'economic fallout of divorce' (Hewlett, 1986: Chapter 3).[4] There are simply more single-parent families as a result of higher divorce rates, and women comprise the overwhelming majority of single parents. In Australia, they headed 85% of single-parent families in 1982 (Cass, 1985: 78).

There is a tendency in some recent literature to link female poverty directly to the no-fault divorce laws introduced in the late 1960s and early 1970s (Weitzman, 1985; Hewlett, 1986). In Britain, the Divorce Reform Bill of 1969 (enacted in 1971) replaced the previous principle that a matrimonial offence such as adultery was the only grounds for divorce with the notion of 'irretrievable breakdown' (Land, 1983: 79). A subsequent 1984 Matrimonial and Family Proceedings Act endorsed the idea of a 'clean break' upon divorce and 'rehabilitative maintenance' to prepare ex-wives for re-entry to the marketplace (Smart, 1984b: 241). In America, divorce after a period of separation was permitted in 21 states by 1961 (East, 1986: 13). California introduced a no-fault divorce law in 1970 and by 1985 most states had followed suit (Minow, 1986: 901). Australia introduced a no-fault Family Law Act in 1975 (Scutt and Graham, 1984: 100–103).

It is not surprising that the single mother's poverty is traced directly to these laws since studies reveal dramatic contrasts between the economic situation of ex-wives and ex-husbands. Leonore Weitzman's figures are the most frequently quoted: 'within the first year of divorce, women and their children experience a 73 percent drop in their standard of living, and men a 42 percent rise' (Wickenden, 1986: 21; Weitzman, 1985). There are several reasons for this contrast, including inadequate child support and the infrequency with which child support payments are met.[5] But several recent studies have attributed the problem to the decline in the number, amount and length of alimony awards. The argument developed by Sylvia Hewlett is that women traded off alimony for so-called 'equitable-distribution' property legislation, and further that women lost a powerful bargaining device in property and alimony settlements when they surrendered the notion of fault. Hewlett quotes Frances Leonard, a spokeswoman for the Older Women's League:

> In the old days women had a marriage contract unless it was broken through adultery, abandonment or cruelty. If her husband wanted out of the marriage she could strike an economic bargain with him—i.e., you support me and I'll give you a divorce. The impolite word for this is blackmail. Nobody feels that it was a good system, but it helped place a value on the marriage contract (Hewlett, 1986: 56).

The next stage in the argument is that feminists blundered by endorsing no-fault laws. Some studies are more careful in their attribution of blame than others. Hewlett definitely implies that feminists 'in the first heady days of women's liberation' erred in embracing no-fault divorce 'as the enlightened path to singleness' (Hewlett, 1986: 56). Weitzman admits that feminist reformers did not discard the idea of alimony but hoped that 'If alimony awards were based on need and the ability to pay, standards reflecting economic equality, the interests of both parties would be protected'. She also slips into a footnote Riane Eisler's observation that the first no-fault divorce laws were passed 'by an almost all-male legislature, before most people had even heard of the women's liberation movement'. Still, the impression is left that 'feminists made a gigantic mistake' (Weitzman, 1985: 363, 366 fn. 30, 179; Eisler, 1977). Bettina Arndt makes no attempt to qualify her conclusion that feminists are responsible for the 'flight from the breadwinner ethic', and for men abandoning the support of their ex-wives: 'By seeking independence, the feminists were aiding the male rebellion' (Arndt, 1986: 68). Not surprisingly, this is an idea which the popular discourse has embraced most enthusiastically. Feminists then are held responsible for women's poverty.

I call this version of events 'the Great Hoax' and would like to proceed to dismantle it in two stages. First, as already mentioned, feminists had little or nothing to do with the shape of no-fault legislation which reflected 1960s enthusiasm for individual self-actualisation and tolerance of sexual 'indiscretion'. Nor were they oblivious to the dangers of the legislation. They did not condemn alimony, but suggested that it ought to be allocated regardless of gender, to the needy spouse (Brown, Emerson, Falk and Freedman, 1971: 952). As Riane Eisler says, spousal support is quite compatible with no-fault legislation (Eisler, 1977: 42).

There was also specific recognition of the fact that 'spouses' who had been responsible for family maintenance in a domestic capacity would need support. The *Spirit of Houston*, a statement of intent issued by the first American National Women's Conference, endorsed the maintenance provisions of the 1970 Uniform Marriage and Divorce Act which specified that the 'amount and duration of payments' should take into account a range of considerations:

> ...the financial resources of the party seeking maintenance, the time necessary to acquire sufficient training to enable the party to find appropriate employment, the standard of living established during the marriage, the duration of the marriage, the age and physical and emotional condition of the spouse seeking maintenance, and the ability of the spouse from whom maintenance is sought to meet his or her own needs while making maintenance payments (National Women's Conference, 1978: 58; see also Brown, Emerson, Falk and Freedman, 1971: 953).

American feminists were also sensitive to the loss of that critical bargaining weapon, 'threatening or seeking divorce on a fault ground', and recommended that the act:

> ...be revised to meet this objection by a directive to the judge to award money for training and education, and related expenses such as day care, so that the woman can bring her earning capacity up to a level commensurate with that of her former husband (Babcock, Freedman, Norton and Ross, 1975: 721).

And in Wisconsin, where the legislation was introduced later, feminists played a leading role in having economic protections written *into* the legislation (Fineman, 1983: 850). In Britain, Ruth Deech, an enthusiastic supporter of no-fault, also insisted upon the need to differentiate between marriages which took place before the date of the reform, 'when a wife might have married in the expectation of lifelong support', and marriages taking place after the date of the reform, 'when it could be said that no term relating to lifelong insulation from self-support could be read into the marriage contract' (Deech, 1977: 232).

Australia's largest organised feminist group, the Women's Electoral Lobby (WEL), welcomed the 1975 Family Law Act. WEL believed that women and men should have equal rights and responsibilities in the area of child custody and maintenance, and that 'the system should no longer assume that a married woman was dependent upon her husband'. But it also acknowledged that maintenance should be provided in certain situations and should take into consideration a list of factors almost identical to those mentioned in the Uniform Marriage and Divorce Act (see above). WEL's enthusiasm was due mainly to the provision that, in property distribution, women's homemaking contribution would now be taken into account. WEL concluded, optimistically it now appears, that 'It means a woman will be automatically entitled to a fair share of the property and income she has helped her husband to acquire' (Scutt, 1983: 236–237; Scutt and Graham, 1984: 61).

So in each case feminists who applauded the introduction of no-fault divorce wanted to guarantee protection for the vulnerable spouse. This is not to say that feminists were unresponsive to the optimistic mood of the period which seemed to portend the imminent onset of genuine egalitarian relationships. It needs to be remembered that in the buoyant economic conditions of the 1960s, and early 1970s, the market appeared eager to absorb female labour. According to Jocelynn Scutt, in lobbying for the passage of the Family Law Act, WEL was aware that 'the legislation might keep women in a position of poverty', but hoped that 'retraining schemes, provision for childcare, and the opening up of the job market to women due to passage of equal opportunity and anti-discrimination legislation would overcome that possibility' (Scutt, 1983: 239).

It is also true that the idea of alimony or spousal maintenance did not sit comfortably with feminist aspirations for women's economic independence. The British group, Rights of Women (ROW), explained the conflict that feminists faced: 'maintenance clearly epitomised the dependency of women in marriage, and we did not want to campaign for the survival of this dependency' (Rights of Women, 1985: 193). Similarly, in America, after noting the dangers of the legislation, some feminist reformers added, almost wistfully: 'On the other hand, isn't it good from a feminist perspective to encourage women toward economic independence and away from reliance on maintenance. . . ?' (Babcock, Freedman, Norton and Ross, 1975: 721).

In the same spirit Ruth Deech considered a maintenance law which 'rests on a foundation of female dependency' incompatible with a concept of marriage as a 'partnership of equals'. Deech had absorbed the individualistic and materialist ethic of the period. She objected to the clause which guaranteed a wife support adequate to maintain her 'previous standard of living' on the grounds that it provided for women 'a career alternative to an economically productive one'. Ultimately, she appealed to the 'responsibility of every person to meet his or her own needs' (Deech, 1977: 230, 233).

The idea of the 'clean break' is attractive and, in the long term, there is no doubt that feminists would want to see spousal maintenance abolished (Smart, 1984b: 227). Even the British socialist feminists, Michèle Barrett and Mary McIntosh, favour the 'clean break' model of divorce, 'where any property is divided as soon as possible and there is no continuing obligation to provide maintenance, except for children until they start work'. Unsurprisingly, given their politics, this is tempered by the recognition that 'women often are unable to support themselves, especially after a long period of marriage when they have kept house and worked outside only intermittently or part-time'. In such cases Barrett and McIntosh wish the courts to be given guidelines on making 'protective settlements' (Barrett and McIntosh, 1982: 155).

While it is possible, therefore, to detect an equal treatment emphasis in some of the feminist responses, there quickly emerged an awareness that, in cases of structural inequality, equal treatment simply would not work. Eleanor Smeal, a former president of NOW, claims that she and other feminists had 'reservations about the equitable divorce laws all along': 'No-fault attempts to treat men and women equally—*or as if they were equal*—at the point of divorce. However, it ignores the *structural* inequality between men and women in the larger society' (Wickenden, 1986: 21, emphasis in original). Betty Friedan, who seems to feel that the women's movement erred initially by being '. . . so concerned with principle—that equality of right and opportunity had to mean equality of responsibility and therefore alimony was out', describes the current view in these terms:

> Alimony? It's a sexist concept, and doesn't belong in a women's movement for equality. But that economic equality we seek is not a reality yet. Half of all women are unpaid housewives still, and the ones who work still earn barely half what men earn, and are still expected to take the entire responsibility of the kids, as well. Maintenance, reimbursement, severance pay— whatever you want to call it—is a necessity for many divorced women, as is child support (Friedan, 1976: 325–326).

There is more agreement than disagreement among feminists on the need to design policy which takes women's differential social location into account in this particular case. If for a time some naively anticipated a rapid improvement in women's situation, it does seem a little unfair to blame them for believing the rhetoric of equality.

Martha Fineman feels that the feminist belief in the ideology of equality surfaced again in the discussion on property distribution, and again to women's disadvantage. American feminists disagreed about whether it was preferable to endorse an 'equitable' or an 'equal' division of assets in the property settlement (East, 1986: 14).[6] According to Fineman, those who supported a simple mathematical division of assets did so because of their adherence to an 'egalitarian model' of marriage and a determination to break down gender stereotypes in family roles. True, they now recognised the need to have women's homemaking contribution acknowledged but, says Fineman, they simply put this on one side of the equation. Such an approach ignored other groups of disadvantaged women, including spouses who made a dual contribution. The chief problem, says Fineman, is that the reformers were uncomfortable invoking the concept of need and yet this was exactly what was required. In her opinion, there is a necessity in divorce for 'special treatment' of certain women. Fineman also calls it 'affirmative action': 'the most appropriate reform would have been one focusing upon the distinctions between the projected positions of the spouses after divorce, thus incorporating the concept of result rather than rule equality' (Fineman, 1983: 796, 827–828, 852, 877). Given the way in which labelling a group 'different' or 'special' implies that they are somehow the problem, the language of affirmative action is more appropriate in this case.

A version of the equal treatment/special treatment debate (see Chapter 5) appears then over property distribution. Fineman represents one group who, like Margaret Thornton in Australia, believes that 'an equal division of assets between parties on divorce is very much within the equal treatment model' and is inadequate since it ignores the fact that 'the former wife is more likely than not to be living in poverty within a short time as a result of her unequal status in the labour market or because of her dependency on welfare' (M. Thornton, 1986: 11). In this view, true equality requires an *inequitable* division of assets in favour of the ex-wife. On the other side are reformers who see a 50/50 split as preferable to trusting judges to evaluate the contribution of the homemaker, which would be necessary under an 'equitable' division law. Representing this approach in Australia, Jocelynn Scutt and Di Graham consider 'equal rights to marital assets' a means of outflanking 'masculine parochialism by curtailing judicial discretion in property division' (Babcock, Freedman, Norton, and Ross, 1975: 721; Scutt and Graham, 1984: 103).

It is possible in these arguments to detect an ideological preference either for 'equality' (sameness) or 'admitting vulnerability (difference)'. The positions are taken up, however, because it is unclear in the existing political system which alternative will most effectively protect women's interests. Equality is endorsed by those who fear the decisions of patriarchal judges; special consideration is recommended by those who realise that an equal distribution of assets will leave many women disadvantaged. I am reminded of

Wendy Chavkin's comment regarding her defence of 'special treatment' in the American maternity leave debate: 'I see where my approach is vulnerable and I see where theirs doesn't get us very far' (see page 149).

It is important to highlight the political imperatives which impel feminists to take sides in these debates instead of leaving the impression that 'equality' and 'difference' are somehow in contention. It is also important to emphasise that both groups are looking for the most effective strategy to protect married women's interests. The politically inspired attempt by conservatives to portray feminists as unconcerned about dependent women needs to be challenged.

The second part of 'the Great Hoax' is the notion that a 'Golden Age' of security and marital bliss preceded the introduction of no-fault laws. Sylvia Hewlett begins her chapter on the 'Economic Fallout of Divorce' with the observation that 'Once upon a time women could rely on marriage to provide a financially secure way of life' (Hewlett, 1986: 51). One wonders if she realised how appropriate the analogy to a fairy tale really was. Opponents of the laws are adamant that the doctrine of 'no-fault' lost for women the common-law presumption that husbands are liable for the support of their wives and children. But men were never, in fact, obliged to support their wives. Criminal sanctions of non-support are almost never invoked and, during marriage, 'the husband, as head of the family, is free to determine how much or how little of his property his wife and children will receive' (Brown, Emerson, Falk and Freedman, 1971: 944–945). Moreover, as far as alimony awards are concerned, the evidence simply does not support the assumption that, since things are bad now, they must have been better before. Alimony awards have always been rare, but somehow this fact gets lost in the overall impression that women are worse off today.[7] Generally enthusiastic in their defence of the traditional family, those intent upon portraying feminists as the villains refuse to acknowledge that 'under the adversary system the vast majority of wives received financial settlements that failed to support them and their children above the poverty level' (Seal, 1979: 13).

The 'old regime' was a disaster for women. Under that regime, the notion of fault had frequently been used to deny 'adulterous' women alimony since they were considered undeserving of support (Babcock, Freedman, Norton and Ross, 1975: 700). The obligation to accept her husband's domicile as her own also meant that a married woman who refused to follow her husband was guilty of desertion and once again was 'justifiably' denied maintenance. Given the division of responsibilities under the marriage contract, moreover, a husband could charge his wife with cruelty if she belittled him or left the home in disarray or ignored her wifely duties (Weitzman and Dixon, 1986: 339, 342).

More women are visibly poor today than previously, quite simply, because there are more divorces. And more to blame than the laws themselves, is the way in which they are implemented. Since the laws made clear provision for the needs of 'displaced' spouses, 'judicial attitudes, rather than the legal provisions themselves, are the immediate culprits' (Taub, 1988: 581). As far as property distribution is concerned, judges tend to undervalue the woman's homemaking contribution to the accumulation of family assets. According to Scutt and Graham, the problem is more socialisation than malice:

> Generally in our society housework and child-care are paid little regard. It is natural that these attitudes should be replicated in the courts. Further, 'woman's work' is virtually invisible. It is commonplace, happens in every household—and occurs in every judge's household usually without the involvement of the (male) judge (Scutt and Graham, 1984: 74).

There is also a reluctance to admit forms of 'new property', such as the 'couple's career and educational investments' (Minow, 1986: 903; see also Friedan, 1985), to the calculations.

In determining alimony or 'spousal support', judges tend to sympathise with the man who often has a new family to support. They also assume that it should be relatively easy for the wife to get back into the workforce. One American judge invoked the rhetoric of women's liberation to justify limiting the duration of maintenance. In 1972 he reversed an award of $100 per week to a 48-year-old alcoholic wife 'because she had had ample time (over two years) since the separation to rehabilitate herself and resume gainful employment':

> In this era of women's liberation movements and enlightened thinking, we have almost universally come to appreciate the fallacy of treating the feminine members of our society on anything but a basis of complete equality with the opposite sex... Whether the marriage continues to exist or is severed through the device of judicial decree, the woman continues to be as fully equipped as the man to earn a living and provide for her essential needs (Davidson, Ginsburg and Kay, 1974: 244).

It is, of course, this kind of statement which has fed the tendency to blame feminists for what is happening, but it does seem unjust to hold them responsible for this implementation of 'equality with a vengeance' (Weitzman, 1985: 366). It is also no coincidence that conservatives are eager to equate feminism with equality, narrowly defined. It allows women to be dealt with unfairly and puts the blame on feminists.

The more direct cause of the poverty of female single parents, in any event, is not the amount of spousal maintenance payments but low or non-existent child support. Women most often assume custody of the children, and child support awards, when they are made, are simply inadequate to compensate for actual costs. Moreover, support orders are often ignored (Fineman, 1983: 828–829; see also Note 5, this chapter). The problem of unenforced child support decrees is a long-standing one and has nothing to do with the introduction of no-fault laws (Minow, 1986: 906). As Karen Seal says, 'there is nothing in the Family Law Act that provides for fathers to be relieved of the responsibility of supporting their children' (Seal, 1979: 14–15).

There are two related problems here, the low amount of awards and the fact that they are seldom enforced. The spiralling increase in the number of divorces has, it seems, caught modern industrial states in a cleft-stick. On the one hand the state does not wish to relieve breadwinners of their duty of support since this is 'the moving force for upward mobility' and the incentive to work (Eisenstein, 1982: 86), and because it would prove costly. On the other hand, in order to facilitate the formation of new family units, there is a desire not to overburden the ex-husband with support obligations for his first family (Smart, 1984b: 114; Minow, 1986: 907). A 'good divorce law', as envisioned by the British Law Commission, would 'buttress' rather than 'undermine the stability of marriage'. To this end, the 'empty shell' of the previous marriage has to be destroyed 'with the maximum fairness, and the minimum bitterness, distress and humiliation' (in Deech, 1977: 231 fn. 21). Clearly, the easiest way to accomplish this goal is, as Weitzman and Dixon say, 'to encourage the divorced woman to become self-supporting (by engaging in gainful employment)' (Weitzman and Dixon, 1986: 347). It is not surprising therefore that the image of the ex-wife as 'alimony drone' is encouraged in public debate. According to the British feminist group, Rights of Women, the ideological content of the 1983 Matrimonial and Family Proceedings Bill, which is now legislation, implied that women regard marriage as a 'meal-ticket for life' and that they required 'some kind of disciplining back into the labour market' (ROW, 1985: 199).

But the contradictions in the system have been exposed in the female poverty figures. Carol Smart is doubtless correct that this poverty facilitates new family formation.[8] In Smart's words, 'There is no real alternative for wives who wish to escape the financial hardship of single parenthood other than to marry again. Thus the family household is reproduced' (Smart, 1984b: 128). The obvious discrepancy between the rhetoric of equality and the reality of poverty, however, is becoming difficult to ignore.

The state has in fact been forced to act. In 1984 the American Congress passed the Child Support Amendments which strengthened enforcement programs in a number of ways, by adopting procedures to withhold income automatically when a parent owing support is more than 30 days late, by intercepting tax refunds and by allowing property liens for overdue support payments (Hunter, 1983). A recent article in the *Scientific American* recommended a more systematic and comprehensive approach:

> ...if a court orders child-support payments, the Federal
> Government automatically sends the mother a monthly support
> check for that amount and collects the money from the father
> through the Internal Revenue Service—with the state
> guaranteeing a minimum level of support whatever the amount
> collected from the father may be (Thurow, 1987: 33).

Australia has just established a Child Support Agency which collects money from non-custodial parents. A recent innovation will allow liability to be calculated as a percentage of income above a basic 'self support exemption' (Hawke, 1988: 8–9).

There are obvious problems with any suggestion that collecting maintenance is all that is necessary. In many cases there will simply not be enough income to go around! While feminists clearly want men to assume some just share of support for their offspring, the timing and the way in which the reforms have been introduced raises questions about the various governments' motivations. In Australia, Sydney's Feminist Legal Issues Group is concerned 'at the effective privatisation of child support responsibilities embedded in these proposals'. The Group also wants the scheme to be voluntary and criticises the proposed penalties for non-cooperation: 'there may well be legitimate reasons for women not wishing to disclose information about the father of their child (for example, that the child was born as a result of rape or incest, or the father has a history of violence)' (Greycar, 1987: 8–9). Nor do the proposals address the problem of the single mother's poverty.

This situation exposes the inadequacy of private law to resolve the problem and challenges an approach which simply shifts 'the hardship of divorce back and forth between individual husbands and wives'. A public solution is necessary:

> As private law in the 1980s continues to fail to provide adequately for marriage breakdown, and as the divorce rate rises, it is increasingly necessary to think again in terms of abolishing private forms of maintenance and replacing them with newly conceived public sources of income maintenance for women (Smart, 1984a: 22–23; see also Greycar, 1987: 11).

Katherine O'Donovan accepts the need for a Guaranteed Maintenance Allowance but goes further than this in her challenge to the privatisation of the family. One possible reform in her view is the introduction of European-style family codes to regulate intra-marriage relationships (O'Donovan, 1978: 184; 1985: 184–187). Other feminists are hesitant to endorse this degree of 'intervention' (ROW, 1985: 202; Smart, 1984b: 238).[9]

The situation of the 'displaced homemaker' illustrates another structural problem which can no longer be ignored. The fact is that women have not *chosen* to be dependants. A whole cluster of welfare, taxation and income support legislation has *constructed* women as dependants (Pascall, 1986: 28). One obvious example is the Dependent Spouse Rebate in Australia, called the 'married allowance' in Britain, which tells a woman that the law recognises her as dependent (Land, 1983: 76; Sharp and Broomhill, 1988: 31, 51). The new divorce laws, however, wish her to behave as if that dependency had never occurred.

The dilemma feminists face therefore in trying to devise proposals which will assist women to assume an active role in the marketplace without disadvantaging women in traditional relationships is not a dilemma of their creation. It is a result of that continuing problem of either/or choices which the system imposes upon women. Practically, then, the government has an obligation to resolve this dilemma. According to Gillian Pascall, this requires a social welfare system that would 'mitigate women's economic dependence without sustaining dependent relationships': 'There are ways of doing this (for example, child benefits). In asking that this should be done women are not asking for the moon' (Pascall, 1986: 29; see also Segal, 1983: 213).

It is not surprising that the right sees the solution to the rising divorce rate and increasing female poverty in a return to traditional sex roles. The nuclear family plays a critical role in the conservative political vision. Because of the desire to reduce the role of the interventionist state and of expenditure, the family, and the woman within the family, is being asked to shoulder more and more of society's caring responsibilities. The family is also considered critical to motivating men to labour. In *Wealth and Property* George Gilder, invoking a touch of biological determinism, explains how the 'claims of family' encourage a married man 'to channel his otherwise disruptive male aggressions into his performance as a provider for wife and children' (in Eisenstein, 1982: 86). So men are portrayed as shiftless and unpredictable, and women are called upon to tame them (Ehrenreich, 1984: 152–170). In a desperate bid to defend the status quo the right looks to woman to resume her role as guardian of the hearth:

> She can prevent delinquency by staying at home to look after the children, she can reduce unemployment by staying at home and freeing jobs for men, she can create a stable family unit by becoming totally economically dependent on her husband so that she cannot leave him. *She* is the answer (Smart, 1984b: 136).

But the model which calls upon women to sacrifice themselves for the system no longer works, if it ever did. Zillah Eisenstein outlines the contradiction within advanced capitalism caused by the requirement for married women to enter the labour force. Put simply, women cannot be in both places, bolstering the family and holding down a job, and yet they are required to be. Therein, says Eisenstein, lies the crisis of liberalism: 'an ideology of (liberal) equality and a contradictory reality of patriarchal inequality is being uncovered by the married wage-earning women' (Eisenstein, 1982: 91). Women can no longer provide that linchpin which holds the uneasy tension between individual self-actualisation and community cohesion in equilibrium. New solutions are required, as the authors of the recent *Habits of the Heart* seem to realise:

> . . . traditionally, women have thought more in terms of relationships than in terms of isolated individuals. Now we are all supposed to be conscious primarily of our assertive selves. To reappropriate a language in which we could all, men and women, see that dependence and independence are deeply related, and that we can be independent persons without denying that we need one another, is a task that has only begun (in Minow, 1986: 916).

It seems then that it is no longer adequate to leave women responsible for caring. Nor is it a solution to encourage women to mimic the 'assertive male' model. Caring still needs to be done. Some form of structural change will have to accommodate this reality. One suggestion is to modify the 'assertive self' model so that both partners can share caring. As mentioned previously, this proposal necessarily involves a complete rethinking of the current conception of paid work as pivotal to self-definition and as separate from personal concerns. The government will clearly have to be involved in facilitating these changes so that 'those who care' are not penalised for doing so. This can be done without surrendering control of people's lives to an impersonal bureaucracy.

These same problems are relevant in the related area of custody. Here, however, some feminists are invoking 'sameness' or 'difference' arguments to defend their position. The history of custody law helps to explain why they do so.

Feminists conducted a number of campaigns in the nineteenth century to challenge the father's absolute right at common law to custody of his legitimate children (women were given automatic custody over illegitimate children, a matter which will be discussed shortly). Their victories were minor ones.[10] In many cases women were probably given guardianship despite the lack of entitlement—that is, they were given the responsibility without the right (Grossberg, 1983: 239).

Towards the end of the century the state became more overtly interventionist in the custody domain, largely because of a growing concern about the health and character of the next generation. Michael Grossberg describes the process as the 'Rise of a Judicial Patriarchy' (Grossberg, 1983; see also Brown, 1986). Judges introduced new standards of child nurture and parental fitness. The 'tender years rule' became popular because of the conviction that mothers had an important role to play in the moral education of the young (Block, 1978). It decreed that 'infants, children below puberty, and youngsters afflicted with health ailments be placed in a mother's care unless she proved unworthy of the responsibility'. This rule was codified in certain states and, says Grossberg, acted as a 'powerful leveler of paternal rights'. Importantly, however, the new rule did not automatically increase *maternal* rights. Rather, 'the law reduced the rights of parenthood itself' (Grossberg, 1983: 247).

Feminists in Britain mounted a vigorous campaign in the 1920s to try to win women equal guardianship rights. The Guardianship of Infants Act (1925) which resulted was in effect a compromise which provided that no parent had a superior claim and that decisions would be made in the 'child's best interest' (Davidson, Ginsburg and Kay, 1974: 271). Australia introduced identical legislation in 1934. The more recent (1971) British Guardianship of Minors Act retains the notion that the welfare of the child is of paramount importance (Smart, 1984b: 120).

An unfortunate consequence of the way in which the legislation has evolved is that it appears as if women's rights are set *against* children's interests. The truth of the matter is that the 'interests of the child', sometimes referred to as the 'welfare principle', is vague and indeterminate despite attempts to define it. Of itself the concept has no meaning and historically judicial opinion has reflected 'social and cultural values and beliefs about the basic institutions of the family and of marriage' (Maidment, 1984: 149). To win their children therefore women have had to conform to a stereotype of 'appropriate' maternal behaviour. Julia Brophy looks at the resultant surveillance of women's sexual behaviour (Brophy, 1985: 97). Nancy Polikoff describes the 'Catch-22' facing many women today. Either they are seen as having insufficient resources to raise the children or, if they work to secure the resources, they are penalised for 'not being sufficiently available to their children'. This becomes even more of a problem when the husband can provide a full-time, live-in replacement, his new wife (Polikoff, 1982: 239–240).

It is true that women 'win' custody in the vast majority of cases, but the word 'win' is not really appropriate since most often custody is not contested. In those cases where fathers do want the children, they stand a good chance of getting them. By 1977 in America close to two-thirds of the fathers who requested custody were awarded it (Minow, 1986: 902). The appearance of groups like Families Need Fathers in Britain suggests that in the future fathers may be seeking custody more often (Brophy, 1982: 149). This prospect predictably troubles many feminists.

Custody is a difficult area for feminists (Brophy, 1985: 98). On the one hand they are forced to appeal to traditional images of womanhood to secure the children. On the other, ideologically, they ought to approve of developments which suggest that fathers are finally taking a greater interest in childrearing. If they follow this path, of course, they stand to lose the children. As Catharine MacKinnon pointedly comments, the one thing the double standard has won for women is their children and this is no small thing (Du Bois et al., 1985: 24). The tension between women's immediate interests and a vision of a different kind of future presents a recurring problem.

Some feminists feel that women ought to exploit their biologically presumptive right to mothering in custody cases (Chessler, 1988), but this essentialist view is not widely supported. A number of feminist psychological studies have presented the negative effects of mother-only parenting both for women and for men, for today and for the future. For example, Nancy Chodorow and Dorothy Dinnerstein suggest that it is the fact that women mother which produces some of 'men's' least desirable character traits, such as their 'more emphatic individuation and a more defensive firming of experienced ego boundaries...' (Chodorow, 1978: 166; Dinnerstein, 1977). Whether or not one accepts these theories, they create at least a hesitancy to endorse the reproduction of traditional parenting patterns. Sylvia Law makes another important point against biological presumption. In her view, mothering is a moral not a biological commitment, and any tendency to invoke a biological imperative makes it impossible 'to attach moral value to the woman's actions or to acknowledge the human and social worth of the nurturing that women do' (Law, 1984: 996).

There is more disagreement among feminists about the appropriate principle to replace the 'tender years presumption' which is being abandoned by the courts because it stereotypes women and men in inappropriate 'sexist' ways.[11] The suggested alternative, a 'primary caretaker' standard, receives a good deal of support. Wendy Williams, for one, finds this solution preferable to upholding a presumption for the mother:

> ...it shares with that presumption some of the predictability
> which discourages custody contests and is important for the
> well-being of children; it permits the reality that women are
> still typically closer to children to carry the day; and yet it does
> not discourage men from risking intimacy with their children
> (Williams, 1982: 190 fn. 80).

Nancy Polikoff accepts these arguments, as do Barrett and McIntosh (Polikoff, 1982: 237; Barrett and McIntosh, 1982: 155).

Others see dangers in the 'primary parenthood' concept. Martha Minow seems to fear that a 'primary parent' presumption could become 'a punishment for women whose husbands share the mothering tasks' (Minow, 1986: 908), since they could lose their children. Annamay Sheppard's concerns are in another direction. She feels that a primary caretaker standard 'assumes the appropriate custodian is the person who has supplied uninterrupted care and nurturance to the child' which could serve to freeze the existing distribution of sex roles. It is also close enough to the presumption in favour of the stay-at-home mother to be exercised against women who depart from this model. Sheppard wants a 'consistent equality theory' (Taub, 1982: 169; Sheppard, 1982: 234).

The alternative of joint custody is even more controversial. Susan Maidment, a strong supporter of joint custody, believes that the evidence is conclusive that 'the most critical factor in the child's successful adjustment to divorce is his [sic] continued contact with both parents'. Therefore in most cases (Maidment specifies that she is talking about 'ordinary' divorces where 'apart from the marriage breakdown there are otherwise two good parents'), she feels, the law ought to require both parents to participate legally and actually in the life of a child (Maidment, 1984: 279; 1985: 45).

Since we are considering 'ordinary' divorces, there is no need to look at cases involving violence or incest where joint custody would find no feminist and few other supporters. There are however still some real concerns about the operation of a joint custody rule. Julia Brophy questions whether an equal treatment, gender-neutral approach is progressive in custody cases. Her main argument is that such an approach ignores 'the considerable advantages which accrue to men from the current sexual division of labour'. Simply to enforce 'legal rights' would not necessarily alter the distribution of domestic responsibilities. Maidment is also sensitive to the difference between 'joint *legal* custody', which would only bestow rights upon fathers, and 'joint actual custody', which would involve sharing the burden of physical childcare. She stipulates that it is the latter she wants enforced. Brophy's point is that this may be only a fond wish given the traditional division of duties in most families. If men are genuine in their desire to change things, she asks them to do something to alter the structural problems facing custodial parents. They could, for example, demand childcare facilities at the *father's* place of work (Brophy, 1985: 115; Maidment, 1984: 257; Brophy, 1982: 165).

Some feminists are also worried that ex-husbands may exploit joint custody orders. They could use them as a pretext for intervening in the lives of their ex-wives. They could also use the threat of such intervention to negotiate lower monetary support contributions. Mothers and children would lose in this event (Brophy, 1985: 110–111; Williams, 1982: 190–191, fn. 81). Women's differential social location which means that in many cases they lack money and hence power must be considered (Sevenhuijsen, 1986: 337).

Some of these same issues are raised in the debate over illegitimacy. The subject became controversial in Britain as a result of a Law Commission Working Paper (1979) which suggested that the status of illegitimacy be eradicated by 'linking each child to a father as though the child was the child of a married father'. ROW members attacked the proposal on two grounds. First they objected to the presumption that a child could gain legitimacy only through attachment to a man. Second they felt that social relations ought to be deemed as relevant as biological relations (ROW, 1985: 194). This is that same point about rights and responsibilities. Julia Brophy develops the argument:

> ...a proposal to give all biological fathers automatic rights would not ensure the actual participation of those men in child care or, of itself, build a good relationship between father and child. It would simply have given such fathers a dimension of power over the child and possibly through that child a certain degree of power over its mother (Brophy, 1982: 164).

Because of her conviction that a child needs two parents, Maidment suggests that this view smacks of 'a certain female exclusivity' (Maidment, 1985: 36).

The problem with these debates is that they are of necessity reactive and are not conceptualised in feminist terms. As a result, feminists are often confronted with unattractive options. In the illegitimacy example, feminists were given the alternative *either* of 'siding with the liberals who wanted to abolish illegitimacy through the device of giving rights to *all* biological fathers regardless of their relationship to the mother', *or* 'of siding with reactionaries who wanted to retain illegitimacy as a last bulwark against permissiveness'. These alternatives are often conceptualised in terms of 'equality' or 'difference'.

Faced with these choices feminists should develop and promote 'a well-defined third alternative' which may not always produce clear-cut solutions but which will at least raise important questions and open up for examination all the problems with apparently straight-forward reforms. This, Carol Smart believes, is what ROW accomplished. The Law Commission changed its mind as a result of their arguments and as yet 'nothing has happened' (Smart, 1984b: 224; ROW, 1985: 196–197).

The development of new reproductive technologies has created a host of new problems for women. Firestone (see page 84) had identified the cybernetic society and test-tube reproduction as keys to women's liberation. Recent analyses have highlighted, rather, the way in which these technologies manipulate women both psychologically and physically (see for example Correa, 1985 and 1986; Arditti, Klein and Minden, 1984). The implications of genetic engineering touch humanity as a whole but, using the inclusion standard developed in Chapter 6, it is enough cause for complaint when they harm women (Rowland, 1987: 7).

Again feminists find themselves positioned between conservatives who categorically deny the appropriateness of artificial

conception because of their concern with the 'preservation of
the conjugal family and the rights of the foetus', and 'liberal
humanists' who accept the technology as benign and wish only
to control its abuses (Martin, 1986: 376–377). The conservative
vision harks back to the organicist *Gemeinschaft* model which rests
firmly upon assumptions about women's natural role. The liberal
humanist model (*Gesellschaft*) sees the world in terms of competing
and free-standing individual units.

Paradoxically feminists who sit more comfortably in the *Gesellschaft* tradition *fear* the new technology because they feel that it will
increase the pressure on women to become mothers and hence
limit their access to the market. This fear is usually expressed by
those who are convinced that women will be liberated only when
they are free of the maternal imperative, when, that is, they can be
more like 'men'. Other feminists insist that it is a woman's 'right'
to 'choose' to use the new technology *because* of the maternal
imperative. Without denying the validity of these positions, there
is a need to interrogate the ideology which lies behind them, to ask
at least why in our society deciding whether or not to become a
mother is such a difficult decision, and whether the language of
rights has any place in a discussion about reproduction.[12]

The political climate produces as alternatives 'de-emphasising'
or 'emphasising' motherhood. This of course is another way of
saying that some feminists minimise and others maximise women's
differences from men. The important point, however, is that these
appear to be the only choices while the political and social system
penalises motherhood. The 'third alternative' in this case would
highlight the *political factors* which set limits on women's choices.
The kinds of questions this analysis might produce include: Is
there any such thing as a 'benign' technology? What are the social
priorities which permit the allocation of huge resources to this kind
of experimentation? Who has access to these resources? (Martin,
1986: 378).

Unfortunately the recent Baby 'M' surrogacy case[13] threatens to
divide the *American* feminist community along familiar lines, into
those who wish to use 'difference' to defend their position and
those who see any invocation of 'difference' as ultimately regressive. The defenders of 'difference' insist that Mary Beth Whitehead has a prior claim to the child because she is the biological
mother. Phyllis Chessler argues that biological motherhood constitutes a 'sacred bond' which begins 'in utero' (Chessler, 1988:
36–38). Ruth Hubbard also insists upon the absolute necessity of
distinguishing between 'the birth-mother and the sperm donor (or
the egg donor, if she is not also the birth-mother)':

Whether or not she has provided the egg, a birthmother has gestated the baby. At birth, the baby is literally her flesh and blood. Until moments before, it was part of her body and nourished like her own organs. To have provided a sperm or egg is trivial by comparison (in Taub, 1989).

Other American feminists fear the consequences of elevating 'gestational ties' above 'genetic or social links'. Nadine Taub asks: '. . . what will be the fallout for reproductive choice in the area of gamete donation, embryo transfer, abortion and genetic screening? What will be the impact on the climate for reproductive choice more generally?' Taub highlights the 'dangers in approaches that risk fostering a mystique about pregnancy': 'Doing so makes it harder for women to choose to forego childbearing by making other types of relationships appear far less attractive, and it makes the inability to experience pregnancy seem more painful' (Taub, 1989). Taub, you will recall, used similar arguments in her critique of maternity leave laws (see page 118).

The same tension apparent in some of the other debates surfaces here. One group fears motherhood because society penalises those who fill the role. Others wish to cling to woman's maternal function as a power base and a protest against an anti-child culture. These tensions are more serious in America where the social supports for reproduction and childrearing are almost non-existent. As a result, positions there become more polarised. The plea here is that feminists involved in these debates bring the political conditions which have impelled them either to downplay or to eulogise motherhood onto the agenda, and not allow the debate to appear to be over women's sameness to or difference from men. To repeat a theme raised several times, a sameness/difference formulation of the problem mystifies the political issues which lie behind it.

9
The sexuality debates

Feminists based in America:

I think sometimes the First Amendment has been carried to extremes.

Catherine East

I have such a dilemma...I'm not hot for censorship and yet I think pornography is pretty criminal. I'm not quite at the Dworkin/MacKinnon stage but I'm not quite at the ACLU (American Civil Liberties Union) stage either.

Leslie Wolfe

Regarding the banning of pornography, 'the cure would have unintended consequences'.

Catharine Stimpson

Regarding pornography, 'it's a good area to illustrate how we have to create new concepts for dealing with these problems. I feel very sympathetic with arguments on both sides because there's a lot of truth on both sides. The debate has gotten stuck because of the inability to think about the fact that there is truth on both sides. Therefore we need the debate but we need to debate it in terms of how difficult it is to create new conceptions dealing with these things in the existing patriarchy.'

Charlotte Bunch

Feminists based in Britain:

Whereas one's natural inclination is that one ought to ban pornography, which is what my own inclination would be, I have actually caught short this inclination because I know the madmen of the Conservative Party are with me on this one.

Lisanne Radici

We must find some way of censoring the pornography of violence.

Mary Stott

I do think there is a linkage between various forms of stimulation and violence but at the same time there is a lot of violence among men who have never seen a single nasty. So it may not be just the overt modern pornography. Mythological pornographies, folk tales, also have the same effect. Nine of ten Indian women are burned or bashed in some way. There is part of the culture that is letting them get away with it.

Georgina Ashworth

If you're talking about violence towards women, any notion of equality is out the window.

Paddy Stamp

What do we do? Do we just sit back and talk about discourse theory and semiotics and let that (pornography) go? I actually feel quite old-fashioned. Heavens, perhaps I'm a left-wing Mary Whitehouse!

Cynthia Cockburn

I came more and more to the view, and it's difficult to justify intellectually if you're a liberal, that pornography ought to be banned.

Elizabeth Vallance

A campaign against pornography should be broadly understood as a campaign against degrading sexual imagery and I do support that. Here [Britain] there has been a very clear split between radical feminists who are broadly speaking against pornography and want it banned, and socialist feminists who say that the dangers of censorship are worse than the dangers of pornography... I am more sympathetic to the radical feminist position on pornography. I think we're being censored all the time anyway.

Michèle Barrett

Feminists based in Australia:

I don't have a libertarian approach to pornography. I think that once violence towards women (or towards anybody but it is usually towards women) is involved, then the right to 'get off' on this is not as important as the right of society to protect itself against these values coming into the community.

Susan Ryan

Regarding the debate in America, 'There has been such bitterness over this. To me, the original strength of feminism was to open women's mouths and have women speak. Here the issue was in fact having the opposite effect. Rather than silencing the pornographers, feminists were silencing each other. I felt that was absolutely tragic... As a socialist feminist

I have a lot of impatience with the lack of any kind of materialist analysis of sexuality... I am not minimising the importance of the debate. It has given rise to an enormous range of statements that haven't been made before... There, is the whole issue of sexual identity, sexual expression, what women want, what men want. I mean, it is terribly profound and important.'

Hester Eisenstein

You have to define pornography and you have to define erotica. Pornography is a form of demeaning, dehumanising of females that is explicit... I am working at the moment to bring up legislation in this state that would prevent inciting to racial hatred. I believe that pornography incites sexual hatred.

Carmel Niland

It is interesting that in Australia the pornography debate really hasn't got off the ground... Here maybe because we feel so ambivalent about it, we prefer not to get involved. Also we have had so many other battles to fight... The other really difficult problem that I have with it is that one is driven straight into the arms of the extreme right, people like the Reverend Fred Nile... Much of the stuff that is disseminated through the media, on television in particular, is ultimately more destructive because it actually gets to a wider audience.

Margaret Thornton

Put simply, the sexuality debates revolve around pornography and what to do about it, and around the nature of sexuality more generally. On one side are those typecast as 'pro-sex', who believe that all forms of sexual expression, including pornography and more exotic forms such as lesbian sadomasochism and butch/femme lesbian relationships,[1] are acceptable. On the other side are a disparate group, labelled 'anti-sex' by their opponents, who object to pornography and to sexual relationships which seem to incorporate displays of power, violence, or dominant/submissive roles.

The first group tend to emphasise women's and men's common sexuality and the need to free people to explore that sexuality. The latter are more likely to identify a benign female sexuality and an aggressive male sexuality, and to see the latter as the cause of many social problems. At this level, the debates are metaphysical and are closely related to the more general question about women's and men's character (Chapter 10). The debates also have policy implications. Those who stress a common human sexuality are keen to introduce gender-neutral legislation in areas such as rape (see page 220). Other feminists are less certain about the trend towards gender-neutrality, for a variety of reasons.

This chapter develops the argument that talking about women's and men's 'similar' or 'different' sexual styles, or the need for 'equal' or 'different' treatment oversimplifies important political problems. It suggests that the metaphysical debate is, in effect, a product of competing social visions. Many defenders of a common sexuality tend to accept an individualistic model for social organisation (*Gesellschaft*). By contrast many of those who identify different sexual styles in women and men support more communitarian values (*Gemeinschaft*), and see female sexuality/character as the repository of those values. Collapsing sexuality into politics in this fashion makes it difficult to say anything meaningful either about sexuality or the different political visions.

Similarly, in the policy/institutional domain, those who insist upon gender-neutrality on every issue tend to accept the idea of equality associated with political liberalism, a notion which abstracts individuals from their particular circumstances. They also use the language of rights, interpreted as zones of non-interference, to try to defend women. Those who identify women as 'different' see problems with the liberal model, but are often content to single women out for special treatment instead of challenging the model. Neither 'sameness' nor 'difference', equal treatment nor different treatment, I suggest, adequately address the full range of women's problems.

The sexuality debates are particularly heated in America, for reasons which confirm their political character. According to Ruby Rich, the debates there have produced 'one of the worst movement splits in recent times' (Rich, 1983: 66). Attitudes toward pornography are pivotal, and are affected by the firm commitment of many Americans to the free speech ideals of the First Amendment of the Constitution.[2] Again we are alerted to the role played by institutions and ideology in the shaping of feminist analysis.

Robert Post sees the problem as the 'ingrained individualism' of American liberal political culture. Post identifies the tension between the individualist and the organicist/pluralist strands within liberalism, noted in the Introduction (see page xii). Either approach, he claims, is compatible with a system of freedom of expression. The question becomes whether we value such freedom because it furthers *individual* or *group* life. The answer to this question is a matter of 'high cultural policy', as Post says, and depends upon the 'kind of social world' Americans wish to use the First Amendment to construct (Post, 1988: 304, 334–335).

Americans to date have pursued the individualist path. Emphasis is placed, therefore, upon freedom and detachment. Sexuality is considered to be integral to personhood and hence every individual is presumed to have a 'right' to explore their sexuality (Bassnet, 1986: 28–29). This is, of course, only one tradition, albeit the dominant one. Because of its strength, some feminists who oppose it have set up female sexuality and women as the symbols of a more caring and communitarian ethic. Where 'sameness' is interpreted to mean the ignoring of a range of human needs, feminists occasionally use an appeal to 'difference' in an attempt to have those needs addressed. There are two unfortunate effects in the sexuality test-case. The political issues get lost in rhetorical appeals to women's 'sameness' or 'difference'. And, the positions become interpreted as alternatives instead of seeking ways to make the model generally more responsive to human needs.

Feminists in each country see pornography as problematic. In the interviews conducted as part of the research for the book, concern was expressed about whether a distinction ought to be drawn between violent pornography and non-violent erotica, the danger of using the state to control its dissemination, and whether or not feminist energy ought to be expended on an anti-pornography campaign. In Britain and Australia, however, there was a consensus that something had to be done. In America, by contrast, there were frequent and firm expressions of belief in the need to preserve freedom of speech.

The issue has become more public and more topical in America as a result of the efforts of two well-known radical feminists, Andrea Dworkin and Catharine MacKinnon, who drafted a city ordinance allowing women and in some circumstances, men, to take pornographers to court. Under the ordinance a woman could sue a pornographer if she were coerced into participating in the production of pornography, if she were forced to view pornography, or if she were assaulted as a direct result of pornography. A final clause would allow a woman to claim the public availability of pornography as a violation of women's civil rights. Indianapolis City Council passed the ordinance, the District Court declared it unconstitutional, and the case is now under appeal. Feminists have submitted briefs on both sides. MacKinnon and Dworkin submitted one supporting the ordinance, while a group called the Feminist Anti-Censorship Taskforce (FACT) has opposed it. FACT includes as members such well-known feminist activists as Linda Gordon, Kate Millett, Adrienne Rich and Gayle Rubin. On the other side MacKinnon and Dworkin have attracted support from Kathleen Barry, Mary Daly, Robin Morgan and Janice Raymond (Kelly, 1985: 5–6).

In Britain, Labour MPs Clare Short and Jo Richardson have been conducting a 'Campaign Against Pornography' for several years. Short introduced a bill, which was defeated, trying to ban 'Page 3' of a daily tabloid which frequently shows provocative pictures of naked women. Jo Richardson explained to me that 'We are starting at the soft porn end, at the images of women stereotyping women' in order to raise consciousness about pornography. She and Short are now considering some broader form of legislation to 'make it an offence punishable by a fine to publish degrading images of women for profit'. Representatives of the radical feminist group, Women Against Violence Against Women (WAVAW), feel that Short's campaign is not radical enough and want pornography to be made a criminal offence. The debate, at this time, 'remains sisterly', probably because of the agreement that some action is necessary (Baxter, 1988: 24–25).

In Australia, Women Against Violence and Exploitation (WAVE) have conducted an active campaign against pornography. Neil Thornton attributes the defeat of the government's attempt to liberalise censorship to 'an alliance of moral conservatives and radical feminists.' The Attorneys-General from around the country voted to ban explicit sex and extreme violence in video films throughout Australia, forcing the Commonwealth to back away from classification proposals which would have allowed non-violent erotica (N. Thornton, 1986: 44; 1985:21; the *Advertiser* [Adelaide], 1 July 1988). The government has recently decided to shelve the ban for the time being and to examine ways to reduce the level of violence in all categories (*Advertiser*, 9 November 1988). Feminist groups are demanding action in this area.

The broader issue of 'appropriate' sexual behaviour is also debated in each country (Ardill and O'Sullivan, 1986), though again the divisions are sharper in America. At the 1982 Barnard conference on the 'politics of sexuality', the two sides engaged in open confrontation. A coalition of anti-pornography feminist groups picketed and leafleted the conference, which had been advertised as a conference on 'women's sexual pleasure, choice and autonomy'. They called for a 'boycott of speakers whose views on sexuality and alleged sexual practice they deemed unfeminist' (Freedman and Thorne, 1984: 103). The organisers of the conference published a *Diary* and a volume, *Pleasure and Danger*, containing many of the papers which had been delivered, documents which attest to the philosophical and ideological complexities of matters relating to sexuality. Towards the end of *Pleasure and*

Danger, a plea was registered against the 'McCarthyite tactics' claimed to have been used by the protestors, and 'for feminists to resist the impulse to censor ourselves, as strongly as we resist the efforts of others to censor us' (Alderfer et al., 1982; Vance, 1984).

It is not surprising that sexuality has posed such an ideological minefield for feminists, given the way in which women have historically been defined through their sexuality. Although it is now clear that attitudes towards women's sexuality, like attitudes to sexuality generally, have changed over time and differ according to the race and class of women being considered (Bacchi, 1988: 43), the dominant theme over the last 100 years has been the contrast between the 'good girl' and the 'bad girl'. In the Victorian era the 'good girl', who was white and middle-class, was also 'asexual'; the 'bad girl' was usually poor or Black, and licentious. The sexologists of the 1920s allowed 'good girls' to become sexual, but within certain constraints and for a specific purpose. According to Anita Grossman, 'Sex Reformers encouraged sexual technique (proficiency) and women's right to orgasm as a means of stabilising and harmonising the heterosexual nuclear family' (Grossman, 1984: 194). The middle-class white woman was 'eroticised' to save the middle-class family (Bacchi, 1988). The 'how to' books of the 1960s (and today) seemed to herald the appearance of the fully sexually liberated woman, but the messages in many of these books were ambivalent. Meryl Altman describes how these texts 'co-opted and transformed' the sexually liberated woman into the 'Sensuous Woman', another sex object, this time dedicated to the sexual satisfaction of her male partner (Altman, 1984: 127).

This history has created understandable tensions within feminism when dealing with matters sexual. There is the tension between trying to discover what sexual 'freedom' means while fending off the image of sex object. There is the tension between a desire to rebel against a moralistic stereotype which has been used to constrain women's sexual activities and the knowledge that in society today women are sexually vulnerable. These tensions are captured in the pleasure/danger dichotomy. How can women seek 'pleasure' in a society where sexuality poses for them explicit dangers, either of sexual aggression, or of unwanted pregnancy? The problem seems to be that women have to 'choose' between 'freedom' and security, between individual self-actualisation and community support (Philipson, 1984: 118; Olsen, 1984: 387). The 'choice' should by now be familiar.

This tension is sometimes expressed as a 'choice' between

'equality' and 'difference'. Lucy Bland claims that feminists have long puzzled over the question:

> Can sexual 'freedom' ever be an equivalent freedom for women as for men? In demanding equality and declaring our 'sameness', how are women to argue simultaneously for recognition of *difference*: our different procreative capacity and our different experience of sexuality? (Bland, 1987: 141, emphasis in original).

As in the other cases in the book where 'sameness' is set against 'difference', this way of thinking makes it difficult to raise questions about fundamental social values. For example, why in our society does a person seem to have to choose between autonomy and security? And why does woman's procreative capacity leave her on the more vulnerable side of this equation? Be this as it may, many in the movement have chosen to explore 'equality' and 'difference'.

To understand why this has happened it is important to remember the historical conditions which produced the 1960s resurgence of feminism. The economic euphoria of the 1960s was accompanied, for reasons which have yet to be adequately explored, by the 'sexual revolution'. The student rebellion against bureaucracy and authority signalled a rebellion also against traditional moral standards. This was the period of 'free love'. Student radicals in the United States produced the epigram 'To Fornicate is Divine' (Evans, 1980: 177).

Women were encouraged to join this revolution. 'Scientific' studies heralded the fact that in sex women could be 'equal' or even 'superior' partners. Sara Evans captured the mood of the period: 'Alfred Kinsey let the cat out of the bag...Women, it turned out, had orgasms'. Masters and Johnson went further and proved that 'the female sexual cycle is capable of multiple orgasms in quick succession' (Evans, 1980: 12; Millett, 1971: 117).

The only 'obstacle' for those women who preferred heterosexual sex, it seemed, was procreation. The new contraceptive device, the pill, promised to bring this 'effect' under 'control'. The abortion campaign also signalled a desire to 'free' women from their biology, to bring their bodies 'under control'. Women were being offered the opportunity to have sex 'like men'. Kate Millett described the goal of the sexual revolution as 'an end of traditional sexual inhibitions and taboos', 'a permissive *single standard* of sexual freedom' (Millett, 1971: 62, emphasis added). Sexuality assumed a 'quasi-mystical dimension'. It became almost a symbol of the liberation women were seeking. Equality seemed to mean the ability to pursue self-actualisation, regardless of consequences.

The heightened awareness which came out of discussions in consciousness-raising groups alerted women to the fact that their sexuality had been constrained for political reasons. The revelation that the clitoris, not the vagina, was the organ specific to women's sexuality raised questions about the political reasons behind the long-standing belief in the 'vaginal orgasm' as the product of a 'superior' kind of sex.[3] The fact that many, if not most, women lived in fear of sexual aggression led to political questions about the inadequacy of rape laws and the unfair way in which women's previous sexual experience became a factor in rape trials. The abortion laws were also singled out as laws designed to control female sexuality. It became clear that 'At the heart of the prohibition against abortion (and birth control) is the deeply held feeling that female sex outside of procreation must be punished' (Shulman, 1980: 26). In a world where women's sexuality had been defined as 'different' by conventional social mores, where women's sex-specific needs were often ignored, and where women's differential social location left them vulnerable, claiming 'equality' was no easy matter.

The rebellion against sexual taboos led to the 'coming out' of female homosexuals. Lesbians made particularly significant theoretical contributions to the understanding of male sexual power. Problems arose, however, when some lesbians claimed that lesbianism was not only or simply a sexual preference, but a political choice. In the words of Martha Shelly, an early Radicalesbian:

> To me, lesbianism is not an oddity of a few women to be hidden in the background of the Movement. In a way it is the heart of the Women's Liberation Movement. In order to throw off the oppression of the male caste, women must unite—we must learn to love ourselves and each other... The idea that women must teach men how to love, that we must not become manhaters is, at this point in history, like preaching pacifism to the Vietcong (quoted in Shulman, 1980: 30).

The message, as Rita Mae Brown put it, was 'You can't build a strong movement if your sisters are out there fucking with the oppressors' (quoted in Echols, 1984a: 68).

The notion of 'political lesbianism' caused predictable problems for heterosexual feminists who did not like to be accused of consorting with the 'enemy'. Some feminists rebelled against the implicit 'prescriptivism', the suggestion that sex could be either 'politically correct' or 'politically incorrect', and that heterosexuality or any behaviour which replicated dominant/submissive sexual styles fell on the 'incorrect' side of the equation (Dimen, 1984; Curthoys, 1988: 24). Hester Eisenstein attributes the 'sex war among women' in part to this 'censoring of people's actual sexual experience':

> if you had fantasies about bondage, or if you had fantasies about being raped, or if you were straight and had lesbian fantasies, or if you were lesbian and had straight fantasies, that was 'wrong think' (Eisenstein interview, 25 August 1987).

There were serious divisions within the movement over the lesbian issue. From the outset Betty Friedan, speaking for the 'straight' faction, wished to disown the lesbian contingent because she feared offending the conservative public. The gay/straight split of the 1970s created problems for the movement which have never gone away, problems which lie behind the current sexuality debates. The divisions are practical and theoretical, and have to do with conflicting beliefs about the ultimate cause of women's oppression, the relationship between sexuality and gender, and strategic decisions about the movement's priorities. Many feminists, of course, stand outside these divisions. I am concerned here to understand what lies behind the open conflict between some feminists over sexual issues.

While it is overly simple to talk about 'pro-sex' and 'anti-sex' feminists, those engaged in the sexuality debates describe each other in these terms. Gayle Rubin identifies two strains of feminist thought on sexuality: the tendency she supports, which she describes as criticising 'restrictions on women's sexual behavior', and the tendency she rejects which, in her words, 'resonates with conservative, anti-sexual discourse' (Rubin, 1984: 301). On the other side, Jayne Egerton of Britain's WAVAW portrays the American 'feminist pro-sexual pleasure lobby' as 'sexual libertarians who believe in the absolute validity of any sexual variation. Their priorities are liberal not feminist . . .' (Rhodes and McNeill, 1985: 211).

Perhaps even more unfortunate has been the tendency to impose present controversies on the past, and to suggest that feminism has always been split into pro-sex and anti-sex factions. To the detriment of historical understanding, both groups of feminists have sought to uncover traditions within feminism which either validate their particular position today or which seem to denigrate that of their opponents. As described in Part I of the book, feminists have often tried to enlist history on their side.

Betty Friedan, a vocal defender of freedom of speech, castigates America's first women's movement for retreating 'behind a cultural curtain of female "purity"', and for 'focusing their energy on issues like prohibition, much like the pornographic obsession of some feminists today' (Friedan, 1985: 12). The historians Ellen Du Bois and Linda Gordon also draw an analogy between the 'revival of social purity politics within feminism' today and the social purity politics of women in the late nineteenth century, a vision which they describe as 'limited and limiting' for women. Feminist anti-pornographers in their view are too closely aligned with the Moral Majority. They accuse them of being even more conservative than their nineteenth-century counterparts for ignoring all the changes to women's situation which make sexual liberation a possibility for women today:

> We have a vision of sexuality that is not exclusively heterosexual, nor tied to reproduction. We have a much better physiological understanding of sexual response, and a vision of ungendered parenting. . . Perhaps most important, we have today at least a chance at economic independence, the necessary material condition for women's sexual liberation (Du Bois and Gordon, 1984: 43).

Among the anti-pornographers, the social purity reformers of the late nineteenth century become, not surprisingly, the heroes. Margaret Jackson praises them for recognising that 'the relationship between sex and power lay at the heart of women's oppression' and for refusing to be seduced by the sex reformers into 'compulsory heterosexuality': 'Many of these women chose to be celibate because they refused to subject themselves to male sexual control, and advocated sexual withdrawal from men as a political strategy' (Jackson, 1984: 49; Rhodes and McNeill, 1985: 222).

This playing out of current disputes on historical battlefields has unfortunate effects. It distorts both the past and the present and is insensitive to change. Du Bois and Gordon are doubtless correct that material variations in women's lifestyles have altered the experience of sexuality, a fact which Jackson ignores. But they in turn overlook developments in technology which have produced dramatic changes in the ways in which information about sexuality is disseminated. Michel Foucault has alerted us to the 'proliferation of discourses' about sexuality in the twentieth century, and has warned that knowledge does not always produce freedom, that in fact the twentieth-century obsession with sexuality is constraining in certain ways. Foucault refers to it as the new 'opiate of the masses' (Foucault, 1981: 128 and *passim*). Du Bois and Gordon fail to acknowledge 'how modern capitalism has harnessed sexuality and sexual "liberation" for dehumanizing purposes' (Philipson, 1984: 115).

Perhaps most seriously these accounts leave the impression that women have always had, and hence will always have, to *choose* between these two options, sexual freedom or social repression. Moreover, they imply that such a choice is possible. Irene Philipson objects to this representation of the problem: 'In a society characterised by male domination it is impossible to want just freedom, on the one hand, or just protection, on the other'. Frances Olsen makes a similar point. She explains that 'in conditions of sexual inequality, women are oppressed by both sexual freedom and societal control of sexuality'. Feminists ought not to be disputing which is worse—social control of women's sexuality or male sexual exploitation—but should be devising strategies to overcome both (Philipson, 1984: 118; Olsen, 1984: 430).

The first step in this process must involve a clearer theorising of sexuality. The theorising of sexuality on both sides of this debate is inadequate which is surprising since both sides are familiar with social construction theory (see page 236). In fact, the social construction of sexuality which sees sexual behaviour, like other behaviour, as shaped and determined by *cultural* rather than *biological* forces, is a starting point for any feminist analysis of sexuality (Wilson, 1983: 136). The problem seems to be that each group is more assiduous in applying this theory to their opponents than to themselves. As a result, both lapse into positions which are closer to essentialism.[4]

The pro-sex lobby, a label adopted for the sake of argument, accuses the anti-pornographers of being essentialists. Du Bois and Gordon, for example, criticise the tendency to attribute women's sexual victimisation to 'some violent essence labelled "male sexuality"' (Du Bois and Gordon, 1984: 43). The Barnard Conference *Diary* represents the anti-pornography movement as believing that male sexuality is 'naturally' different from that of women (Alderfer et al., 1982: 7). Gayle Rubin meanwhile challenges 'sexual essentialism—the idea that sex is a natural force that exists prior to social life...' She denounces the notion of a 'natural libido subjected to inhumane repression' and calls upon feminists to develop a radical critique of sexual arrangements 'that has the conceptual elegance of Foucault and the evocative passion of Reich' (Rubin, 1984: 277–278). In the Introduction to *Pleasure and Danger* Carole Vance also insists that sexuality is a social construction and 'not simply a "natural" fact, as earlier, essentialist theories would suggest' (Vance, 1984: 7).

However, some of the representatives of the pro-sex group tend themselves to talk about sex as a 'natural drive' which has been 'repressed', and also frequently lack sensitivity to the cultural location of their own views. Linda Gordon and Allen Hunter state, in one article, that 'we can be in principle unequivocally pro-sex because sex itself is a human activity that has its own worth...' Gayle Rubin has also been accused of 'ignoring the historical and cultural construction that she otherwise espouses' for comments such as, 'sex is fundamentally okay until proven bad' (both quotations from Diamond and Quinby, 1984: 122–123). Ellen Willis is outspoken in her endorsement of sexuality as a 'fundamental force', and of 'erotic impulses' as 'fundamentally benign and necessary for human happiness'. Pornography, in Willis's view, is a form of resistance, 'a protest against the repression of non-marital, non-procreative sex'. Moreover she finds it depressing, 'one hundred and fifty years after Freud', 'to have to insist that sex is not an unnecessary, morally dubious self-indulgence but a *basic human need*, no less for women than for men' (Woodruff et al., 1986: 36; Philipson, 1984: 114; Willis, 1984: 94, emphasis added).

Even Carole Vance who appears to be fully aware of the implications of social construction theory is troubled by it. She asks, 'What is the nature of the relationship between the arbitrariness of social construction and the immediacy of our bodily sensations and functions?' At the Seventh Berkshire Conference on the History of Women, she pursued this query and concluded that, while 'we must combat any return to biological determinism', we must also reject 'a move towards total disembodiment'. Susan Magarey and Susan Sheridan commented on Vance's session: 'The ghost of Freud lurked on the perimeters of this whole session, but was never summoned in for consultation' (Vance, ed., 1984: 9; Magarey and Sheridan, 1987: 149–154).

Vance has made an important point which will come up again. There is no doubt that one of the most stubborn problems facing feminists and social theorists generally is how to theorise the body. For the time being, however, the point I wish to make is how difficult it is, despite good intentions, to recognise the ways in which attitudes are influenced by contemporary conceptual systems. The pervasive current belief that sexuality provides the key to our essence as a person, which lies behind much of the pro-sex theorising, is a relatively recent phenomenon (Diamond and Quinby, 1984: 120; 1988: 198). It also has to be more than co-incidental that this attitude is reinforced by, and suits so well the individualist impulse which characterises contemporary capitalism.

Speaking for the 'anti-sex' faction, Margaret Jackson makes that very point, that our 'notions of sexual pleasure, desire etc., should not be accepted as given, but examined as social constructs'. Catharine MacKinnon is also aware of the way in which Freudian assumptions have shaped our understanding of sexuality: 'The social problem posed by sexuality since Freud has been seen as the problem of the repression of innate desire for sexual pleasure by the constraints of civilisation' (Rhodes and McNeill, 1985: 217; MacKinnon, 1983: 28). But the radical feminist message is consistently portrayed as itself essentialist. Is this representation unjust?

The answer to this question depends, in part, upon the radical feminist under consideration. For Susan Brownmiller, rape is clearly a function of male biology: 'By anatomical fiat—the inescapable construction of their genital organs—the human male was a predator and the human female served as his natural prey' (Brownmiller, 1975: 16). Biology also plays a crucial role in Adrienne Rich's reassessment of motherhood: 'I have come to believe...that female biology...has far more radical implications than we have yet come to appreciate' (Rich, 1976: 39).[5]

Other radical feminists are more careful in their analysis. Anne Koedt, for example, attributed male oppression not to men's biology but to the way in which men '*rationalise*' their '*supremacy* on the basis of that biological difference'. Robin Morgan also refers to the 'patriarchally trained male's' sexuality. Unfortunately, she does not carry over this analysis to women's sexuality, which appears as 'naturally' sensual and tender (Echols, 1984a: 65, 71).

Andrea Dworkin is difficult to pin down. In 1978 she wrote a powerful essay condemning biological determinism. The experiences of Dworkin's family in the concentration camps of Auschwitz and Birkenau doubtless affected her views on the subject: 'it is dangerous—because genocide begins, however improbably, in the conviction that classes of biological distinction indisputably sanction social and political discrimination' (Dworkin, 1978: 51; see also Rogers, 1987: 14). But in her most recent book, *Intercourse*, Dworkin seems to be saying that the act of male/female, penis/vagina intercourse creates or at least perpetuates inequality. She is at best ambivalent on the subject. At times she refers specifically to the fact that she is talking about 'sex for women under male dominance as a social system'. At other times the consequences are described as possibly 'intrinsic, not socially imposed'. Most clearly essentialist is her description of the way in which a woman engaging in coition is 'a space inhabited, a literal territory occupied literally: occupied even if there has been no resistance, no force'. Her only answer to the disturbing question—'can those with metaphysically compromised privacy have self-determination?'—is that 'Intercourse is not necessary to existence anymore' (Dworkin, 1987: 76, 145, 146, 157, 163). This conclusion ignores recent feminist criticism of the new reproductive technologies (see page 199). It also seems a little strange to build a 'radical' feminist analysis of sexuality upon privacy, a contemporary American cultural artifact and a fundamental tenet of liberalism.

Clarifying their position on biological determinism, radical feminists often make explicit disclaimers. MacKinnon states: '. . . men are the way they are because they have power, more than that they have power because they are the way they are'. WAVAW also claims that men's sexual behaviour is not 'natural and biological' but 'has been socially constructed to be aggressive, exploitative, objectifying'. There is however a rather unfortunate circularity in the argument which then proceeds to explain that the 'system is constructed by men, in men's interests, for the benefit of all men'. MacKinnon's final conclusion is that 'the mainspring of sex inequality is misogyny', and Dworkin refers to an 'unexplained, undiagnosed, mostly unacknowledged' hatred of women 'that pervades sexual practice and sexual passion' (MacKinnon, 1987: 5, 220; Rhodes and McNeill, 1985: 7; Dworkin, 1987: 164). If this is not essentialism, it is something so like it that the differences do not seem to matter. It is not *male biology* which is responsible for all the pain and anguish women experience; it is *men*.[6]

It is possible then to conclude that, despite claims to the contrary, both groups are essentialist. The two camps reify 'male' and 'female' sexuality and thus 'fail to appreciate the way in which sexuality is an historically culturally specific construct' (Sawicki, 1986: 34; Ferguson, 1984: 110). They do, of course, reify these sexualities differently, which is important for this particular study. The pro-sex group posits, by implication if not directly, a *common* human sexual essence ('sameness') which ought to be liberated; the anti-sex group sees two separate essences: a male essence which is aggressive and a female essence which is placid and benign.

Ann Ferguson offers a useful comparison of the two paradigms. Radical (anti-sex) feminists, she claims, espouse a 'primacy of intimacy' theory which emphasises the communication of emotion; libertarian (pro-sex) feminists on the other hand adopt a 'primacy of pleasure' approach which focuses upon the exchange of 'physical erotic and genital sexual pleasure'. The former emphasise feelings; the latter, bodily sensations. Both sides are caught then in a version of the mind/body dichotomy, an idea feminists have been keen to challenge. As with so many dichotomies, the 'truth' is hidden by the construction: 'neither emotions nor physical pleasures can be isolated and discussed in a vacuum' (Ferguson, 1984: 109).

There seems little likelihood that a resolution to the sexuality debates lies down some 'middle path' (Rubin, 1984: 303). A closer scrutiny of the ideological foundations of sexual attitudes is, however, essential. Instead, feminists are finding 'their arguments trivialised into a line-drawing debate' (Olsen, 1984: 390), similar in some ways to the 1920s debate on protective legislation. Not that the issues are identical, but that the hardening of positions is foreclosing constructive dialogue.

According to Liz Kelly, neither side is even addressing the questions raised by the other. In the pornography debate, FACT pays little attention to the accumulated evidence 'of the coercion of women into the sex industry and of the abusive use of porn by men in heterosexual relationships'. FACT also stresses the negative impact of censorship, almost ignoring the fact that MacKinnon's and Dworkin's anti-pornography ordinance is designed to put more power into the hands of women than into the hands of the state. On the other hand, Dworkin and MacKinnon have said little about the difficulties involved in implementing the anti-pornography ordinance (Kelly, 1985: 7).

As a first step to reopening dialogue, it may prove helpful to bring to the surface the political values which lie subsumed beneath the sexuality debates. It then becomes possible to discuss the different political visions, their strengths and limitations, a project which is difficult so long as we believe that the dispute is about whether women and men share a common sexuality, or have conflicting sexual styles, whether they are the 'same' or 'different'.

In effect, on both sides, sexuality has become a metaphor for a political stance. The radical feminist view of sexuality as 'competitive and greedy' represents their political commentary on contemporary capitalism, on the 'hunger, war and ecological disasters' (Echols, 1984a: 64). Once sexuality has been constructed in this way, as self-indulgent and compulsive, it becomes necessary to describe women as 'anti-sex'. Otherwise they could be seen as condoning the political status quo. And so women are described as 'more concerned with ecology and peace and less with sexuality'. A capacity for 'abstinence, repression or suppression' becomes, in this framework, adaptive over 'male hypersexuality' (Echols, 1984a: 62, 72). Sadomasochism and butch/femme roles have then to be condemned for apparently replicating an undesirable value system. Alice Echols is correct that the real culprit in radical feminism is not sexuality at all but individualism. Unfortunately, her only response is a *defence* of individualism (Echols, 1984a: 76).

She does not seem to realise that both sides have collapsed sexuality into politics, constraining both the analysis of sexuality and the political vision.

By turning a critique of capitalism into an exhortation against male sexuality, radical feminists forego a more sophisticated political commentary. They also fall into the trap of leaving women responsible for the world's caring values in much the same way as the ancient *Gemeinschaft* tradition counted on women's altruism to service the family and the community. This is seen most obviously in the way in which radical feminism copies moral conservatism. While many authors have stated that, in the anti-pornography campaign, feminists and the Moral Majority make 'strange bedfellows' (Wilson, 1983: 154; Faust, 1981: 6), I am suggesting more than this. In both analyses, men are seen as uncontrollable and unpredictable, and women are given the task of taming them. In the tension between individual self-actualisation and community standards women are again allocated responsibility for maintaining social stability. Female sexuality has often been seen this way, 'as a sort of glue to hold structures together' (Janeway, 1980: 5). Feminists ought not, however, to endorse uncritically the role traditionally assigned to women. They ought rather to analyse the way in which that role has been constructed, and the political uses it serves.

On the other side, a model which says simply that people should be free to pursue self-interest (*Gesellschaft*), sexual and otherwise, has limitations. It is this model which motivates some liberal feminists to cling to a 'coherent theory of equality' (Williams, 1982: 175). The problems which this approach can create are apparent in the pornography debate and in two other test cases, statutory rape and abortion. These will be considered first.

America acquired statutory rape laws under English common law. These laws make it an offence for a man to have sex with an under-age female. The 'age of consent' has varied over the years. One of the most important nineteenth-century feminist campaigns was to raise this age to eighteen or preferably to 21. The majority of American feminists today want to *remove* the laws which, they claim, restrict young women's activities since they make it illegal for them to engage in sexual intercourse. The laws are also criticised for reinforcing the stereotype that men initiate sex and women resist. Representatives of the equal treatment school (see Chapter 5) insist that in this, as in other matters, men and women must be treated identically, that feminists must be consistent in their search for equality. Most states have now made the laws gender-neutral and some have decriminalised sex among teen-agers.[7] But some laws remain on the books and, in a recent court case, *Michael M. v. Sonoma County* (1981), the Supreme Court upheld California's gender-based legislation on the grounds that it deterred teenage pregnancy (Olsen, 1984: 403–404; Goldstein, 1988: 267–282).

As in maternity leave (Chapter 5) and protective legislation (Chapter 6), it is easy to understand why some feminists insist that women reject any law which designates them as 'different' since that construction has consistently been used against them. In the area of sexuality, the case of *Dothard v. Rawlinson* (1977) is exemplary. In that case (see page 160), a woman security guard was denied her job on the grounds that, as part of her 'very woman-hood', she was more vulnerable to rape than a man and hence would be unable to perform the job properly. The supposition that women are vulnerable and the assumption that women should be assimilated into the status quo, meant that the court did not even consider alternatives, such as training female employees in self-defence or segregating sex offenders to reduce the risk (Littleton, 1981: 494–495). Cases like *Dothard* have convinced many feminists that women admit 'difference' at their peril. As a result, many have condemned the decision of *Michael M.* on the grounds that it singles out women for 'special treatment', and have endorsed the view of the dissenting judges that equality demands that women be considered *equally culpable* in statutory rape cases (Olsen, 1984: 421).

This understandable reluctance to identify women as 'different', however, has unfortunately blinded some feminists to certain reali-ties. Most importantly, in the world today, men frequently have more monetary, social and hence psychological power, and some-times use it to extract sex from women. A selection from the testimony in *Michael M.* illustrates the point. The plaintiff, Sharon, related what happened:

> We was laying there and we were kissing each other...And he told me to take my pants off. I said, 'No,' and I was trying to get up and he hit me back down on the bench and then I just said to myself, 'Forget it,' and I let him do what he wanted to do...(quoted in Olsen, 1984: 416 fn. 132).

While it would have been difficult to prove Michael M. guilty of rape, the statutory rape laws provided in this instance a tool to equalise the power imbalance.

The key then is the need to recognise and address the disadvan-tages which result from women's differential social location.

Frances Olsen believes that 'we should acknowledge the present reality of pervasive male sexual aggression in our society and devise ways to change it rather than denying it as an "outmoded stereotype"'. This is another case (see page 163) where parts of the stereotypes are 'true' and to pretend that they are false perpetuates inequality. To quote Olsen again:

> It is a mistake to believe that feminists have only two choices: to reject a generalisation about women and call it an 'outmoded stereotype' ['sameness'], or to accept the generalisation and embrace it as true and good ['difference']...Instead, feminists can acknowledge the elements of truth in the generalisation and attempt to change the conditions that make it true (Olsen, 1984: 424; 428 fn. 197).

The search for a 'coherent equality theory' makes this type of analysis difficult. ERA supporters admit that 'To be sure, the singling out of women (in statutory rape cases) probably reflects sociological reality', but they are trapped by the formality of their proposal:

> ...the Equal Rights Amendment forbids finding legislative justification in the sexual double standard, and requires such statutes to be framed in terms of the general human need for protection rather than in terms of crude sexual categories (Brown, Emerson, Falk, and Freedman, 1971: 958).

In the search to have women treated 'equally', some feminists have accepted the narrow understanding of equality which abstracts people from their particular circumstances. Their political analysis is constrained by this principle. This is not to say that statutory rape laws should remain unamended. The law could give under-age women control over the prosecution decision. It is also possible to consider extending the same protection to young men (Olsen, 1984: 409, fn. 103).

Gender-neutrality has become an issue in other rape legislation. Over the past decade, feminists in America and Australia have recommended replacing the word 'rape' with the less emotive term 'sexual assault', and introducing several categories of sexual assault (Scutt, 1976; Naffin, 1984). The purpose of the reforms is to shift the focus away from the commonsense understanding of rape, as penetration of the vagina by a penis, to a more sensitive awareness of the varieties of sexual violation and degradation perpetrated upon both women and men. Levels of sexual assault with graded punishments, it is hoped, will also increase the number of success-ful prosecutions. Gender-neutrality, of course, also fits into a 'coherent theory of equality' which calls for the 'de-institutional-isation of sexual differences'. Alison Jaggar endorses this approach:

> . . . to suggest that the right to freedom from assault and rape is a specifically female right is to presuppose that women alone are desirable sexual objects or that women alone are incapable of defending themselves. Such suggested female rights are far better viewed as applications of general human rights. . .
> (Jaggar, 1977: 95, 101).

Other feminists are more cautious. Margaret Thornton is con-cerned that the 'harm suffered by the female victim is likely to be undervalued and trivialised'. Britain's Rights of Women (ROW) opposed removing the word 'rape' on these grounds (M. Thorn-ton, 1986: 12; Wilson, 1983: 192).

We are at an experimental stage with some of this legislation. As a result, we need to monitor its effects. Any 'good' which is achieved by drawing attention away from the sex of the actors may be counterbalanced by diminishing women's power in some way. Setting up gender-neutrality as a goal in and of itself is premature, since feminists still have a great deal to do to uncover and correct gender biases in supposedly neutral rules and laws.[8]

There is no area in which the question of gender-neutrality is more problematic than abortion. The 'special treatment' theorists, Linda Krieger and Patricia Cooney, use abortion to support their prop-osition that 'a *failure* to acknowledge that pregnancy is in some ways unique and deserving of special treatment could lead to disastrous consequences'. The insistence that women and men always be treated the same, which is the 'analytical mainstay of the equal treatment approach', can and has led, in Krieger's opinion, to a direct assault on women's reproductive freedom. In the case of *Fritz v. Hagerstown Reproduction Health Services* (1982), for ex-ample, the court ruled that a husband could prevent a wife from having an abortion by withholding consent. The judgment rested upon an analogy between paternity and maternity which then required that the 'two be treated the same' (Krieger, 1987: 54–55; see also Krieger and Cooney, 1983: 539–541).

Equal treatment theorists avoid talking about abortion in equal treatment terms, for obvious reasons. Instead they invoke another mainstay of liberal individualism, individual rights. At a recent symposium on reproductive rights, Nadine Taub reported that 'one of the day's understood premises was that "the right to safe, legal abortion is the *sine qua non* of a woman's ability to control her personal destiny"' (Taub, 1982: 169).

Arguing in terms of individual rights suited the individualist spirit which characterised the sexual revolution. Women had a right to 'take control of their bodies'. They had a right to be 'free' to have sex without consequences, *like men* (Diamond and Quinby, 1984, 1988; Martin, 1986: 382). Moreover, given America's legal heritage, it is completely understandable why feminists there would explore the possibility of extending particular rights to cover abortion (Goldstein, 1988: Chapter 4). The decision in *Griswold v. Connecticut* (1965) that a right of privacy existed in matters of marital intimacy determined the approach taken in *Roe v. Wade* (1973) where women won the 'right' to abortion as part of their 'right to privacy'.

This line of argument has some problems, however. Most clearly, the notion of privacy assumes the separation into private and public spheres which has had disastrous consequences for women (Benhabib and Cornell, 1987: 7). For example, it allows 'wifebeating' and incest to be considered outside the field of 'appropriate' state intervention. Putting abortion into the private side of the public/private social model has meant that the government could proceed to deny public (Medicaid) funding of abortions (*Harris v. McRae, 1980*). Catharine MacKinnon describes the outcome:

> To guarantee abortions as an aspect of the private, rather than of the public sector is to guarantee women a right to abortion subject to women's ability to provide it for ourselves. This is to guarantee access to abortion only to some women on the basis of class, not to women *as* women... (MacKinnon, 1983: 24).

Moreover, for many poor and Black women, the 'right to choose' to *have* children has been as problematic as the 'right to choose' *not* to have children. Lack of resources is one concern. Compulsory sterilisation programs and the active *promotion* of contraception and abortion by some governments among designated 'less desirable' groups is another. Zillah Eisenstein recognised that 'for all women to be free to choose abortion or childbirth, they have to have the actual freedom from economic want, sexism and racism' (Eisenstein, 1981: 238; see also Riley, 1981).

The 'Moral Majority' uses rights rhetoric to set women's rights *against* foetal rights, which is completely inappropriate given the interdependent relationship of mother and foetus (Smith, 1983: 265–266). Some women, primarily those on the political right, have decided that women's vulnerability, which is in large part due to pregnancy, means that women cannot afford to risk staking out a claim to individual rights ('sameness'). These women tend to oppose abortion because they see it as a threat to the 'bargain' women have had to strike with men, a promise of support in exchange for dependency (English, 1984; Luker, 1984). A group of 'pro-life' feminists has now emerged which agrees that women are 'different' and need 'social support'. The initial feminist emphasis on individual rights has in their opinion been overdone.[9]

The problem, as I see it, is not in pressing for 'rights', but the narrow way in which 'rights' are interpreted in the dominant liberal discourse as zones of non-interference, as 'rights' *against* another person. If 'rights' were broadened to include the right to freedom from social harm, women could count on the social supports which they need in order to have children. There would then be no necessity to appeal to 'difference'.

While the individualistic (*Gesellschaft*) approach to abortion clearly has limitations, the communitarian (*Gemeinschaft*) solution also has dangers. Some feminists in this tradition, who wish to see reproduction considered a social responsibility, seem willing to have women surrender control of the process. Alison Jaggar is an example:

> . . . if the community as a whole came to assume responsibility for the welfare of children (and mothers), then the birth or non-birth of a child would affect that community in a much more direct and immediate way than it does at present. In this case, it would seem reasonable to allow the community as a whole to participate in decisions over whether children were born and how they should be reared. In these changed social circumstances, it would no longer be even plausible to interpret reproductive freedom as a 'right' of individual women (Jaggar, 1983: 320).

The way in which communitarian solutions can absorb and subsume women has been mentioned several times. We need a model which offers social support for reproduction without removing women's control over their bodies.[10] Rosalind Petchesky offers a model which achieves this balance.

Petchesky describes reproduction as, by 'its very nature', *social* and *individual* at the same time: 'that is, it operates "at the core of social life" as well as within and upon women's bodies'. Therefore, even where society might bear equal responsibility for nurturance and childcare (Petchesky, 1980: 108, 116), Petchesky defends women's 'personal and bodily integrity'.

The demand to acknowledge women's bodily integrity is not an essentialist demand. There is a critical difference between arguing that biology creates particular kinds of persons, such as nurturant women or violent men, and recognising that bodies do not exist outside of political structures. Petchesky is not talking about a benign or 'natural' biology, but biology 'mediated by social and cultural organisation' (Petchesky, 1980: 98).

Abortion is and has always been a political issue, not a private one. It has *not* always been regulated. Laws making it illegal were introduced in the late nineteenth century at the behest of physicians who wanted to bring unlicensed practitioners under control (Mohr, 1978). But abortion is political, even when the government does nothing, as in the case of the removal of Medicaid funding in America. The state often allows certain social conditions to flourish by its very inaction (Olsen, 1985). Seen in this context, the feminist position on abortion should aim to achieve recognition of the fact that female reproduction is controlled for political reasons and to assert that women must be able to challenge that control.[11] If women's sex-specific needs were included in the human standard, 'equality' would include bodily integrity.

As in abortion, so in pornography, feminists have to bring into sharper analytical focus the meaning of concepts like 'rights' or 'freedom' before they are made the basis of political stances. Rights to free speech, for example, upheld so strongly by anti-pornographers, are not enjoyed equally (MacKinnon in Gaze, 1986: 126). The 'right' of access to the mass media is dependent upon resources and hence upon class, race, and gender. Perhaps, as with abortion, feminists ought to be working to shift the pornography debate out of the field of rights altogether. Perhaps it makes more sense to consider some pornography as similar to the 'hate propaganda' directed against racial minorities, or as group libel (Gaze, 1986: 126; Wilson, 1983: 220). Another approach might be to shift the debate from freedom of speech to the equality domain by showing how some pornography encourages sex discrimination (Minow, 1985: 1097; Scutt, 1984: 16). If sex is a social construct, as social theory suggests, it is obviously still in the process of being constructed. Pornography plays a part in this construction and thus contributes to the creation of an image of women which encourages their exploitation (Frost, 1983: 10).

A chief concern among anti-pornography feminists, and one which engages those who are not strict civil libertarians (I would include Kate Millett and Adrienne Rich in this category), is the question of tactics. Some are justifiably hesitant to give the state additional power, particularly in an area where women and minorities are often more severely regulated.[12] Ellen Willis is convinced that 'In a male supremacist society the only obscenity law that will not be used against women is no law at all' (Willis, 1984: 87). The

MacKinnon/Dworkin ordinance suggests, however, that there may be some techniques of intervention which are less dangerous than others. Carol Smart sees this as another area where feminists should be seeking a 'third alternative', something other than liberal advocacy or reactionary prohibition (Smart, 1984b: 224).

A number of feminists do not want pornography to become a single-issue campaign and wish rather to locate it within the broader problem of the sexist representation of women (Coward, 1982: 53). These feminists are also concerned about the shifting definition of pornography and the need to differentiate between pornography and erotica. Some of these problems could be resolved by establishing several campaigns in tandem. The problem of violent pornography seems the more urgent priority and ought to be opposed as a separate case. A parallel campaign could draw to the attention of the public, much in the way Jo Richardson and Clare Short are doing in Britain, the role some soft pornography and some advertising plays in the creation of a depersonalised and hence dehumanised image of women. To those who keep insisting that pornography is 'effect', not 'cause', Catharine Mac-Kinnon has a convincing retort: 'They do not say apartheid should be ignored as effect rather than cause because white racism pre-dates it and happens elsewhere in different form' (MacKinnon, 1987: 222).

Behind the tactical disagreements, however, lies a dispute which is more difficult to resolve. At one level it is a difference of opinion about the fundamental cause of women's oppression. Is it man? Is it the system? One's politics will determine where one ends up in this debate. At an even deeper level there is disagreement about the potential to achieve change. Anti-pornography feminists see radical feminists like MacKinnon and Dworkin as preaching ultimately a 'rhetoric of despair' (Wilson, 1983: 161). The concentration upon violence, male aggression, female victimisation and female complicity in their victimisation (both Dworkin and Mac-Kinnon describe women as 'collaborators' in the perpetuation of their subservience—see Dworkin, 1987: Chapter 7; MacKinnon, 1987: 6–7) seems to rob women of any semblance of agency. Carole Vance asks: 'Can women be sexual actors?...Or are we purely victims, whose efforts must be directed at resisting male depredations in a patriarchal culture?' (Vance, 1984: 6–7). For MacKinnon it is simply unrealistic to deny the oppression which women face:

> To those who think 'it isn't good for women to think of
> themselves as victims', and thus seek to deny the reality of their

victimization, how can it be good for women to deny what is happening to them? Since when is politics therapy? (MacKinnon, 1987: 220).

In response, Linda Gordon insists that 'To be less powerful is/ not to be power-less, or even to lose all the time' (Gordon, 1986: 24). The agency/victim or free will/determinism dispute lingers behind the sexuality debates. For Barbara Ehrenreich the sexual revolution was a victory for women, and to see it as otherwise, to see it as a 'victory for men', 'a joke on women', 'to see women as victims even of their self-chosen ventures, is not only to falsify the past but to foreclose the future' (Ehrenreich et al., 1986: 192). For WAVAW, on the other hand, the sexual revolution was the means by which men 'invalidated any challenge to their dominant sexual values' (Coward, 1982: 54). According to Barbara Ehrenreich, sadomasochism and butch/femme practices proved that 'roles can be assumed as easily as costumes', and hence 'male power is not the majestic theme our bodies are molded to express, inescapably, time after time' (Ehrenreich et al., 1986: 205). Catharine MacKinnon, on the other hand, sees such practices as contributing to the construction of a false notion of 'freedom' (MacKinnon, 1987: 15). For the pro-sex faction, sex is a 'vector of oppression', not reducible to gender (Rubin, 1984: 293); for the anti-sex faction, sex is oppression. In MacKinnon's words, '...the social relation between the sexes is organised so that men may dominate and women must submit and this relation is sexual—in fact, is sex' (MacKinnon, 1987: 3).

Much as I admire Catharine MacKinnon's analysis, I find her explanation of male behaviour unsatisfactory. The suggestion that men's violence may be due to the fact that they have power (see page 216) is unconvincing, especially since cross-cultural studies of rape (see Sanday, 1986) suggest that the problem may be the reverse, that rape may be due to the attempt to disguise vulnerability. We need more and closer studies of violence, not a categorical statement which explains nothing. Even more disturbing is the implication that women have so internalised dependency that they are incapable of acting. If the message is that the only solution is to give up traditional heterosexual intercourse altogether, that if you do not you are 'unliberated', but that you will probably not be able to make this decision because of your internalised dependency, it is little wonder that some feminists are despairing of sexual politics altogether (Stacey, 1986: 244, fn. 9). This is unfortunate since sex is the site of much discrimination and exploitation.

On the other hand we need to be careful not to recreate a model of individual agency which suggests that people are completely free of structural constraints. We have to remain ever wary of falling back onto liberal assumptions about the transcendent individual, the 'gloriously autonomous' 'sole author of history' (Moi, 1985: 8).

What is required is a theory of the subject which avoids setting up 'free will' and 'victim status' as options. Social construction theory is inadequate because it provides little room for personal experience. Judith Grant feels that the pornography debates have been so painful for women 'because they exposed what should have been an obvious problem—our theory: what happens when two women or groups of women have conflicting experiences of the same thing, in this case—sex?' (Grant, 1987: 111). Nor does social construction theory provide a framework for action. The question becomes: what does one do once one recognises that what we are, how we feel, how we act, are all the effects of accumulated history and experience? Teresa de Lauretis describes being a woman as becoming something which we know does not exist, becoming in other words a construct.[13] How much is me? How much is stereotype? How do we design laws to dismantle stereotypes without disadvantaging those for whom the stereotype is in some sense 'true'? These are the difficult theoretical questions feminists face, and they are the questions which lie behind the current dispute about the meaning of 'woman', a dispute taken up in the next, the last chapter.

This chapter has established the importance of recognising the way in which political value systems infect the sexuality debates. Feminists who embrace the traditional liberal ideal of equality transpose this ideal to sexual relations. Freedom becomes the goal and people's particular situations disappear into the background. A more subtle understanding of the way in which sexuality is a part of other social processes seems necessary.

On the other side, some feminists who have rebelled against liberal individualism associate its principles solely with men and proceed to use male sexuality as a shorthand for values they condemn. 'Women's' more benign sexuality is put forward as the basis of a new social ethic. There are two problems here: first, if sexuality serves as a metaphor for political debate, it becomes difficult to say anything meaningful about sexuality; and second it becomes difficult to debate the merits of the political visions. Untangling the politics from the sexuality suggests there are problems both in aspiring to make all people abstracted, competing individuals and in designating women as the ones responsible for congealing the social order. To repeat a theme, we need a model which recognises people's interdependence without appointing women the carers.

10
The construction of 'Woman'

Feminists based in America:

We as feminists and we as human beings want to understand more about where we are and who we are and what our culture is. We talk about preserving 'women's culture'—what is it? where did it come from? what parts of it should we try to save?

Mary Jean Collins

It's not good for women's psychology to keep thinking of themselves as inferior.

Jessie Bernard

What is the desire for difference?...I think much of it was the seeking of what seemed to be a better world...That female difference became inseparable from female betterment in both senses of the word. Females were better and females would better themselves if they recognised their femaleness...There's a sense of reaction and reconstruction that are inescapable from each other.

We have to be more careful not only with our own theorising but also with what we think to be true, since we can theorise without giving our theories the truth status.

Catharine Stimpson

Regarding the question of sexual difference, 'the creativity about the problem would come if we could understand that this problem arises in part from the limitation of the terminology and the approach that we are using and therefore move beyond it.'

Charlotte Bunch

Differences, when they existed, have been reconstructed in society to create inequality.

Veena Oldenburg

Maybe women right now are a different kind of person and there's this tremendous ambivalence within individuals and tremendous disagreement about whether you want to retain that.

Nadine Taub

What worries me about this stuff about women being more nurturant is—what do we do with that? Maybe we are more nurturant but then by God let's start teaching men how. We may be told to stay home and take care of the children on no pay because we are more nurturant.

Leslie Wolfe

Feminists based in Britain:

These are civilised values and they are values and skills which women have had, caring values and nurturing values...which frankly we disparage at our peril.

Elizabeth Vallance

I think we won't really solve the woman question until we try to make men more human, indeed more feminine, because they are vulnerable in their own way but they express it as aggression and violence...that again rebounds on women and we get blamed!

Georgina Ashworth

Men have greater opportunities available to them, men have more money, men have more power...These differences are the kind we're concerned to address.

Paddy Stamp

People have got very very polarised around difference...My inclination would be to give some credence to what is obviously true in what they [Gilligan, Dale Spender] say. A direct appeal to someone's experience is very powerful.

Michèle Barrett

The whole concept of what the male role is about is not one that I think women should emulate.

Ann Oakley

Society loses a lot by having a whole section of its population whose values which may be, which *are* different from male values are looked upon as O.K. but not to be regarded very highly.

Jo Richardson

There's absolutely no reason to throw difference out, like the baby with the bathwater, just because some people use it in an essentialist way. Difference is cultural and historical and it's not just a phenomenon of our oppression. It's not that one would argue for 'women's' values in some unchanging way but that the values that women have developed through their particular cultural and historical position in their subordination actually gives us a kind of foothold, a much better vantage point with which to develop a politics for the whole world.

What women are doing today which is revolutionary is neither saying we're equal with men, in other words stepping into the men's half, nor is it saying we're different from men, in the sense of keeping our own half, it's actually stepping clean out of the complementary mode.... What we're doing is forcing everybody else and ourselves to think of differences which are not convergences on the other sex but which are genuine differences, something new and something various and something which gives scope for feminist, not just women's, for feminist cultural inventions.

Cynthia Cockburn

Feminists based in Australia:

We say women have this nurturing capacity, which I think in general is true, because we have been socialised to have it. Now what happens ten, twenty years out when maybe the education is different? Are we going to lose that capacity or the reverse, which I hope will be true? Is it going to be valued in a way that it hasn't been valued?

Valerie Pratt

From what I believe and experience at the moment, we [women and men] experience the world differently. I have, compared to the man I live with, a sense of generational change. I carry within me eggs that I had when I was born... and they have potential for human life which will also carry them forward. Now somewhere above that is my centre of femaleness, so I carry the world of the past and the world of the future.

Carmel Niland

I am not interested in a social transformation that means that everyone is aggressive and competitive... In dealing with the 'difference', I think the important thing is to say continually, Why are women in this position? Why are men in that position?

Helen Campbell

On 11 March 1985, women's history went on trial.[1] On that date Professor Rosalind Rosenberg, Associate Professor of History,

Barnard College, appeared as an expert witness in the case of *EEOC v. Sears, Roebuck and Company* (hereafter referred to as Sears). The company had been charged with discrimination on two grounds: the under-representation of women in commission sales, where the selling of high ticket items netted high commissions and hence better pay than ordinary wages, and the salary differential between men and women in managerial and administrative jobs (Dowd Hall et al., 1986: 753–754).[2] Sears' lawyers did not dispute the statistical imbalance between women and men in commission sales but argued that, despite Sears' best efforts,[3] women were disinclined to choose these jobs. They argued that the EEOC started from an *a priori* assumption that was simply untrue, that men and women were the *same* 'with respect to preferences, interests, and qualifications' (Dowd Hall et al., 1986: 754). Professor Rosenberg was called in to provide historical evidence to support Sears' claim that women have *different* attitudes towards paid labour which explained their under-representation in certain kinds of jobs.

Rosenberg made two main points: first, that because women tended to be primarily responsible for housework and childcare, they chose jobs that complemented their family obligations 'over jobs that might increase and enhance their earning potential'; and, second, that women had 'internalised' different values which made certain kinds of work unappealing: 'Women tend to be more relationship-centred and men tend to be more work-centred'; 'Women are seen by themselves and by society as less competitive than men and more concerned with protecting personal relationships'. Her 'Offer of Proof'[4] concluded that it was naive 'to believe that the *natural effect* of these *differences* is evidence of discrimination' (quotes from Rosenberg in Dowd Hall et al., 1986: 761, 763, 764, 766, emphasis added). The EEOC brought in Dr Alice Kessler-Harris, who at the time was Professor of History, Hofstra University, to rebut Rosenberg's testimony. On 3 February 1986 Judge Nordberg ruled that the EEOC had not proven its charges against Sears. The EEOC has appealed to the Supreme Court (Dowd Hall et al., 1986: 756).

Feminism is in crisis about the meaning and usefulness of the concept 'woman' (Delmar, 1986: 28; Alcoff, 1988), about whether the term has any transhistorical meaning which should be valued, whether there is or is not a 'female essence' which is benevolent. The outlines of this metaphysical debate were foreshadowed in Chapter 4. On one side cultural feminists, who include radical, some liberal and some socialist feminists, believe that women have unique values which the world sorely needs. Some attribute these values to women's biology; some to women's socialisation. On the other side many liberal feminists fear that this reincarnation of 'difference' will be used to women's disadvantage. Black 'and socialist feminists are concerned that the notion ignores important 'differences' *among* women, and hinders the possibility of political allegiance with men, who become the natural purveyors of aggression in much cultural feminist writing. Poststructuralists also object to the adoption of a concept, 'Woman', which in their terms is a social construct and hence a fiction in the sense that it is an idealised version of what women should be (Alcoff, 1988: 417).[5]

The Sears antidiscrimination case has been selected as a way into this debate. It is useful for several reasons, not the least of which is an opportunity to observe the interaction between feminist theory and the 'real' world. Rosenberg's testimony opens up for examination the implications of using a concept of 'Woman' as somehow different and superior to 'Man', and the other complex problem of women's positioning as the primary caretakers in society today. The case is also central to this particular study because of the way in which some feminist scholars have located it within the sameness/difference debate. Sara Evans describes the 'explosive case' as exposing 'a basic, historical disagreement (among feminists) over whether women and men are fundamentally the same or fundamentally different' (Evans, 1988: 171). Ruth Milkman opens her article on the case with questions directly linked to equal treatment/special treatment concerns:

> Are women's interests best served by public policies that treat women and men identically, ignoring the social and cultural differences between them? Or should we view those differences positively and seek greater recognition and status for traditionally female values and forms of behavior? (Milkman, 1986: 375).

These quotations illustrate the tendency noted previously among some feminists to describe the women's movement as historically divided over the question of difference, and to identify women's problem as selecting between equal treatment and different treatment. This characterisation of the issues at stake in Sears, it will be argued, is not only inappropriate but dangerous. Sears' lawyers described women as 'different', as less competitive and more relationship-centred than men, and as natural childcarers. These 'differences' then became the explanation/justification for women's absence/exclusion from certain kinds of jobs. Women were offered the 'choice' of gaining access to the marketplace on existing terms or opting out. The alternative of changing marketplace rules to make them more humane and responsive to people's needs was not considered.

The Sears case, therefore, clearly illustrates the central hypothesis of the book, that reducing social analysis to discussions about women's sameness to or difference from men deflects attention from general social problems which need to be addressed. These include the unresponsiveness of the market to the personal side of people's lives, and the disproportionate value placed upon competitiveness. It also shows that describing women as nurturant and men as aggressive in overly simple terms allows women to be labelled as the problem so that nothing has to be done. A more useful political analysis would draw attention to the way in which the current economic system encourages certain behaviours and discourages others. This chapter uses the Sears case, therefore, to comment upon a number of interrelated theoretical issues: the relationship between free will (agency) and determinism (victim), the problems associated with socialisation and social construction theory, the encounter between feminism and antidiscrimination law, the challenge of writing women's history, the meaning of 'Woman', and the meaning of feminism.

Despite the innuendo about Rosenberg's compromised motives because of her ex-husband's connection with the law firm representing Sears (Milkman, 1986: 385), the analysis starts from the premise that both Rosenberg and Kessler-Harris acted in good faith. In fact, it will be suggested that what happened to Rosenberg could have happened to any feminist. At least half of my interviewees felt that, in substance, Rosenberg's argument was valid; they objected only to her telling the court. Granted, most of those interviewed had little knowledge of the case beyond a brief summary. Still, a large number sympathised with the view that, given women's domestic obligations and their upbringing, they probably *would not want* the commission sales jobs at Sears. Many who believed this still felt that Sears had 'discriminated' however, for reasons which will be looked at later.

Rosenberg's testimony contained much with which most feminist historians would agree. In fact, she offered a rather standard interpretation of the impact of domestic ideology on women.[6] 'Throughout American history', she explained, 'there has been a consensus, shared by women, that, for women, working outside the home is subordinate to family needs.' Beyond this kind of general statement which few would dispute, Rosenberg acknowledged the role of the state in reinforcing this ideology. She noted

that during the Depression of the 1930s, 'Legislation was introduced in many states to restrict employment of married women'.
She went even further in identifying 'American individualism' as
to blame for standing 'in the way of government policies that
would make it easier for married women and women with small
children to work' (Rosenberg in Dowd Hall et al., 1986: 758, 760).
Nor would anyone disagree that many women 'must choose jobs
with flexible hours to meet what they perceive to be their responsibilities at home' (Rosenberg presented evidence showing the
numbers of women seeking part-time work), or that few young
women in 1968 'expected to work in occupations that were not
"typical" for females' (Rosenberg in Dowd Hall et al., 1986: 761,
757 fn. 1).

To support her contention that women had 'different' values,
Rosenberg quoted Kessler-Harris (which was one of the reasons
Kessler-Harris felt compelled to offer testimony):

> ...even after women were 'sucked into the competitive
> maelstrom...they continued to rationalize their activities in
> terms of familiar humane and nurturing values'. These values,
> which were suited to family succor, tended to foster
> 'inappropriate behavior patterns for participation in a
> competitive world'.

Carol Gilligan features prominently in Rosenberg's footnotes, as
does Nancy Chodorow (Dowd Hall et al., 1986: 757 fn. 1; 763
fns 17 and 19a; 764 fn. 19c). Rosenberg also draws attention to
a theme which has been central in this book: 'that men still tend to
define themselves in terms of "agency" [or self-actualisation] and
that women still tend to define themselves in terms of "com-
munion" [or family/community responsibilities]' (Rosenberg in
Dowd Hall et al., 1986: 763 fn. 17). Any difference of opinion
arises predictably over the *interpretation* of these ideas.

Several assumptions underlying Rosenberg's interpretation have
to be questioned: that women *completely* absorb the ideas about
their 'appropriate' role, that these ideas are consistent and unam-
biguous, and that women have the freedom to 'choose' whether or
not to engage in paid labour. Kessler-Harris is most angered by the
last of these. She accused Rosenberg of writing 'as if all women
were middle class' and white. For many immigrant, poor and
Black women, explained Kessler-Harris, the luxury of conceiving
of 'family needs' as 'separable from the productive labour of
women, inside or outside the home' was not an option (Kessler-
Harris, 1987: 56–57). These women worked when they had to

and, for obvious reasons, sought jobs which paid as much as possible.[7]

In her written testimony, Kessler-Harris attributed Rosenberg's interpretation to the fact that she was a historian of ideas and that 'her expertise does not lie in the history of wage-earning women' (Kessler-Harris in Dowd Hall et al., 1986: 768 fn. 1). Rosenberg's most important book is a study of a small, relatively unknown group of early female sociologists who were among the first to examine the impact of 'cultural conditioning' on women (Rosenberg, 1982: xiv). Her evidence in the Sears case, which assumes the strength of conditioning as a social process, was perhaps affected by this earlier research. Moreover, as for most of us who have studied ideas held about women, although we are well aware that the messages are elite, ethnocentric, and prescriptive, there is usually little opportunity or inclination to test the *impact* of these messages *upon the women* receiving them. Perhaps there is a lesson here—the desperate need for studies 'from below', despite the difficulties involved in writing them. Otherwise, descriptions of the domestic ideology might appear, as they do in Rosenberg's testimony, as self-fulfilling prophecies.

Accusations about underlying ideological assumptions and professional ineptitude flowed in both directions. Rosenberg described Kessler-Harris' scholarship as 'of questionable validity' and as 'written in the service of the larger cause of opposition to capitalism itself'. In support of her claim she quoted a 1979 article in which Kessler-Harris wrote 'hopefully' that women 'harbor values, attitudes and behavior patterns potentially subversive to capitalism' (Milkman, 1986: 388). The place of political ideology in women's history and in the debate about the meaning of 'Woman' will be taken up later in this chapter.

The agency/victim question became a part of the disagreement in a rather unusual way. *Both* women claimed that they wished to *retain* a role for women's agency. Rosenberg argued that blaming employers for the condition of women in the way Kessler-Harris did made women into victims. She felt that her testimony, in contrast, 'emphasised the complexity of the world in which women make decisions—choices—about their work'. Kessler-Harris however allied herself with a strong defender of agency, Natalie Zemon Davis, who wrote: 'I want to show that even when times were hard, people found ways to cope with what was happening and maybe to resist it...Especially I want to show that it could be different, that there are alternatives'. Kessler-Harris sees the role of feminist historians as, in part, asking questions about 'how women have pushed at the boundaries of opportunity' (Milkman, 1986: 388; Kessler-Harris, 1987: 53). To sort out these apparently contradictory interpretations, it becomes necessary to take a closer look at the theory being employed.

The world in which women make decisions is complex indeed. And what the Sears case suggests more than anything else is the urgent need for a usable *theory of the subject*, something accessible and something which rings true with experience. Feminists and other social theorists have made significant contributions to the development of such a theory, but unfortunately only some of these ideas filter through to a larger public, and then endure long after new developments have appeared (Connell, 1987).

Such, for example, is the case with socialisation theory. Chapter 4 described how socialisation theory became the theoretical linch-pin of early second-wave feminism (see page 82). The common understanding of socialisation was invoked by feminists to explain why women and men were the way they were. The theory also suggested that women's behaviour and character could be in-fluenced by changes in the messages from the agents of socialisa-tion. In this way it became the basis of many strategies for change, such as removing sexist language from school texts. In Veena Oldenburg's words, 'I am a believer in socialisation because I am a believer in education' (Oldenburg interview, 18 March 1988).

Socialisation, however, has deterministic implications. While it made a useful contribution by moving the discussion of behaviour beyond speculation about the role played by innate biology, it left behind passive individuals, shaped by a series of social cues (Hen-riques et al., 1984: 103). The theory explained that women 'feared success', were 'apolitical', 'insecure', 'lacked initiative', while men became 'assertive' and 'politically committed'. If we create fixed categories of masculine and feminine behaviour in this way, and talk as if every person fits those categories perfectly, we do two things. Inadvertently we strengthen the power of sex roles by convincing ourselves and others of their significance, even when experience challenges their power.[8] We also convey the impression that people are more or less trapped by sex roles (Connell, 1987: 50). Vicky Randall calls this kind of interpretation 'sex-role reduc-tionism'. Arthur Brittain and Mary Maynard are equally critical of what they label 'strong socialisation' theory (Randall, 1982: 86; Brittain and Maynard, 1984: 71–74).

Developments in social construction theory offered a more soph-isticated account of social relations. Whereas socialisation theory had implied that a biological entity *acquired* gender characteristics (so that a 'female' became a 'woman'), it was now suggested that you could not separate the physical being from socially acquired characteristics. Since there is no 'pre-social' individual, there is no 'pre-social' biology. Put simply, if the social cue is that it is unsuitable for women to engage in vigorous exercise, it stands to reason that, physically, women develop fewer muscles. Even biology therefore is 'socialised' to an unascertainable extent (Henriques, et al., 1984: 151; Lambert, 1978: 105; Grosz, 1989: x). The categories 'male' and 'female' are themselves socially constructed and reinforced by scientists and social behaviour.[9] Although this explanation is more sophisticated than socialisation, it too has deterministic implications. The message is really much the same: women become women as a result of growing up in a gendered society (Birke and Vines, 1987: 564).

There are comparable problems with poststructuralist theory since it also emphasises the 'social dimension of individual traits and intentions'. In Linda Alcoff's opinion, poststructuralists are therefore similarly neodeterminists:

> The idea here is that we individuals really have little choice in the matter of who we are, for as Derrida and Foucault like to remind us, individual motivations and intentions count for nil or almost nil in the scheme of social reality. *We are constructs—* that is, our experience of our very subjectivity is a construct mediated by and/or grounded on a social discourse beyond (way beyond) individual control (Alcoff, 1988: 416, emphasis added).

Every deterministic theory, however, encounters a puzzle which must be solved: *change does indeed take place*. The difficult task is to discover the mechanism behind the process. We need a theory which accounts for 'resistance and political change' (Barrett, 1987: 35).

Feminists have been particularly concerned to find a way out of deterministic models. This is partly because of the power of sex roles in women's lives. Women more than men are told that what they are determines what they will become ('biology is destiny'). Women's activities have also been severely constrained by expectations about their responsibility for family maintenance. There is a desire then to rescue 'feminine subjects' from 'their social and communal persona' (Benhabib and Cornell, 1987: 12). Feminists have also had direct experience of women's ability to challenge social expectations about appropriate female behaviour. Experiences in consciousness-raising groups, for example, reaffirmed women's ability to change.

The first step beyond determinism is the discovery that the messages women receive about appropriate behaviour are ambiguous and contradictory, which opens up the space for an active response (Connell, 1987: 193). Women receive mixed messages. At one and the same time they are treated as both the same as and as different from men, providing 'the psychological source of women's resistance to their social subordination' (Sayers, 1986: x). We do not automatically assume a gender identity; we negotiate one, given our perception of our needs.[10] People take up positions because 'there will be some satisfaction or pay-off or reward'. Social changes, such as the development of an oral contraceptive, open up contradictions and opportunities which may alter women's understanding of which position is the 'best investment' (Hollway, 1984: 239, 260). Other major dimensions of social 'difference' including class, race and age 'intersect with gender to favour or disfavour certain positions'.

This understanding recovers some room for the 'subject' to manoeuvre. At the same time it does not fall back upon some notion of a 'gloriously autonomous' self, operating free from social constraints. Rather, ideology has become a 'contradictory construct, marked by gaps, slides and inconsistencies' (Moi, 1985: 8, 26). These inconsistencies, or 'chinks and cracks', as Teresa de Lauretis calls them, in the messages women receive provide the opportunity to alter or challenge those messages (de Lauretis, 1987: 10, 25). The kind of history which feminists must have therefore, the kind of writing which is required in every field, is work which captures 'the complexity of power and weakness in women's lives' (Gordon, 1986: 25). History, particularly if it enters the courtroom, ignores theory at women's peril, as the Sears case demonstrates.

In her testimony Rosenberg seemed to be saying at one and the same time that women *fully absorb* the message about their appropriate domestic role (Scott, 1988: 42), and yet retain *choice*. On the one hand she ignored the 'chinks and cracks', the mixed messages which mean that women do not all emerge as clones of the 'ideal mother'; on the other she somehow simultaneously underestimated the social constraints which set the parameters for 'choice'. Kessler-Harris had less trouble 'Reconciling the notion that women could simultaneously operate within and against their society' (Kessler-Harris, 1987: 59). Women *are* constrained by domestic ideology and absorb *parts* of its message, but they also *reject* it when it contradicts their needs and/or desires. Unfortunately, as we will see, Kessler-Harris had greater difficulty translating that understanding into courtroom testimony.

Rosenberg maintained that she was employing a 'multicausal' view of history, 'one in which socialisation, family responsibilities, educational practices, government policies, cultural attitudes and employer discrimination all played a part in shaping the contemporary labor force'. Hence she could not say that discrimination *alone* accounted for the relative absence of women in commission sales: 'disparities in the sexual composition of an employer's workforce, as well as disparities in pay between men and women in many circumstances, are consistent with an absence of discrimination on the part of the employer'. This seems obvious. Equally obvious is that they are also consistent with the *presence* of discrimination. A 'multicausal' approach 'begs the question of how to order and assess' causes. While it may be appropriate in a classroom text, in a courtroom where the question—is there discrimination?—must be answered 'yes' or 'no', it is positively dangerous: 'to argue that discrimination was not the likely explanation is to lend one's expertise to the argument that other explanations are more plausible' (Kessler-Harris, 1987: 53, 54, 59–60). Kessler-Harris outlined the potentially disastrous repercussions of the Sears decision:

> . . . if defendants could justify the absence of women in certain kinds of jobs on the grounds that insufficient numbers of women possessed any interest in them, one could foresee the resulting cycle. Expectations and aspirations conditioned by generations of socialisation and labor market experience would now be used to justify continuing discrimination against women (Kessler-Harris, 1987: 47).

The EEOC conducted elaborate statistical analyses, factoring out 'supply' problems such as identifiable 'differences' between women and men including job applied for, age, education, job type experience, product line experience, and commission product sales experience. Still, statistically significant disparities remained unexplained. In some previous discrimination cases (for example A.T. & T.) a statistical discrepancy between women and men had been adequate to establish indirect discrimination. Sears, however, argued that the EEOC had to establish 'intention' to discriminate, which is not usually required in indirect discrimination cases (see page 164). The fact that the EEOC did not protest and that the judge accepted the argument lends support to the hypothesis that the EEOC wanted to lose the case (Milkman, 1986: 381, 383).[11]

The discrimination model which allowed Sears to be found 'not guilty' is one we should recognise (see Chapter 7). Sears claimed that they had not discriminated against women because women and men were *not similarly situated* insofar as perception of work and social roles were concerned. Rosenberg's evidence was useful because it supported the contention that women were indeed 'different', and therefore treating them differently did not constitute discrimination.

Most of the women I interviewed agreed that on average women probably were 'different' in the ways Rosenberg had suggested, but that Sears was guilty of discrimination anyway because it was unfair to judge *all* women by the characteristics of *some*. They accused the company of applying a stereotype which frustrated the ambitions of women who had broken free of the stereotype. There is certainly evidence that this is true. Although the company emphasised that *women* did not want commission sales jobs, it is at least equally clear that *Sears* did not want *women* in those jobs. Whether or not the depiction of women as non-competitive and nurturant is accurate, the company believed that women were this way, making them 'unsuitable' for commission sales. Sears described the type of person who made a successful commission 'salesperson':

> Although virtually all noncommission sales jobs can be filled by a sociable person with a pleasant, helpful personality...the combination of technical skills and specific personal characteristics found in effective commission salespersons distinguishes the latter as an elite among retail salespeople...
> One of the most important personal qualities a commission salesperson must possess may be variously described as aggressiveness, drive, 'hunger', or more generally, motivation.

Applicants were given a number of aptitude tests. One, the Vigor scale, seeking the appropriate degree of aggressiveness, asked questions such as, 'Do you swear often?', 'Have you ever done any hunting?', 'Have you participated in wrestling?' Women were almost balloted out of contention by the masculine bias in the hiring procedures, and yet Sears proceeded to persuade the court that *women* were generally not interested in commission sales because *they* feared or disliked 'the competitive, "dog-eat-dog" atmosphere' and because of 'their distaste for the type of selling they believed was required in commission divisions' (Milkman, 1986: 382, 384–385). Shifting the focus to women's 'choices' somehow allowed Sears to escape the obvious conclusion that the *company's* fears about women were more significant in keeping women out of commission sales than the *women's* fears about the nature of the jobs.

Choice is a difficult concept, encountered previously in the discussion about whether anyone really 'chooses' to work long or unsocial hours (see page 140). In her testimony Kessler-Harris argued that women's 'choices' are affected by available opportunities and by their *perception* of available opportunities (Dowd Hall et al., 1986: 777). American lawyer, Elizabeth Holtzman, makes a similar point. There are two factors at work in discrimination, she suggests: first, discrimination and second, discriminatory attitudes that help shape women's own views of what is appropriate, which may discourage them (*New York Times*, 29 March 1987).

The suggestion that women are influenced by their *perceptions* of what is appropriate behaviour leads back into that tricky area, socialisation. For, if women do in fact internalise messages about their lack of competence and their unsuitability for certain jobs, it seems that in part at least the stereotypes are 'true'. Social construction theory confirms that growing up in a gendered society has an impact, even on biology. Pretending that this is not the case reinforces rather than challenges the status quo. Single-sex education classes designed to counteract the negative effects of socialisation are based upon this premise. Dealing with these sorts of problems requires, however, a *broader conception of discrimination* than the 'stereotype' model, which says simply that individual women should be judged, not by stereotypes, but by personal abilities. How do we deal with the fact that many women do lack confidence? How do we respond when many women do 'choose' jobs which fit in with 'their' domestic responsibilities?

One way to deal with the first of these problems is to acknowledge that women's perceptions about job choices are, in part, 'themselves products of employers' assumptions and prejudices about women's roles' and, since employers are an 'important part of this world', they are 'complicit in the socialisation process' (Kessler-Harris, 1987: 57). Several of my interviewees developed this line of argument. Helen Campbell said that in many instances a *work culture* exists which ensures that women 'choose' *not* to put themselves forward for certain jobs, and 'that's why the concept of discrimination, that is, treating someone less favourably on grounds of sex, is not adequate to deal with the structural position of women' (Campbell interview, 24 August 1987). Hence, it needs to be established that companies have a responsibility to create a work culture which is non-threatening and even appealing. Holding companies responsible for guaranteeing that the workplace is free from sexual harassment is an indication of the kind of policy which is required, although here I am talking about the creation of *positive* images for jobs rather than simply eliminating *negative* conditions.

Many people would challenge the feasibility and the legitimacy of charging companies with this degree of social responsibility but, as Mary Jean Collins put it, 'the corporation...is the most radical-ising, change-oriented institution in our society...They cannot but know that they themselves are people who change the role of people in society' (Collins interview, 18 February 1988). Paddy Stamp agreed that 'Employers have a social role as much as anyone else' (Stamp interview, 29 March 1988).

There is also an important question here about workplace values. In the Sears case, defining women as 'nurturant' was used to justify the retention of a 'dog-eat-dog' competitive environment. Since women were 'different', the implication was that there was nothing wrong with this environment. Instead we should be asking why aggressive and even unethical sales techniques are approved and rewarded.

Similarly, insofar as 'women's' domestic duties are concerned, it has been argued earlier (see pages 126–127) that companies have an obligation 'to make jobs more accommodating to people who have families' (Holcomb interview, 18 March 1988). An employer who designs work conditions so that employees cannot fulfil domestic obligations is guilty of discrimination, though perhaps another term is more appropriate to describe the behaviour. Perhaps 'socially irresponsible' is more accurate. Rosenberg made almost this same point on one occasion: 'if women aren't taking certain jobs, perhaps corporations have to change the conditions of those jobs (for instance, by providing child care)' (Sternhell, 1986: 51). It is unfortunate that, instead of pursuing this line of think-ing, she persisted in emphasising simply that 'men's and women's lives are still fairly different' and 'Avoiding the truth will not bring equality any sooner' (Sternhell, 1986: 89). Neither, I would sug-gest, will avoiding the causes of that inequality which in this case is the assumption that companies have no obligation to design jobs which take into account people's family responsibilities.

As mentioned at the outset, the Sears case has been presented as yet another example of the problems caused feminists by the question of difference:

> ...where Kessler-Harris stresses equality and argues that the 'difference' in women's interests was created by the needs of the market itself, Rosenberg stresses difference and argues that

an assumption of equality would only assure that women's special needs are ignored (Sternhell, 1986: 89).

However, presenting the debate in this way distorts both the issues at stake and the positions of both Rosenberg and Kessler-Harris. The issue, to repeat the argument developed throughout the book, is not whether women are the same as or different from men, but that society ought to adjust to the fact that people are not the abstract automatons of liberal theory, that they do have personal characteristics which have to be taken into account. A rephrasing of the sameness/difference question may clarify this point: do women, because of 'their' domestic roles, require 'special treatment'? or should they be treated the same way as men (i.e. should domestic roles be ignored)? Neither alternative is satisfactory.

Rosenberg defends a 'special treatment' approach, but the very limitations of this approach are indicated by the fact that her focus on 'difference' distracted her from the more dramatic structural reforms which flowed potentially from her analysis. It should be remembered that the 'special treatment' Sears offered women was exclusion from better-paying jobs. And, while Kessler-Harris believes in equality, it misrepresents her views to ally her too closely with those who are generally reluctant to institute large structural changes. She must find it strange to be accused of being a Marxist and an equal treatment theorist at one and the same time.

The debate was never really a sameness/difference debate at all. Both Kessler-Harris and the EEOC stated clearly that there were 'differences' in women's experience which needed to be taken into account (Milkman, 1986: 381, 387). The EEOC's statistical analyses acknowledged those differences. The more important question then becomes how the debate was made to *look like* a debate about sameness or difference. Kessler-Harris related to me that the publicity surrounding the case 'used arguments from difference in a way the case never did. The press and Rosenberg said the EEOC believes women are *just like men*. That then became the issue':

> The way that idea of 'difference' was picked up was itself a political issue. People fastened onto it as 'difference versus sameness'. While the EEOC carefully didn't play into that game, it got caught anyway (Kessler-Harris interview, 17 March 1988).

Clearly Sears *wanted* the case to be argued in terms of sameness and difference so that the company could then appeal to the public that the problem was not discrimination but women's 'natural differences'. As Helen Lambert explains, we are encouraged to believe that compensatory action for disadvantages which are 'natural' is inappropriate (Lambert, 1978: 113). The care of children therefore became women's 'difference' as a first step towards justifying the company's lack of attention to the problems facing workers with children.

Sears set Rosenberg an assignment which would be likely to produce an analysis which focused on women's 'differences'. Rosenberg explained that she was never asked if Sears were guilty of discrimination: 'I started with a straight-forward question—did the EEOC err in assuming that all men and women applying for sales positions at Sears were equally interested and available for commission sales? I believe they did' (Sternhell, 1986: 51).

'Given the nature of adversarial proceedings', Kessler-Harris was then compelled to remove ambiguity and nuance from *her* argument (Scott, 1988: 41): 'Any attempt I made to introduce controversy, disagreement and analysis merely revealed that history was an uncertain tool and invalidated both its findings and my conclusions' (Kessler-Harris, 1987: 61).[12] The adversarial system polarises positions. There is no room for a common view or compromise. It forces people into extreme positions to defend their case and, therefore, exaggerates discrepancies in points of view. Each party is out to discredit the other so neither can afford to concede doubt. Consequently, the case ended up *looking* much more like an instance of 'sameness versus difference' than it in fact was. Not surprisingly, remembering the constellation of traditional social values likely to be held by the judiciary (see page 161), the judge came down on the side of 'difference'.

The problems which women face are infinitely more complex than asking if they are the same as or different from men. In fact, perceiving the situation in those terms avoids all the real issues, such as how families are to be cared for. That is why those in power wish to present it this way. It allows them to avoid responsibility for the human side of people's lives. The way in which the powerful can use the media to distort issues puts feminists into a difficult position. But it does not put them into an impossible position. They must struggle to avoid having their analyses reduced to a sameness/difference dichotomy. With Ruth Milkman, I would conclude that we ignore the political dimensions of the sameness/difference debate at our peril (Milkman, 1986: 394).

The metaphysical debate on the meaning of 'Woman' is closely implicated in the Sears case. Rosenberg's use of Carol Gilligan to defend an image of women as nurturing and non-competitive, an image which was subsequently exploited to disadvantage women, raises practical questions about the wisdom of laying claim to 'female' uniqueness. Politically, as Toril Moi suggests:

> ...this projection of male and female as unquestioned essences is surely always dangerous for feminists: if any sex difference were ever to be found, it could always (and always would) be used against us, largely to prove that some particularly unpleasant activity is 'natural' for women and alien to men (Moi, 1985: 154).

Or, conversely, as in the Sears case, to prove that some particularly lucrative activity is 'natural' to men and alien to women.

The way in which the idea of 'difference' is integrated into popular discourse is also worrying. The sexologist, Bettina Arndt, is one of the worst offenders. In an article on the complexities of the courtship ritual for men, Arndt uses 'difference' to 'explain' (excuse?) rape:

> Girls growing up are expected to learn to be sensitive to how others feel, to observe and interpret people's behaviour. Boys often miss out on this training and now they pay the price as they wallow in confusion, trying to negotiate their way into women's hearts and beds...
>
> Perper [Timothy Perper, biologist and author of *Sexual Signals—The Biology of Love* (ISI Press, 1985)] believes that in some men this anger and resentment builds up, and can lead to rape (*Adelaide Advertiser*, 6 October 1987).

In another article Arndt questions why women should assume that their 'voice' is in any way superior to men's voice. Surely , she suggests, there is room for both:

> No matter that, for generations many happy marriages have flourished on men and women employing different emotional strategies, she the interpreter, the talker, he playing a more silent but equally crucial role.
>
> The new female expectation leads to fights. She says 'I want to talk', and he, knowing he will be outmanoeuvred in any battle over emotions, retreats in silence (*Adelaide Advertiser*, 10 November 1987).

Of course, it would be unfair to hold Gilligan responsible for the way in which corporate lawyers or the popular press make use of her work. Still, there is a need to be aware of the dangers involved in oversimplifying Gilligan's analysis. While every feminist would accept that parts of the feminine stereotype are 'true', that living in a gendered society makes it a 'wise investment' at times to act upon social cues about 'appropriate' gender behaviour, a tendency has appeared in some feminist literature to replace serious political analysis with generalisations about the way women and men 'are'. Bob Connell calls this tendency 'categoricalism' (Connell, 1987: 56–58). Lynne Segal labelled it 'psychic essentialism' (see page 90).

Most of the women I interviewed were sympathetic to Gilligan's analysis but would have vigorously disclaimed the label 'essentialist'. They attributed the character differences they perceived between women and men to contrasting social roles and socialisation. Segal's point is that this kind of analysis has a similar effect to essentialism if it simply stops at the identification of character differences. I share Segal's concern. In effect, talking in overly simple terms about women's sameness to or difference from men recreates the sameness/difference framework at a metaphysical level and shares its limitations. Women are told that they can either be like 'men' and join the system, or opt out and be 'women'. There is no way in this framework to challenge the masculine behavioural norm.

A number of feminist authors have pointed out that the generalisations commonly drawn about women's caring nature and male detachment are based upon gender stereotypes which have been created by men and which have been used to constrain women. Classic Western philosophers, all men, were the ones, as Genevieve Lloyd shows (*Man of Reason*, 1984), who equated woman with nature, body and emotion, and man with culture, mind and rationality. This constitution of 'womankind' as responsible for the warm and emotional side of human needs has functioned historically to repress women in certain ways (Lloyd, 1984: 105). Women, for example, were excluded from civic rule on the grounds that their character unsuited them for it. To rule, one had to be 'rational' not emotional, 'objective' not caring. Drawing attention to women's nurturing capacity also reinforces the traditional sexual division of labour. In fact, there are echoes of that ancient *Gemeinschaft* tradition which allocated women domestic and nurturing responsibilities.[13]

On the other hand the idea that women may be more caring appeals to a large number of women who are disillusioned with the excessive competitiveness and corruption they observe in business and government today. The idea that women may be able to offer a counter-ethic creates a sense of sex solidarity and mobilises some women for political action. Is this reason enough to risk invoking 'difference'? Or is a political analysis which simply equates women with caring values and sees this as a way to change the world inadequate or even potentially regressive? Is the concept ultimately dangerous or useful?

Similar questions are being asked within the feminist historical community. As mentioned in Part I (see page 99), cultural feminism, with its celebration of women's shared experience, has produced a new emphasis in women's history. Loosely labelled 'women's culture', it involves an exploration of the historical interaction among women, in clubs and societies and through women's networks for example (see Blair, 1980; Vicinus, 1985). A dispute has arisen over how to interpret that experience. In brief, the disagreement is about whether 'women's culture' ought to be *underplayed* because it represented the status quo and hence was inherently conservative, or whether it ought to be *extolled* because it provided the necessary sense of solidarity which impelled women to act on their own behalf.

Ellen Du Bois sees women's culture, with its focus on 'domesticity and morality', as 'self-defeating and reactionary'. Feminism in her opinion, or at least nineteenth-century women's rights feminism, grew out of a *critique* of this culture. Hence she is sceptical of the tendency today to romanticise it. Nancy Cott on the other hand (and Carroll Smith-Rosenberg would agree) believes that 'woman's sphere' provided the basis for a subculture among women which 'led to the development of women's consciousness as a group' and 'which was a necessary *prerequisite* for the emergence of a feminist movement' (Du Bois et al., 1980: 26–30, 55–58, emphasis added). The question again is whether feminists ought to eschew or enshrine the notion of what it means/has meant to be a woman. To what extent is that identity valuable? To what extent is it restrictive?

For a large part of recent history (see Chapters 1, 2 and 3), the maternal ethos supplied an identity which most closely described women's experiences and which, because of the 'respect' accorded the maternal function, gave women a certain amount of prestige. Women seeking an improvement in their social status logically exploited this mystique. Those who rejected it were a distinct minority. Even those equal rights feminists of the 1920s and 1930s, who campaigned for the opportunity to participate in the marketplace, spoke warmly about woman's maternal character. A number of early feminists who were political progressives set up the maternal ethic as a counter to the visibly corrupt practices of the world. Many objected to the partisanship which produced dishonest politics, and the excessive individualism which threatened the environment and the health of their families. They campaigned for consumer rights, for parks and playgrounds, and against war (Bacchi, 1983: Chapter 6).

The way in which the maternal mystique became a 'role

typology' has already been described (see page 27). This had the effect of politically marginalising women by locking them into a service role (Stoper and Johnson, 1977: 207). Women became identified with the 'social' sphere which was conceptualised as some place between the private and the public, but which was carefully demarcated against 'high politics'. Winning a ballot did 'little to disturb this otherness' (Riley, 1987b: 42–43).

The maternal ethos was also steeped in racism and class prejudice. Suffragists promised that good Protestant Anglo-Saxon women would help outvote the pauper and the foreigner. Many were eugenists. Sandra Harding reminds us that 'our concepts of "womanliness" and "manliness" are always racial as well as class-based' (Harding, 1986: 166). Nor should it be forgotten that the maternal ethos was a historically specific identity—'motherhood has not always been a dominant feminine ideal' (Block, 1978: 101). Identifying with 'women's' experiences or women's culture was therefore *simultaneously* politicising and limiting. It posed a challenge to certain parts of the traditional order and reinforced others. It mobilised some women but alienated others: 'This was a world in which identification as a woman was complex indeed' (Smith-Rosenberg in Du Bois et al., 1980: 62).

And so it is today. Some historically specific factors have contributed to the appeal of 'difference'. Alice Echols identifies part of the explanation: 'For any oppressed group it is tempting to seek solace in the reclamation and rehabilitation of that identity which the larger culture has systematically denigrated' (Echols, 1984a: 62). The promise of unity in a period of divisiveness and set-backs increases its allure. But, as at the turn of the century, the 'woman as superior' construct is primarily a metaphor for a political alternative which remains poorly defined. It represents a disillusionment with the world as it is today and offers an inadequate program for social change based upon a vague hope that women will make a difference.

Cultural feminism, you may recall (see page 86), emerged out of a critique of the system to which women had been seeking access. Many feminists in the 1970s became politically aligned with the anti-war movement, the pro-ecology movement, the anti-big business and the anti-multinationals movement. As in the radical feminist analysis of sexuality (see Chapter 9), men became the symbols of everything which was wrong with the world and women became the symbols of salvation. In Elizabeth Gould Davis, for example:

> Man is the enemy of nature: to kill, to root up, to level off, to
> pollute, to destroy are his instinctive reactions. . . .
> Woman, on the other hand, is the ally of nature and her
> instinct is to tend, to nurture, to encourage healthy growth,
> and to preserve ecological balance (Davis, 1973: 335–336).

In a world frightened by superpower hostilities, women became
the 'natural' pacifists. 'Because of her gift for personal relationships she deals more effectively with injustice, war, prejudice'
(Nin, 1972: 26, 28). Because of their capacity to give birth, they
were described as knowing the cost of human flesh and by nature
'unwilling to kill' (Cambridge Women's Peace Collective, 1984: 3).
Or, the 'positive energy' women gained from taking responsibility
for children became an explanation of their 'concern for peace'.

In much of this writing political analysis is subsumed beneath
gender metaphors. The way in which this happens is demonstrated
in the disagreement among American feminists about whether or
not women should be eligible for the military draft. Catharine
MacKinnon who opposes the draft admits that:

> The draft, then, is not the only, nor even the primary issue.
> The real question is what the foreign and domestic policy of
> this country is, and whether we can assent to it (MacKinnon in
> Williams, 1982: 189 fn. 77).

And yet, subsequent to this political analysis, she simply rejects
the 'war reflex' as an instance of 'male hysteria'. Similarly, in
feminist discussion about whether women should join men's sports
or organise separately, the issue is whether you want women to
become rugged individualists, not whether you wish them to become like 'men'. And yet the two types of analysis get collapsed.
According to MacKinnon, 'athletics to men is a form of combat',
'it's competitive', and radical feminism is not satisfied with women
emulating that image (MacKinnon, 1987: 119, 121).

Now it might seem strange to criticise cultural feminism for a
political analysis which equates men with the system when that is
precisely their political message. The appeal which the 'woman as
superior' construct has attracted in the wider feminist community,
however, reflects only a rather vague revulsion against contemporary political values which has not been adequately analysed. Man is
equated with the 'system' and woman becomes the embodiment of
a countervailing ethic, and the analysis stops there.

Somewhat paradoxically Rosalind Rosenberg, whose testimony
explored 'women's social and cultural differences' from men, rejects the current interest in women's culture: 'I was and I continue

to be skeptical of the utility of conceiving of men and women living in separate cultural worlds' (Kessler-Harris, 1987: 58; Milkman, 1986: 394). Kessler-Harris on the other hand feels that women's culture *should be* 'the subject of historical analysis', and she is angry that Rosenberg 'presented its role as preserving the status quo'. Kessler-Harris sees female culture as both 'malleable' and 'as part of the process of change' (Kessler-Harris, 1987: 58, 60).

This paradox is resolved when we examine the two women's political values. Rosenberg supports the social status quo and is neither attracted to nor excited at the prospect of a countervailing female ethic; Kessler-Harris on the other hand is hopeful that women 'harbor values, attitudes and behavior patterns potentially subversive to capitalism' (Milkman, 1986: 388). Kessler-Harris thus becomes the *real* defender of 'difference'. The dilemma she gets herself into offers a warning to those who have begun to see women as the key to transforming the world into a 'caring' place without pursuing the political analysis further. As Sandra Harding says, 'we have become preoccupied with gender symbolism at the expense of complex political realities' (Harding, 1986: 176).

The kind of analysis which increases political understanding focuses upon the varieties of masculinity and femininity, the ways in which they are expressed, and the political uses they serve. In other words, unless we are content with a political analysis which says simply that all men *are* a particular way—independent, unfeeling, individuated—and which implies that women's caring values will save the world,[14] we need to study the processes which produce these values. Unless we find ways to challenge and change the masculine behavioural norm, women will face the options of mimicking it or abandoning the places where it regulates behaviour. The situation replicates exactly the more obvious dilemma facing women with childcare obligations. Neither assimilation to a system which ignores those obligations nor opting out and assuming those obligations is a workable alternative. Neither 'sameness' nor 'difference' is adequate. The original model has to be challenged.

Some recent work on the construction of masculinity is useful here. Paul Willis, for example, has looked at the way in which 'Discontent with work is turned away from a political discontent ...into the symbolic sexual realm', and how the wage packet has become 'a kind of symbol of machismo' (Willis, 1979: 196, 197). Andrew Tolson considers how work for working-class men is 'made palatable only through the kinds of compensation masculinity can provide' (Tolson, 1977: 48; see also Cockburn, 1983).

Men, like women, receive mixed messages. On the one hand they are encouraged to think of themselves as the unfettered automatons of liberal theory; on the other they are reminded of their breadwinner role. Culture sometimes dictates which message is the stronger.[15] 'Home life' serves as a motivator for men's public duties in the workplace[16] and, as Genevieve Lloyd suggests, in the war machine (Lloyd, 1986; Morgan, 1986: 183). Men are compensated for their lack of real autonomy in the 'public' sphere with domination of the 'private'. Battered women pay the cost.

It seems inadequate then simply to equate 'man' and individualism. Is masculinity not also a construct? There have been many male critics of individualism—think of Marx, for example (Grimshaw, 1986: 68; see also page 27). Nor are all men happy with existing norms of masculine behaviour (Grimshaw, 1986: 193).[17]

In Carol Gilligan's most recent work, *men and women* use both voices, the caring voice and the voice of justice, in defining and resolving moral problems. But men remain more inclined to invoke the justice voice to defend their decisions. Now Gilligan wants to know: 'Why are men not representing in their formal decision-making procedures what in fact is present in their thinking?' (Du Bois et al., 1985: 47, 49). This question shifts the analysis from 'men' to the institutions which shape and constrain value systems and behaviour.

Moreover, leaving women responsible for nurturing values will not effect real change. Equating women with 'self-sacrifice' neatly 'perpetuates the system' (Du Bois et al., 1985: 46). A genuine transformation requires extending caring values to the public sphere (O'Donovan, 1985: 207), which cannot happen until men are encouraged/allowed/required to transform their consciousness. While in a final desperate search for a political alternative to the status quo, women might be encouraged to take 'the risk of essence', an inadequate political analysis will leave the world much as it is (Jardine, 1987: 58).

This is not to suggest that women surrender 'difference' for 'sameness'. The limitations of the dominant liberal tradition, which the 'sameness' alternative endorses by implication, especially the way in which this tradition ignores people's interdependency, has provided a central theme in this book. It is important to acknowledge the contribution cultural feminism has made to the critique of liberal individualism. Sandra Harding aptly describes the 'feminine' as a 'category of challenge' (Harding, 1986: 181–183). Alice Kessler-Harris agrees that the concept has helped feminism make some real breakthroughs in challenging commonly accepted values which she calls 'male' universals (Kessler-Harris, 1987: 65). Barbara Sichtermann describes cultural feminism as a 'moment of hesitation' in the evolution of feminist theory when feminists took 'a critical view of patriarchal history'. But, whereas Sichtermann believes that we still need both approaches—'the pragmatic one and the Utopian one, the political one and the aesthetic one, the one which insists on equality and the one which insists on difference' (Sichtermann, 1986: 107–108), I suggest that the two approaches work at cross-purposes, and that neither offers an adequate political analysis.

As in the institutional equal treatment/special treatment debate, setting equality *against* difference makes it difficult to question the nature of the equality which is on offer. Similarly, seeking out samenesses and differences diverts attention from the conditions which produce the norm against which women are being compared. Without such an analysis, little will change. The project of feminism, as I understand it, is to learn from the encounter with 'female' values and 'female' experience and to extend the lessons to society at large.

For example, women have in large part been given social responsibility for the 'private' parts of lives, those parts not accommodated by the dominant tradition in liberal theory. As they have moved into the marketplace they have experienced the contradiction of trying to live 'like a man', while maintaining 'their' domestic responsibilities. The difficulty of balancing the two roles is leading some women to look for new solutions. The alternatives they suggest, from community-based childcare to flexible hours, are hemmed in by institutional constraints. Even feminists within a strong equal rights tradition are flirting with more collectivist solutions as a result. At the same time feminists schooled in socialism are searching for alternatives to excessive bureaucratisation (Dale and Foster, 1986: 79), because of many women's day-to-day experience with public welfare institutions.

The way in which women have been penalised by a system which allocates to them the world's caring work is leading feminists to construct alternative models of the relationship between the individual and society so that *Gemeinschaft* values can be retained without leaving women responsible for them. They are looking for models in which autonomy and dependency, freedom and security are no longer offered as either/or 'choices'. Marjorie Weinzweig develops the idea of 'relational self-actualization', based on 'interdependence rather than domination and submission' (Weinzweig, 1987: 90). Lucinda Finley also wants a new approach to gender issues, 'based on a richer conception of human nature and needs than the view of humans as atomised individuals...' (Finley, 1986: 1122). Carol Gilligan's 'inclusion' model, which brings together care and justice, implies a radical transformation in standards of moral philosophy and perhaps in future judicial practice:

> The inclusion of two voices in moral discourse, in thinking about conflicts, and in making choices, transforms the discourse. It is no longer either simply about justice or simply about caring; rather it is about bringing them together to transform the domain. We are into a new game whose parameters have not been spelled out...(Du Bois et al., 1985: 45).

These examples show that it is possible to insist upon the necessity of 'different' political values without suggesting that women embody them. The insights of cultural feminism have moved the dialectic along; it is necessary to keep it moving.

Rejecting the idea of 'Woman' as it has been constructed creates several problems, however. Denise Riley explains that 'Woman' is not just some ethereal notion which can be eliminated from feminist analysis since it has a concrete impact on women's lives (Riley, 1987b). In our attitudes to mothering and caring we act out to an extent the messages about what being a 'woman' means. As a result feminists face a difficult task. They want to challenge an ideology which has been imposed on women, but also wish to assist women for whom that ideology forms part of their lives.

The poststructuralist challenge complicates the situation. If 'Woman' is indeed a fiction and we are called upon to recognise our 'fractured identities' and 'multiple subjectivities', just whom does feminism represent? On what grounds can feminism claim to speak for 'women'? Biddy Martin's advice is that feminists carefully tread the line between 'the dangers of theories about the endless subversion of identity [that is, poststructuralism] *and* the dangers of theories that promote sexual difference [such as categoricalism]'. She along with many other feminists rejects 'Woman' because of the way in which it falsely universalises women's experience and appears to be a fixed identity. But at the same time she is unwilling to allow this poststructuralist insight to undermine her feminist commitment: 'We cannot afford to refuse to take a political stance "which pins us to our sex" for the sake of an abstract theoretical construct...'(Doane and Hodges, 1987: 12–13).

From this position the option of developing a carefully constructed *political identity* based upon women's shared disadvantages begins to emerge. A number of feminists are thinking along these lines.[18] A political identity permits the necessary flexibility to remain attentive to women in a variety of situations, those in waged labour, those in unpaid domestic labour, those combining both labours, and to women differentiated by class, race, culture, creed and age. It builds upon the commonalities which feminists have identified in women's experiences. Gayatri Spivak, for example, who is sceptical about women finding a common purpose, promotes a 'sense of our common yet history-specific lot', based upon 'the (sex) objectification of women' on a scale which ranges from sexist advertising to clitoridectomy (Spivak, 1981: 182, 184). Carole Pateman has identified the way in which 'the social and legal meaning of what it is to be a "wife" stretches across class and racial differences' (Pateman, 1988: 18). All the women I interviewed agreed that a priority for feminist political action today is female poverty. Even Bell Hooks, who is particularly attentive to the differences among women, believes that

> Ending economic exploitation could become the feminist
> agenda that would address the concerns of masses of women,
> breaking down the barriers separating those small groups of
> women who actively participate in feminist organizations from
> the larger group of women in society who have not participated
> in organized feminist struggle (Hooks, 1987: 10)

This list of 'common causes' could be extended. Of course, designing 'consistent' policy may be difficult. However, a flexible approach to policy which recognises the contradictions in women's lives may prove more relevant.

A political identity for women could accommodate the claim that they have a distinctive contribution to make to politics, so long as the distinction is not essentialised. The sexual division of labour means that at an obvious level most women's experiences are different from most men's. As our theory tells us, this will have *some effect* upon lifestyles and viewpoints. Hence women in government demonstrate a better understanding of childcare requirements, for example.

To those who consider retaining the idea of innate 'difference' because of the way in which it inspires some women to collective action, I suggest that an emphasis upon the political insights of feminism is potentially *more* inspiring since it attributes to women a degree of moral judgment and decision-making. It seems important to acknowledge that the women who choose 'to denounce violence and domination and its ultimate expression, war, are political thinkers making political decisions and choices' (Hooks, 1987: 128). To suggest otherwise, to suggest that women are naturally this way, denies them moral authority.

The challenge in this chapter to the identification of women as 'different' forms part of the book's central message. This is that an analysis which reduces social problems to a sameness/difference framework is inadequate. The argument is recapitulated in the Conclusion which follows.

Conclusion

Feminists based in America:

I have believed for twenty years that unless women have their
own pay cheques, they are very very disadvantaged...Now I
see people who are ten years younger than I am, struggling
with a job on one hand and a kid on the other hand and
husbands with very busy schedules and they've got very busy
schedules...Who is supposed to raise the children?
Mary Jean Collins

Regarding the next generation, 'we have left them in a very
difficult position. They think the doors are open. At the same
time they know, at some level, that there aren't supportive
structures, social institutions that will make it possible for them
to do what they think we've made it possible for them to do.
They say–I want a career, I want a family, I want a husband, I
want children, I want it all. We know it's often not possible to
have it all, especially not all at once.'
Ruth Mandel

I don't think ideology does any good now. You have to be
willing to compromise on legislation.
Catherine East

Feminism started with women asking for equality to get into
the system we had been excluded from. This has moved to a
much more basic question of how indeed we redefine the
structure of society so we don't have the whole dynamic of
domination of one group by another.
Charlotte Bunch

Feminists based in Britain:

The question of difference is itself unavoidable. It is going to
be asked. The real question is whether we're self-aware enough
to realise that 'difference' has a whole lot of meanings.

We kid ourselves and we kid our daughters if we say that it's all fine, the problems have all been ironed out because we understand and we recognise that there *are* differences between men and women or indeed that there are *no* differences between men and women and leave it at that.

Elizabeth Vallance

I don't think I agonise over whether we're the same or different, just over the practical problems the present society provides...We just look at ways in which society ought to be changed so that women don't suffer disadvantage.

Tess Gill

I regard a feminist as a Human Rights campaigner. It's partly because I think women's rights, women's issues, and the woman question get marginalised and I like to put them right there as major concerns of humanity.

Georgina Ashworth

It's not that women want more of the cake. They want to change the recipe!

Jo Richardson

Feminists based in Australia:

The only way to stay optimistic as a feminist is to take a very very long historical view and to start understanding the depth of the kind of issues that were taken on. It is almost as if we stumbled into them and in a very naive way. As we now move into an era where there have been feminist successes and triumphs and there has been a reaction to them, we are measuring what we are up against. It is very important for us to be quite clear what our objectives are...The way forward has to include a much more nuanced notion of what 'difference' means.

Hester Eisenstein

How have feminists engaged in the debate on sexual difference? More precisely, when and why have they invoked arguments about women's sameness to or difference from men in debate with each other? Feminists argue in these terms when political conditions impel them to do so. 'Sameness' and 'difference' are strategic responses to a limited range of political options. The alternatives are shaped by the interaction of political culture, legal doctrine and historical circumstance. Sometimes feminists struggle against the limitations created by these forces and try to find openings for change. Sometimes they share some of the fundamental political values which then affect the shape of their arguments. Many feminists are not involved in these disputes. The debates arise in certain contexts and, when these are examined closely, the way in which politics and political 'choice' set the terms of debate becomes clear.

The women's movement then, contrary to some interpretations (for example, Banks, 1981), has not debated constantly whether women are the same as or different from men, or at least not always in the same way. Serious disputes about woman's sex-specific function, whether all women should mother, did not arise until the inter-war years. Serious debate about woman's character, whether all women share a maternal, caring nature, is more recent still. It is important to identify the historically specific conditions in which divisions appear in order to understand their causes.

The inter-war dispute was a result of the demand by some married women to enter the marketplace. The available models for social organisation (*Gesellschaft/Gemeinschaft*) meant that these women would *either* enter the market free of responsibility for family and living arrangements, *or* remain home and shoulder these responsibilities. The organised women's movement produced two factions, the equalitarians and the reformers, to present these alternatives. Those who were called 'sameness' advocates believed that women could expect no more than to compete in the market on its terms, which meant that no provisions would be made for living arrangements. They therefore downplayed pregnancy and childcare, anything which seemed to suggest that women were less employable than men. Feminists who emphasised 'difference' denied that these conditions could be avoided and, therefore, tried to suggest social supports such as family endowment to allow women to remain home. Both groups sought to increase women's autonomy. They were constrained in constructing alternative visions, however, by their acceptance of some of the underlying social values of the period. Some agreed that women had a duty to remain home; others, that the economic system could not be expected to acknowledge the personal details of people's lives. They were also constrained by the legal doctrine which said that, to be 'equal', you had to deny 'difference', and by the lack of institutional alternatives.

Contemporary sameness/difference debates are somewhat different in character. Few feminists today would suggest that it is an option for women to remain home. Sometimes, however, this suggestion finds its way into the literature. Elizabeth Wolgast and Jean Elshtain are examples (see pages 94, 120). Some British feminists also wonder if it remains possible to provide adequate social supports to allow women to remain home. 'Wages for house-work' still attracts a good deal of support in some quarters.

Amongst the majority, however, the question at the institutional level has become how to fit women to the marketplace. The op-tions described by those debating the question are either asserting explicitly 'women's' needs or trying to analogise these to men's requirements. The constraints shaping the debate are much the same as in the earlier period—social values, legal doctrine, and the lack of institutional alternatives. The problem is also the same—to find some way to get the market to acknowledge that people have children and lives outside paid work. The contemporary meta-physical debate about woman's character is more elusive. However, the central point of contention, albeit at a symbolic level, remains the same. Should women join the market or remain outside as its critics?

Sameness/difference debates are therefore substantive debates about the shape of the social order. They become expressed as debates about women's sameness to or difference from *men* because of the general assumption that marketplace rules either suit men or are unchallengeable. This is a critical point. Debates *among femin-ists* along sameness/difference lines surface in contexts where there appear to be only two options, joining the system on its terms or staying out. The debates dissolve, or never even surface, when it is possible to expect humane living conditions for everyone.

The book uses case-studies to illustrate that important politi-cal issues lie subsumed beneath a sameness/difference analysis, and that feminists get locked into debate with each other along sameness/difference lines when political alternatives are severely constrained. In the historical section (Part I), two examples stand out: wages and maternity leave. In Australia, where minimum wages existed for all workers, feminists did not divide over the issue as they did in Britain and in America. They did not have to argue either that women were the 'same' as men, out of a fear that if they received a minimum wage, employers would not hire them. Nor did they have to maintain that women were 'different' in a desperate bid to gain a decent wage. Similarly, in Britain, once the Beveridge reforms introduced basic support for maternity leave, feminists no longer had to insist either that maternity was irrelevant, because they feared employers would penalise pregnant women, or that maternity made women 'different' in order to win some support.

Amongst the 'Contemporary Controversies', most dramatic is the American equal treatment/special treatment case-study where feminists are engaged in trying to defeat each other's reform proposals. The dispute closely replicates divisions in Britain prior to the Beveridge reforms. American feminists remain divided over the issue of maternity leave because they are unable to call upon an interventionist state to provide basic protection for maternity. They continue then to face the alternatives of either denying 'difference' or insisting upon it.

In part, this dilemma helps to explain why some feminists, again mainly in America, divide over custody, reproductive technologies, and surrogacy (Chapter 8) along sameness/difference lines. Those who most fear the way in which the market penalises maternity try to downplay the condition. Others insist upon the uniqueness of maternity in the hope that women might win some recognition. Similarly, in the metaphysical debate, some who are uncomfortable with the trend among some feminists to eulogise maternity are concerned by the way in which mothering has been used to constrain women. Those who commit themselves to a maternal ethic often do so as a symbolic protest against an uncaring society.

The British dispute over hours limitations and nightwork (Chapter 6) confirms that feminists resort to sameness/difference arguments when political conditions make them necessary. Given the Conservative Government's commitment to deregulation, some feminists are pursuing 'equal treatment' (nightwork for everyone) while others are holding out for 'special treatment' (hours limitation for women). As several participants in the debate make clear, however, if reasonable hours of work existed for all workers, the debate would dissolve. The 'equality' which is being offered is the equal right to work unsocial hours.

These examples illustrate the way in which political culture and political climate set the terms of the debates. America experiences the sharpest divisions because feminists there have had less success in getting the government to accept even a modicum of social responsibility for a range of human needs, including reproduction. It therefore becomes necessary to argue 'difference' to try to have women's needs addressed, or 'sameness' because of the fear that any admission of vulnerability will be interpreted as weakness and punished. And, when the social supports are being removed, as in Britain today, feminists have to rethink their strategies. In times of economic recession and growing political conservatism, when it is more difficult to envisage the kinds of structural changes necessary so that everyone can lead more human lives, feminists start thinking in terms of either/or alternatives. 'Difference' sometimes *looks* to achieve more than the 'equality' on offer.

The important point here is that feminists have to find their way within shifting political institutions and ideologies, and to take their chances where they find them. Because of America's solidly liberal political culture, American feminists have had some success in entrenching equality ('equal rights') legislation there. Britain has a strong Labour tradition and its reforms have been weighted in favour of a welfare approach, based upon a recognition of woman's maternal role. Australia has both traditions. This is not to suggest that Australian women inhabit Nirvana, however. As presently conceived, both approaches retain a blindspot. Pressing for equal opportunity ('sameness') without acknowledging people's particular circumstances and living arrangements will leave women shouldering these responsibilities. Alternatively, seeing maternity as *women's* responsibility ('difference') leaves women vulnerable and disadvantaged in other ways.

Still, a clear message in this study is that countries with a tradition of state intervention are more likely to implement the kinds of changes which are necessary. As one example, Australia's recently announced national women's employment strategy calls for the 'improvement of working conditions and arrangements for workers with families' (*Financial Review*, 18 November 1988: 46). Despite the higher profile of the women's movement in America, I for one would hesitate to endorse the 'liberal/equal rights' model as women's best hope (see Gelb, 1986).

Although feminists adopt sameness/difference strategies because of political imperatives, in some cases they have absorbed the values and assumptions of their political culture. In some cases, then, they genuinely believe either that the market should ignore personal circumstances or that mothering is woman's duty. It is clearly difficult to distinguish between conviction and exigency. The book contains a number of examples, however, where feminists declared either the need for a 'coherent theory of equality' (see pages 167, 197, 221), or that 'sex roles are natural to us' (see page 120). In these cases, the limitations of a 'sameness' or a 'difference' approach are clear.

Those pursuing a coherent theory of equality ('sameness') tend to concentrate upon challenging 'outmoded' stereotypes of femininity and appropriate female behaviour, and insist that women not be judged or constrained by them. They want every 'individual' woman to have the opportunity to prove her worth. As a result they underestimate or deny the extent to which stereotypes are 'true' to an extent. 'What', Martha Minow asks, 'is equal treatment for the woman who is correctly identified, not stereotyped, and who differs from nonstereotyped persons in ways that are relevant to the workplace?' (Minow, 1988: 53). Some in this group are also incapable of responding adequately to the structural disadvantages many women face, because of the reluctance to identify women as 'different' in any way. A few, for example, reject affirmative action (see page 167). Others, in their eagerness for gender-neutral legislation, downplay women's differential social location (see page 219). Concomitant parts of liberal political ideology, such as narrow conceptions of liberty and rights, also produce problems for some 'equal rights' feminists in the pornography debate (see page 206).

On the other side, some 'difference' proponents tend to *overestimate* the extent to which stereotypes are 'true' and, in the process, freeze the system in its present form. Even those who do not overtly endorse traditional sex roles see women as defined by pregnancy in a way many women would reject. The close ties drawn between *women* and procreation also imply that men are disconnected from this process. The assumption seems to be that we can recreate a social order in which men pursue self-actualisation in the marketplace while women find solace, comfort and meaning in a separate world. This approach threatens to 'carve a new norm that produces new exclusions' (Minow, 1988: 54). Moreover, by ignoring the connections between the marketplace and living arrangements, and the ways in which the two have been *constructed* as separate, it offers an inadequate political analysis.

The 'sameness' alternative is insufficiently critical of the status quo. The 'difference' option *is* critical of the status quo, but seems to conjecture that women can exist in some sort of separate world. Seeing women as the 'same' as men prevents us *challenging* the model against which women are being compared; seeing women as 'different' prevents us *changing* it. Talking in terms of 'sameness' or 'difference' skirts the issue, rather than confronting it.

These comments apply both to the institutional and to the metaphysical debates, though the weaknesses are more obvious in the former. The argument developed in Chapters 9 and 10 is that the metaphysical debate about woman's nature recreates the institutional equal treatment/special treatment debate at a symbolic level. The 'woman as superior' construct posits a woman-centred society in which women take responsibility for the world's caring work. Those who oppose the construct may unthinkingly be insufficiently critical of contemporary political and social values. Neither produces a political analysis which seriously challenges those values, or provides a way to influence them.

The central hypothesis, then, is that, when feminists resort to arguments about women's 'sameness' or 'difference', the real problem is that society caters inadequately for living arrangements and human needs generally. Debates about 'sameness' or 'difference' can, in effect, distract attention from the fact that this is the problem. Instead, the problem becomes 'women' or 'difference'. The debates seem to be about some sort of human destiny instead of about the necessary institutional arrangements to make life humane. Martha Minow puts it this way: by 'encapsulating complex realities in simple dichotomies', you risk accepting the rhetoric that what matters is 'sameness' or 'difference', rather than the way in which society is organised. Efforts to reach beyond the concepts of 'sameness' and 'difference' 'can lead to more searching debate over how we should live, how we should raise our children...' (Minow, 1985a: 1093). There is an important insight here into the way in which 'ideology operates by excluding whole areas of debate' from people's very consciousness (Wilson, 1980: 69).

It is no coincidence then that social conservatives encourage the reduction of complex social problems to a sameness/difference or equality/difference framework. The book contains several examples where this occurs. In the divorce case-study (Chapter 8), anti-feminists suggest that women erred in trying to be 'equal' to men and that they should settle for dependence. Feminists are castigated for leading women down the equality road. 'Difference' is offered as a viable alternative. A closer study reveals that a more sensitive institutional response to the structural inequalities of women and men is required, and that most feminists are well aware of this necessity.

The anti-feminist use of the sameness/difference framework is most sinister in attempts to portray antidiscrimination legislation and affirmative action as contradictory (Chapter 7). The argument, and it is one used against other disadvantaged groups, is that you cannot have 'equal treatment' and 'different treatment' at the same time. Another popular phrasing of the claim is that it is inconsistent to ask simultaneously *not* to be discriminated against, and *for* discrimination in your favour.

Clearly the problem is the nature of the equality being offered. Equality here is meant to imply some kind of identical treatment of abstract human essences. Women have the greatest difficulty with this understanding of equality because of the long-standing assumption that they will take care of the personal circumstances of life which the model ignores. Feminist analysis then should focus upon the inadequacy of the model, and not whether women can live 'up' to it. Women do not wish to be singled out and treated disadvantageously, but they do wish to have their sex-specific disadvantages addressed. There is no inconsistency here. Setting equal treatment *against* different treatment is conceptual and semantic deceit.

The last example which illustrates the use social conservatives make of the sameness/difference framework is the Sears antidiscrimination case (Chapter 10). Here, the substantive issues were whether employers ought to be held responsible for providing jobs which acknowledge workers' family commitments, and which provide a psychologically healthy (not 'dog-eat-dog') environment. By identifying childcare and non-competitive values as woman's 'difference', the company successfully absolved itself of those responsibilities.

In the Sears case, the employers scored a double victory. They managed to convey the impression that women's 'sameness' or 'difference' was at issue, *and* that *feminists agreed* that this was the issue. Feminists who describe the Sears case in sameness/difference terms instead of drawing attention to the wider political questions about the employers' social irresponsibility, foster this interpretation of events. History which tells us that the question of difference has *constantly* befuddled feminists (see page xi) encourages feminists to think in these terms. Both the interpretation and the history reflect a common problem—how difficult it is in a world where men hold most of the positions of power to conceive of a point of reference *other than man*. Think, for example, of how difficult it is to think of women as *other than 'different'*. Instead of accepting the language of 'difference', however, we need to examine the processes which turn sex-specific characteristics into disadvantages. So long as women are identified in relation to men, we get oppositions which limit our understanding. As Catharine MacKinnon says, we need to criticise 'the standards that set us up to be either the same as or different from men' (MacKinnon in Du Bois et al., 1985: 34).

While it is understandable that some feminists pursue assimilation or accommodation or even segregation to help women because of political constraints on the options available, the argument here is that the political forces which dictate these circumstances have to be brought centre-stage. Otherwise, the problem will be translated to the public as a problem about *women* and their 'sameness' or 'difference'. Political discussion about the inadequacy of the institutional response to people's needs is thereby curtailed. Similarly, if 'woman' is used as a symbol of a 'different' world, 'man' becomes the problem and the social values which need to be challenged have somehow slipped from the political agenda.

There is a tendency when we observe the obvious power imbalances between women and men to describe the world as constructed to suit male needs. We refer to a 'male norm' in politics, in social arrangements, in phallocentric philosophy. At several points in this analysis, it has become clear that the 'male norm' does not suit all men. Rather, social arrangements accommodate a particular construction of masculinity as autonomous and detached from other persons, as strong and impervious to ill health. If the observation is accurate that some men are not this way and that others may not want to be this way, the question becomes why the political and economic system encourages men to aspire to this norm of behaviour.

'Sameness' and 'difference' in some abstract sense therefore are not in dispute. In dispute is the nature of the social arrangements which inadequately cater for the personal side of people's lives. In dispute are the political and social values by which we choose to live. The message of this book is that the sameness/difference framework does feminism a disservice since it mystifies these political issues. And so we would be well advised to avoid describing the movement in these terms. It is far preferable to discuss openly disagreements about strategies and political visions than to create the impression, first, that the problem is whether or not women are like men and, second, that women must (or can) choose *either* to replicate contemporary male lifestyles and values *or* take responsibility for the world's caring work. The way to get beyond sameness/difference debates is to bring to the surface the political conditions which force women into these alternatives. The way to stop the 'pendulum swing' between 'same as' and 'different from' (Eisenstein and Jardine, 1980: xxiii) is to confront the changes required to allow all people to live fully human lives.

It is disheartening to find young female undergraduates still puzzling over the question the *Smith College Weekly* posed in 1919: why it seemed fixed 'in the nature of things that a woman must choose between a home and her work when a man may have both' (Solomon, 1985: 174). Less privileged women ask why they have to perform both jobs and are inadequately compensated for either. Women, it seems, are still being asked to resolve that tension in the middle-class mind between a belief in the free market and a desire for social cohesion (see page xii). Women try either to mimic the 'male' model or to accept a sex-specific role as carers or, as most women do, try to balance these roles. A new model is required in which the market is compelled to respond to human needs. A way has to be found to provide social supports for the commitments of day-to-day living and to allow women and men to share these commitments.

A social model which *includes* women in the human standard could achieve this goal. In this model it will be possible to speak about women as women, in their own right, and not as 'not men' (Finley, 1986: 1159). Including women in the standard changes our way of thinking about the nature of people and what they require to flourish. It means that society will have to take on board that women reproduce and people have children, and that all workers want safe and humane working conditions. It helps to ensure that our living and working conditions reflect the full range of humanity in all its diversity—a humanity which comprises two sexes, not one.

The questions addressed in this book are both highly political and fundamental to all our lives. They include how home and paid work are to be related, and which values our political and economic system should encourage. It is time to demystify these issues. Challenging the sameness/difference framework is a necessary step towards achieving this purpose.

Appendix

List of Interviewees

The following list includes all the women interviewed in Britain, America, and Australia in alphabetical order, and their occupations. I wish to repeat my thanks to those who gave so generously of their time and thoughts. Interviewees were given the opportunity to alter inaccurate or misleading wording.

ASHWORTH, GEORGINA   Writer, editor, publisher, lobbyist, now living in London; Founding Director of *CHANGE*; development consultant.

BARRETT, MICHÈLE   Author and sociologist; Senior Lecturer, Department of Social Science and Humanities, The City University, London.

BERNARD, JESSIE   Author and sociologist; currently working on a new book in Washington, DC.

BRADLEY, DENISE   Author, teacher and administrator; Academic Director, South Australian College of Advanced Education, Adelaide.

BROOKS, SUZANNE MAY   At the time of the interview, First Assistant Secretary, Office of the Status of Women, Department of the Prime Minister and Cabinet, Canberra, ACT.

BUNCH, CHARLOTTE   Author, teacher, theorist and activist; currently The Blanche, Edith and Irving Laurie New Jersey Chair in Women's Studies, Voorhees Chapel, Douglass College, New Brunswick, New Jersey.

CAMPBELL, HELEN MARGARET   Liaison Officer (Higher Education), Affirmative Action Agency, Sydney, NSW.

CASS, BETTINA   Associate Professor of Social Policy in the Department of Social Work, University of Sydney; Consultant Director of the Social Security Review.

CHAVKIN, WENDY, MD, MPH   Director, Bureau of Maternity Services and Family Planning, New York City Department of Health.

COCKBURN, CYNTHIA   Author, academic and activist; Senior Research Fellow, Department of Social Science and the Humanities, The City University, London.

COLLINS, MARY JEAN   Lobbyist, former Vice-President of NOW, currently Director of Public Affairs, Catholics for a Free Choice, Washington, DC.

CURTHOYS, ANN   Author, editor and teacher; Head, School of Humanities and Social Sciences, University of Technology, Sydney.

DENNIS, SHIRLEY M.   Former Director, Women's Bureau, US Department of Labor, Washington, DC; currently Resident Fellow, Institute of Politics, John F. Kennedy School of Government, Harvard University.

EAST, CATHERINE   Senior staff member for all presidential advisory commissions on women from 1962 to 1977; ERA lobbyist; consultant and former legislative director, National Women's Political Caucus.

EISENSTEIN, HESTER   Author; Leader (Chief Education Officer), Equal Employment Opportunity Unit, Department of Education, New South Wales until 1988; now Visiting Professor of Women's Studies at the State University of New York, Buffalo.

GILL, TESS   Author and unionist; Group Secretary, National Union of Civil and Public Servants, London.

GOLDSMITH, JUDY   Former President of NOW; currently Director of Communications, National Center for Policy Alternatives, Washington, DC.

HOLCOMB, H. BRIAVEL   Author and lecturer; former Acting Director, Women's Studies Program, Rutgers University; Associate Professor, Department of Urban Studies, Rutgers University, New Brunswick, New Jersey.

KESSLER-HARRIS, ALICE   Author and teacher; Professor of History, Temple University, Philadelphia.

MANDEL, RUTH B.   Author and teacher; Director, Center for the American Woman and Politics, Eagleton Institute of Politics, Rutgers University, New Brunswick, New Jersey.

MEEHAN, ELIZABETH, M.   Author and lecturer; Lecturer in Politics, School of Humanities and Social Sciences, University of Bath, UK.

NILAND, CARMEL J.   Author and teacher; President, Anti-Discrimination Board, Premier's Department, Sydney, NSW.

OAKLEY, ANN R.   Author, sociologist; Deputy Director, Thomas Coram Research Unit, London.

OLDENBURG, VEENA T.   Author and teacher; currently Rockefeller Humanist-in-Residence, Institute for Research on Women, Rutgers University, New Brunswick, New Jersey.

PLATT, BARONESS, OF WRITTLE   Engineer and educationist; Chairman of the Equal Opportunities Commission, London.

PRATT, VALERIE   Former personnel manager and consultant; Director, Affirmative Action Agency, NSW.

RADICE, LISANNE   Author, lecturer and activist; Department of Government, Brunel University, London.

RICHARDSON, Jo   Labour MP, Shadow Minister for Women, London.

RYAN, SUSAN   Former lecturer; Senator for ACT since 1975; at time of interview Minister Assisting the Prime Minister on the Status of Women.

SHINN, RUTH   Chief, Division of Legislative Analysis, Women's Bureau, US Department of Labor, Washington, DC.

STAMP, PADDY Positive Action Officer, Women's Rights Unit, National Council for Civil Liberties, London.

STIMPSON, CATHARINE R. Author and academic; Professor of English, Dean of the Graduate School, and Vice Provost for Graduate Education at the New Brunswick campus of Rutgers University, New Jersey.

STOTT, MARY Author, journalist and activist; former Chair of the Fawcett Society, London.

SUMMERS, ANNE Author, lecturer, activist; currently Editor in Chief, *Ms* Magazine, New York, NY.

TAUB, NADINE Author and academic; Professor, Rutgers Law School, Newark, New Brunswick.

THORNTON, MARGARET R. Author and academic; Senior Lecturer, School of Law, Macquarie University, NSW.

VALLANCE, ELIZABETH Author and academic; Reader in Politics and Head of Department of Political Studies, Queen Mary College, University of London.

WOLFE, LESLIE R. Lobbyist and administrator; Executive Director, Center for Women Policy Studies, Washington, DC.

Notes

Introduction

1 As only one of many possible examples, a recent Australian Broadcasting Commission 'Science Show' reported that male rats succeeded better in 'mastering' mazes far from the home base whereas female rats did better closer to home, and speculated that the research provided insights into human behaviour (ABC 'Science Show', 20 February 1989).

2 Katherine O'Donovan describes some of the tragic consequences which follow from the determination to categorise as 'male' or 'female' people who do not slot easily into one of these categories. The most obvious problems arise where there are ambiguous genitalia (O'Donovan in Edwards, 1985: 12).

3 With Joan Scott, I feel that 'it is a mistake for feminist historians to write this debate uncritically into history for it reifies an "antithesis" that may not actually have existed' (Scott, 1988: 50 fn. 8).

4 Neither describes an actual existing society, but only a dominant tendency within a society (Kamenka and Tay, 1986: 289).

5 It is important to remember that liberalism is not a monolithic ideology. Stuart Hall identifies a dominant, 'establishment liberalism', based upon the image of 'bourgeois rational man', and a subdominant tradition, commonly called pluralism, which recognises the importance of group status (Hall, 1986: 49–53).

6 Katherine O'Donovan reminds those of us keen to revive the communitarian values of *Gemeinschaft* not to overlook the 'hierarchical and dependent relationships traditionally associated with self-abnegation' (O'Donovan, 1985: 5).

7 This is clear in the following quotation from Tonnies:

> The realm of life and work in *Gemeinschaft* is particularly benefiting to women; indeed, it is even necessary to them. For women, the home and not the market, their own or a friend's dwelling and not the street, is the natural seat of their activity (in O'Donovan, 1985: 2).

8 Frances Olsen describes how the acceptance of a market/family dichotomy constrains reform initiatives (Olsen, 1983: 1560).

9 Karen Offen uses the terms 'relational' and 'individualist' modes of feminist discourse to refer to the two traditions I have just described.

Offen, in my view, does not pay enough attention to the *political constraints* which shaped these discourses. Hence, at times, she seems to be offering them as alternatives, with relational values her preference. I argue that both discourses, as constructed, disadvantage women. I am therefore more sympathetic to Offen's conclusion that 'We must collapse the dichotomy that has placed these two traditions at odds historically and chart a new political course'. As my argument develops, however, it will become clear that, in my opinion, this necessarily involves challenging a definition of woman as 'the nurturing sex', a definition Offen finds acceptable (Offen, 1988: 156).

10 Julia Brophy and Carol Smart make the point: 'we are equally located in the languages and practices of our time' (Brophy and Smart, 1985: 46). Karen Hunt adds: 'To build a feminist political theory it is important to analyse how theories and ideologies have constructed our understanding of society. It is only on this basis that society can be changed' (Hunt, 1986: 47).

11 Littleton uses Kuhn to raise the more general point that 'the formulation of any question determines the range of answers that will be sought' (Kuhn, 1970 in Littleton, 1981: 487). In Elizabeth Meehan's words, 'the concepts and categories we use to describe the world also serve to limit our understanding of it and, therefore, influence what can be regarded as possible social practice' (Meehan, 1986: 121).

12 Catharine MacKinnon states that talking about women's sameness to or difference from men are simply two ways of having man as your standard:

> In effect, if not intent, the law has conceptualized women workers either in terms of their 'humanity', which has meant characteristics women share with men, or in terms of their womanhood, which has meant their uniqueness... When women have been defined 'as women' their human needs have often been ignored... Alternately, when women have been analysed as 'human', their particular needs as women have often been ignored (MacKinnon, 1979: 3).

More recently, Elizabeth Grosz challenged the representation of women as either the 'opposites or negatives of men' or 'in terms the same as or similar to men' or 'as men's complements': 'In all three cases, women are seen as variations or versions of masculinity...' (Grosz, 1989: xx).

13 Here, I am building upon Martha Minow's solution to what she calls the 'difference dilemma'. Minow asks whether the problems faced by disadvantaged groups are 'better remedied by separation or by integration of such groups with others'. 'Either remedy', she says, 'risks reinforcing the stigma associated with assigned difference by either ignoring it or focusing on it.' A way out of the dilemma, she suggests, may be to locate 'difference in the relationship rather than in the person or group called "different"'. The problem then becomes the 'shared context in which difference appears'. Speaking

specifically about the problem of children with special needs, Minow wants to 'somehow locate all the students on the same side of the problem, as part of the solution'. She claims this approach would work 'to the educational benefit of every student in the classroom (Minow, 1985b: 157, 207). Similarly, the idea of positioning women on the same side as men so that their needs become part of a common human standard would, I suggest, have beneficial effects for everyone.

14　Michèle Barrett has written about the several ways in which the concept of 'difference' is used in recent feminist writing, and recommends that feminists specify their intention when they use it to avoid confusion (Barrett, 1987). Here, I am asking for greater clarity with reference to the several meanings of 'difference' *within* discussion about sexual difference, which is only one of Barrett's categories.

15　Colette Guillaumin distinguishes between the 'idea of difference' and the empirical 'reality of difference'. Linda Gordon speaks about 'making the difference a derivative rather than a primary category' (Guillaumin, 1987: 65; Gordon, 1986: 26). I suggest that references to women's 'differential social location' are less ambiguous.

16　Teresa de Lauretis credits Black feminists with shifting feminist consciousness to an awareness of and a desire to work through 'feminism's complicity with ideology' (de Lauretis, 1987: 10).

1 The nineteenth century: equal but different

1　It would seem desirable, as a result of the way in which suffragists could endorse both entry to the 'public' world of politics and yet suggest that in an ideal world married women would not engage in the 'public' marketplace, to be far more careful in applying the notion of a public–private dichotomy. With Frances Olsen I find a family–market dichotomy a more accurate representation of attitudes towards sex roles (Olsen, 1983).

2　Essentialist arguments are those which make reference to a male or female essence and are usually connected with biological determinism. Both anti-feminists and some feminists use an essentialist framework (Eisenstein, 1984: xvii–xix).

3　It should become clear from this paragraph that the author has dramatically altered her interpretation since the publication of *Liberation Deferred?* in 1983. She believes this reflects both the discovery of the 1980s, that equal opportunity and justice were further apart than at first estimated, and the quite remarkable outpouring of feminist analyses in the last decade.

4　Jane Lewis develops a similar argument in *Women in England, 1870–1950: Sexual Divisions and Social Change*, Wheatsheaf Books, Sussex, 1984. See especially pp. 88–90.

5　The number of political theorists who have produced volumes trying to give the notion of 'equality' some precision attests to its ambiguity. Douglas Rae and others in *Equalities* suggest that the complexity arises not *within* the abstract idea of equality but in its confrontation with the world (Rae et al., 1981). Rozann Rothman believes the very ambiguity of the notion somehow explains its success:

> Americans throughout their history have juggled the somewhat contradictory cluster of conceptions that surround the symbols 'liberty' and 'equality'. . . For most of our history, we have been able to devise neat formulas which obscure the contradiction of our belief system so that Americans can easily believe themselves to be both free and equal (Rothman, 1981).

6 Schreiner wrote an important introduction to *Woman and Labour* which was published in 1911. In it she explains that the bulk of the manuscript had been destroyed by fire in 1898. This volume is basically all that remains. The missing sections paid more attention to women's 'domestic labour' and the fact that it is not 'adequately recognized or recompensed' (Schreiner, 1911: 22).

7 Sandra Harding has developed the concept 'feminist standpoint' to describe those feminists who argue that 'men's dominating position in social life results in partial and perverse understandings, whereas women's subjugated position provides the possibility of more complete and less perverse understandings' (Harding, 1986: 26).

8 The term 'maternal ethos' will be used as a shorthand for that conviction that woman's connection with reproduction made her unique.

9 It would be impossible to provide a comprehensive list. Readers are directed to the footnote references in Davin, 1978; Bacchi, 1980; and Dyhouse, 1976.

10 Selma Sevenhuijsen discovered similar attitudes among Dutch first-wave feminists:

> Whereas feminists tried to argue from the standpoint of women, their way of thinking about 'women' was, in differing degrees, influenced by the discourse of other political forces, in which a fear of the life-styles of the urbanised working class, and a corresponding anticipation that illegitimate children might become criminals and prostitutes, mingled with a clear explosion of anti-socialism and fear of social disruption (Sevenhuijsen, 1986: 333).

11 According to Gillian Pascall, the threat of a demand by women for individual rights is just this: '. . .it offers a threat to the fabric of interdependence on which men's rights depend' (Pascall, 1986: 9).

2 The split (part I): 'equalitarian' versus 'reform' feminism

1 Guy Alchon from the University of Delaware's History Department is writing a book on the lives of Lillian Gilbreth and Mary Van Kleeck. I am indebted to him for much of my information on both of these women.

2 Hayden calls them 'material' feminists because they 'dared to define a "grand domestic revolution" in women's material conditions' (Hayden, 1983: 1).

3 Jane Lewis describes the protective legislation debate as one between 'middle class feminists' and 'the women's trade union movement'. I agree with Bob Connell that there is no reason why the latter should not also be called feminist: 'It articulates women's interests and involves an extensive critique of the power of men' (Lewis, 1984: 91; Connell, 1987: 269).

4 Although many men participated in the suffrage movement and by some definition could be labelled 'feminist', this study is primarily concerned with the way in which women sorted out their relationships with politics and the world.

5 Babcock, Freedman, Norton and Ross quote William O'Neill (*Everyone Was Brave*, 1969: 280–281) to the effect that 'the argument that protective legislation was desirable when equally applied to men and women was made so often by the militants [O'Neill's label for the NWP] that their sincerity on the point seems hardly open to question' (Babcock, Freedman, Norton and Ross, 1975: 250).

6 The Shephard-Towner Maternity and Infancy Protection Act of 1921 allocated federal funds to the states to set up programs for instruction in the hygiene of maternity and infant care (Lemons, 1973: 158).

7 On the issue of equal pay the equal rights feminists appear inconsistent in the other direction. That is, despite their insistence on equal treatment in every area, the NWP hung back in its support of the equal pay campaign largely, says Cynthia Harrison, because the Women's Bureau, their arch-opponents, had instigated it. It seems that the Bureau had intended to use the issue to divert attention from the ERA. Another equal rights group, the Business and Professional Women, joined the national equal pay committee from its founding (Harrison, 1988: 41–45).

8 It is clearly difficult to unravel the complex motivations involved in the dispute, but one motivation seems to have been the understandable commitment to a reform which had absorbed one's energy over many years. At a 1927 investigation into the labour laws the representative for the American Federation of Labor, Sara Conboy, declared in exasperation: 'What do any of you know about labor conditions? Nine out of ten of you are professional women that never knew what it meant to feel fatigue. *We have struggled for this legislation for years*. I am willing to say every inch of it has been put on the statute books by the trade union movement' (Technical and Advisory Committee, *c*.1927: 44, emphasis added).

9 During the meeting Van Kleeck admitted that the Secretary of Labor had 'ruled that he did not wish public hearings in the Department' (Technical and Advisory Committee, *c*.1927).
   My thanks to Guy Alchon for allowing me to see this document.

3 The split (part II): 'ultra' versus 'new' feminism

1 The Charity Organisation Society developed a philanthropic approach which saw 'poverty as a product of the individual's own moral failings' (Macnicol, 1980: 17).

2 See for example Nicole Cox and Silvia Federici, *Counter-Planning from the Kitchen: Wages for Housework—A Perspective on Capital and the Left*, Falling Wall Press, Bristol, 1975.

3 The Woman Patriots accused the Women's Bureau of trying to 'Bolshevize America by destroying the family' with their proposal for a maternity grant (Lemons, 1973: 213).

4 An exception to this generalisation, the socialist feminist, Marion Phillips, said that, if working-class women wanted economic independence, they would get it only by struggling to establish their right to work and to be paid equally, *mothers or not* (Mann, 1974: 33). Dora Marsden of the Women's Freedom League was also suspicious of the idea of a state endowment of motherhood, fearing that it 'would confirm the domestic role and keep women dependent on men' (Garner, 1984: 71).

5 Smyth presents an excellent example of the difficulties involved in trying to recapture feminist motivations. It is impossible to determine to what extent she might have been manipulating current attitudes about national health to serve women's interests. Her speeches explicitly endorsed the eugenist proposal that those with hereditary diseases should not have families. At the same time she told her mainly female audience that in her shop (she was a local Melbourne merchant) she stocked a full range of preventatives including the rubber 'French Pessarie Preventatif', 'the only article of the kind that can be used without the knowledge of the husband' (Kelly, 1988: 43). It seems foolhardy to give a ranking to such a complex mix of feelings and attitudes.

6 The 'differential birth rate' referred to the fact that, using an occupation scale, blue-collar workers were outbreeding white-collar workers and professionals. The Australian Birth Rate Commission of 1903–1904 placed a great deal of the blame for this trend upon the 'new women' and their preoccupation with extra-maternal interests (Bacchi, 1980a: 202–203).

7 Feminists have found what I call the 'veteran analogy' appealing in making demands for maternity provisions. See, for example, Jaggar in Scales, 1981: 428 and Finley, 1986: 1176. The point is not that the analogy is completely inappropriate but that like all comparisons it has to be used carefully with full awareness of the implications.

8 Nancy Cott focused upon a small sub-cultural collective in New York which earned the label 'Feminist' with a capital 'F', but the non-capitalised version was frequently used early in the century to refer to women with a wide range of views (Cott, 1987a: 35–50).

9 In the interviews conducted in Britain several feminists who endorsed a program of equal opportunity and even affirmative action said they were uncomfortable with the label 'feminist'. Australian feminists from every location on the political spectrum seemed content to adopt the title though, as in America, those with socialist views insisted on expanding their definition beyond a 'narrow' equal rights focus.

4   The 1960s resurgence: from equal rights to post-feminism

1   By 1977 women comprised 36% of the South Australian labour force
and of these two-thirds were married (Bacchi, 1986: 426). In Britain
by 1978 some 62% of married women were classified as economically
active (Lewis, 1984: 218).

2   Esther Peterson explained her opposition to including 'sex' in the Act:

> 'I was fearful that adding in women's rights would defeat the Bill.
> Sex was added on as an amendment to the Bill by Howard Smith,
> an outspoken opponent of civil rights in an attempt to kill the Bill.
> I just could not risk advancing women's rights on the backs of my
> black sisters. . . Of course I was wrong' and 'I am very pleased that
> it turned out that I was wrong' (Peterson, *c*.1976: 18).

3   Hester Eisenstein provides a most useful analysis of these developments in feminist thought (Eisenstein, 1984).

4   Segal refers here to her 1979 volume *Beyond the Fragments* which she
wrote with Sheila Rowbotham and Hilary Wainwright. She sees this
volume as asserting the validity and potential of the experience of
social movements including feminism, 'but alongside the validity and
potential of working-class experience and struggle' (Segal, 1987: 209–
210).

5   I agree with Judith Stacey that it is appropriate to call Elshtain a
feminist because she claims the title and because, in my opinion, she is
trying to negotiate a resolution of the conflict between family and paid
work. The fact that most feminists may not approve of her resolution
in no way changes this (Stacey, 1986: 220).

6   Susan Hekman provides a useful summary of the ideas associated with
this position (Hekman, 1987).

Denouement

1   As mentioned previously (see p. 19), I would include my early work
in this category.

2   I wish to be fair to the authors of *Sex Discrimination and the Law*.
They, like most historians of the period, find it difficult to maintain a
consistent line given the inconsistencies they discover. And so Babcock, Freedman, Norton and Ross admit, in parentheses, that the idea
of equal competition between women and men may not have been a
desirable and practical goal 'at that point in history'. I don't think they
would dispute my conclusion however that, in their view, a 'difference' line of argument was (and is) dangerous and that an insistence
upon 'sameness' was (and is) the appropriate strategy to adopt (Babcock, Freedman, Norton and Ross, 1975: 41).

3   Banks occasionally admits that the 'sameness' feminists did not extend
their analysis to sex roles:

> . . .in neither Britain nor America did the feminist movement
> concern itself with changes in marriage and the family.
> . . .the equal rights tradition, in spite of its Englightenment
> emphasis on the fundamental similarities of men and women, has

tended, like the evangelical tradition, to leave unchanged, and indeed at times even unchallenged, the traditional division of labour and the traditional role of women (Banks, 1981: 58, 243).

II Current Controversies—Prologue
1 The most recent statistics from the South Australian Women's Adviser's Office illustrate trends elsewhere. As of December 1987, 67.2% of women worked in three occupational categories—'Clerks', 'Salespersons and Personal Service Workers', and 'Labourers and Related Workers'. According to the report, 'There has been little change in occupational and industry segregation for female employees'. The weekly total earnings for all employed women was 66% of the male wage. Part of the reason for the differential is the large proportion of female workers who work part-time and the relatively poorer wages and benefits attached to part-time work. Women comprised 78% of all part-time workers in South Australia in December 1987. Once this is factored out, female ordinary time earnings rise to 84% of those of men (Women's Adviser's Office, 1987).
2 I would like to thank all the women who gave generously of their time to help with this project. A list of those interviewed and their occupations appears in the Appendix.

5 'Equal' versus 'special' treatment
1 Participants in the debate use other labels for their positions though I have decided to retain 'equal treatment' and 'special treatment' because they are most familiar. Recently Christine Littleton and Wendy Williams agreed that 'asymmetry' and 'symmetry' best described their respective positions (Littleton, 1987: 1287 fn. 42).
2 It is important to note that 'Britain's family leave entitlements are the most restrictive of any in Europe (Eastern or Western)'. Here, however, the contrast is with America where provisions are non-existent. In a 1984 ILO survey of 118 countries, only the United States 'lacked any national legislation regarding maternity rights and benefits' (Stoiber, 1989: 6).
3 California, Hawaii, New Jersey, New York, Rhode Island and Puerto Rico provide statutory benefits for working women at childbirth. A large number of private employers also offer some benefits, usually basic hospitalisation insurance (Kamerman, Kahn and Kingston, 1983: 4–5).
4 Chapter 7 will look in detail at the impact of discrimination theory on feminism and feminist debates.
5 The equal protection clause of the Fourteenth Amendment states that no state shall 'deny to any person within its jurisdiction the equal protection of the laws' (Goldstein, 1988: 626).
6 Babcock, Freedman, Norton and Ross refer in 1975 (pre-PDA) to the dangerous line being developed by some feminists who 'supported special programs of aid to pregnant workers without realizing that their theory...could just as easily support discrimination against

pregnant workers' (Babcock, Freedman, Norton and Ross, 1975: 315).

7   Lucinda Finley makes the point that the equal treatment solution could have the same adverse impact on pregnant women as special treatment due to 'cost factors':

> If a company increases its allowed disability leave time to encompass time for maternity, or makes parenting leave available to workers of both sexes, far more women than men will avail themselves of the benefit. Thus, it will still be more expensive to employ women, in the sense that women may take more time off from work (Finley, 1986: 1151).

8   American College of Obstetrics-Gynecology Guidelines now specify that the traditional approach is 'to certify disability beginning two weeks before delivery and ending at six weeks postpartum', but they can only recommend this approach; they cannot enforce it (*ACOG Technical Bulletin*, no. 58, May 1980, 4).

9   Some of the qualms about the intent behind the legislation may be justified. Wendy Williams points out that the MMLA emerged directly out of the 'doubts and fears of many citizens' who wanted to protect 'the rights of individuals who wish to assume traditional roles in the family and society...' (Williams, 1982: 195, fn. 109).

10   More will be said about disparate effects in Chapter 7.

11   In debate with Carol Gilligan, MacKinnon confesses that she was troubled by the possibility of women identifying with 'what is a positively valued feminine stereotype': 'Given existing male dominance, those values amount to a set-up to be shafted' (Du Bois et al., 1985: 74–75). The usefulness and limitations of cultural feminist theory will be pursued in Chapter 10.

12   Feminists owe a debt of gratitude to Ann Scales for the way in which she openly demonstrated the need to push constantly at the boundaries of conceptualisations (Scales, 1981 and 1986).

13   In the American constitution, if a classification is subjected to 'strict scrutiny', as race is, then it is justified only if it serves important governmental objectives and must be 'substantially related to achievement of these objectives' (Goldstein, 1988: 165).

14   In a footnote Finley explains that here she is talking about only the majority of relationships and does not wish to disparage lesbian or single mothers where, she argues, her model holds since other human beings are still affected by how society treats the pregnant woman (Finley, 1986: 1137 fn. 92). While Littleton does not make the same disclaimer she also sees the usefulness of emphasising the '*interaction of the sexes*' in the case of pregnancy (Littleton, 1987: 1327).

15   Christine Littleton describes the amount of restructuring which each approach would involve and, although she is quite right that some models go further than others, none in my opinion adequately challenges traditional workplace values and rules. Littleton's 'parallel' female workforce which might incorporate a new value system for

women would still leave the 'male' workforce model intact (Littleton, 1987: 1301).

16 In 1979 the European Commission informed the British Government that it needed to amend its 1975 Equal Pay Act to bring it into line with EEC policy. The 1975 Act called only for equal pay for equal work. This had to be modified to include the concept of equal pay for work of equal value (Scorer and Sedley, 1983: 7).

17 *The South Australian Equal Opportunity Act*, 1984, specifies that it is not unlawful to grant women 'rights or privileges in connection with pregnancy or childbirth' (Equal Opportunity Act, 1984, Part III, Division VII, item 46). The Commonwealth Sex Discrimination Act (1984) has a similar provision (section 31, SD Act) (Ronalds, 1987: 153).

18 Paid maternity leave is available for teachers in NSW, Victoria, the ACT and the Northern Territory. NSW public servants receive six weeks' full pay and six weeks' half-pay (Women's Electoral Lobby, South Australian branch, April, 1987; Women's Bureau, 1985: 39).

19 In 1985, 47% of female employees were unionised compared to 63% of male employees. Women currently represent one-third of all unionists. Since September 1987, the 38-member ACTU Executive has included five women ('Women in Australia—Statistical Summary', made available by Senator Susan Ryan).

20 Although Hewlett presents the decision to have a child as 'both a private and a public decision', her emphasis is upon the female contribution: 'It is true, only women can have babies; it is both the privilege and the *responsibility* of the female sex...' (Hewlett, 1986: 149, emphasis added).

21 Wendy Williams seems to accept that, if maternity benefits are provided out of public funds or a mandatory insurance system, this would reduce the extent to which employers 'will be tempted not to hire women in the peak childbearing years' and hence eliminate one of the chief dangers of such benefits (Williams, 1984: 376 fn. 200).

6   Protective legislation and industrial health hazards

1   The details about the design and implications of sex discrimination legislation are contained in the following chapter.

2   When Title VII was enacted almost half the state minimum wage laws, fifteen out of 32, applied to women only. By 1976 39 laws covered both men and women (US Department of Labor, 1976: 11). While there are no limitations on weekly hours, there are rules covering overtime wages.

3   These same battles are being fought elsewhere. In Japan a recent equal employment opportunities law abolished a regulation forbidding women to work at night. Factory workers will now have to work at night or lose their jobs. The feminist leader of the Japan Socialist Party, Takako Doi, campaigned unsuccessfully to eliminate the law's harmful effects (Rose, 1988: 44).

4   The declared purpose of the *Occupational Safety and Health Act* is 'to

assure so far as possible every working man and woman in the Nation safe and healthful working conditions and to preserve our human resources' (Williams, 1981: 663–664).

5 Catharine MacKinnon said also that: 'The affirmative form of the argument is that the health needs of women workers should be accommodated equally with men' (MacKinnon, 1979: 118).

6 While Christine Littleton's idea of 'equality as acceptance' avoids some of the problems associated with the assimilation and segregation models, it does not in my view go far enough. It still constructs a parallel system for women and ignores the need to challenge the values which lie behind the 'male' side of the equation. To repeat, *inclusion* does not mean adding women to existing standards; it means reformulating standards with women as full and participating members in the process.

7 Sex discrimination and affirmative action

1 Federal antidiscrimination laws include the *Equal Pay Act* (1982), Title VII of the *Civil Rights Act* (1964), Title IX of the Education Amendments of 1972, the *Equal Credit Opportunity Act* (1982), the *Fair Housing Act* (1976) and the *National Housing Act* (1982) (Freedman, 1983: 916).

2 In Britain the Labour government introduced the Sex Discrimination Act in 1975 and the Race Relations Act in 1976. Section 5(3) of the former provides that like must be compared with like. In Australia the Whitlam Labor Government intended to follow the framework of its *Racial Discrimination Act* (1975) in sex discrimination legislation but lost office before it had a chance to do so. Australia's Sex Discrimination Act was finally introduced in 1984 (Gregory, 1987: 2; Ronalds, 1987: 14; McGinley, 1986: 420).

3 Selma Sevenhuijsen blames 'liberal legal discourse' for forcing feminist lawyers 'to think in terms of individuals, persons and parents, as if the legal system had "banned" structural power relations between the genders' (Sevenhuijsen, 1986: 339).

4 Wendy Williams explains the three frameworks used to analyse alleged discrimination. The first, facial discrimination, occurs when an employer adopts a policy which 'treats certain classes of workers differently from other classes of workers on the grounds of race, religion, national origin, or gender'. The second which would still be classed as 'direct discrimination' occurs when a plaintiff alleges that an apparently neutral policy is a 'mere pretext for forbidden discrimination'. The third framework, indirect discrimination, applies when a genuinely 'facially neutral' policy has a disparately adverse effect on a group protected from discrimination (Williams, 1981: 668–669).

5 The wording in the British SDA (1975) and the Australian SDA (1984) is close enough to allow an extract from the former to suffice:

1 (1) A person discriminates against a woman in any circumstances relevant for the purposes of any provision of this Act if:

(a) on the ground of her sex he treats her less favourably than he treats or would treat a man, or

(b) he applies to her a requirement or condition which he applies or would apply equally to a man but

    (i) which is such that the proportion of women who can comply with it is considerably smaller than the proportion of men who can comply with it, and

    (ii) which he cannot show to be justifiable irrespective of the sex of the person to whom it is applied, and

    (iii) which is to her detriment because she cannot comply with it.

(Gregory, 1987: 184. For the Australian legislation see Ronalds, 1987: 99).

6 The opposition predictably insisted that 'objectives' were only quotas by another name, though there appears to be an obvious difference between a standard imposed by penalty and a voluntarily set forward objective (Ronalds, 1987: 23).

7 According to the Inner London Education Authority:

> It is neither possible nor desirable to definitely support or reject single groupings per se. Their success or otherwise can only be measured in relation to the particular pupil, teacher, curricular needs and the school concerned . . . single sex grouping alone will not solve the problem of inequality or underachievement by groups of pupils in schools. It should be regarded as one of many possible strategies that can be adopted, and should be firmly placed within the context of an overall anti-sexist anti-racist policy for the school (ILEA, 1987: 1).

8 These may appear to be 'voices in the wilderness' in the present economic climate and given the Australian Labor Government's commitment to 'economic rationalism', but they are still voices which deserve to be heard. For a critical discussion of the Australian Government's 'initiatives' in education, see Yeatman, 1988: 39–41.

9 Sadurski distinguishes between 'equality before the law', which simply means the 'correct' or non-arbitrary application of a general rule, and 'equality in law', which implies that legal rules should not contain 'any discriminating and privileging provisions'. It is 'equality in law' which is in contention here (Sadurski, 1986: 131).

8 Divorce, custody, and Baby 'M'

1 In 1978–1979, in Australia, 19% of non-aged single women were poor compared with 7% of men (Cass, 1985: 80).

2 Meredith Edwards challenges the commonly-accepted assumption that 'the income of a household is pooled and spent for the benefit of its members (or at least of both partners in a marriage). . .' (Edwards, 1984: 120).

3 In America women and children account for 77% of the poor and half of those live in families headed by females with no husband present (Thurow, 1987: 31). In Britain 'the second largest single group of women on Supplementary Benefits is single women' (the largest

group is the elderly) (Pascall, 1986: 204). In Australia one half of women-headed single parent families are living in poverty (Cass, 1985: 83).

4 Bettina Cass notes that 'the great majority (85%) of single parent families are formed after the cessation of a marriage or a marriage-like relationship', and therefore 'the increase in numbers represents changes in the social institutions of marriage and parenthood, not an increase in ex-nuptial births' (Cass, 1985: 78).

5 In Australia in 1986 the 'absurdly low going rate' for child support was $20 per child a week. Moreover, 'An estimated 40 percent of maintenance orders are never paid' (Arndt, 1986: 70). Concerning America, Dorothy Wickenden notes that 'child support is grossly inadequate and between 60 and 80 percent of fathers refuse to comply with court-ordered payments' (Wickenden, 1986: 21).

6 Britain and Australia use the common law in the division of marital property. Starting from Blackstone's premise that 'By marriage, the husband and wife are one person in law' and that person was the husband, subsequent legislation such as the Married Women's Property Acts (late nineteenth century) gave a woman the right to control the property she owned before marriage, and property she earned or received by gift during the marriage. Since then other forms of protection of a marital share in the property have been instituted. The final decision for 'equitable' division rests on judicial discretion.

Most American states have a common law system but eight, with Spanish or French origins, employ the European model entitled 'community of property'. Under this approach, 'property acquired by each spouse during the marriage is owned in common by both husband and wife' and upon divorce there is an 'equal' sharing of assets. Unless modified by reform, during the marriage, the husband controls the management of the property (Brown, Emerson, Falk and Freedman, 1971: 937; 946–949; Eisler, 1977: 33; Smart, 1984b: 46–49).

7 Sylvia Hewlett concedes that 'Alimony has always been rather less common than folklore would have us believe' and refers to a 1919 study which found that 'alimony was awarded to only 32 percent of divorcing women'. Catherine East points out that this study was based upon one county in California and that there has really been no significant change in alimony awards since 1922: 'In 1922, 14.7 percent of divorced women were awarded alimony. The percent for 1983 is 13.9. The highest percentage recorded was in 1916 when 15.3 percent was the figure.' Riane Eisler adds that in most respects 'no-fault need not—and indeed has not—made that much difference in the division of property upon divorce' (Hewlett, 1986: 55; East, 1986: 14; Eisler, 1977: 33).

8 Smart acknowledges the important contribution of Christine Delphy to the theorising of divorce. According to Delphy, 'divorce is not the opposite of marriage nor even its end, but simply a change or a transformation of marriage' (in Smart, 1984b: 127; see also Delphy, 1976 and Delphy, 1984).

9 Frances Olsen makes the important theoretical point that, since the 'state is responsible for the background rules that affect people's domestic behaviours', it makes no sense to consider the policies referred to as 'noninterventionist' as any less interventionist than policies referred to as 'interventionist'. That is, the state is as active in creating social relations by not doing things as by doing things. The notion of the 'private' family is therefore an ideological construct and a myth (Olsen, 1985: 837–838).

10 For example an 1895 Act provided that a wife could be awarded custody if she could prove a matrimonial fault against her husband. However she had first to separate from her husband and was not entitled to take her children with her. 'In effect', Julia Brophy explains, 'this provision proved futile for the vast majority of women who had no means of establishing a separate residence' (Brophy, 1982: 151).

11 In America a West Virginia Court was forced to abandon the tender years presumption as a result of a sex discrimination challenge and to replace it with a gender-neutral standard. The primary caretaker standard was adopted (Williams, 1982: 190 fn. 80).

12 I realise the provocative nature of a comment like this given the stand of the women's movement on abortion. I am not saying that it is inappropriate to talk about rights in certain contexts but that we need to sort out the contexts. Linda Martin talks about the potency of the 'rights discourse', how it has been appropriated by IVF researchers who now talk about the 'right to reproduce', and the implications for women. I will say more about abortion 'rights' in the next chapter (Martin, 1986: 382–383; see also Diamond and Quinby, 1988).

13 'On February 6, 1985, Mary Beth Whitehead signed a surrogacy contract agreeing to be artificially inseminated with sperm from biochemist William Stern and to turn over to him the child she gave birth to. She agreed to assume all medical risks, and to submit to amniocentesis or abortion on demand. In return, she would receive $10 000 if she gave birth to a healthy baby. In March 1986, Mary Beth gave birth to a baby girl and decided she wanted to keep her' (*Ms Magazine*, May 1988: 36).

9 The sexuality debates

1 Lesbian sadomasochism is a term used to cover a wide range of physical and/or emotional power relations, usually of a temporary, contractual and reversible kind. The phrase 'butch/femme' is commonly used to describe a permanent adoption of roles by partners in a relationship, in which one partner apparently approximates stereotypical masculinity and the other stereotypical femininity. The reality may, of course, be very different from the image. The relative rarity of both these forms of relationship among a wide range of more equal lesbian relationships should also be noted.

2 The First Amendment, added to the Constitution in 1791, reads: 'Congress shall make no law respecting an establishment of religion, or prohibiting the free exercise thereof; or abridging the freedom of

speech, or of the press, or the right of the people peaceably to assemble, and to petition the Government, for a redress of grievances' (Goldstein, 1988: 624).

3   Anne Koedt's important essay, 'The Myth of the Vaginal Orgasm' claimed that the truth about women's sexuality had not been popularised for 'social reasons':

> The establishment of clitoral orgasm as fact would threaten the heterosexual institution. For it would indicate that sexual pleasure was obtainable from either men *or* women, thus making heterosexuality not an absolute, but an option. It would thus open up the whole question of *human* sexual relationships beyond the confines of the present male-female role system (Koedt, 1970: 166, emphasis in original).

4   As with any study of this sort it is difficult to do justice to nuances in arguments. The setting up of contending sides also means that people sometimes get shoved into categories where they do not quite fit. Leading spokespeople for the contending views have been selected in an effort to be fair, but it is certainly not implied that everyone who supports a particular position in the pornography debate, for example, supports these views. As will be discussed later it is patently clear that Kate Millett and Adrienne Rich have lined up with FACT more for tactical reasons than for ideological ones.

5   In a recent ABC (Australian Broadcasting Commission) radio program Rich claimed that she is now placing less importance on biology. 'Mum's the Word', Coming Out Show, 1986.

6   As Ardill and O'Sullivan put it, 'In revolutionary feminism, male sexuality was, for the foreseeable future, irredeemable'. Elizabeth Wilson also finds the theories used by anti-pornography feminists inadequate: 'although, that is, they do not explain male violence as stemming from a male instinct of aggression—they merely replace biology with a transhistorical, universal "male supremacy" expressed and manifested in "patriarchy". This is either to say something very similar or to say something too general to be helpful' (Ardill and O'Sullivan, 1986: 39; Wilson, 1983: 218).

7   The whole question of juvenile and childhood sexuality, while important, is one which will not be considered.

8   The best case to illustrate this point is the law of provocation. Margaret Thornton explained to me that traditionally the law applied only where the accused acted in the 'heat of passion'. Feminists, however, pointed out that women simply were unable to respond in the same way as men if they were attacked: 'Many women were first the subjects of domestic violence, suffered thus for years and years but they couldn't respond. They could only respond if the man was drunk or asleep and then self-defence and provocation were not open to them...' The law in some Australian states has since been reformed to allow consideration of 'subjective factors like race, educa-

tion and so on as well as the sex of a person' (Thornton interview, 28 August 1987; see also Edwards, 1986).

9 In the debate between pro-life feminist, Sidney Callahan, and pro-choice feminists, Ellen Willis and Linda Gordon, the moderator asked if any compromises were available. Gordon mentioned that in Wisconsin a 'pregnancy options' bill emerged from the 'collaboration of feminists and right-to-lifers'. The bill makes it possible for teen-agers to be openly presented with a variety of options, including abortion and adoption (Woodruff et al., 1986: 43).

10 Frances Olsen argues that rights for women, including 'individualis-tic' and 'alienating' rights, may be necessary as 'an expression of the social practice of allowing women to resist forced community'. Seyla Benhabib and Drucilla Cornell explain why feminists need to be wary of simple communitarianism: 'If unencumbered males have difficul-ties in recognizing those social relations constitutive of their ego identity, situated females often find it impossible to recognize their true selves amidst the constitutive roles that attach to their persons' (Olsen, 1984: 394; Benhabib and Cornell, 1987: 12).

11 Gayatri Spivak concurs that the political mission of feminism is to reveal the 'political function of the biological':

> At the moment, the fact that the entire network of advanced capitalist economy hinges on home-buying, and that the philosophy of home-ownership is intimately linked to the sanctity of the nuclear family, shows how encompassingly the uterine norm of womanhood supports the phallic norm of capitalism (Spivak, 1981: 182–183).

12 A recent decision by the US Supreme Court giving public school officials broad power to censor student newspapers is unlikely to assist the anti-pornography cause: 'the case stemmed from the dele-tion of two pages concerning teen pregnancy and divorce in a Mis-souri high school paper...' (*The Review*, University of Delaware, 15 January 1988: 8).

13 To use de Lauretis's precise words:

> That women continue to become Woman, continue to be caught in gender as Althusser's subject is in ideology, and that we persist in that imaginary relation even as we know, as feminists, that we are not *that*, but we are historical subjects governed by real social relations, which centrally include gender—such is the contradiction that feminist theory must be built on, and its very condition of possibility (de Lauretis, 1987: 10).

10 The construction of 'Woman'

1 For additional background details on the Sears case refer to Dowd Hall et al., 1986; Sternhell, 1986; Milkman, 1986; Scott, 1988.

2 Rosenberg's testimony was used against the commission sales charge, upon which this chapter will focus. The salary differentials here were substantial. Ruth Milkman records that 'Between 1973 and 1980,

first-year commission salespersons had median earnings about twice those of *all* noncommission salespersons' (Milkman, 1986: 381).

3   Under instruction from the government, Sears had instituted an affirmative action plan in 1974. The EEOC claimed that the company had not really attempted to put it into action (Milkman, 1986: 378).

4   An 'Offer of Proof' is a written document which is drawn up before a witness appears and which summarises the arguments she/he intends to make (Dowd Hall et al., 1986: 755).

5   This is obviously an oversimplification of some very complex theory. Readers wishing to delve deeper into feminist poststructuralism should read de Lauretis, 1987 and Moi, 1985.

6   I have written a similar description of the strength of the 'cult of domesticity' in South Australia (Bacchi, 1986a).

7   Anne Phillips' point that part-time work is taken up mainly by white women adds weight to Kessler-Harris's interpretation (Phillips, 1986: 6).

8   Margrit Eichler relates an anecdote which explains her reservations about 'strong socialisation' theory:

> Not too long ago I attended a conference which brought together fifty Canadian women who were considered leaders in their fields in government, from the business world, in the publicity business and from academia. At some point, this larger group broke up into smaller discussion sections. The section of which I was a part started to discuss the failure of women to assert themselves, their fear of success, their inability to speak in public etc. There were earnest nods all around when one speaker said that we as women did not know how to behave in public and how to be successful in various types of organizations. The ironic aspect of this was that there was not a single woman in that group who had not successfully made her way against all odds in a formal organization and who did not frequently speak in public (Eichler, 1980: 10).

9   Suzanne Kessler and Wendy McKenna develop a powerful and convincing defence of the social construction of gender. Here they describe the self-fulfilling practice of psychological studies of sex differences:

> For a psychologist to ask the question 'How are girls different from boys?' overlooks the fact that in order to ask the question, she or he must already know what boys and girls are...
> [S]cientists would not be able to talk about differences in the first place unless they knew how to classify the incumbents of the two categories which they are comparing. And we will never be able to say how this is done by making more and detailed lists of differentiating factors (e.g. males are more competitive, females admit to a wider range of feelings) because in order to make these lists *we must have already differentiated* (Kessler and McKenna, 1978: ix, emphasis added).

10 Jean Anyon interviewed students in five elementary schools to test the attitudes of female students toward sex roles. She found working-class girls particularly rebellious against prescriptive messages. Almost all of the girls said they would work or wanted to work when they grew up although all but one said their husbands would not want them to work (Anyon, 1983).

11 The chair of the EEOC, Clarence Thomas, publicly 'questioned the validity of the Sears suit, particularly its reliance on statistical evidence to demonstrate discrimination'. The *Washington Post* reported that Thomas and other Reagan administration officials 'privately make little secret of their desire to lose the [Sears] case, and lose it in a way that would explode any chance for future EEOC officials to bring class-action suits on the basis of statistics'. Judge Nordberg was another Reagan appointee (Milkman, 1986: 377, 390).

12 A few quotations from Kessler-Harris' testimony indicate this loss of nuance: '...ideas about women's traditional roles are neither deeply rooted in women's psyche nor do they form a barrier that inhibits women's work force participation'; 'Where opportunity has existed, women have *never* failed to take the jobs offered'; 'there is little evidence that expressions of belief in traditional roles have *any* bearing on the labor market behavior of women who need to work' (Dowd Hall et al., 1986: 771, 772, 773, emphasis added).

13 Sandra Harding concludes: '"Woman" and "femininity" are concepts created through and central to masculine domination projects' (Harding, 1986: 172).

14 'Fortunately—what luck!—', Christine Delphy comments sarcastically:

> feminine values, the above-mentioned gentleness, understanding, concern for others, innate aptitude for washing nappies, and other Platonic ideals, will counterbalance, if they are needed, the violence (dynamic) and closeness to death (promethean nature) of masculine values (Delphy, 1984: 207).

15 Elizabeth Meehan disputed the suggestion that all men operate on the basis of an 'ethic of rights':

> that may be so in the United States where there's a much stronger tradition of rights. In other societies which are shaped by other political theories and political philosophies, I would have thought that the notion of duties is very important. Men often think they have a duty to support a wife and family. It's a dignified and honourable thing to be fulfilling that duty. In Britain we've got quite a long tradition of what we call the family wage (Meehan interview, 7 April 1988).

16 '...the construction which defines the home as a woman's place may have as much to do with the market as the family itself' (Bottomley, Gibson and Meteyard, 1987: 55).

17 While it is important to remember that women suffer most from the

present construction of gender relations, this does not mean that no men suffer. I agree with Bell Hooks that 'This suffering should not be ignored', especially if it may be causally linked to the violence which is subsequently perpetrated on women' (Hooks, 1987: 72).

18   As Teresa de Lauretis explains, this feminist concept of identity:

> . . . is not at all the statement of an essential nature of Woman, whether defined biologically or philosophically, but rather a political-personal strategy of survival and resistance that is also, at the same time, a critical practice *and* a mode of knowledge (de Lauretis, 1986: 9).

Sandra Harding offers similar guidelines:

> Once 'woman' is deconstructed into 'women', and 'gender' is recognised to have no fixed referrent, feminism itself dissolves as a theory that can reflect the voice of a naturalised or *essentialized* speaker. It does not dissolve as a fundamental part of our political *identities*, as a motivation for developing *political solidarities* (Harding, 1986: 246, emphasis added).

Bibliography

Books and pamphlets

Abbott, E. and Bompass, K. (1943) *The Woman Citizen and Social Security* London: Rydal Press

Alderfer, H. (et al.) (eds) (1982) *Diary of a Conference on Sexuality* New York: Faculty Press

Alpern, S. (1987) *Freda Kirchway: A Woman of the Nation* Cambridge: Harvard University Press

Antler, J. (1987) *Lucy Sprague Mitchell* New Haven: Yale University Press

Apter, T. (1985) *Why Women Don't Have Wives: Professional Success and Motherhood* Essex: Macmillan

Arditti, R., Klein, R. and Minden, S. (1984) *Test-Tube Women: What Future for Motherhood?* London: Pandora Press

Atkinson, M. (1914) *The Economic Foundations of the Women's Movement* Fabian Women's Group series no. 4, London: Fabian Society

Babcock, B. A., Freedman, A. E., Norton, E. H. and Ross, S. C. (1975) *Sex Discrimination and the Law: Causes and Remedies* Boston: Little Brown & Co.

Bacchi, C. (1983) *Liberation Deferred? The Ideas of the English-Canadian Suffragists 1877–1918* Toronto: University of Toronto Press

Baer, J. (1978) *The Chains of Protection: The Judicial Response to Women's Labor Legislation* Westport: Greenwood Press

Banks, O. (1981) *Faces of Feminism* Oxford: Martin Robertson

Barrett, M. (1980) *Women's Oppression Today* London: Verso

Barrett, M. and McIntosh, M. (1982) *The Anti-social Family* London: Verso

Bassett, S. (1986) *Feminist Experiences: The Women's Movement in Four Cultures* London: Allen & Unwin

Becker, S. (1981) *The Origins of the Equal Rights Amendment: American Feminism Between the Wars* Westport: Greenwood Press

Benhabib, S. and Cornell, D. (eds) (1987) *Feminism as Critique: Essays on the Politics of Gender in Late-Capitalist Societies* Cambridge: Polity Press

Benn, S. I. and Gaus, G. F. (1983) *Public and Private in Social Life* London: Croom Helm

Berger, P. and Luckmann, T. (1979) *The Social Construction of Reality* Harmondsworth: Penguin

Blair, K. (1980) *The Clubwoman as Feminist: True Womanhood Redefined, 1868–1914* New York: Holmes & Meier

Bondfield, M. (1940) *A Life's Work* London: Hutchinson & Co.

Brittain, A. and Maynard, M. (1984) *Sexism, Racism, and Oppression* Oxford: Basil Blackwell

Broom, D. H. (ed.) (1984) *Unfinished Business—Social Justice for Women in Australia* Sydney: George Allen & Unwin

Brophy, J. and Smart, C. (eds) (1985) *Women-in-Law: Explorations in Law, Family and Sexuality* London: Routledge and Kegan Paul

Brown, J. and Small, S. (1985) *Family Income Supports Part 9: Maternity Benefits* London: Policy Studies Institute

Browne, A. (1987) *The Eighteenth Century Mind* Brighton: Harvester Press

Brownmiller, S. (1975) *Against Our Will: Men, Women and Rape* New York: Simon and Schuster

Bryant, M. (1979) *The Unexpected Revolution: A Study in the History of the Education of Women and Girls in the 19th Century* London: University of London, Institute of Education

Burstall, S. (1907) *English High Schools for Girls: Their Aims, Organisation and Management* London: Longman's Green & Co.

Burton, C., Hag, R. and Thompson, G. (1987) *Women's Worth: Pay Equity and Job Evaluation in Australia* Canberra: Australian Government Publishing Service

Cambridge Women's Peace Collective (1984) *My Country is the Whole World* London: Pandora

Campbell, B. (1984) *Wigan Pier Revisited: Poverty and Politics in the 80's* London: Virago

—— (1987) *The Iron Ladies: Why Do Women Vote Tory?* London: Virago

Carr, E. H. (1976) *What Is History?* Harmondsworth: Penguin

Charvet, J. (1982) *Feminism* London: J. M. Dent & Sons

Chavkin, W. (ed.) (1984) *Double Exposure: Women's Health Hazards on the Job and at Home* New York: Monthly Review Press

Chodorow, N. (1978) *The Reproduction of Mothering: Psychoanalysis and the Sociology of Gender* Berkeley: University of California Press

Clarke, E. (1873) *Sex in Education; or, a Fair Chance for the Girls* Boston: Osgood & Co.

Cockburn, C. (1983) *Brothers: Male Dominance and Technological Change* London: Pluto Press

Connell, R. W. (1987) *Gender and Power: Society, The Person and Sexual Politics* Sydney: Allen & Unwin

Cook, B. (ed.) (1978) *Crystal Eastman: On Women and Revolution* Oxford: Oxford University Press

Coote, A. (1972) *Women Factory Workers: The Case Against the Protective Laws* London: Rye Express

Correa, G. (1985) *Man-made Women* London: Hutchinson

—— (1986) *The Mother Machine* New York: Perennial Library

Cott, N. (1987a) *The Groundings of Modern Feminism* New Haven: Yale University Press

Coussins, J. (1979) *The Shift Work Swindle* NCCL Rights for Women Unit London: Redesign

Coussins, J., Durward, L. and Evans, R. (1987) *Maternity Rights at Work* 3rd rev. ed., National Council for Civil Liberties, South Norwood: Yale Press

Cox, N. and Federici, S. (1975) *Counter-Planning From the Kitchen: Wages for Housework—A Perspective on Capital and the Left* Bristol: Falling Wall Press

Creighton, W. B. (1979) *Working Women and the Law* London: Mansell Publishing

Cross, B. M. (ed.) (1965) *The Educated Woman in America: Selected Writings of Catherine Beecher, Margaret Fuller and M. Carey Thomas* New York: Teachers College Press

Curthoys, A. (1988) *For and Against Feminism* Sydney: Allen & Unwin

Dahlerup, D. (ed.) (1986) *The New Women's Movement: Feminism and Political Power in Europe and the USA* London: Sage Publications

Dale, J. and Foster, P. (1986) *Feminists and State Welfare* London: Routledge & Kegan Paul

Davidoff, L. and Hall, C. (1987) *Family Fortunes: Men and Women of the English Middle Class 1780–1850* London: Hutchinson

Davidson, K., Ginsburg, R. and Kay, H. (1974) *Sex-Based Discrimination: Test Cases and Materials* St Paul: West Publishing Co.

Davies, E. (1910) *Thoughts on Some Questions Relating to Women 1860–1908* Cambridge: Bowes and Bowes

Davies, M. (ed.) (1978) *Maternity: Letters From Working Women* first published 1915, London: Virago

—— (ed.) (1984) *Life As We Have Known It By Co-operative Working Women* first published 1931, London: Virago

Davis, E. (1973) *The First Sex* Baltimore: Penguin

de Beauvoir, S. (1961) *The Second Sex* New York: Bantam Books

Delamont, S. (1980) *Sex Roles and the School* London: Methuen

de Lauretis, T. (ed.) (1986) *Feminist Studies: Critical Studies* Bloomington: Indiana University Press

—— (1987) *Technologies of Gender: Essays on Theory, Film and Fiction* Bloomington: Indiana University Press

Delphy, C. (1984) *Close to Home: A Materialist Analysis of Women's Oppression* Amherst: University of Massachusetts Press

Dinnerstein, D. (1977) *The Mermaid and the Minotaur: Sexual Arrangement and Human Malaise* New York: Harper & Row

Doane, J. and Hodges, D. (1987) *Nostalgia and Sexual Difference* New York: Methuen

Dobkin, M. (1979) *The Making of a Feminist: Early Journals and Letters of M. Carey Thomas* Kent: Kent State University Press

Donovan, J. (1985) *Feminist Theory: The Intellectual Traditions of American Feminism* New York: Frederick Ungar Publishing Co.

Dowdy, Mrs H. A. (1914) *The Higher Education of Women* Adelaide: Women's Liberal Education Union

Duchen, C. (1987) *French Connections: Voices from the Women's Movement in France* Amherst: University of Massachusetts Press

Dworkin, A. (1981) *Pornography: Men Possessing Women* New York: Perigee and G. P. Putnam's

—— (1987) *Intercourse* London: Arrow Books

Dworkin, R. (1978) *Taking Rights Seriously* London: Duckworth

Edelman, M. (1971) *Politics and Symbolic Action* Chicago: Markham Publishing Company

—— (1977) *Political Language: Words that Succeed and Policies that Fail* New York: Academic Press

Edwards, S. (ed.) (1985) *Gender, Sex and the Law* London: Croom Helm

Ehrenreich, B. (1984) *The Hearts of Men: American Dreams and the Flight From Commitment* New York: Anchor Books

Ehrenreich, B., Hess, E. and Jacobs, G., (1986) *Re-making Love: The Feminization of Sex* New York: Anchor Press/Doubleday

Eichler, M. (1980) *The Double Standard: A Feminist Critique of Feminist Social Science* London: Croom Helm

Eisenstein, H. (1984) *Contemporary Feminist Thought* London: Unwin Paperbacks

Eisenstein, H. and Jardine, A. (eds) (1980) *The Future of Difference* Boston: G. K. Hall & Co.

Eisenstein, Z. (1981) *The Radical Future of Liberal Feminism* New York: Longman

—— (1984) *Feminism and Sexual Equality* New York: Monthly Review Press

Eisler, R. T. (1977) *Dissolution: No Fault Divorce, Marriage and the Future of Women* New York: McGraw Hill

Engels, F. (1968) *The Origins of the Family, Private Property and the State* Moscow: Progress Publishers

Evans, J. (et al.) (1986) *Feminism and Political Theory* London: Sage Publications

Evans, M. (1985) *Simone de Beauvoir: A Feminist Mandarin* London: Tavistock

Evans, S. (1980) *Personal Politics: The Roots of Women's Liberation in the Civil Rights Movement and the New Left* New York: Vintage Books

Faust, B. (1981) *Women, Sex and Pornography* Ringwood: Penguin

Flowers, M. (1977) *Women and Social Security: An Institutional Dilemma* Washington: American Enterprise Institute for Public Policy Research

Foucault, M. (1981) *The History of Sexuality: Vol. I An Introduction* London: Penguin

Friedan, B. (1965) *The Feminine Mystique* first published 1963, Harmondsworth: Penguin

—— (1976) *It Changed My Life* New York: Random House

—— (1982) *The Second Stage* first published 1981, London: Michael Joseph

Fuller, M. (1972) *Woman in the 19th Century and Kindred Papers Relating to the Sphere, Condition and Duties of Woman* Freeport: Books for Libraries Press

Garner, L. (1984) *Stepping Stones to Liberty: Feminist Ideas in the Women's Suffrage Movement* London: Heinemann Education Books

Gerson, K. (1985) *Hard Choices: How Women Decide About Work, Career and Motherhood* Berkeley: University of California Press

Gilligan, C. (1982) *In a Different Voice: Psychological Theory and Women's Development* Cambridge: Harvard University Press

Gilman, C. P. (1911) *The Man-Made World or Our Androcentric Culture* New York: Charlton Company

Goldmark, J. (1913) *Fatigue and Efficiency: A Study in Industry* New York: Survey Associates

Goldstein, L. (1987) *The Constitutional Rights of Women: Cases in Law and Social Change* Madison: University of Wisconsin Press

Gollancz, V. (ed.) (1917) *The Making of Women: Oxford Essays in Feminism* London: George Allen & Unwin

Goodnow, J. and Pateman, C. (eds) (1985) *Women, Social Science and Public Policy* Sydney: George Allen & Unwin

Goodsell, W. (1923) *The Education of Women: Its Social Background and its Problems* New York: Macmillan Co.

Gordon, L. (1977) *Woman's Body, Woman's Right: A Social History of Birth Control in America* Harmondsworth: Penguin

Greer, G. (1971) *The Female Eunuch* New York: Bantam Books

_____ (1985) *Sex and Destiny* London: Picador

Gregory, J. (1987) *Sex, Race and the Law: Legislating for Equality* London: Sage

Grimshaw, J. (1986) *Feminist Philosophers: Women's Perspectives on Philosophical Traditions* Sussex: Wheatsheaf Books

Grosz, E. (1989) *Sexual Subversions: Three French Feminists* Sydney: Allen & Unwin

Harding, S. (1986) *The Science Question in Feminism* Ithaca: Cornell University Press

_____ (ed.) (1987) *Feminism and Methodology: Social Science Issues* Bloomington: Indiana University Press

Harding, S. and Hintikka, M. (eds) (1983) *Discovering Reality: Feminist Perspectives on Epistemology, Metaphysics, Methodology and Philosophy of Science* London: D. Reidel Publishing Company

Harman, H. (1978) *Sex Discrimination in School: How to Fight it* London: National Council for Civil Liberties

Harrison, B. (1978) *Separate Spheres: The Opposition to Women's Suffrage in Britain* London: Croom Helm

Harrison, C. (1988) *On Account of Sex: The Politics of Women's Issues 1945–1968* Berkeley: University of California Press

Hayden, D. (1983) *The Grand Domestic Revolution* Cambridge: MIT Press

Henriques, J., Hollway, W., Unwin, C., Venn, C. and Walkerdine, V. (eds) (1984) *Changing the Subject: Psychology, Social Regulation and Subjectivity* London: Methuen

Henry, A. (1971) *Woman and the Labor Movement* first published 1923, New York: Arno

Hewlett, S. A. (1986) *A Lesser Life: The Myth of Women's Liberation in*

America New York: William Morrow & Co.

Hochschild, J. (1981) *What's Fair? American Beliefs About Distributive Justice* Cambridge: Harvard University Press

Holcombe, L. (1973) *Victorian Ladies at Work* Newton Abbot: David & Charles

Hole, J. and Levine, E. (1971) *Rebirth of Feminism* New York: Quadrangle Books

Holton, S. (1986) *Feminism and Democracy: Women's Suffrage and Reform Politics in Britain 1900–1918* Cambridge: Cambridge University Press

Hooks, B. (1981) *Ain't I a Woman: Black Women and Feminism* Boston: South End Press

——— (1987) *Feminist Theory: From Margin to Center* 3rd printing, Boston: South End Press

Hyam, R. (1976) *Britain's Imperial Century 1815–1914* London: Batsford

Jaggar, A. (1983) *Feminist Politics and Human Nature* Sussex: The Harvester Press

Jancar, B. W. (1978) *Women Under Communism* London: Johns Hopkins University Press

Kamerman, S. B., Kahn, A. and Kingston, P. (1983) *Maternity Policies and Working Women* New York: Columbia University Press

Kelley, F. (1905) *Some Ethical Gains through Legislation* New York: Macmillan Co.

Kessler, S. and McKenna, W. (1978) *Gender: An Ethnomethodological Approach* Chicago: University of Chicago Press

Klatch, R. E. (1987) *Women of the New Right* Philadelphia: Temple University Press

Kraditor, A. (1971) *The Ideas of the Woman Suffrage Movement 1890–1920* New York: Anchor Books

Kuhn, T. (1970) *The Structure of Scientific Revolutions* Chicago: University of Chicago Press

Lasch, C. (1979) *Haven in a Heartless World: The Family Besieged* New York: Basic Books

Lemons, J. S. (1973) *The Woman Citizen: Social Feminism in the 1920s* Urbana: University of Illinois Press

Lewis, J. (1980) *Politics of Motherhood: Child and Maternal Welfare in England 1900–1939* London: Croom Helm

——— (ed.) (1983) *Women's Welfare, Women's Rights* London: Croom Helm

——— (1984) *Women in England 1870–1950: Sexual Divisions and Social Change* Brighton: Wheatsheaf Books

——— (1987) *Before the Vote Was Won: Arguments For and Against Women's Suffrage* New York: Routledge & Kegan Paul

Lloyd, G. (1984) *The Man of Reason: 'Male' and 'Female' in Western Philosophy* London: Methuen

Lorde, A. (1984) *Sister Outsider* New York: Crossing Press

Luker, K. (1984) *Abortion and the Politics of Motherhood* Berkeley: University of California Press

Maccoby, E. E. and Jacklin, C. N. (1974) *The Psychology of Sex Differences* Stanford: Stanford University Press

Mackinnon, A. (1984) *One Foot on the Ladder* St Lucia: University of Queensland Press

MacKinnon, C. (1979) *Sexual Harassment of Working Women: A Case of Sex Discrimination* New Haven: Yale University Press

_____ (1987) *Feminism Unmodified: Discourses on Life and Law* Cambridge: Harvard University Press

Macnicol, J. (1980) *The Movement for Family Allowances—1918–45* London: Heinemann

Magarey, S. (1985) *Unbridling the Tongues of Women—A Biography of Catherine Helen Spence* Sydney: Hale and Iremonger

Maidment, S. (1984) *Child Custody and Divorce: The Law in Social Context* London: Croom Helm

Marks, E. and de Courtivron, I. (eds) (1981) *New French Feminisms: An Anthology* Sussex: Harvester Press

Maternity Alliance (1987) *Working Parents' Rights* London: Maternity Alliance

Matthews, J. (1985) *Health and Safety at Work* Sydney: Pluto Press

Mead, L. (1895) *Awakening Womanhood* Adelaide: Hussey & Gillingham

Meehan, E. (1985) *Women's Rights at Work: Campaigns and Policy in Britain and the United States* London: Macmillan

Midgley, M. (1981) *Heart and Mind: The Varieties of Moral Experience* Brighton: Harvester Press

Mill, J. S. (1929) *On the Subjection of Women* London: Dent

_____ (1975) *Three Essays: On Liberty, Representative Government, the Subjection of Women* London: Oxford University Press

Miller, J. B. (1976) *Towards a New Psychology of Women* Boston: Beacon Press

Millett, K. (1971) *Sexual Politics* New York: Equinox Books

Mitchell, J. (1984) *Women: The Longest Revolution* London: Virago

Mohr, J. (1978) *Abortion in America: The Origins and Evolution of National Policy, 1800–1900* New York: Oxford University Press

Moi, T. (1985) *Sexual/Textual Politics: Feminist Literary Theory* London: Methuen

Money, J. and Ehrhardt, A. A. (1972) *Man and Woman, Boy and Girl* Baltimore: Johns Hopkins University Press

Murray, J. and Clark, A. (1985) *The Englishwoman's Review of Social and Industrial Questions: An Index* New York: Garland Publications

Noddings, N. (1984) *Caring: A Feminine Approach to Ethics and Moral Education* Berkeley: University of California Press

O'Brien, M. (1981) *The Politics of Reproduction* London: Routledge & Kegan Paul

O'Donovan, K. (1985) *Sexual Divisions in Law* London: Weidenfeld & Nicolson

O'Donovan, K. and Szyszczak, E. (1988) *Equality and Sex Discrimination Law* Oxford: Basil Blackwell

O'Neill, W. (1969) *Everyone Was Brave: A History of Feminism in America* Chicago: Quadrangle Books

Owen, M. and Shaw, S. (1979) *Working Women: Discussion Papers from the*

Working Women's Centre Melbourne: Sisters Publications

Pascall, G. (1986) *Social Policy: A Feminist Analysis* London: Tavistock Publications

Pateman, C. (1988) *The Sexual Contract* Cambridge: Polity Press

Phillips, A. (1986) *Divided Loyalties: Dilemmas of Sex and Class* London: Virago

—— (ed.) (1987) *Feminism and Equality* London: Basil Blackwell

Pickens, D. (1968) *Eugenics and the Progressives* Nashville: Vanderbilt University Press

Rae, D. (et al.) (1981) *Equalities* Cambridge: Harvard University Press

Randall, V. (1982) *Women and Politics* London: Macmillan

Rathbone, E. (1927a) *The Ethics and Economics of Family Endowment* London: Epworth Press

—— (1927b) *The Case for Family Endowment* Harmondsworth: Penguin

Reeves, M. P. (1979) *Round About a Pound a Week* first published 1913, London: Virago

Refshauge, C. (1984) *Protective Legislation at Work* NSW: Anti-Discrimination Board

Rendall, J. (ed.) (1987) *Equal or Different: Women's Politics 1800–1914* London: Basil Blackwell

Rendel, M. (et al.) (1968) *Equality for Women* Fabian Research Series, Middlesex: Walrus Press

Rhodes, D. and McNeill, S. (eds) (1985) *Women Against Violence Against Women* London: Onlywoman Press

Rich, A. (1976) *Of Woman Born: Motherhood as Experience and Institution* New York: W. W. Norton

Riley, D. (1983) *War in the Nursery: Theories of the Child and Mother* London: Virago

Ronalds, C. (1987) *Affirmative Action and Sex Discrimination: A Handbook on Legal Rights for Women* Sydney: Pluto Press

Rose, S., Kamin, L. J. and Lewontin, R. C. (1984) *Not in Our Genes: Biology, Ideology and Human Nature* Harmondsworth: Penguin

Rosenberg, R. (1982) *Beyond Separate Spheres: Intellectual Roots of Modern Feminism* New Haven: Yale University Press

Rossi, A. (1982) *Feminists in Politics: A Panel Analysis of the First National Women's Conference* New York: Academic Press

Rowbotham, S., Segal, L. and Wainwright, H. (1980) *Beyond the Fragments: Feminism and the Making of Socialism* London: Merlin

Royden, A. M. (1917b) *Women and the Sovereign State* London: Headley

Rupp, L. and Taylor, V. (1987) *Survival in the Doldrums: The American Women's Rights Movement* New York: Oxford University Press

Sachs, A., and Wilson, J. H., (1978) *Sexism and the Law* Oxford: Martin Robertson

Sapiro, V. (ed.) (1985) *Women, Biology and Public Policy* Beverly Hills: Sage Publications

Sawer, M. (ed.) (1985) *Program for Change: Affirmative Action in Australia* Sydney: Allen & Unwin

Sayers, J. (1986) *Sexual Contradictions: Psychology, Psychoanalysis and*

Feminism London: Tavistock Publications

Schramm, S. (1979) *Plow Women Rather than Reapers: An Intellectual History of Feminism in the United States* Metuchen: The Scarecrow Press

Schreiner, O. (1911) *Woman and Labour* London: T. Fisher Unwin

Scorer, C. and Sedley, A. (1983) *Amending the Equality Laws* Nottingham: Russell Press

Scott, H. (1982) *Sweden's Right to Be Human* London: Allison & Busby

Scutt, J. and Graham, D. (1984) *For Richer, For Poorer: Money, Marriage and Property Rights* Ringwood: Penguin

Sealander, J. (1983) *As Minority Becomes Majority: Federal Reaction to the Phenomenon of Women in the Work Force 1920–1963* Westport: Greenwood Press

Searle, G. (1971) *The Quest for National Efficiency* London: Oxford University Press

＿＿＿ (1976) *Eugenics and Politics in Britain* Leyden: Noordhoff International Publishers

Segal, L. (1983) *What Is to Be Done About the Family?: Crisis in the Eighties* Harmondsworth: Penguin

＿＿＿ (1987) *Is the Future Female?: Troubled Thoughts on Contemporary Feminism* London: Virago

Sharp, R. and Broomhill, R. (1988) *Short Changed: Women and Economic Policies* Sydney: Allen & Unwin

Showalter, E. (ed.) (1978) *These Modern Women: Autobiographical Essays from the Twenties* New York: Feminist Press

Sichtermann, B. (1986) *Femininity: The Politics of the Personal* John Whitlam (trans.) Cambridge: Polity Press, first published in German in 1983.

Six Point Group (1945) *Dorothy Evans and the Six Point Group* London

＿＿＿ (1968) *In Her Own Right* London: George C. Harrap and Co.

Skolnick, A. S. (1987) *The Intimate Environment: Exploring Marriage and the Family* 4th Edition Boston: Little Brown & Co.

Smart, C. (1984b) *The Ties that Bind: Law, Marriage and the Reproduction of Patriarchal Relations* London: Routledge & Kegan Paul

Smyth, B. (1894) *The Social Evil: Its Cause and Cure* Melbourne: Rae Brothers

Solomon, B. (1985) *In the Company of Educated Women: A History of Women and Higher Education* New Haven: Yale University Press

Spence, C. (1878) *Some Aspects of South Australian Life* Adelaide: R. Kyffin Thomas

Spencer, A. G. (1923) *The Family and its Members* Philadelphia: J. B. Lippincott Co.

＿＿＿ (1972) *Women's Share in Social Culture* first published in 1913, New York: Arno Press

Spender, D. and Sarah, E. (eds) (1980) *Learning to Lose: Sexism and Education* London: Women's Press

Spivak, G. C. (1987) *In Other Worlds: Essays in Cultural Politics* New York: Methuen

Staten, H. (1985) *Wittgenstein and Derrida* Oxford: Basil Blackwell

Stimpson, C. (ed.) (1972) *Women and the Equal Rights Amendment* New York: R. R. Bowker Co.

Stocks, M. D. (1949) *Eleanor Rathbone: A Biography* London: Victor Gollancz

Stoiber, S. A. (1989) *Parental Leave and 'Woman's Place': The Implications and Impact of Three European Approaches to Family Leave Policy* Washington: Women's Research & Education Institute

Summers, A. (1975) *Damned Whores and God's Police: The Colonisation of Women in Australia* Ringwood: Penguin

Swanwick, H. (1914) *The Future of the Women's Movement* London: G. Bell and Sons Ltd

—— (1971) *The War in its Effect Upon Women* and *Women and War* New York: Garland Publishing Company

Taylor, B. (1983) *Eve and the New Jerusalem: Socialism and Feminism in the Nineteenth Century* London: Virago

Tilly, L. A. and Scott, J. W. (1978) *Women, Work and Family* New York: Holt, Rinehart and Winston

Tocqueville, A. (1966) *Democracy in America* New York: Harper and Row

Tolson, A. (1977) *The Limits of Masculinity: Male Identity and the Liberated Woman* New York: Harper & Row

Vance, C. (ed.) (1984) *Pleasure and Danger: Exploring Female Sexuality* Boston: Routledge & Kegan Paul

Vicinus, M. (1985) *Independent Women: Work and Community for Single Women 1850–1920* London: Virago

Walsh, C. M. (1917) *Feminism* New York: Sturgis and Walton

Ware, S. (1981) *Beyond Suffrage: Women in the New Deal* Cambridge: Harvard University Press

Webb, B. (ed.) (1902) *The Case for the Factory Acts* London: Grant Richards

Weiner, G. (ed.) (1985) *Just a Bunch of Girls: Feminist Approaches to Schooling* Milton Keynes: Open University Press

Weitzman, L. (1985) *The Divorce Revolution: The Unexpected Social and Economic Consequences for Women and Children in America* New York: Free Press

White, R. (ed.) (1986) *Psychology and the Prevention of Nuclear War* New York: New York University Press

Wilson, E. (1977) *Women and the Welfare State* London: Tavistock Publications

—— (1980) *Only Halfway to Paradise: Women in Postwar Britain 1945–68* London: Tavistock

—— (1983) *What Is to Be Done About Violence Against Women?* Harmondsworth: Penguin

Wilson, E. and Weir, A. (1986) *Hidden Agendas: Theory, Politics and Experience in the Women's Movement* London: Tavistock

Wolgast, E. (1980) *Equality and the Rights of Women* Ithaca: Cornell University Press

Wollstonecraft, M. (1983) *A Vindication of the Rights of Women* Harmondsworth: Penguin

Zimmern, A. (1898) The Renaissance of Girls' Education in England London: Innes

Articles

Abbott, E. (1924) 'Real Not Pseudo-Protection for Women: The Case Against Differential Legislation for Women in Industry', London: NUSEC

ACOG Technical Bulletin (1980) 'Pregnancy, Work, and Disability', 58

Adams, C. and Arnot, M. (1986) 'Investigating Gender in Secondary Schools: A Series of In-Service Workshops for ILEA (Inner London Education Authority) Teachers', London: ILEA

Alcoff, L. (1988) 'Cultural Feminism Versus Post-Structuralism: The Identity Crisis in Feminist Theory' *Signs*, 13, 3, pp. 405–436

Altman, M. (1984) 'Everything They Always Wanted You to Know: The Ideology of Popular Sex Literature', in C. Vance (ed.) *Pleasure and Danger: Exploring Female Sexuality* Boston: Routledge & Kegan Paul

Anderson, M. C. (1925) 'Should There Be Labor Laws for Women? Yes' [US] *Good Housekeeping* September, pp. 49–52

Anyon, J. (1983) 'Intersections of Gender and Class', in S. Walker and L. Barton (eds) *Gender, Class and Education* Lewes: Falmer Press

Ardill, S. and O'Sullivan, S. (1986) 'Upsetting An Applecart: Difference, Desire and Lesbian Sadomasochism' *Feminist Review* 23, pp. 31–57

Arndt, B. 'High Cost of the Collapse of the Breadwinner Ethic' *Bulletin* 3 June 1986, pp. 66–71

Bacchi, C. (1980a) 'The Nature-Nurture Debate in Australia, 1900–1914' *Historical Studies* 19, 75, pp. 199–212

—— (1980b) 'Evolution, Eugenics and Women: the Impact of Scientific Theories on Attitudes Towards Women 1870–1920', in E. Windschuttle (ed.) *Women, Class and History* Melbourne, Fontana/Collins

—— (1986a) 'The "Woman Question" in South Australia', in E. Richards (ed.) *The Flinders History of South Australia: Social History* Netley, SA: Wakefield Press

—— (1986b) 'Women and Peace through the Polls' *Politics* 21, 2, pp. 62–67

—— (1988) 'Feminism and the "Eroticization" of the Middle-Class Woman: The Intersection of Class and Gender Attitudes' *Women's Studies International Forum* 11, 1, pp. 43–53

Barrett, M. (1987) 'The Concept of "Difference"' *Feminist Review* 26, pp. 29–40

Baxter, S. (1988) 'Women Against Porn' *Time Out* March 23–30, pp. 24–25

Benn, S. and Gaus, G. (1983) 'The Liberal Conception of the Public and Private', in S. Benn and G. Gaus (eds) *Public and Private in Social Life* London: Croom Helm

Bertin, J. (1986) 'Review of W. Chavkin (ed.) *Double Exposure: Women's*

Health Hazards on the Job and at Home', Women's Rights Law Reporter 9, 1, pp. 89–93

—— (1989) 'Reproductive Laws for the 1990's—Reproductive Health Hazards in the Workplace: Proposals for Legislation, Education, and Public Policy Initiatives', in S. Cohen and N. Taub (eds) *Reproductive Laws for the 1990s* New Jersey: Humana Press

Birke, L. and Vines, G. (1987) 'Beyond Nature Versus Nurture: Process and Biology in the Development of Gender' *Women's Studies International Forum* 10, 6, pp. 555–570

Black, C. (1902) 'Some Current Objections to Factory Legislation for Women', in B. Webb (ed.) *The Case for the Factory Acts* London: Grant Richards, pp. 192–222

Blackburn, J. (1984) 'Schooling and Injustice for Girls', in D. Broom (ed.) *Unfinished Business: Social Justice for Women in Australia* Sydney: Allen & Unwin

Bland, L. (1987) 'The Married Woman, the "New Woman" and the Feminist: Sexual Politics of the 1890s', in J. Rendall (ed.) *Equal or Different: Women's Politics 1800–1914* London: Basil Blackwell

Block, R. (1978) 'The Rise of the Moral Mother' *Feminist Studies* 4, 2, pp. 101–126

Bottomley, A., Gibson, S. and Meteyard, B. (1987) 'Dworkin, Which Dworkin? Taking Feminism Seriously' *Journal of Law and Society* 14, 1, pp. 47–60

Bremner, J. (1982) 'In the Cause of Equality: Muriel Heagney and the Position of Women in the Depression', in M. Bevege, M. James, and C. Shute (eds) *Worth Her Salt: Women at Work in Australia* Sydney: Hale and Iremonger

Brill, A. (1987) 'The Loss of the ERA: Different Conversations of Equality' *Women's Rights Law Reporter* 10, 1, p. 97

Bromley, D. 'Feminist—New Style' *Harper's Magazine* October 1927, pp. 552–560

Broom, D. (1986) 'The Occupational Health of Houseworkers' *Australian Feminist Studies* 2, pp. 15–35

—— (1987) 'Gender and Inequality—An Overview: Another Tribe', in C. Jennett and R. Stewart (eds) *Three Worlds of Inequality: Race, Class and Gender* Melbourne: Macmillan

Brophy, J. (1982) 'Parental Rights and Children's Welfare: Some Problems of Feminists' Strategy in the 1920's' *International Journal of the Sociology of Law* 10, pp. 149–168

—— (1985) 'Child Care and the Growth of Power: the Status of Mothers in Child Custody Disputes', in J. Brophy and C. Smart (eds) *Women-In-Law: Explorations in Law, Family and Sexuality* London: Routledge & Kegan Paul

Brown, B. A., Emerson, T. I., Falk, G. and Freedman, A. E. (1971) 'The Equal Rights Amendment: A Constitutional Basis for Equal Rights for Women' *The Yale Law Journal* 80, 5, pp. 871–985

Brown, C. (1986) 'Mothers, Fathers and Children: From Private to Public

Patriarchy', in L. Sargent (ed.) *The Unhappy Marriage of Marxism and Feminism* London: Pluto Press

Burns, E. (1917) 'Education' in V. Gollancz (ed.) *The Making of Women: Oxford Essays in Feminism* London: George Allen & Unwin

Burville, C. (1985) 'Women and Protective Legislation' *Refractory Girl* 28, pp. 27–29

Caine, B. (1987) 'From "A Fair Field and No Favour" to "Equal Opportunity": or a New Look at Campaigns to Improve the Employment Opportunities of Women' *Refractory Girl* October, pp. 36–40

Callahan, S. (1986) 'Is Abortion the Issue?' *Harpers Magazine* July, pp. 35–43

Cass, B. (1983) 'Redistribution to Children and to Mothers; a History of Child Endowment and Family Allowances', in C. Baldock and B. Cass (eds) *Women, Social Welfare and the State in Australia* Sydney: Allen & Unwin

—— (1985) 'The Changing Face of Poverty in Australia: 1972–1982' *Australian Feminist Studies* 1, pp. 67–89

Chavkin, W. (1986) 'Work and Pregnancy: Review of the Literature and Policy Discussion' *Obstetrical and Gynaecological Survey* 41, 8, pp. 467–472

Chessler, P. (1988) 'What is a Mother?' *Ms Magazine* 17, 11, pp. 36, 38–39

Chesterman, C. (1981) 'Women at Work: In Need of Protection', in M. Hatton (ed.) *Work and Health: Issues in Occupational Health* Canberra: ANU Centre for Continuing Education

Cockburn, C. (1981) 'The Material of Male Power' *Feminist Review* 9, pp. 41–58

—— (1988a) 'Macho Men of the Left' *Marxism Today*, 32, 4, pp. 18–23

—— (1988b) 'Masculinity, the Left and Feminism', in R. Chapman and J. Rutherford (eds.) *Male Order: Unwrapping Masculinity* London: Lawrence & Wishart

Cole, D. (1984) 'Strategies of Difference: Litigating for Women's Rights in a Man's World' *Law and Inequality* 2, 33, pp. 33–96

Cott, N. F. (1987b) 'Feminist Theory and Feminist Movements: The Past Before Us', in J. Mitchell and A. Oakley (eds) *What is Feminism?* Oxford: Basil Blackwell

Coward, R. (1982) 'What is Pornography?' *Spare Rib* 119, pp. 52–55

Coyle, A. (1980) 'The Protection Racket' *Feminist Review* 4, pp. 1–14

Darroch, D. (1981) 'The Occupational Health of Houseworkers', in M. Hatton (ed.) *Work and Health: Issues in Occupational Health* Canberra: ANU Centre for Continuing Education

Davin, A. (1978) 'Imperialism and Motherhood' *History Workshop* 5, pp. 9–59

Deech, R. L. (1977) 'The Principles of Maintenance' *Family Law* 7, 8, pp. 229–233

Delmar, R. (1986) 'What is Feminism?', in J. Mitchell and A. Oakley (eds) *What is Feminism?* Oxford: Basil Blackwell

Delphy, C. (1976) 'Continuities and Discontinuities in Marriage and Divorce', in L. Barker and S. Allen (eds) *Sexual Divisions and Society: Process and Change* London: Tavistock

Diamond, I. and Quinby, L. (1984) 'American Feminism in the Age of the Body' *Signs* 10, 1, pp. 119–125

—— (1988) 'American Feminism and the Language of Control,' in I. Diamond and L. Quinby (eds) *Feminism & Foucault: Reflections on Resistance* Boston: Northeastern University Press, 1988.

Dimen, M. (1984) 'Politically Correct? Politically Incorrect?', in C. Vance (ed.) *Pleasure and Danger: Exploring Female Sexuality* Boston: Routledge & Kegan Paul

Dowd Hall, J., Cooper, S., Rosenberg, R. and Kessler-Harris, A. (1986) 'Women's History Goes to Trial: EEOC v. Sears Roebuck and Company' *Signs* 11, 4, pp. 751–779

Du Bois, E., Buhle, M., Kaplan, T., Lerner, G. and Smith-Rosenberg, C. (1980) 'Politics and Culture in Women's History: A Symposium' *Feminist Studies* 6, 1, pp. 26–64

Du Bois, E. and Gordon, L. (1984) 'Seeking Ecstasy on the Battlefield: Danger and Pleasure in Nineteenth-century Feminist Sexual Thought', in C. Vance (ed.) *Pleasure and Danger: Exploring Female Sexuality* Boston: Routledge & Kegan Paul

Du Bois, E., Dunlop, M., Gilligan, C., MacKinnon, C., Menkel-Meadow, C. (1985) 'Feminist Discourse, Moral Values and the Law—A Conversation' *Buffalo Law Review* 54, 11, pp. 20–28, 37–49, 73–75

Dworkin, A. (1978) 'Biological Superiority: The World's Most Dangerous and Deadly Idea' *Heresies* 6, pp. 46–51

Dyhouse, C. (1976) 'Social Darwinistic Ideas and the Development of Women's Education in England 1880–1920' *History of Education* 5, 1, pp. 41–58

Echols, A. (1984a) 'The New Feminism of Yin and Yang', in A. Snitow, C. Stansell, and S. Thompson (eds) *Desire: The Politics of Sexuality* London: Virago

—— (1984b) 'The Taming of the Id', in C. Vance (ed.) *Pleasure and Danger: Exploring Female Sexuality* Boston: Routledge & Kegan Paul

Edgar, D. (1987) 'The Family in Between: The Hidden Factor in Employer/Employee Relationships' *Business Council Bulletin* 30, pp. 19–23

Edwards, M. (1984) 'The Distribution of Income Within Households', in D. Broom (ed.) *Unfinished Business: Social Justice for Women in Australia* Sydney: Allen & Unwin

Edwards, S. (1986) 'Provoking Her Own Demise: From Common Assault to Homicide', in J. Hanmer and M. Maynard (eds) *Women, Violence and Social Control* London: Macmillan Press

EEC (1987) 'Protective Legislation for Women' *European Industrial Relations Review* 162, pp. 18–21

Ehrenreich, B. (1981) 'The Women's Movements: Feminist and Anti-feminist' *Radical America* 15, 1 & 2, pp. 93–101

—— (1986) 'Accidental Suicide' *Atlantic Monthly* 258, 4, pp. 98–100

—— (1988) 'The Heart of the Matter' *Ms Magazine* May, pp. 5–6

Eisenstein, H. (1985 and forthcoming) Feminism and Femocrats: Theorising Women and the State, Paper presented at the Women's Studies Conference, University of Sydney, 20–22 September; forthcoming in *Practising Feminism on Two Continents* (working title) Sydney: Allen & Unwin

Eisenstein, Z. R. (1982) 'The Sexual Politics of the New Right: Understanding the "Crisis of Liberalism" for the 1980's', in N. O. Keohane, M. Z. Rosaldo and B. C. Gelpi (eds) *Feminist Theory: A Critique of Ideology* Brighton: Harvester Press

Elshtain, J. B. (1982) 'Antigone's Daughters' *Democracy*, pp. 46–59

—— (1985) 'The New Feminist Scholarship' *Salmagundi* 70–71, pp. 3–43

English, D. (1984) 'The Fear that Feminism Will Free Men First', in A. Snitow, C. Stansell and S. Thompson (eds) *Desire: The Politics of Sexuality* London: Virago

Evans, S. M. (1988) 'The Woman Question' *The Nation* 6 February, pp. 171–172

Fawcett, M. (1918) 'Equal Pay for Equal Work' *Economic Journal* 28, pp. 1–6

Ferguson, A. (1984) 'Sex War: The Debate Between Radical and Libertarian Feminists' *Signs* 10, 1, pp. 106–112

Ferguson, A., Philipson, I., Diamond, I., Quinby, L., Vance, C. and Snitow, A. B. (1984) 'Forum: The Feminist Sexuality Debates' *Signs* 10, 1, pp. 106–135

Fineman, M. L. (1983) 'Implementing Equality: Ideology, Contradiction and Social Change: A Study of Rhetoric and Results in the Regulation of the Consequences of Divorce' *Wisconsin Law Review*, pp. 789–886

Finley, L. M. (1986) 'Transcending Equality Theory: A Way Out of the Maternity and the Workplace Debate' *Columbia Law Review* 86, 6, pp. 1118–1182

Fiss, O. M. (1977) 'Groups and the Equal Protection Clause', in M. Cohen, T. Nagel and T. Scanlon (eds) *Equality and Preferential Treatment* Princeton: Princeton University Press, pp. 84–154

Fowlkes, D. (1987) 'Feminist Epistemology is Political Action' *Women and Politics* 7, 3, pp. 3–10

Freedman, A. (1983) 'Sex Equality, Sex Differences and the Supreme Court' *The Yale Law Journal* 92, 6, pp. 913–968

Freedman, E. and Thorne, B. (1984) 'Introduction to "The Feminist Sexuality Debates" *Signs* 10, 1, pp. 102–105

Friedan, B. (1985) 'How to Get the Women's Movement Moving Again' *New York Times Magazine* 3 November; reprinted in Women's Electoral Lobby, *National Bulletin* January 1986, pp. 11–14

Frost, W. (1983) 'Censorship: Closing More Options for Women' *Priorities* March, pp. 10–12

Game, A. and Pringle, R. (1986) 'Beyond Gender at Work: Secretaries', in N. Grieve and A. Burns (eds) *Australian Women: New Feminist Perspectives* Melbourne: Oxford University Press

Gaze, B. (1986) 'Pornography and Freedom of Speech: An American Feminist Approach' *Legal Services Bulletin* 11, 3, pp. 123–127

Gelb, J. (1986) 'Feminism in Britain: The Politics of Isolation', in G. Moore and G. Spitze (eds) *Women and Politics: Activism, Attitudes and Office Holding* Greenwich, Connecticut: Jai Press

Ginsburg, R. (1978) 'Sex Equality and the Constitution: The State of the Art' *Women's Rights Law Reporter* 4, pp. 143–147

Goldstein, L. (1987) 'Europe Looks at American Women 1820–1840' *Social Research* 54, 3, pp. 519–542

Goodman, J. and Taub, N. (1986) 'For Women Only? The Recurring Debate Over Sex-Specific Laws' *New Jersey Law Journal* 117, 25, pp. 1, 22–23

Gordon, L. (1986) 'What's New in Women's History', in T. de Lauretis (ed.) *Feminist Studies: Critical Studies* Bloomington: Indiana University Press

Grant, J. (1987) 'I Feel Therefore I Am: A Critique of Female Experience as the Basis for a Feminist Epistemology' *Women and Politics* 7, 3, pp. 99–112

Graycar, R. (1987) 'Towards a Feminist Position on Maintenance' *Refractory Girl* September/October, 30, pp. 7–13

Grossberg, M. (1983) 'Who Gets the Child? Custody, Guardianship, and the Rise of a Judicial Patriarchy in Nineteenth Century America' *Feminist Studies* 9, pp. 235–260

Grossman, A. (1984) 'The New Woman and the Rationalization of Sexuality in Weimar Germany', in A. Snitow, C. Stansell, and S. Thompson (eds) *Desire: The Politics of Sexuality* London: Virago

Guillaumin, C. (1987) 'The Question of Difference', in C. Duchen (ed.) *French Connections: Voices from the Women's Movement in France* Amherst: University of Massachusetts Press

Hacker, A. (1986) 'Women at Work' *New York Review* 14 August, pp. 26–33

—— (1987) 'Women at Work' *Dialogue* 3, pp. 2–7

Hacker, S. L. (1982) 'Sex Stratification, Technology and Organizational Change: A Longitudinal Case Study of A.T. & T.', in R. Kahn-Hut, A. K. Daniels and R. Colvard (eds) *Women and Work: Problems and Perspectives* New York: Oxford University Press

Hall, S. (1986) 'Variants of Liberalism', in J. Donald and S. Hall (eds) *Politics and Ideology* Milton Keynes: Open University Press

Hamilton, A. (1984) 'Protection for Women Workers', in E. Pleck, E. Fox-Genovese, J. Hoff-Wilson and H. Woodman (eds) *Restoring Women to History* Bloomington: Organization of American Historians

Hammerton, A. J. (1977) 'Feminism and Female Emigration, 1861–1886', in M. Vicinus (ed.) *A Widening Sphere* Bloomington: Indiana Press

Hartsock, N. C. (1983) 'The Feminist Standpoint: Developing the Ground for a Specifically Feminist Historical Materialism', in S. Harding and M. B. Hintikka (eds) *Discovering Reality* D. Reidel Publishing Company

Hartz, L. (1986) 'The Concept of a Liberal Society', in P. Nivola and D. Rosenbloom (eds) *Classic Readings in American Politics* New York: St Martins Press

Hekman, S. (1987) 'The Feminization of Epistemology: Gender and the Social Sciences' *Women and Politics* 7, 3, pp. 65–84

Hepple, B. (1983) 'Judging Equal Rights' *Current Legal Problems* 36, pp. 71–90

Hollway, W. (1984) 'Gender Difference and the Production of Subjectivity', in J. Henriques et al. *Changing the Subject* London: Methuen

Humphries, J. (1977) 'The Working Class Family, Women's Liberation, and Class Struggle: the Case of Nineteenth Century British History' *Review of Radical Political Economics* 9, 3, pp. 25–41

—— (1981) 'Protective Legislation, The Capitalist State, and Working Class Men: The Case of the 1842 Mines Regulation Act' *Feminist Review* 7, pp. 1–33

—— (1982) 'The Working-Class Family: A Marxist Perspective', in J. Elshtain (ed.) *The Family in Political Thought* Sussex: Harvester Press

Hunt, K. (1986) 'Crossing the River of Fire: The Socialist Construction of Women's Politicisation', in J. Evans (et al.) *Feminism and Political Theory* London: Sage

Hunter, N. D. (1983) 'Child Support and Policy: The Systematic Imposition of Costs on Women' *Harvard Women's Law Journal* 6, 1, pp. 2-27

Hutchins, B. (1902) 'The Historical Development of the Factory Acts', in B. Webb (ed.) *The Case for the Factory Acts* London: Grant Richards, pp. 75–123

Jackson, M. (1984) 'Sex Research and the Construction of Sexuality: A Tool of Male Supremacy?' *Women's Studies International Forum* 7, 1, pp. 43–51

Jaggar, A. M. (1977) 'On Sexual Equality', in J. English (ed.) *Sex Equality* New Jersey: Prentice-Hall

Janeway, E. (1980) 'Who Is Sylvia? On the Loss of Sexual Paradigms', in C. Stimpson and E. Person (eds) *Women, Sex and Sexuality* Chicago: University of Chicago Press

Jardine, A. (1980) 'Prelude', in H. Eisenstein and A. Jardine (eds) *The Future of Difference* Boston: G. K. Hall and Co.

—— (1987) 'Men in Feminism: Odor di Uomo or Compagnons de Route?', in A. Jardine and P. Smith (eds) *Men in Feminism* New York: Methuen

Jennett, C. (1987) 'The Feminist Enterprise', in C. Jennett and R. Stewart (eds) *Three Worlds of Inequality: Race, Class and Gender* South Melbourne: Macmillan

Johnson, C. and Wajcman, J. (1986) 'Comment on "A Comparative Analysis of Equal Pay in the United States, Britain and Australia"' *Australian Feminist Studies* 3, pp. 91–95

Kahn, P. (1985) 'Unequal Opportunities: Women, Employment and the Law', in S. Edwards (ed.) *Gender, Sex and the Law* London: Croom Helm

Kamenka, E. and Tay, A. (1986) 'The Traditions of Justice' *Law and*

Philosophy 5, pp. 281–313

Karst, K. (1984) 'Woman's Constitution' *Duke Law Journal* 3, pp. 447–509

Kay, H. H. (1985) 'Equality and Difference: The Case of Pregnancy' *Berkeley Women's Law Journal* 1, 1, pp. 21–38

Kelley, F. (1922) 'Shall Women be Equal Before the Law—No!' *The Nation* 12 April, p. 421

Kelly, F. (1988) 'Brettena Smyth', in H. Radi (ed.) *200 Australian Women: A Redress Anthology* Sydney: Women's Redress Press

Kelly, L. (1985) 'Feminist vs. Feminist' *Trouble and Strife* 7, pp. 4–9

Kenney, S. (1986) 'Reproductive Hazards in the Workplace: the Law and Sexual Difference' *International Journal of the Sociology of Law* 14, pp. 393–414

Kerber, L., Greeno, C., Maccoby, E., Luria, Z., Stack, C., and Gilligan, C. (1986) 'On *In A Different Voice*: An Interdisciplinary Forum' *Signs* 11, 2, pp. 304–333

Kessler-Harris, A. (1984) 'Protection for Women: Trade Unions and Labor Laws', in W. Chavkin (ed.) *Double Exposure: Women's Health Hazards on the Job and at Home* New York: Monthly Review Press

—— (1987) 'Equal Employment Opportunity Commission v. Sears Roebuck and Company: A Personal Account' *Feminist Review* 25, pp. 46–69

Koedt, A. (1970) 'The Myth of the Vaginal Orgasm', in L. Tanner (ed.) *Voices from Women's Liberation* New York: Mentor Books

Koziara, K. (1987) 'Women and Work: The Evolving Policy', in K. Koziara, M. Moskow, and L. Tanner (eds) *Working Women: Past, Present, Future* Washington: Bureau of National Affairs

Krieger, L. (1987) 'Through a Glass Darkly: Paradigms of Equality and the Search for a Woman's Jurisprudence' *Hypatia* 2, 1, pp. 45–61

Krieger, L. J. and Cooney, P. N. (1983) 'The Miller-Wohl Controversy: Equal Treatment, Positive Action and the Meaning of Women's Equality' *Golden Gate University Law Review* 13, 3, pp. 513–572

Lambert, N. (1978) 'Biology and Equality: A Perspective on Sex Differences' *Signs* 4, 1, pp. 97–117

Land, H. (1983) 'Who Still Cares for the Family? Recent Developments in Income Maintenance, Taxation and Family Law', in J. Lewis (ed.) *Women's Welfare, Women's Rights* London: Croom Helm

Law, S. A. (1984) 'Rethinking Sex and the Constitution' *University of Pennsylvania Law Review* 132, 4, pp. 955–1040

Lehrer, S. (1985) 'Protective Labor Legislation for Women' *Review of Radical Political Economics* 17, 1–2, pp. 187–200

Lewis, J. (1983) 'Dealing with Dependency: State Practices and Social Realities, 1870–1945', in J. Lewis (ed.) *Women's Welfare, Women's Rights* London: Croom Helm, pp. 17–37

Littleton, C. (1981) 'Toward a Redefinition of Sexual Equality' *Harvard Law Review* 95, pp. 487–508

—— (1987) 'Reconstructing Sexual Equality' *California Law Review* 75, 4, pp. 1279–1337

Lloyd, G. (1986) 'Selfhood, War and Masculinity', in C. Pateman and E. Gross (eds) *Feminist Challenges: Social and Political Theory* Sydney: Allen & Unwin

Lorber, J. (1981) 'Minimalist and Maximalist Feminism' *Quarterly Journal of Ideology* 5, 3, pp. 61–66.

____ (1986) 'Dismantling Noah's Ark' *Sex Roles* 14, 11/12, pp. 567–580

McFadden, M. (1984) 'Anatomy of Difference: Toward a Classification of Feminist Theory' *Women's Studies International Forum*, 7, 6, pp. 495–504

McGinley, G. P. (1986) 'Judicial Approaches to Sex Discrimination in the United States and the United Kingdom—a Comparative Study' *Modern Law Review* 49, 4, pp. 413–445

MacKenzie, C. (1986) 'Simone de Beauvoir: Philosophy and/or the Female Body', in C. Pateman and E. Gross (eds) *Feminist Challenges: Social and Political Theory* Sydney: Allen & Unwin

MacKinnon, C. (1983) 'The Male Ideology of Privacy: A Feminist Perspective on the Right to Abortion' *Radical America* 17, 4, pp. 23–35

Magarey, S. and Sheridan, S. (1987) 'The Seventh Berkshire Conference on the History of Women' *Australian Feminist Studies* 5, pp. 149–154

Mahoney, P. (1983) 'How Alice's Chin Came to be Pressed Against her Foot: Sexist Processes of Interaction in Mixed-Sex Classrooms' *Women's Studies International Forum* 6, 1, pp. 107–115

Maidment, S. (1985) 'Women and Childcare: The Paradox of Divorce', in S. Edwards (ed.) *Gender, Sex and the Law* London: Croom Helm

Mappen, E. (1986) 'Strategies for Change: Social Feminist Approaches to the Problems of Women's Work', in A. John (ed.) *Unequal Opportunities: Women's Employment in England 1800–1918* Oxford: Basil Blackwell

Martin, G. (1914) 'Education of Women and Sex Equality' *The Annals of the American Academy* 56, November, pp. 38–46

Martin, L. (1986) 'Reproductive Rights and New Technologies: Lessons From Law Reform' *The Australian Quarterly* 58, 4, pp. 375–387

Meehan, E. (1983) 'The Priorities of the EOC' *Political Quarterly* 54, 1, pp. 67–76

____ (1986) 'Women's Studies and Political Studies', in J. Evans et al. *Feminism and Political Theory* London: Sage

Milkman, R. (1986) 'Women's History and the Sears Case' *Feminist Studies* 12, 2, pp. 375–400

Minow, M. (1985a) 'Rights of One's Own' *Harvard Law Review* 98, 5, pp. 1084–1099

____ (1985b) 'Learning to Live with the Dilemma of Difference: Bilingual and Special Education' *Law and Contemporary Problems* 48, 2, pp. 157–211

____ (1986) 'Consider the Consequences' *Michigan Law Review* 84, February/April, pp. 900–918

____ (1988) 'Feminist Reason: Getting it and Losing it' *Journal of Legal Education* 38, 1 & 2, pp. 47–60

Morgan, D. (1986) 'Masculinity and Violence', in J. Hanmer and M.

Maynard (eds) *Women, Violence and Social Control* London: Macmillan

Nin, A. (1972) 'Notes on Feminism', in L. Edwards (ed.) *Woman: An Issue* Boston: Little Brown & Co.

Oakley, A. (1983) 'Millicent Garrett Fawcett: Duty and Determination (1847–1929)', in D. Spender (ed.) *Feminist Theorists: Three Centuries of Women's Intellectual Traditions* London: The Women's Press, pp. 184–202

O'Donnell, C. and Golder, N. (1986) 'A Comparative Analysis of Equal Pay in the United States, Britain and Australia' *Australian Feminist Studies* 3, pp. 59–90

O'Donovan, K. (1978) 'The Principles of Maintenance: An Alternative View' *Family Law* 8, pp. 180–184

—— (1982) 'Should All Maintenance of Spouses Be Abolished?' *Modern Law Review* 45, pp. 424–433

—— (1984) 'Protection and Paternalism' in M. D. A. Freeman (ed.) *The State, the Law, and the Family: Critical Perspectives* London: Tavistock Publications

—— (1985) 'Transsexual Troubles: the Discrepancy Between Legal and Social Categories', in S. Edwards (ed.) *Gender, Sex and the Law* London: Croom Helm

Offen, K. (1988) 'Defining Feminism: A Comparative Historical Approach' *Signs* 14, 11, pp. 119–157

Olsen, F. E. (1983) 'The Family and the Market: A Study of Ideology and Legal Reform' *Harvard Law Review* 96, 7, pp. 1495–1578

—— (1984) 'Statutory Rape: A Feminist Critique of Rights Analysis' *Texas Law Review* 63, 3, pp. 387–432

—— (1985) 'The Myth of State Intervention in the Family' *University of Michigan Journal of Law Reform* 18, 4, pp. 835–864

—— (1986) 'From False Paternalism to False Equality: Judicial Assaults on Feminist Community, Illinois 1869–1895' *Michigan Law Review* 84, pp. 1518–1541

Petchesky, R. (1980) 'Reproductive Freedom: Beyond "A" Woman's Right to Choose', in C. Stimpson and E. Person (eds) *Women: Sex and Sexuality* Chicago: University of Chicago Press

Philipson, S. (1984) 'The Repression of History and Gender: A Critical Perspective on the Feminist Sexuality Debate' *Signs* 10, 1, pp. 113–118

Polikoff, N. (1982) 'Why Are Mothers Losing: A Brief Analysis of Criteria Used in Child Custody Determinations' *Women's Rights Law Reporter* 7, 3, pp. 235–243

Poole, R. (1984) 'Markets and Motherhood: The Advent of the New Right', in A. Burns, G. Bottomley and P. Jools (eds) *The Family in the Modern World: Australian Perspectives* Sydney: Allen & Unwin, pp. 103–120

Post, R. C. (1988) 'Cultural Heterogeneity and Law: Pornography, Blasphemy, and the First Amendment' *California Law Review* 76, 2, March, pp. 297–335

Ranald, P. (1982) 'Feminism and Class: the United Associations of Women and the Council of Action for Equal Pay in the Depression', in

M. Bevege, M. James, and C. Shute (eds) *Worth Her Salt: Women at Work in Australia* Sydney: Hale and Iremonger

Rathbone, E. (1917) 'The Remuneration of Women's Services', in V. Gollancz (ed.) *The Making of Women: Oxford Essays in Feminism* London: George Allen & Unwin

Ratner, R. S. (1980) 'The Paradox of Protection: Maximum Hours Legislation in the United States' *International Labour Review* 119, 2, pp. 185–198

Redgrove, J. (1984) 'Women are not from Lilliput or Bedlam' *Ergonomics* 27, 5, pp. 469–473

Refshauge, C. (1984) 'Bearers of Burdens: Occupational Safety Without Discrimination', in Women and Labor Publications Collective (eds) *All Her Labours—One—Working it Out* Sydney: Hale and Iremonger

Rich, R. (1983) 'Anti-Porn: Soft Issue, Hard World' *Feminist Review* 13, pp. 56–67

Richards, J. R. (1983) 'Why Should Women Have the Monopoly On Virtue?' *Guardian* (London) 10 May, p. 8

Rights of Women, Family Law Subgroup (1985) 'Campaigning Around Family Law: Politics and Practice', in J. Brophy and C. Smart (eds) *Women-In-Law: Explorations in Law, Family and Sexuality* London: Routledge and Kegan Paul

Riley, D. (1981) 'Feminist Thought and Reproductive Control: the State and the "Right to Choose"', in The Cambridge Women's Studies Group (eds) *Women in Society: Interdisciplinary Essays* London: Virago

—— (1987a) '"The Serious Burdens of Love?" Some Questions on Childcare, Feminism and Socialism', in A. Phillips (ed.) *Feminism and Inequality* Oxford: Basil Blackwell

—— (1987b) 'Does a Sex Have a History? "Women" and Feminism' *New Formations* pp. 35–45

Robinson, R. (1988) 'America and Extreme' Review of M. A. Glendon *Abortion and Divorce in Western Law*, *New York Times Book Review* 2 March 1988, pp. 7, 9

Rogers, B. (1987) 'Pornography: Propaganda Against Women?' *Everywoman* May, pp. 13–17

—— (1988) 'Pornography and Sexual Violence: Causes and Effects' *Everywoman* February, p. 15

Rose, P. (1988) 'Takako Doi' *Savoy* August, pp. 42–44

Rosenberg, H. (1984) 'The Home is the Workplace: Hazards, Stresses and Pollutants in the Household', in W. Chavkin (ed.) *Double Exposure: Women's Health Hazards on the Job and at Home* New York: Monthly Review Press

Rosewarne, S. (1988) 'Economic Management, the Accord and Gender Inequality' *Journal of Australian Political Economy* 23, August, pp. 61–86

Rothman, R. (1981) 'Political Symbolism', in S. Long (ed.) *The Handbook of Political Behavior* vol. 2, New York: Plenum Press, pp. 285–340

Royden, A. M. (1917a) 'The Future of the Woman's Movement', in V.

Gollancz (ed.) *The Making of Women: Oxford Essays in Feminism* London: George Allen & Unwin, pp. 128–146

—— (1917c) 'Modern Love', in V. Gollancz (ed.) *The Making of Women: Oxford Essays in Feminism* London: George Allen & Unwin, pp. 17–63

Rubin, G. (1984) 'Thinking Sex: Notes from a Radical Theory of the Politics of Sexuality', in C. Vance (ed.) *Pleasure and Danger: Exploring Female Sexuality* Boston: Routledge & Kegan Paul

Ruddick, S. (1980) 'Maternal Thinking' *Feminist Studies* 6, 2, pp. 342–367

Sadurski, W. (1986) 'Equality Before the Law: A Conceptual Analysis' *The Australian Law Journal* 60, March, pp. 131–138

Sanday, P. (1986) 'Rape and the Silencing of the Feminine', in S. Tomaselli and R. Porter (eds) *Rape* Oxford: Basil Blackwell

Sawicki, J. (1986) 'Foucault and Feminism: Towards a Politics of Difference' *Hypatia* 1, 2, pp. 23–36

Scales, A. (1981) 'Towards a Feminist Jurisprudence' *Indiana Law Journal* 56, 3, pp. 375–444

—— (1986) 'The Emergence of Feminist Jurisprudence: An Essay' *Yale Law Review* 95, pp. 1373–1403

Schor, N. (1987) 'Dreaming Dissymetry: Barthes, Foucault, and Sexual Difference', in A. Jardine and P. Smith (eds) *Men in Feminism* New York: Methuen

Scott, J. (1988) 'Deconstructing Equality—Versus—Difference: Or, the Uses of Poststructuralist Theory for Feminism' *Feminist Studies* 14, 1, pp. 33–50

Scutt, J. (1976) 'Reforming the Law of Rape: The Michigan Example' *The Australian Law Journal* 50, 12, pp. 615–624

—— (1983) 'Legislating for the Right to be Equal: Women, the Law and Social Policy', in C. Baldock and B. Cass (eds) *Women, Social Welfare and the State* Sydney: George Allen & Unwin

—— (1984) 'Pornography: Condoning Abuse of Women's Rights' *National Times* 720, pp. 15–16

Seal, K. (1979) 'A Decade of No Fault Divorce' *The Family Advocate* 10, 14, 4, pp. 10–15

Segal, L. (1983) 'The Heat in the Kitchen', in S. Hall and M. Jacques (eds) *The Politics of Thatcherism* London: Lawrence and Wishart

Segers, M. C. (1979) 'Equality, Public Policy and Relevant Sex Differences' *Polity* 11, pp. 319–339

Sevenhuijsen, S. (1986) 'Fatherhood and the Political Theory of Rights: Theoretical Perspectives of Feminism' *International Journal of the Sociology of Law* 14, 3/4, pp. 329–340

Sheppard, A. (1982) 'Unspoken Premises in Custody Litigation' *Women's Rights Law Reporter* 7, 3, pp. 229–234

Shimmin, S. (1984) 'Pressures on Factory Women: Between the Devil and the Deep Blue Sea' *Ergonomics* 27, 5, pp. 511–517

Shulman, A. (1980) 'Sex and Power: Sexual Bases of Radical Feminism', in C. Stimpson and E. Person (eds) *Sex and Sexuality* Chicago: University of Chicago Press

Smart, C. (1984a) 'Marriage, Divorce and Women's Economic Dependency: A Discussion of the Politics of Private Maintenance', in M. D. A. Freeman (ed.) *The State, the Law and the Family: Critical Perspectives* London: Tavistock Publications

Smith, D. E. (1979) 'A Sociology for Women', in J. Sherman and E. Beck (eds) *The Prism of Sex* Madison: University of Wisconsin Press

Smith, J. (1983) 'Rights-Conflict, Pregnancy and Abortion', in C. Gould (ed.) *Beyond Domination: New Perspectives on Women and Philosophy* New Jersey: Rowman & Allenheld

Spender, D. (1978) 'The Facts of Life: Sex Differentiated Knowledge in the English Classroom and the School' *English in Education* 12, 3, pp. 1–21

Spivak, G. (1981) 'French Feminism in an International Frame' *Yale French Studies* 62, pp. 154–184

—— (1985) 'Feminism and Critical Theory', in P. Treichler, C. Kramarae and B. Stafford (eds) *For Alma Mater: Theory and Practice in Feminist Scholarship* Urbana: University of Illinois Press

Spritzer, A. D. (1972) 'Equal Employment Opportunity vs. Protection for Women: A Public Policy Dilemma' *Alabama Law Review* 24, 3, pp. 567–606

Stacey, J. (1986) 'Are Feminists Afraid to Leave Home? The Challenge of Conservative Pro-Family Feminism', in J. Mitchell and A. Oakley (eds) *What is Feminism?* Oxford: Basil Blackwell

Sternhell, C. (1986) 'Life in the Mainstream: What Happens when Feminists Turn Up on Both Sides of the Courtroom?' *Ms Magazine*, 15, 1, pp. 48–91

Stevens, D. (1984) 'Suffrage Does Not Give Equality', in E. Pleck (et al.) *Restoring Women to History* Bloomington: Organization of American Historians

Stoper, E. and Johnson, R. (1977) 'The Weaker Sex and the Better Half: The Idea of Women's Moral Superiority in the American Feminist Movement' *Polity* 10, pp. 192–217

Summers, Anne (1986) 'Mandarins or Missionaries: Women in the Federal Bureaucracy', in N. Grieve and A. Burns (eds) *Australian Women: New Feminist Perspectives* Melbourne: Oxford University Press

Tapper, M. (1986) 'Can a Feminist be a Liberal?' *Australasian Journal of Philosophy* Supplement to 64, June, pp. 37–47

Taub, N. (1980) Review of MacKinnon, C. (1979) *Sexual Harassment of Working Women: A Case of Sex Discrimination* New Haven: Yale University Press in *Columbia Law Review* 80, 5, pp. 1686–1695

—— (1982) 'A Symposium on Reproductive Rights: The Emerging Issues' *Women's Rights Law Reporter* 7, 3, pp. 169–173

—— (1984) 'From Parental Leaves to Nurturing Leaves' *New York University Review of Law and Social Change* 13, 2, pp. 381–405

—— (1985) 'Dealing With Employment Discrimination and Damaging Stereotypes: A Legal Perspective' *Journal of Social Issues* 41, 4, pp. 99–110

—— (1988) 'Review of L. Weitzman *The Divorce Revolution*', *Signs* 13, 3, pp. 578–582

—— (1989) 'Feminist Tensions: Concepts of Motherhood and Reproductive Choice', in J. Zuckerberg (ed.) *Gender in Transition* New York: Plenum

Taub, N. and Williams, W. W. (1985) 'Will Equality Require More than Assimilation, Accommodation or Separation from the Existing Social Structure?' *Rutgers Law Review* 37, 4/1, pp. 825–844

Tenenbaum, S. (1982) 'Women Through the Prism of Political Thought' *Polity* 15, 1, pp. 90–102

Thornton, M. (1982) 'Sex Discrimination Legislation in Australia' *The Australian Quarterly* Summer, pp. 393–403

—— (1985) 'Affirmative Action, Merit and the Liberal State' *Australian Journal of Law and Society* 2, 2, pp. 28–40

—— (1986) 'Feminist Jurisprudence: Illusion or Reality' *Australian Journal of Law and Society* 3, pp. 5–29

Thornton, N. (1986) 'The Politics of Pornography: A Critique of Liberalism and Radical Feminism *ANZJS* 22, 1, pp. 25–45

Thurow, L. (1987) 'A Surge in Inequality' *Scientific American* 256, 5, pp. 26–33

Uglow, J. (1983) 'Josephine Butler: From Sympathy to Theory (1828–1906)', in D. Spender (ed.) *Feminist Theorists: Three Centuries of Women's Intellectual Traditions* London: Women's Press

Van Kleeck, M. (1921) 'Women and Machines' *The Atlantic Monthly* pp. 3–14

Vogel, V. (1986) 'Rationalism and Romanticism: Two Strategies for Women's Liberation', in J. Evans (et al.) *Feminism and Political Theory* London: Sage Publications, pp. 17–46

Wajcman, J. and Rosewarne, S. (1986) 'The "Feminisation" of Work' *Australian Society* September, pp. 15–17

Wallace, M. (1985) 'The Legal Approach to Sex Discrimination', in M. Sawer (ed.) *Program For Change* Sydney: Allen & Unwin

Wallis, C. (1987) 'The Child-Care Dilemma' *Time* (Australia) 2, 25, pp. 54–61

Wasserstrom, R. A. (1977) 'Racism, Sexism, and Preferential Treatment: An Approach to the Topics' *UCLA Law Review* 24, pp. 581–622

Weiner, G. (1985) 'Equal Opportunities, Feminism, and Girls' Education: Introduction', in G. Weiner (ed.) *Just a Bunch of Girls: Feminist Approaches to Schooling* Milton Keynes: Open University Press

Weinzweig, M. (1987) 'Pregnancy Leave, Comparable Worth, and Concepts of Equality' *Hypatia* 2, 1, pp. 71–101

Weitzman, L. and Dixon, R. (1986) 'The Transformation of Legal Marriage Through No-Fault Divorce', in A. S. and J. H. Skolnick *Family in Transition* 5th Edition, Boston: Little, Brown and Co.

Westen, P. (1982) 'The Empty Idea of Equality' *Harvard Law Review* 95, 3, pp. 537–588

Wickenden, D. (1986) 'What Now?' *The New Republic* 5 May, pp. 19–25

Williams, W. (1981) 'Firing the Woman to Protect the Fetus: The Reconciliation of Fetal Protection with Employment Opportunity Goals Under Title VII' *Georgetown Law Journal* 69, 1, pp. 641–704

—— (1982) 'The Equality Crisis: Some Reflections on Culture, Courts and Feminism' *Women's Rights Law Reporter* 7, 3, pp. 175–200

_____ (1984) 'Equality's Riddle: Pregnancy and the Equal Treatment/ Special Treatment Debate' *New York University Review of Law, Society and Change* 13, pp. 325–380

Willis, E. (1984) 'Abortion: Is a Woman a Person?', in A. Snitow, C. Stansell and S. Thompson (eds) *Desire: The Politics of Sexuality* London: Virago

Willis, P. (1979) 'Shop Floor Culture, Masculinity and the Wage Form', in J. Clarke, C. Critcher and R. Johnson (eds) *Working Class Culture: Studies in History and Theory* Birmingham: Hutchinson of London

Wilson, G. and Sapiro, V. (1985) 'Occupational Safety and Health as a Women's Policy Issue', in V. Sapiro (ed.) *Women, Biology and Public Policy* Beverly Hills: Sage Publications

Wolff, R. (1980) 'There's Nobody Here But Us Persons', in C. Gould and M. Wartofsky (eds) *Women and Philosophy* Harmondsworth: Penguin

Woodruff, J. (et al.) 'Is Abortion the Issue?' *Harper's Magazine* 273, 1634, pp. 35–43

Wulff, M. (1987) 'Full Time, Part Time, or Not Right Now?' *Newsletter of the Australian Institute for Family Studies* 19, pp. 14–26

Wyndham, D. (1981) 'Health Problems of Women In and Out of the Workforce', in M. Hatton (ed.) *Work and Health: Issues in Occupational Health* Canberra: ANU Centre for Continuing Education

Yeatman, A. (1988) 'The Green Paper on Higher Education: Remarks Concerning its Implications for Participation, Access and Equity for Women as Staff and Students' *Australian Universities Review* 1, pp. 39–41

Miscellaneous

ACTU Congress (1983) *Working Women's Charter* Melbourne: ACTU

ACTU Action Program for Women Workers (1985) *BHP—Australian Iron & Steel Equal Opportunity Case: Implications for Union* Melbourne: ACTU

ACTU (1986) *Action Program for Women Workers* Melbourne: ACTU

Caust, L. (1989) 'Beyond Equality: A Study of Equal Opportunity (Gender) in One Workplace', Paper presented at Australian Political Studies Association Conference, University of New South Wales

Citizens' Advisory Council on the Status of Women, *Annual Reports to the President* 1971, 1972, 1973 Washington, DC: US Government Printing Office

Conference on Legislative and Award Restrictions to Women's Employment (1986) *Report* Canberra: Department of the Prime Minister and Cabinet

Davies, E. (1868) 'Special Systems of Education for Women', Emily Davies Papers, Reel 5, Box x, no. 9

East, C. (1986) 'Critical Comments on *A Lesser Life, The Myth of Women's Liberation in America*' Washington, DC: National Women's Political Caucus

Equal Opportunities Commission (1979) *Health and Safety Legislation:*

Should We Distinguish Between Men and Women? Manchester: Equal Opportunities Commission

—— (1982) *Towards Equality: A Casebook of Decisions on Sex Discriminations and Equal Pay 1976–1981* Manchester: EOC

—— (1985) 'Parental and Family Leave: the Proposed EC Directive' Manchester: Equal Opportunities Commission

—— (1987) news release, 'Over £3000 Compensation for Sacked Mums-to-be', 20 August, Manchester

—— (1988) *Equal Treatment for Men and Women: Strengthening the Acts* Manchester: Impact Print Services

Fawcett, Mrs H. (*c.* 1895) 'The Story of the Opening of University Education to Women', Emily Davies Papers, Reel 11, Box xx, no. 5

Fawcett, M. G. (1921) 'Miss Emily Davies' *Women's Leader* 22 July, Emily Davies Papers, Box vi, no. 81–17

Hawke, R. (1988) *Towards a Fairer Australia: Social Justice Budget Statement 1988–89* Canberra: Australian Government Publishing Service

Inner London Education Authority (1987) 'Single Sex Groupings in Mixed Schools: A Discussion Document and Case Studies' London: ILEA

Mann, S. *Trade Unionism, the Labour Party and the Issue of Family Allowances, 1925–1930*, MA thesis, University of Warwick, 1974

Maternity Alliance (1988) 'Response to the Department of Employment's Consultative Document on the Restrictions on the Employment of Young People and the Removal of Sex Discrimination in Legislation', London: Maternity Alliance

Naffin, N. (1984) *An Inquiry into the Substantive Law of Rape* Adelaide: Women's Adviser's Office, Department of the Premier and Cabinet

National Council for Civil Liberties, Women's Rights Unit (1988) *Restriction or Protection?* London: NCCL

National Women's Conference (1978) *The Spirit of Houston* Washington, DC: National Commission on the Observance of International Women's Year

Nicholson, M. (1983) *Woman's Politics in South Australia: The Ideas of the Women's Non-Party Association 1919–1933*, Honours thesis, University of Adelaide

Niland, C., 'Maternity Leave: a Feminist Perspective', Paper presented at Women's Electoral Lobby Seminar (Sydney) 20 October 1979

Open Door International for the Economic Emancipation of the Woman Worker (1935) *Report of the Fourth Conference* held in Copenhagen, 19–23 August, printed in London

Peterson, E., undated speech (*c.*1976) unpublished, held by Women's Bureau, Washington, DC

Stimpson, C. (1988) 'What Am I Doing When I Do Women's Studies in 1988?', unpublished speech delivered at Rutgers University, New Brunswick, New Jersey

Technical and Advisory Committee for the Investigation of the Effect of Special Legislation on Employment of Women in Industry, *Minutes of Joint Meeting*, 31 March *c.*1927 from the papers of Lillian M. Gilbreth,

Purdue University, photocopy in the possession of Guy Alchon, University of Delaware

Thornton, N. (1985) 'Enforcing the Moral Consensus: The Case of Video Pornography', paper delivered at Australian Political Studies Association Conference, Adelaide, August 1985

US Department of Labor (1976) *State Labor Laws in Transition: From Protection to Equal Status for Women* Washington: US Government Printing Office

Van Kleeck, M. (1919) 'Suffragists and Industrial Democracy' New York: National Women's Suffrage Publishing Co., Mary Van Kleeck Papers, Box 24, Folder 487, photocopy in the possession of Guy Alchon, University of Delaware

Women's Adviser's Office (1987) 'Women's Employment in South Australia' Adelaide: Department of the Prime Minister and Cabinet

Women's Bureau (1984) 'Women and Existing Retirement Income Systems', Submission to the Senate Standing Committee on Social Welfare, Canberra: Department of Employment and Industrial Relations

_____ (1985), 'Maternity and Parental Leave' *Information Paper No 3*, Canberra: Department of Employment and Industrial Relations

Index